WESTMORELAND

Glass

Chas West Wilson

COLLECTOR BOOKS

A Division of Schroeder Publishing Co., Inc.

The current values in this book are intended to reflect and not to set prices. They are estimates and should be used only as a guide. Dealer prices as well as auction prices can vary greatly according to the section of the country and the selling situation. They will be affected by condition and will change with demand. Neither the author nor the publisher assumes responsibility for losses that could be incurred through the use of this guide.

These current value estimates are for clean, unchipped, uncracked, unrepaired pieces with cold decoration or matt gold in good-to-excellent, but not exceptional, condition. Value estimates for period carnival pieces assume iridizing is in original condition, however.

As the understanding of any collectible grows, the range of its prices will broaden: seemingly minor differences will result in large value disparities. This can be expected with much of Westmoreland's glass in the future.

Searching For A Publisher?

We are always looking for knowledgeable people considered to be experts within their fields. If you feel that there is a real need for a book on your collectible subject and have a large comprehensive collection, contact Collector Books.

On the Cover:

The bowl and the sugar and cream set are from the 1820 line, which is pictured in several sections of this book. The glass is cased in Westmoreland's "Transparent Rose" — one of five translucent sprayed glass colors the company introduced in 1927 (see the Cased Glass section). The cutting is Westmoreland's copper wheel engraving; the roses have been selectively polished. Joseph Racinger is the probable engraver.

Book design by Terri Stalions
Cover design by the author

Printed in the U.S.A. by Image Graphics

In Memory of my Grandfather,

Charles Howard West

Charles Howard West and the author.

Over nearly half a century, Mr. West had given of his time and abilities to the glassware industry generally....

A real gentleman of the old school, Charles West in his glassware career was a partisan only against those things which were harmful or lacked beauty. He felt his best interests were the best interests of all and his conciliatory and up-building attitudes often were of the greatest value....

— China Glass & Lamps, Sept. 1937 (Written in the year of his retirement as first president of the Associated Glass & Pottery Manufacturers, and as owner and president of the Westmoreland Glass Co.)

Preface

When I was a child, my grandfather, Chas Howard West, was my special buddy. I spent my first four years in his house — at the time when he was still Westmoreland's president, and essentially its sole owner. When he returned from work each day, he would draw pictures and tell me stories as I sat on his knee. His stories were always fresh; they were never repeated. He would bring me glass from work, and I can especially remember the lanterns filled with colored candy. One evening in 1936 he took me on the train to visit the factory. I can still recall the semi-darkness, the fire, the pot furnace with men gathered around it, and the fuss these men made over me as Chas West's grandson. I can even recall wanting to stay there all night. What my father, a research chemist at Mellon Institute, did for a living was beyond my comprehension; but what my grandfather did was something I could really grasp.

Nevertheless, in the years that followed, Westmoreland was something I thought very little about. In late 1936 our family moved out of my grandparents' house; then one year later the company passed into other hands. From that point on in my family, Westmoreland was simply not discussed. But things like this have an odd way of surfacing eventually, and that is the best reason I can give for returning to the company and its glass.

As I began to explore Westmoreland's past, I became aware of the importance it once had in the industry — an importance that cannot be explained by its size or sales. I found Westmoreland had a story to tell that was not being told. In so many ways Westmoreland was a pioneer, and its pioneering went beyond the clever novelties and fanciful candy containers that, deservedly, have long been familiar to glass collectors. Perhaps this book will help stretch today's definition of "Westmoreland" and encourage others in the future to stretch it right out to its elastic limit!

I would like to express my deepest appreciation to the following people who, through their help, made this book possible:

Thelma Armstrong
R.H. (Bud) Ashmore, Jr.
Connie Carter
Frank Chiarenza
Frank M. Fenton
Karen and Freeman Frey
Ruth Heindel
Dwight Johnson
The late Robert Jones
Jim Miller
Ann Porreca
The late Geraldine West Powell
Robin at Qualax
Robert Rupp
Elaine Shick
Martha and John Smith
Dean and Mary Watkins
Avis (Mrs. George L., III) West
The late George Lauman West
Helen (Mrs. George L., Jr.) West
The late S. Brainard West, Jr.
Berry Wiggins
Dr. Alex L. Wilson
Virginia Wright

I would particularly like to thank Phil J. Rosso, Jr., for the 1915 decorating department pictures and permission to photograph fifteen pieces of his glass. These pieces can all be seen at his Westmoreland Museum in Portvue, Pennsylvania. Dwight Johnson, Westmoreland's last chemist, also has a Westmoreland museum in Jeannette, just a short distance from the plant.

Chas West Wilson
400 Park Hill Drive
Mechanicsburg, PA 17055

Contents

Usage Guide

In the glass section:

Date estimates are in parentheses at the top of the information in the outside margin. Support for these estimates appears in bold in the photo caption. "c." stands for "circa" (about).

Glass names and numbers in bold type are all authentic designations.

"1904," "1932," "1940," are the dates of three Westmoreland price lists. "1932" may be the last West period price list, whereas "1940" may be the first Brainard period price list.

"Asstd Colors" is a term used throughout Westmoreland's 1932 price list. Colors for that year were, "Green, Amber, Roselin, Aquamarine Blue, Black, Opal, Belgian Blue, Moonstone." Color choice was evidently Westmoreland's rather than the customer's, and it was probably based as much on production as on marketing considerations. This should be kept in mind when assessing relative scarcity today.

In 1932, Moonstone (opalescent) was probably restricted to the **77 Hobnail** line because it was specifically listed there and nowhere else. While black was undoubtedly restricted to certain pieces, it must have been selectively included with the "Asstd Colors" for it was rarely listed separately. Opal (milk glass), however, was given its own special section. Ruby, made in late 1932 for 1933, was not among the colors listed, nor was it penned in. Ruby, with its high selenium content, is the only transparent color with a significantly higher material cost than crystal.

To help cover added inventory costs, the "Asstd Colors" were priced at 20% over crystal. Opal in 1932 was typically priced at 44% over crystal because of its material cost, but this percentage was frequently higher owing to the high reject rate on large and complicated pieces. (Opal tends to set up quickly.)

The special significance of the "Asstd Colors" is this: glass available in colors in 1932 was probably also available in colors for a number of years before and after this date; the particular colors, however, would have depended on the year. Glass available only in crystal in 1932 was unlikely to be available in colors in other years.

From late 1937 to the end of 1960, Westmoreland made no colored transparent glass. This is reflected in the 1940 price list which listed only crystal and opal.

Most of the glassware listed in the 1932 price list, yet not listed in the 1940 price list, was probably discontinued shortly after August 1937. While most of these discontinued pieces were never made again, some were reissued many years later.

Dimensions shown include those that could be helpful for identification. Since Westmoreland never used metric measurements, none appear in this book.

Weights are shown if they are unusual or useful for identification.

I have used Westmoreland's (and the industry's) contemporary terms such as, "jug," "comport," "cutting" (for both cutting and engraving), "candleholder" (for candlesocket), and "opal" (for milk glass prior to World War II).

I have also adhered to spellings used by Westmoreland and most of the industry: "matt," "mould," "sulphur," "kryolite," and "lustre," for example.

Since Charles West abbreviated his first name, I have referred to him as "Chas West" throughout. I have also abbreviated "William," and other first names when I have used three names. First name abbreviations as well as initials were usual before c. 1910, but became less common later.

While I have tried to avoid repetition within each section, I have deliberately repeated, or at least used cross-referencing between the sections. This is for the benefit of many readers who may want to refer just to particular parts of the book.

Footnotes, always a distraction but important for future research, have been made as inoffensive as possible. (I am indebted to the late Wm Heacock for pointing the way to the method I used.) The two trade journals, *China, Glass & Lamps* and *Crockery & Glass Journal* were the sources of most of my cited material, and I have employed the letters "L" and "J" to represent them. The dates that appear with these letters show the periods of the citations without my having to mention them. With books, the numbers are page numbers — or plates in the case of the three milk glass texts. All coded references are listed in the back, and this listing is restricted to them.

George L. West's Story

I would like to begin this book with a selection from George West's remarkable story. Geo. Lauman West, the older of the two sons of Geo. Robinson West, cofounder of Westmoreland, wrote and mailed me his Westmoreland story shortly before his death in 1982. I am sorry that I knew him for only a few short years.

I would like to think he was a clone of his father. What I will always remember is a true polymath, with an inventive, curious mind, eager to converse on any subject. He had a strong aesthetic sense which I recall extended to the furniture of Duncan Phyfe, and the same warm, whimsical sense of humor his father displayed in his ads and his Shriners collectibles. He took up gourmet cooking in the last year of his life, and he drove his Volvo station wagon till the end.

In his account he failed to point out that he was employed at Westmoreland from about 1917 to mid-1921. Following his graduation from college as an engineer, his father and his uncle (my grandfather) put him in charge of West Bros, where he was responsible for the thenexploding candy packaging operations at the factory. In later years he was the manager of Building Product sales (architectural glass) at PPG, where he invented and patented the "West Tension Door."

George Robinson West in 1890.

"*The history of the Westmoreland Glass Company has, as far as I know, never been authentically recorded. There have been allegations and many assertions, some of them untrue, concerning its early beginnings. I feel that I am qualified to write its valid history since I was born on November 13, 1895, just six years after the Westmoreland Glass Company was incorporated. Furthermore, George R. West (George Robinson West, 1863 – 1929), the president of the fledgling company, was my father. He was very close to me and from the time I was in my early teens I spent many Saturdays at the glass plant in Grapeville, the little community in southwestern Pennsylvania where Westmoreland Glass still stands. I knew every inch of the factory and all the personnel. I learned how to blow and how to press glass, how to make molds, and even tried my hand at making a barrel in the cooper's shop.*

*It would be impossible to write a history of Westmoreland Glass Company, formerly Westmoreland Specialty Company, without including the biographical data of George R. West, for he organized the company and had the drive and ingenuity to make it financially a very successful opera-*tion. My father was born in 1863, in a brick house on Penn Avenue on the site now occupied by the Roosevelt Hotel in down-

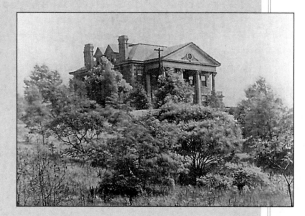

town Pittsburgh. His father, Joseph Lafayette, had a carriage shop on Duquesne Way at a spot which is now part of Joseph Horne's department store.

My father must have engaged in commercial activities at an early age because he had acquired a sizable sum of money before he was 20 years old. Some of his transactions were noted in one of his diaries. At one point he was in a mercantile business with Mr. M.C. Cozad, and when he withdrew from that company in

Westcliff, George West's home on Heberton Avenue, Pittsburgh from 1907. It was situated on the highest point in Allegheny County adjoining Highland Park. The seven-acre grounds included a tennis court, a swimming pool, an Italian sunken garden, an artificial lake, and a log cabin. The house was torn down in 1932, the middle of the Depression.

(John & Vernie West)

1883 he received $4,000 as his share of the venture. Notes in the diary also concern interest he received from promissory notes which he had outstanding.

"Westmoreland Specialty Company - Glass Works" c. 1891 from the southeast.

(Avis West)

The first of George West's 16 patents. A George West violin should be recognizable since the patent inscription reads, "The mouth or opening C of the bottle is found at the end opposite to the neck of the violin." Note, too, the scroll, and yet the absence of the four pegs.

It must have been about this time that he and Caldwell McFarland (a brother-in-law) decided to begin a dry goods business and opened the shop of West & McFarland on Penn Avenue in East Liberty near North Highland where the Woolworth Store now stands. For those times it was a pretentious undertaking. Into this venture George R. West took with him his younger brother (Charles Howard West, 1865 – 1943). The dry goods store was a two-story building with an elevator, but what was more remarkable to me as a small boy was a fascinating device used in making change. When the clerk made a sale she would place the money in a small box hanging from a wire attached to the ceiling. When she pulled a lever the small box was sent at

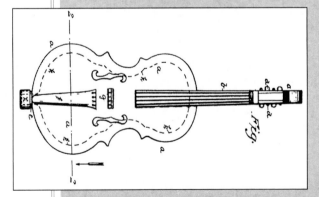

great speed to the cashier's room in the rear of the store. In due course it returned with the proper change. The McFarland store was active until recent times, and is remembered by most older East Liberty residents. (East Liberty is in the east end of Pittsburgh; the Wests moved to that area about 1870.)

I don't know how my father learned that there had been a new glass factory just completed at Grapeville in Westmoreland County where a successful business might be developed without having to invest an excessive amount of capital. By realizing a sum from his interest in West & McFarland and another sum from the sale of his share of a large piece of property at Pinkerton on the Youghigheny River (near the Mason & Dixon Line) he had a total large enough to make a very fair investment....

Records show that the factory in Grapeville and surrounding land were purchased by George M. Irwin, George R. West, and Charles H. West on October 14, 1889. The site selected for the factory was not ideal since it was on a relatively steep hillside, but it was as close as possible to the mainline of the Pennsylvania Railroad. The chief reason for the selection of that particular site was the fact that a gas well located nearby would provide cheap fuel. A gas well was an uncommon event at that time, as indicated by the fact that my father told me that a boardwalk and a platform had been built at the railroad track so that a train could stop there to allow President McKinley to view the new phenomenon. (This platform was built and the well was lit Sept. 30, 1887, for President Cleveland and his new bride; it, apparently flared up 50 feet. Thirteen years later a newspaper reported, "The Lady of the White House was in ecstasies.") (JD 8/3/00)

Westmoreland Specialty had glassmaking underway in a very short time. I have proof of that since I am fortunate to have in my possession an early piece which is dated and carries a patent inscription. This particular piece was patented by my father in 1892. It is a beautiful design, a small violin of amber glass with an opening in the bottom end and a cork stopper so that it could be filled with perfume. I asked my father what the perfume was, and as I recall he said it was alcohol and oil of bergamot. I questioned what the price may have been and was told that it was about one dollar a gallon. (1995: $20)

After his induction to the board of directors there is no further record of George M. Irwin, so it is logical to assume that before too long he had withdrawn whatever assets he had. This was no doubt the time when the company was seeking additional capital and sold a block of stock to Mr. Ira Brainard, who lived on North

Highland Avenue, a short distance from where the West's lived. He did not have any part in direct management of Westmoreland Specialty, and I am sure it was a rare occasion if he ever visited the plant. I myself never met him nor did I ever see him at the plant.

There were actually two companies shipping out of Westmoreland Specialty; one, Westmoreland Glass, and the other, the West Brothers. West Brothers were primarily interested in supplying novelties and low cost items for the trade, such as Woolworths, Union News Company, and others whose sales were directed toward children. Candy filled glass toys accounted for a significant increase in sales volume for the West Brothers. My father was the pioneer in this development, and it became an almost explosive success when he designed and patented the candy filled glass toy telephones. The telephone consisted of a glass bottle for the base, capped with a pewter mouthpiece, and small wooden earphone hanging from the side. It was so popular that it was bound to be copied as far as the patent allowed, but the copies were crude and never surpassed the original in beauty of design.

The one real exception in volume in sales to the children's novelties were the West Brothers containers filled with mustard. The mustard was added to increase the glass sales, unlike present merchandising with the glass container solely a necessity. It was interesting to see the long battery of the stone grinding mills added to keep pace with the increasing sales. Before long it became necessary to build a vinegar factory on the other side of the railroad tracks so the vinegar would be readily accessible for the making of mustard. It was said at the time that West Brothers was one of the largest manufacturers of prepared mustard in the United States. Wouldn't it be nice if today you could buy an iced tea glass filled with mustard for ten cents? All of the various products shipped by West Brothers became large volume business and were a great factor in keeping the large 16-pot furnace and two day tanks operating to capacity.

While fine tableware glass, both pressed and blown, was the prime product of Westmoreland Glass, there was also a large volume of sales of commercial ware. I remember the headlight lenses for Pierce-Arrow automobiles which had prisms to deflect the light toward the highway. I also remember making for the inventor the first small red disks with the word "Stop" imposed on them. These were sold directly to vehicle owners because at that time car manufacturers did not install stop lights in the vehicle's mechanism. Another good commercial item which had steady sales was pressed and cut door knobs. (Some of these moulds, overlooked in two scrap drives, survived at the factory in 1991.)

From its very inception Westmoreland manufactured and shipped a steadily increasing volume of opal glass, more commonly known as milk glass. The "Hen on Nest" has now become a common decorative piece for the home, but in the early days there was a demand for it particularly in the rural areas where its functional use was on the breakfast table filled with boiled eggs. A substantial sale of milk glass was to the distributors of dental products. Many of us recall the ever-present milk glass bowl with the accompanying instrument tray. (Moulds for some of these also survived.)

My father had a very loyal group of employees whose high quality of workmanship contributed to the success of Westmoreland. There were Dan Jenkins, the day factory superintendent, and his brother Dave who handled the night turn, and Fred Becker, a master mechanic who could design and fabricate most of the metal pieces needed. Fred was also a skilled diemaker and was responsible for the blanking and stamping dies for the metal shop. Fred became a good friend of mine because, when I was only a teenage boy, my father arranged for me to accompany Fred on visits to the parts factories, suppliers of various materials. (Fred Becker was responsible for three of Westmoreland's patents.) Gustav Horn educated me in the art of decorating, enameling, and engraving glass. I am grateful to have known him and to have benefitted from

Annie Bell Lauman (Mrs. Geo. R.) West, 1869 – 1932. (Avis West)

Founded in 1852, C. West & Co. was still in business making carriages as late as 1913. (Pittsburgh City Directory, 1864)

his teaching. (Gustav Horn, head decorator during the West years, was responsible for two of Westmoreland's patents.) An outstanding employee was Benjamin Bennett, the head of the mould shop, who was respected throughout the industry as one of the top mould makers of his time. It was not uncommon for potential customers to come to Westmoreland to ask Ben to make a mould that had been judged too difficult by others.

Westmoreland had a special group of skilled artisans, engravers, and cutters *who produced the fine pieces of heavy cut glass so much in demand. When glass is manufactured it is molten and must be annealed or cooled slowly so that it is not under strain that would cause it to break down when subject to shock or to a sharp change in temperature. Blanks or pieces of glass used in making heavy cut glass had to be handled with extreme care since they were heavy and massive. They were cooled in special ovens, usually for days, instead of just the hours needed for ordinary glassware."*

Chas H. West's Diary

Helen Baker (Mrs. Chas H.) West, 1867 – 1948, from a photograph called "Solitude," taken and exhibited by Chas West.

Charles Howard West in 1890.

Charles and Helen West took their honeymoon in New England in 1893. The following entries are from Charles' diary.

"Wednesday 2/15/1893
Sold 1000 paper weights in Boston today @ 20 cents to Jones, McDufee & Stratton and a car of glassware.
Thursday 2/16/1893
(Portland, Maine) Made an agency here with W. W. Marong & sold three bills *of mustard.*
Friday 2/17/1893
Saw Carthill & Otis in Boston & sold some mustard (a car load) also Barstow Mfg. Co. & sold them half car glassware."

QUICK SELLER,
ELITE SUGAR BOWL MUSTARD.

Packed 2 doz. to Case.
Write us for Prices,
WESTMORELAND SPECIALTY CO.,
GRAPEVILLE PA.

Trade card, c. 1896.

Just five months before Westmoreland was founded, Jones, McDuffee & Stratton bought the entire stock of glassware and moulds from the Boston & Sandwich Glass Co (J 5/9/89). They sold all the glassware for a third off the wholesale price, and the moulds must have ended up somewhere. A member of the family, not directly connected to the company, told me she understood Westmoreland began with some Sandwich moulds. Granted, the timing is right; but then she grew up in the era when everyone was trying to tout a Sandwich connection. I believe this claim has to be treated with the same care as the more recent claim that Westmoreland possessed some original Atterbury moulds.

While the Wests were in Massachusetts, Charles insisted on visiting Fall River, where Lizzie Borden had turned the expression "Life begins at 40" on its head just a few months before!

The West Brothers' Vinegar Operation

1895 — The Beginning

"Recently a factory for the manufacture of vinegar was established, the vinegar being made from grain by a secret process, and a high class article turned out. The factory is operated to the fullest extent all the time to supply the great demand, the vinegar finding ready sale with wholesale grocers and pickle manufacturers" (JD 5/3/95).

1900

"The Grapeville vinegar factory owned by West Bros is one of the most steady factories in the whole country. It never shuts down for repairs; its machinery does not stop even on Sunday and throughout the year it is never idle one day. Four carloads of vinegar are shipped from the factory every week, averaging seventy-five barrels each and three hundred barrels a week is a pretty fair output, even for Grapeville. The present factory is possibly three times as large as it was originally....

The corn is carried from the P.R.R. siding to the basement of the building by a cleverly designed chute. In the basement is the mill which grinds the corn into meal and it is then carried by a grain elevator to the top floor where it is ready for use. The water for the factory is obtained from the P.R.R. reservoir, below Sadler's crossing, which has been leased from the railroad company. Some time ago one of the leading merchants of the town sent to their supply house in Pittsburgh for a barrel of good cider vinegar. In due time the cider vinegar came and after paying the freight charges the merchant was astonished to find that the vinegar originally came from the Grapeville factory which is not a hundred yards from his store. The moral of this story is to patronize home industries and it will at least save freight charges" (JD 1/13/00).

1905 — Big Sunday Evening Fire at Grapeville

Fire Sunday evening destroyed the Grapeville vinegar works, which is operated by Charles H. and George R. West, of Pittsburg, in connection with the Westmoreland Specialty works, two cattle stables owned by the Pittsburgers, a dwelling of George W. Croushore and a stable of Dr. Joseph B. Wakefield, in addition to damaging the freight station of the Pennsylvania Railroad Company. West Brothers' vinegar works building was a four-story frame structure and the loss is placed at $25,000 (1995: $425,000). It contained about 40 carloads of vinegar which were destroyed.... The works had a capacity of a carload of vinegar a day....

The heat was so intense that a passenger train was scorched as it passed.... Charles H. West said that as soon as the losses had been adjusted by the insurance companies the works would be rebuilt" (JD 12/7/05).

West Bros. vinegar building, 1895 – 1905.

(Avis West)

After the vinegar building burned to the ground in December 1905, the operations were restored, in part, across the track: The glass factory building was extended to the east to accommodate the mustard and vinegar activities. At this time the vinegar operation seems to have been reduced to what was needed for making mustard. (Vinegar made up three-quarters of Westmoreland's mustard.)

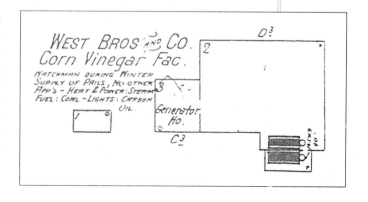

Life in Grapeville

Two Grapeville Farmers

"West Bros. purchased the four acre meadow of E.J. Bricker last week for a handsome price. They intend to enlarge their present 'stock yard' and the meadow is to be used for grazing for a short time" (JD 7/28/99).

Two Grapeville Hunters

"Mr. Thomas McKenan, the genial book keeper of the Westmoreland Specialty works, and Mr. Charles West, of the same company (secretary and treasurer at that time), have just returned from a three day hunting trip in the wilds of Northern Pennsylvania. Mr. Mc-Kenan covered himself with glory bringing home a total of 3 rabbits, 3 pheasants and 1 opossum. It doesn't matter haw many Mr. West bagged as Tom claimed them all as his right of superior experience, and claims that he would have shot more game than both could have carried home if he had not fallen into a creek and wet his ammunition" (JD 12/8/99).

The Grapeville Literary Society

"The Grapeville Literary Society has been unable to hold a meeting during the last two weeks. On the first meeting most of the members were busy talking over the recent election and forgot all about it. Last Monday night just as the exercises were about to begin the lights went out, not having been filled with oil. Those on the program instantly and emphatically refused to speak giving as a reason that their gestures on which they had been practicing could not be observed" (JD 4/27/00).

The Grapeville Baseball Nine

"The Grapeville Baseball Nine with a score of rooters drove over to Arona last Saturday in a hay wagon. They drove slowly back in the evening and sorrowfully said that they had been defeated by a large score. The score boy had lost count of a run or two in the excitement and none of the boys knew exactly what it was. In the second inning the Arona boys made eight runs and would have made more had they not knocked the cover off the ball. Well, we got done up Saturday, but just wait until next time" (JD 5/4/00).

"The Grapeville Baseball team did not get beaten last Saturday. Various reasons for the phenomenon are assigned and the one usually accepted is because they did not play" (JD 6/22/00).

Raymond Jenkins

"Raymond, the four-year-old hopeful of Daniel W. Jenkins, the well-known foreman in the Specialty works has secured a steady job in the mould shops. The young man was seized with a mighty desire to earn some Christmas spending money and applied to his father for a lucrative position. Accordingly, he took his dinner pail Monday morning and started to work. All Monday morning he was as busy as any one in the shops engaged in making marks on a piece of iron with a chisel and hammer. At noon he demanded his wages and was presented with a regulation envelope containing the hoard he had earned" (JD 12/28/00). (Workmen were paid for many years in cash. I understand Westmoreland was the only plant in the Jeannette area never to have been robbed.)

I have heard Dan Jenkins described as a "glassmaker's glassmaker." In 1895 he appears to have replaced George Gleis, Westmoreland's first superintendent. In 1932 he celebrated his golden wedding anniversary. When he retired after 40 years as Westmoreland's superintendent at the end of 1935, it was said he had spent 60 years in the glass business (L 11/35).

C.H. West Band

"The recently reorganized C.H. West Band of Grapeville is making preparations for an active spring and summer. They are always willing to help out in a good cause, having led may delegates at the time of the Peacock evangelical campaign, based on numerous public serenades...for which they received no pay. However, they do not expect that all their work will be charity and are open for engagements that may present themselves..." (JD 2/13/17).

C.H. West Band, 1917. Chas West, who played the violin, is believed to have bought the band players their new uniforms, and perhaps some of their instruments as well. Robert Jones identified the three in this picture as the Fulmer brothers: Howard ("Duchy"), Eddie, and Bill — none of whom worked at Westmoreland. (Family picture)

A Little Journey to Santa Claus' Workshop

A Westmoreland Factory Tour of May 1915

"West is the name of two brothers (George R. is president and Chas H. treasurer) who have kept the wheels of industry whirring busily for some 27 years in the Westmoreland Specialty Company but their product has gone north and south and at present a good deal of it is going east across the Atlantic to the Allies.

With which prelude (as the story books say) is introduced the story of a 'little journey' a la the late lamented Fra Elbertus to Grapeville station and the plant where some 500 Jeannette men, boys, and girls find employment... ("Fra" Elbert Hubbard, who died in 1915, established a "commune" in upstate New York where he made "Craft-Style" [Mission] furniture and published The Roycrofts and The Philistine.)

The 11:11 train at Jeannette will land the passenger — if he's so minded — before the very door of the Specialty plant because it stops for water at the tank on the opposite side of the track.

Then if properly introduced and shown around from department to department will be disclosed a remarkable establishment.

'I have little to tell you' said Chas H. West, who has personal charge of the plant. His brother, George R., is the business getter on the road to a great extent. Both the brothers are hustlers.

'Except,' he continued, 'that we are busy and selling pretty much of our staple goods to the Allies. The Allies won't allow us to sell to the Germans.' (The war in Europe began in August 1914, nine months before; the Lusitania was sunk in May 1915.)

'Little to tell,' but the plant of the modest manufacturer spoke volumes for the business ability of the two brothers. The plant puts out about a half million dollars worth ($7.6 million in 1995 dollars) of manufactured products each year.

The plant makes its own gas in huge furnaces in the basement and also produces its own electric light and power. Everything which enters into the articles manufactured must be "right." The sand dug from the mountains of central Pennsylvania fine as pin heads, the lime from Centre County and other ingredients which enter into glass manufacture are of the first grade.

Glass men quickly will grasp the extent of the glass blowing and moulding departments with the statement that the plant has a 16 pot furnace, three four pot furnaces and two day tanks. And as for the products, well there are something like 5000 different varieties of articles manufactured from the finest of cut glass table ware, vases and candlesticks down to the hundreds of glass candy filled revolvers, lanterns, vases, autos and toy glass watches. These articles are turned out by the gross and retail at ten cents. There are egg beaters, lemon cups and squeezers and dear knows what not which must make glad the five and ten cent store merchants and the frugal housewife and children who buy them. The specialties include glass receptacles filled with mustard made in the plant. (Early that summer the Wests discontinued their mustard operations.)

At present the big drawing card is a Keupie tub candy receptacle. First the Keupie and its tub are molded. Then the article passes through several hands and is

Westmoreland Decorating department, August 1915. If early accounts give the impression of a melange of Westmoreland glassware being made and worked on together, this photograph confirms it. On the left, Charlie Chaplin candy containers; on the right, 1700 Colonial vases in black glass receiving enamel. By the rear windows, unidentified vases; and in the center, unidentified handled three-footed black glass bowls. Most interesting of all, though, is that white opal (white "Carrara marble") standard which must be three feet tall. What was the reject rate for such a thing? What did the mould look like? How did it fit into the lehr? Can any have survived? (P.J. Rosso)

This was probably the "auto" referred to. It is the first of two similar town cars patented by George West.

Westmoreland's Story

The Kewpie doll mould must already have been made by the time George Semler applied for his patent in April 1915. At about the same time Semler also received a patent on a similar Charlie Chaplin.

Both patents were assigned to Geo. Borgfeldt & Co. of New York. A Kewpie mould still survived at the plant in 1991.

painted, touched up, filled with candy, wrapped and shipped. Fine hand painted vases are a delight to the eye. Gustavus Horn has charge of the decorating department. William Harrison heads the cutting department and Ben Bennett has charge of the mould shop. They are experts every one of them in their line. For that matter everybody in the plant goes busily about his or her work with that "know how" efficiency which means so much in the final analysis of any plant and its product. Much of the efficient production system is due to the careful supervision of D.W. Jenkins, factory manager.

A detailed description of the various departments would sound like a tale dealing with Santa Claus' mythical workshop at the North Pole for that's what the Westmoreland Specialty company plant is — a Santa Claus workshop, and hundreds of children all over this broad land every Christmas have some article manufactured at Grapeville station in their stocking when they waken Christmas morn. And many older folk, too, are delighted with the high grade table ware the Christmas brings them — just as the housewife takes pride in the other articles she buys which are made at this plant.

The tour of inspection under the able direction of paymaster T.R. Stoughton ended, the visitor pauses a moment to watch the swarm of girls punch the time clock at 11:45. The girls stop work a short while before the men in order to comply with the 54 hour a week state law governing the employment of women.

And then on an upper floor Mr. West, heads of departments and office force gather around the luncheon table.

Here Mr. West, Mr. Jenkins, Mr. Stoughton, H.G. Horn, bookkeeper; F.J. Rock, division factory manager; Mary Marshall, Frances Wolfe, Gertrude Yingling and Mary Baker and others of the office force enjoy the noon day lunch. (Gertrude Yingling, head of the office force, died in 1931. She had been employed at Westmoreland 25 years.)

Mr. West is merely one of the employes at this noonday affair. Business is forgotten and this particular day the possibility of Italy entering into the great war and the circus coming to Pittsburgh were the chief topics of conversation, although everybody was so busy discussing the menu there was little opportunity for any other discussion. And then the courtesy extended to a visitor may have precluded shop-talk.

Realizing that time meant money literally the visitor borrowed no more attention from the men who do things at the Westmoreland Specialty Company's plant but asked station agent Henry to flag the 12:42 train and soon was back in Jeannette.

The 'Little Journey' to Santa Claus' workshop was ended" (JD 5/25/15).

Westmoreland's 35th and 40th Anniversaries

These three anniversary write ups from the '20s allow us to see just how Westmoreland's glass was regarded 65 and 70 years ago. It seems clear that Westmoreland prided itself, then, in being an innovative company, and these accounts confirm that the trade viewed them this way as well.

Westmoreland's 35th anniversary — 1924

"An unusual record in the glassware industry is that of the Westmoreland Specialty Co. at Grapeville, Pa., which will observe within a few months its thirty-fifth anniversary....

In the variety of its product, the Westmoreland Specialty Co. also is unusual... and it has one of the largest decorating shops in the country. The line of decorated crystal and colored glass offered by this factory is most extensive, probably containing more items than any factory of similar size....

All the presently popular forms of glass decorating are done in the Westmoreland plant. There is a glass-cutting section where men work in front of large windows with plenty of natural light. Copper-wheel engraving also is done here. This is a high form of the cutting art.

The decorating department proper has various sections and employs a large number of men and women performing all kinds of decorating, from aerographed colors to gold encrustations. Because of the many kinds of decorated ware listed in the company's catalog, the decorating force is extremely flexible and includes in its number some operatives of high skill. The decorating department is entirely separate from the glass-manufacturing section. When an order is received, if the blanks are not in stock, they must first be made and then taken to the decorating department.

Not only does the decorating department exercise its art on table ware and decorative pieces in large numbers, but it also decorates a great number of specialties and novelties...

The Westmoreland Specialty Co... also makes its own molds... at the Westmoreland Plant, the mold shop has 12 employees, who are kept busy all the time, not only in designing and making molds for new wares, but also in replacing and refinishing worn and used molds. The mold equipment here is most extensive, necessarily so because of the great variety of shapes and sizes produced.

While both crystal and colored glass are made regularly, crystal forms the bulk of the output. The colors made cover a wide variety, running from opal or white to black....

Charles H. West, the president of the company, has been with it since the beginning.... Mr. West always has taken a lively interest in the affairs of the glassware industry and is serving his second year as president of the Associated Glass & Pottery Manufacturers....

The Westmoreland Specialty Co. takes its name from the county in which it is located — Westmoreland — but the name also includes the family — West — which has conducted it for nearly 35 years" (L 6/16/24).

Westmoreland's 40th anniversary — 1929

In this article written five years later, note the correction made to the earlier article concerning the origin of the company name.

"The Westmoreland Glass Co., on October 1 observed the 40th anniversary of its start in the glassware production field. For 40 years it has continued at Grapeville, establishing a record for continuance which is equalled by few factories in the glassware industry....

The Westmoreland Glass Co. also is unusual for the variety and distinctiveness of its products. It has for many years been a leader in the introduction of new things in glassware, including not only wares that have grown to be staples in glassware fac-

tory lines but also specialties.... If you could look over the new things that have come one after another in quick succession from the Westmoreland factory, you would only begin to realize the work and effort necessary to keep the trade supplied with new and attractive wares.

In the variety of its product, no factory of equal capacity has done more than the Westmoreland Glass Co. Not only does it produce varied lines of tableware in unusual designs in all the popular colors, but from its decorating shops come an extensive array of modern decorations, including engraving, cutting and etching. Many specialties also are produced, giving the Westmoreland line a unique variety.

Not only does the Westmoreland factory make all the glassware used in its decorating shops, but it makes its own moulds for its line of staples and novelties....

The factory... location is due to the big field of natural gas developed in and around Jeannette 40 or more years ago. The natural gas supply still is adequate.

The name of the Westmoreland Glass Co. is derived from its location and not from the West family which has been identified with it throughout its existence. The factory is in Westmoreland County, the original county of western Pennsylvania.

Charles H. West, president of the Westmoreland Glass Co., has been with the factory since its beginning. During the 40 years, there never has been any labor trouble and there are many employes who have been with the factory 30 years or more (Westmoreland's first strike was in

1950).... Charles H. West is assisted in the management by James J. Brainard as vice president and treasurer and by his son, S. Brainard West, as secretary..." (L 10/29).

Westmoreland's Story

(L 8/3/25)

There seems to be some confusion about Westmoreland's term "Silver Rose." It was first applied to the 1706 line of tableware, and then applied to the silver decoration used on their black glass — which included the 1211 Octagon console set. However, the "Silver Rose" decoration was used on other glass, and the 1211 Octagon line came with other decorations. (L 2/30)

15

The Skill of Forty Years Glassmaking

In contrast to the 1924 review which focused on Westmoreland's decorating, note the shift in emphasis towards the tableware lines and colored glassware, both of which were so much in vogue in the late '20s.

It is hard to believe the following review was written two months into the Depression; it could never have been written, say, 10 years later. Fifteen minutes after the Titanic struck the iceberg, no one seemed to understand the gravity of what had happened and what lay ahead. Except for those who had bought stock on margin, this also seems to have been the case shortly after the Oct. 29, 1929 Crash. Nevertheless, ahead lay a cataclysmic shake-up second only to what the country went through in the 1860s. Among the many changes brought about by the Crash: people no longer wrote this way!

Taking Like Wild Fire
Glass Hen and Toy Chicks

The vogue for reproductions has brought back these fascinating dishes into greater popularity than ever.

No. 3 Toy Chick

Quaint, ornamental and useful—gives them a three-fold purpose in the home of good taste.

To see them is to want to own them.

Made in etched crystal and beautiful shades of amber, green or blue, with decorated combs and eyes.

WESTMORELAND GLASS CO.
GRAPEVILLE, PA.

Representatives

NEW YORK — H. C. Gray Co., 200 Fifth Avenue
BOSTON — H. P. & H. F. Hunt, 11 Pearl Street
Traveling Representatives
R. B. Reibeck, 1422 E. Marquette Rd.
R. A. Keel, 403 Lincoln Ave.
CHICAGO

PHILADELPHIA — Fred Stott, 1007 Filbert Street
SAN FRANCISCO — Himmelstern Bros., 718 Mission Street
LOS ANGELES — Himmelstern Bros., 643 S. Olive Street
SEATTLE, WASH. — Himmelstern Bros., Terminal Sales Bldg.

No. 2 medium size and large

(J 1/28/26)

A POPULAR ITEM FOR JUNE GIFTS

No. 1211/12½ CONSOLE SET

Among the great variety of individual pieces, combinations and sets in the WESTMORELAND line, we stress for June selling the Console Set illustrated.

We have taken the very attractive Silver Rose decoration and applied it to shining black glass in a new shape. The octagon-shaped bowl has a foot similar to the foot of the candlesticks.

This Console Set sells on sight. We suggest a good supply on hand when gift buying starts late in May.

WESTMORELAND GLASS CO.
GRAPEVILLE, PENNA.

REPRESENTATIVES

New York—H. C. Gray Co., 200 Fifth Avenue.
Chicago—Ira A. Jones Co., 208 W. Randolph Street.
Philadelphia—Fred Stott, 1007 Filbert Street.
Boston—H. P. & H. F. Hunt Co., 72 Summer Street.
Baltimore, Md.—John A. Dobson & Co., 110 Hopkins Place
San Francisco—Himmelstern Bros., 718 Mission Street.
Los Angeles—Himmelstern Bros., 643 South Olive Street.
Seattle—Himmelstern Bros., Terminal Sales Building.
R. A. Keel, 65 E. Walnut Lane, Germantown, Philadelphia.

—Twenty-seven miles east of Pittsburgh on Penna R. R.—

(L 4/30)

"Comparison of the earliest product of our foremost glassware factories with the ware they produce today brings to the impartial observer a grateful sense of progress and improvement... and the vast difference... is, perhaps, nowhere better illustrated than in the present product of the factory of the Westmoreland Glass Co., Grapeville, Pa., one of the leaders in the glassware industry.

The Westmoreland factory was established in 1889.... The factory produced in those days what might be classed as common glassware: beer mugs, jelly glasses, jars for kitchen use, and four-piece table sets comprising sugar bowl, cream pitcher, butter dish and spoon holder. Many specialties also... such as glass guns and lanterns and similar toys, intended to be filled with candies, were brought out to a market composed of the younger members.... (Candy containers actually were made and filled at Westmoreland to the end of the West period.) *Oil lamps, too, were a mainstay of production in the dear departed days.... It was characteristic of those pressed glass lamps, wherever made, that they could not lay claim to much beauty of shape or decoration, except those of a strictly simple colonial design which was not duly appreciated in the ornate 80's!*

Still another item which this company made in lesser quantity forty years ago (from about 1902) *was the opalescent* (opal) *hen and nest: a dish which if memory serves us aright, was intended to hold matutinal eggs and keep them properly hot. It was made for the trade continuously for about four or five years... but now this quaint ornament of the breakfast table has disappeared from the market.... Sold nowadays as antiques, these glass hens and homely glass lamps and so forth reflect the taste and needs of a simpler, less 'sophisticated' generation, a more limited age which, if blessed with better manners and morals, lacked the virtue of truly artistic taste in many articles of household equipment.* (In 1935 in *American Home Magazine*, Westmoreland's hens and other animals on baskets were shown used as individual soup tureens in two table settings.) *What a contrast with present preferences and requirements — met so successfully by the wares produced by the Westmoreland factory today!...*

In their showrooms! One's first impression is of the great diversity of lines on display: here in pressed and blown glass, cut glass, art vases, bowls, candlesticks, jugs and jars, compotes and condiment sets, cheese and cracker dishes, relish dishes, asparagus dishes, sandwich plates, flat or tri-footed cake plates, cracked-ice buckets, toilet bottles which, by the way, includes a very complete line, tobacco jars, cigarette boxes... glass that is pink... green... blue....

(There) *is a line of pressed glass stemware (**555** line) so expertly wrought as to invite comparison with fine cut glass. The sparkling glasses are ebony footed* (for 1930 and 1931), *some with a circlet of laurel leaves white against the glossy black,* others without the decoration of leaves. Black glass plates complete this attractive luncheon set.

Another line consists of finger bowls of various colors, shaped to resemble an opened lotus blossom (**1921 Lotus** line). And there are graceful candlesticks, the design of which is borrowed from the famous dolphin candlesticks of Venetian manufacture (No. **1049**).

There are tobacco jars, blue and amber, with cameo decorations. There are ice buckets of plain glass, blue, green, or of etched or frosted glass; some of the plain and frosted buckets are ornamented with icicles in relief (No. **200**), as if hanging over their rims.

A large assortment of salad plates in rose, amber, green and blue includes some that have clusters of grapes and pears in relief on their under sides (**1058 Fruit** line), and similar fruit decoration is applied to certain pressed vases, while others are adorned with raised long-stemmed roses and buds (**1706 Silver Rose** line). Bowls, almost without number, round and octagonal (**1211 Octagon** line), plain or etched or moulded in flower and fruit ornament in relief; octagonal bowls with the rim of each side bent toward the center, giving them the appearance of morning-glory blossoms; other eight-sided bowls, two with quaint down curling handles growing out of the point of junction of two sides; round bowls with flanges covered with

gold encrustations....

It is interesting to recall to mind the fact that a distinct preference for colored

(J 3/28)

glassware was started about twenty-five years ago and lasted two or three years, then died out for a time. Its revival within recent years is still 'going strong,' and bids fair to continue in widespread popularity — according to the expressed view of one of the officers of the Westmoreland Co....

It was in 1910 that the transition from what we have termed common glassware to finer glassware, as well as the marked diversification of their line took place..."

Alden Welles (J 1/30).

James H. Brainard's Story

The following account deserves its place here — not because of its content accuracy, but because of the importance of its author to Westmoreland's history. Jas Heaton Brainard, son of Jas Jacob Brainard, went to work at Westmoreland in October 1933, in the depths of the Depression, four months after graduating from college. He began, and worked for 20 years directly under his father (initially as assistant treasurer) until the latter's death in November 1953. At that time he

succeeded his father as president and remained in that capacity until he sold the company in March 1981. His span of time with Westmoreland was just five months shy of Chas West's 47 years and 10 months.

I found this personally-typed, one-page history filed with the Jeannette Public Library. Evidently, this is the way J.H. Brainard wanted Westmoreland's story told and remembered.

"A copy of the earliest record is herewith enclosed, and it indicates that in the Spring of 1889 a group of men operating the Specialty Glass Company in East Liverpool, Ohio, migrated to Grapeville because of Gas being on the property where our plant is now located. In October of 1889 construction of the plant started, and actu-

al production occurred in early 1890.

My grandfather, Ira F. Brainard, lived in Pittsburgh — about 25 miles west of Grapeville, and had many interests and was instrumental in financially helping two sons with a widowed mother, participate in the development of the factory here at Grapeville. The men from East Liverpool

**James Heaton Brainard,
1968.** (Company photograph)

sold out their interest in the very early 90's and the two West brothers, backed by my grandfather's finances, operated the plant successfully until 1920. At that time friction developed between the West brothers, and one sold his interest to the other and my grandfather.

In 1924, it was voted to change our name from Westmoreland Specialty Company to WESTMORELAND GLASS COMPANY, as the former had become somewhat of a misnomer because they began to get inquires on many different types of products, going so far as Flat Silverware for use in the Railroad's Pullman Dining Cars. I believe that even a request was made for Guns during World War I. By that time people began to feel that we manufactured most any item. Actually, glassware was the only real item manufactured, although early in the 1900's many condiments such as vinegar, mustard, baking powder, lemon flavor, etc. were processed here; but it is difficult to say whether such things were supplied in the containers for the purpose of selling the glassware of the condiment involved.

During World War I, many glass items contained Candy and were distributed by the News Stands and Dime stores throughout the country. Such diversification was not profitable because, as mentioned above, glass was the primary product of the Company. It was of high quality, manufactured by hand from the Pot Furnaces. Milk Glass, such as our Hens and other pieces illustrated in the enclosed booklet, was probably the outstanding material produced; although in the 1920's we did make some high quality decorated ware and crystal. We still manufacture some decorated ware in addition to Colored Crystal such as Amber, Blue, Green, and Pink. During the last thirty years our manufacturing has been 90% Milk Glass, and the quality today is undoubtedly superior to that of years ago.

In the years following the Civil War, there were a number of Milk Glass producers in the Pittsburgh, Pennsylvania area, and one of the outstanding plants was the Atterbury Company. They made high quality Milk Glass and our Company came into it a year or so after they went out of existence. So, in a sense, we carried on where they left off.

During the depression in the 30's our company, like many plants, was badly hurt, but we never stopped operations and re-organization took place in 1937 after the West financial interest became worthless and considerable investment was being risked by the Brainard interest. My father, James J. Brainard, who joined the company in 1920 as treasurer, became President in 1937. I took over as treasurer after joining the company in 1933 following graduation from Yale University.

My father's death occurred in 1953, and I became President of the Company shortly afterwards. My grandfather died in 1927.

J.H. Brainard, President

Four Significant Years

1889 — The Founding

In the beginning it was all Grapeville — miles of woods and farmland in Pennsylvania's Westmoreland County surrounding a general store and post office (which still stands) just a short walk from Pennsylvania Railroad's tiny Grapeville station. Then in early 1888, thanks to natural gas discoveries, it rapidly began to change.

Much would later be written about the activities of H. Sellers McKee and James A. Chambers that year. With the help of a syndicate formed for the purpose, they bought close to 800 acres of Grapeville farmland, laid out a town which they named after McKee's wife, Jeannette, and then sold off building lots to finance the construction of two plants. This land profiteering in the absence of zoning, seems to have benefited everyone at the time. Grapeville's farmers were paid up to $600 an acre (1995: $11,900) for their land, and it was said that some of those that paid $400 for each of the subdivided lots in 1888 were able to resell them less than a year later for four times that amount. In America in the late nineteenth century, you certainly could make a silk purse out of a sow's ear!

Incredibly, in mid-May 1888, just a few months after the enterprise began, a new Chambers-McKee window glass plant was reported to be in operation. Then four months later, the relocated McKee glass plant began to turn out the first of its Jeannette glass. It was said that over the summer the entire McKee glass facility was moved out in 40 box cars from Pittsburgh, 27 miles to the west.

What is of particular interest to us here is an almost identical, though less publicized development, which took place about a year and a quarter later in part of the remaining area of Grapeville. But before examining this, let us turn back to March 1888, to East Liverpool, Ohio, a pottery center located about 60 miles to the west.

Specialty Glass

In early 1888, a group of Pittsburgh businessmen bought a nearly new but abandoned glass factory from the Masonic Bank of Pittsburgh. They agreed on a name, the "Novelty Glass Co.," but before the month was out they had to change it to the "Specialty Glass Co." for they found their chosen name was already chartered (J 3/22/88). A.J. Stevenson, described as a "wealthy retired oil merchant," was the first president, and a Major George Irwin was the business manager. Stevenson held a 17 percent interest against Irwin's 10 percent, but Irwin was also a "trustee" over another 45 percent. Apparently, Stevenson was just a figurehead, for by year-end Irwin was president — a position he held until he left Specialty Glass in January 1891. After 1888, Stevenson's name appeared only as a director.

A trade reporter wrote at the time, "Here was lying idle an almost new and very valuable glass plant right in the very heart of the natural gas field." (J 3/22/88). True. But the reporter (as well as the investors) should have continued digging. The glass plant he described so glowingly had been built six years before by a newly-formed group headed by George Fry (H.C. Fry's brother) of nearby Rochester, Pa. This group was chartered as the Liverpool Glass Mfg. Co., Ltd. Owing to particularly stiff import competition, pottery wages had always been well below glass wages. For this reason America's two pottery centers, Trenton and East Liverpool, were located away from glassmaking. Nevertheless, when the Liverpool Glass works were completed in late 1882, the new company roused this issue out of its dormancy when it hired pottery workers, then involved in a

labor dispute, and paid them glass workers wages. Within a few months this company was forced to close because of financial problems, possibly related to the supply of gas; and the new facility apparently sat unused for more than five years.

After the Specialty group bought the buildings, they began to make glass there in April 1888 — presumably with glass workers brought in from outside. But their serene beginning was soon followed by a succession of misfortunes, only some of which were accidental. In May that year there was a major fire that was successfully put out. Then, a year and a half later the crown of the furnace caved in causing a three-week shutdown. This was followed by another shutdown two months after that when the company could not get soda. Over the years there were a number of shutdowns caused by gas shortages as the town fathers made sure the glass company was the first to be shut off whenever the pressure was reduced. One such shut-off in 1896 destroyed six pots. Finally, since the town would never build Specialty an access road, the plant finally burned to the water line in March 1898 during a flood when it caught fire and firemen were unable to get to it.

Over the years Specialty had not been without its own supply of darts, however. For example, in 1891 they complained to the Board of Health about the "awful stench" of burning bones from the pottery companies. (This complaint was picked up by the local Democratic newspaper, but totally ignored by the Republican

"W.S. Co - Glass Works," c. 1895 from the southwest taken by the Pennsylvania Railroad. (family photo)

Westmoreland's Story

This ad appeared in the Greensburg Daily Tribune every day from June 26, 1889 through October 23, 1889. "East Jeannette" was an early attempt to rename the rest of Grapeville; it was no longer used after 1890.

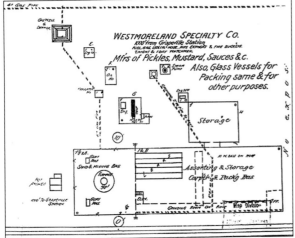

Sanborn fire insurance map of 1891.

newspaper.) The town council, however, did nothing even after the Board of Health requested a local ordinance prohibiting the burning of bones at the potteries. Clearly they were unwilling to interfere with the pro-bono work at the olfactory!

Fourteen months after they began, Specialty decided to do something about two of their problems: the price and the uncertainty of their gas. They began in late May 1889 to drill for gas on the plant property. But shortly afterwards, when they came up dry and were unable to negotiate more favorable terms, they decided to relocate. In early June they purchased about 20 acres of land, just to the east of the railroad station in Grapeville, and before the month was out they began to excavate for a new plant there. Just as the Chambers and McKee interests had laid out much of Jeannette and sold off lots the year before, Specialty now did the same in Grapeville. They laid out 13 acres in 40' x 100' lots and offered them for sale to their workers in East Liverpool. In a letter of June 1889 to the workers (copy on file at the Jeanette Public Library) George Irwin offered to sell them lots in advance of an auction to be held July 1st at "a price... agreed upon." He offered as an inducement, free gas to every house built within a year as long as the supply lasted, and he projected this could be for "at least 20 years." He predicted the lots would sell at auction "from $300 upward," and speculated that buyers could "double or triple their money on every purchase made within the next year." The purpose of Irwin's hype, of course, was to finance the construction of the new plant. The local paper reported that 70 lots were sold at the July 1st auction at an average price of $330 each, which meant Specialty grossed $23,000 (1995: $458,000) that day alone (JD 7/5/89). Construction of the plant seems to have begun just after the auction brought in the needed capital, but individual lot sales continued long after the auction. An ad for lots appeared in a local newspaper from June 26th every day for four months.

Westmoreland Specialty

When Specialty closed for summer recess in early July, they evidently had no intention of reopening in East Liverpool, for they advertised their plant in the Pittsburgh newspapers. The West brothers, George and Charles, must have seen and responded to this ad, but they apparently insisted on buying the new Grapeville plant — the one not advertised. Perhaps rumors of the difficulties of East Liverpool reached the brothers, or perhaps it was simply the prospect of an easier commute from the East Liberty station to Grapeville each day. But sometime in August, the East Liverpool works were back in operation and Specialty was presumably reconciled to the sale of Grapeville (J 8/1/89).

From the time they saw the ad, the brothers had three months to sell their interest in a family dry goods business and prepare for a new career. This transition from dry goods to glass proved to be no more a problem for the Wests than to Deming Jarvis, 60-some years before. In the nineteenth century, American businessmen seemed to be regularly venturing into new, unrelated businesses — without the help of twentieth century cost accounting systems to guide them.

By October 14th, the date of Westmoreland's incorporation, Specialty Glass was out of the picture. The West brothers brought $40,000 to the new company and George Irwin, evidently representing himself, brought the buildings and land. The press noted, "The Specialty Glass works have decided not to move away from East Liverpool. Major Irwin has disposed of the new works at Jeannette, Pa... together with all the real estate they owned at a nice advance over cost..." (J 10/17/89). The choice of the new company's name has never really been explained. But "Specialty" was probably chosen for the company that put up the buildings, and "Westmoreland" (rather than the more obvious "Grapeville") may have been chosen as subtle encouragement to the brothers who put up the cash. Major Irwin's contribution to the company was valued at $35,000 — giving him an ownership plurality of 47 percent. The Wests raised their 53 percent share on their own; they were not "backed."

The original 100' x 220' building, finished or nearly finished on October 14th, deserves some mention here, for it still survives (1995) as part of an enlarged complex. The 16-pot, 16-ton, Nicholson-type furnace described as "perhaps the largest furnace of the kind in the United States" (JD 10/11/89), was constructed by 20 men under the supervision of W.J. Kemp of Pittsburgh. J.W. Douthitt, also of Pittsburgh, was the contractor. The contractor for the the carpentry work was Benz Brothers, and the supervisor was J.W. Coleson (JD 10/11/89). The imposing cathedral-like ceiling with its original wood beams spanning 80 feet with only a single scarf joint survives today unaltered. We know that "gas was turned on the ovens for the first time" on Friday, November 15, 1889 (JD 11/22/89), and this furnace was used continuously to the late '20s when it was replaced by another furnace almost identical to it. Except for summer breaks, glass was made at the Westmoreland factory from February 1890 (Chas West's cited date) continuously to May 30, 1982, and from July 12, 1982 to June 6, 1984 — a total of 94 years. It appears glass was made at that plant for a longer period of time than in any other surviving glass factory in the country. Also, glass may have been made there continuously for a longer period of time than in any other surviving glass factory in the world. Despite water damage and substantial vandalizing in 1992, it was still intact in 1995 with both furnaces, the lehr, the glory holes, and many moulds, snaps, and other tools that were used over the years.

The ultra-kinetic George Irwin was the president of both Specialty Glass and Westmoreland Specialty from October 1889 to January 1891. That year and a quarter must have been an exciting one for both companies. By mid-1890, Westmoreland was turning out paper boxes in a separate paper box building. Then in December the press reported that they made "an article of food called egg custard... put up in every conceivable shape. They also manufacture an excellent quality of cologne... paper boxes... cologne bottles, etc. The food articles find a market in all parts of the United States as well as Europe" (JD 12/17/90). The next year on the Sanborn fire insurance map, Westmoreland was described as "Manufacturers of pickles, mustard, sauces etc. Also glass vessels for packing same and for other purposes." Earlier that year it was, perhaps, more accurately reported, "They manufacture glassware for preparations of egg custard, candy, mustard, and cologne" (L 2/25/91). Since the article excerpt-ed from the local paper mentions the names of Westmoreland's three founding owners, we can be sure Major Irwin was still there through mid-December 1890.

It is interesting that before the February 1891 press report, there is little mention of Westmoreland's glass. Yet, several press reports on Specialty Glass before January 1891 mention only their glass. While it appears Specialty did no packaging themselves, they made a variety of novelties and containers intended for packaging, as well as light bulbs, arc globes, battery jars, etc, never to my knowledge made by Westmoreland. Nevertheless, a "Revolver Flask" of Specialty's appears to have been the basis of a later Westmoreland candy container. Also, George Irwin's patented glass screw cover was used by both concerns.

Non-manufacturing activities of Westmoreland in 1890 are even more interesting than the products they made. A few months into the year, a decision was made to expand the factory. On June 6th excavation began for a major addition which was completed within several months. In late 1890 the main building, which had measured 100' x 220' at the beginning of the year, now measured 100' x 400'. In order to pay for this, the Major, as before, proved equal to the challenge. In July 1890 Westmoreland's capital stock was increased to $150,000 by the sale of 750 — $100 shares of Class B (non-voting) stock to workers and townspeople. What was not used for the plant or for working capital was used to construct a hotel (which stood until the '30s across from the plant) and a number of houses, which were then sold off. Initially, 40 houses were built by the company followed by 90 more. At the end of the year it was reported that the three original stockholders received a dividend of 15 percent. Company records show this class B stock was bought back by Westmoreland and by the end of 1898, seven-eighths of it had been retired.

In January 1891 there was no record of Major George Irwin in either company. On January 22 Specialty Glass held their annual election of officers: Jno G. Quay was elected president and business manager. That same week Westmoreland's stockholders held their annual meeting. It was simply reported that George R. West "was elected president in place of Major Irwin" (L 1/28/91). Major Irwin seems to have disappeared. But had he?

Westmoreland's Story

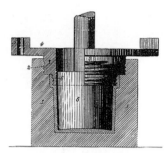

This patent of Major Irwin's, applied for in August 1889, made possible the glass screw-on cap used by Specialty Glass and also by Westmoreland in their Columbus, Isabella, and Brunswick jars in the '90s.

Westmoreland's Story

Chas Howard West and Ira Fitch Brainard, c. 1923.

(taken by Helen West Wilson)

This ad, with its bold Shakesperean lead, suggests George West was personally responsible for Westmoreland's spirited early advertising. The stand was very likely made in Westmoreland's blacksmith shop. (JC 5/21/24)

In May, a large ad appeared in the Jeannette paper which was worded, "Irwin — Those Seeking Profitable Investments... the Mammoth Plate Glass Works Costing over a million dollars will soon be completed and will necessitate the erection of fully 400 dwellings..." (JD 5/29/91). While there is a nearby town named "Irwin," its name going back to the eighteenth century, this ad certainly seems to be covered all over with the Major's fingerprints!

At some point after the founding, Ira Brainard came into the company, and I believe January 1891 was the date. Apparently, Major Irwin sold 16 percent of his stock to George West, for the 1909 reorganization papers show that George West's proportion was then 37 percent — up from 33 percent at the time of the founding. But the rest of Irwin's shares must have been sold then to Ira Brainard, for in 1909 he owned 39 percent of the business. Chas West's share rose insignificantly from 20 percent to 21 percent over the 20-year period.

Ira Brainard, who had earlier made money investing in the Bourbon Stockyards of Louisville, lived in Pittsburgh at 301 North Highland Avenue a few blocks from George West. Nevertheless, because of their later close, personal friendship, it must have been Chas West who brought him into the company. I do not know how Charles, or perhaps the West brothers, first met Ira Brainard, but it could have been through a Masonic connection. Ira Brainard and the two Wests were all Shriners, and therefore Masons, and I have speculated they could have been fellow lodge members. If this is correct, it was the Wests rather than Major Irwin who found this congenial partner — one, unlike Major Irwin, with no interest in the operation of the business. Since I could find no record of George Irwin in Pittsburgh's Syria Temple, I have assumed there was probably no connection between these two men.

1921 — The Change of Management

"Announcement was made last week that George R. West had resigned as president of the Westmoreland Specialty Co... and that he had been succeeded as head of the company by his brother, Charles H. West, who has been treasurer. In retiring from the Westmoreland Specialty Co., Mr. George West takes with him his sons, George L. West and Charles H. West II.... James J. Brainard will take the place of C.H. West as treasurer. It is understood that R. B. Reineck, as sales manager, and D.W. Jenkins, as factory manager, will continue in their present places" (L 5/16/21).

Two days later the local paper reported, *"George R. West and sons, Charles and George Jr... have purchased the building and grounds comprising about two acres of the Jeannette Union Planing Mill Co.... The firm name is George R. West & Sons.... Within a short time the manufacture of high grade decorated glass ware will be begun.... Mr. West for many years has been associated with his brother Charles West in the Westmoreland Specialty Co. works at Grapeville. He will retain his interests in that concern..."* (JD 5/18/21).

In his short history, Jas Heaton Brainard wrote that "Friction developed between the West brothers" and that this lead to George West's departure. True. But this "friction" was the direct result of his grandfather, Ira, asking if a place could be found in Westmoreland for his father, Jas Jacob, who had moved to Pittsburgh with his family not long before.

In terms of Westmoreland's direction, both West brothers had evidently seen eye-to-eye for 32 years. And of course they had been partners in a wide variety of West Brothers ventures since, at least, 1895. Where the two differed sharply, however, was in their views of the proper role of Ira Brainard, Westmoreland's third stockholder, in their company.

Charles and Helen West were socially very close to Ira Brainard and his wife, Fanny. The Wests named their only son Sam'l Brainard West in 1900. The two couples played bridge together once a week for years. In my research I found Charles and Helen West's signatures on Ira's home-typed 1917 will, and again on related legal documents following his death (just six months after Fanny's) in 1927. But there seems to have been no comparable link between the Brainards and the George Wests. George L. West wrote in his *Westmoreland Story* that he had never met Ira Brainard and had never seen him at the plant. Apparently, even though the families lived just a few blocks apart, Ira Brainard had never visited the George West home. In 1921 Westmoreland was still prospering from its record earnings of the World War I era, and in that halcyon period both of George West's sons were employed there. It is not hard to understand why Charles agreed to create a position for Jas Jacob Brainard when he was asked by his friend, Ira.

Perhaps it was prescience; perhaps it was just personal. But for whatever reason, George West adamantly refused to go along with his brother's decision In fact, George L. West told me his father gave Charles the ultimatum, "It's him or me," and then made good his threat when Charles refused to back down. Company records seem to support George L. West's account: they show that J.J. Brainard began his employment in May 1921, within days after George West left with his two sons.

Although the Brainard ownership share was down to just 13 percent at the time of Ira's death in 1927, it had been almost 40 percent in 1909, and it was presumably still that high in 1921. With about 40 percent of the stock controlled by Ira Brainard and the remaining 60 percent split between the Wests, any two of these stockholders were in a position to outvote the third. And so, if this matter had come to a formal vote, George West could not have prevailed.

Ira's request must have been made that spring. In January, George West was interviewed by a trade publication where he boasted of Westmoreland's being "The largest decorating factory in the United States" and he added, "We are running at capacity with orders contracted months ahead" (B 1/29/21). If George

West's suitcase was then half packed, he was certainly showing no signs of it to the reporter.

With George's departure, Charles moved up from his secretary-treasurer position, which he had held since Westmoreland's founding, to president. He sent for his son in Texas, then beginning a career as an engineer for Gulf Oil, and made him Westmoreland's secretary. Then when J.J. Brainard arrived, Charles made him treasurer, and added the honorary, "vice president" to his title.

Initially, George decided to hold on to his Westmoreland stock, but later he changed his mind and sold his entire interest to his brother. By October it was reported his new company, George R. West & Sons, had spent $100,000 (1995: $860,000) in remodeling and installing equipment (L 10/17/21). The bulk of this money must have come from the sale of his stock in Westmoreland.

Some of the decorating done at George R. West & Sons in the '20s seems to have paralleled the decorating done at Westmoreland. Glass cutting, however, which was expanded at Westmoreland under Chas West, was not done there at all. Since his new facility was in operation within a matter of weeks, George West must have taken with him his pick of Westmoreland's decorators. Initially, all of its decorating was done on American china and imported free-blown glass blanks, but later it bought blanks from Westmoreland. According to Robert Jones, who began his Westmoreland employment in 1924, the West brothers continued to ride up together in the train each morning. George, he said, would get off in Jeannette, while Charles would stay on till the next station, Grapeville.

Westmoreland's Story

Top : Sam'l Brainard West at Chautauqua, c. 1922.
(taken by Helen West Wilson)

Center: James Jacob Brainard at Pike Run, c. 1922. (taken by Helen West Wilson)

These bath bottles, Westmoreland's 1105, confirm George R. West & Sons was using Westmoreland's blanks for their decorating. (JC 1/2/24)

1925 — The Change of Name

Westmoreland Specialty Co.
GRAPEVILLE, PA.

In the Westmoreland line of high grade glassware there are many items most suitable for gifts and remembrances.

No. 1820—Relish Dish With Cocktail Center

The illustration shows only one of hundreds of items in crystal and colors most suitable for decorators and cutters. Many new pieces for 1925.

REPRESENTATIVES—
New York—H. C. Gray Co., 200 Fifth Avenue.
Philadelphia—Fred Stott, 1007 Filbert Street.
Boston—H. P. & H. F. Hunt, 41 Pearl Street.
San Francisco—Himmelstern Bros., 718 Mission Street.
Los Angeles—Himmelstern Bros., 643 S. Olive Street.
Seattle—Himmelstern Bros., Terminal Sales Building.
Trav. Rep.—R. B. Reineck, 1422 E. Marquette Rd., Chicago.
Trav. Rep.—W. R. Renouf, East Liverpool, Ohio.

(L 1/26/25)

WESTMORELAND GLASS CO.
GRAPEVILLE, PA.

In the Westmoreland line of high grade glassware there are many items most suitable for gifts and remembrances.

No. 1820—Relish Dish With Cocktail Center

The illustration shows only one of hundreds of items in crystal and colors most suitable for decorators and cutters. Many new pieces for 1925.

REPRESENTATIVES—
New York—H. C. Gray Co., 200 Fifth Avenue.
Philadelphia—Fred Stott, 1007 Filbert Street.
Boston—H. P. & H. F. Hunt, 41 Pearl Street.
San Francisco—Himmelstern Bros., 718 Mission Street.
Los Angeles—Himmelstern Bros., 643 South Olive Street.
Seattle—Himmelstern Bros., Terminal Sales Building.
Trav. Rep.—R. B. Reineck, 1422 E. Marquette Rd., Chicago.
Trav. Rep.—W. R. Renouf, East Liverpool, Ohio.

L 2/23/25

At a meeting of the directors held on March 14, 1924, it was *"Resolved that the name, style, and title of this corporation be changed from Westmoreland Specialty Company to Westmoreland Glass Company."* Almost a year later on February 10, 1925, Chas West and his son S. Brainard West, secretary, signed a Letter of Patent making the name change official. The press reported that *"Announcement was made February 20 that hereafter the Westmoreland Specialty Co... will be known as the Westmoreland Glass Co.... The name had been found somewhat misleading and in order that the buying trade and public should recognize it readily as a glass manufacturer, the name henceforth will be the Westmoreland Glass Co."* (L 2/23/25). Another trade magazine wrote that *"The former name did not convey the correct impression, that the concern were glassware manufacturers..."* (J 2/26/25).

Is there any particular significance to this 1925 date? At the time of the name change Westmoreland was operating at capacity; its new 16-pot furnace had been operating for more than a year together with its original 1889 furnace. Westmoreland's employment was at its all-time peak of about 500 — up from about 400 before the new furnace and lehr were put in service. Westmoreland's 1924 catalog, its last "Specialty" catalog, had 124 pages, and with a 21-page supplement, it continued to be used through 1925. Westmoreland's 1926 catalog, its first "Glass Co." catalog, had 172 pages, and it contained everything shown in the earlier catalog. Then a year later a 49-page supplement added the new glass items for 1927. Three ads were printed in the trade journals shortly before February 20 that used the "Specialty" name; the same three ads appeared just after this date with the new "Glass" name. The ads were otherwise identical.

Nevertheless, primarily due to renewed import competition, major changes were occurring just beneath this placid surface. The 1924 catalog showed a large number of fairly plain blanks created primarily for decorating. But from that point on, many of the new items were more complex pieces — many intended to be sold "as is" without decoration. In order to meet competition, more of Westmoreland's color had to come from its glass and more of its "decoration" had to be built into its pressings. But Chas West seems to have been obstinately unwilling to abandon decorative handwork to the Central Europeans. Some of Westmoreland's finest decorating was done in that difficult decade from 1925 on.

1937 — The Change of Ownership

In a letter of commendation to a long-term employee, Jas Jacob Brainard wrote in 1949; "You have seen many changes both in the executive and operating departments. You have seen the decline of the company to an all but a dissolution and a point where it didn't seem as if it could possibly survive. Then the company took on new life...until it has advanced to the most prosperous years since its organization...." Was this, indeed, the case? Was Westmoreland ever at a point of "dissolution?"

When Ira Brainard died in 1927, an inventory of his estate shows he held 110 shares of Westmoreland — just 13 percent of the company. However, he also held two notes against the company totaling $15,000. His two sons, Jas Jacob and Edward Heaton, each received 55 shares of the stock; J.J. received the $5,000 note and E.J. (with no working connection to Westmoreland) received the $10,000 note. The remaining seven-eighths of Westmoreland stock was owned by Chas West, who retained his original shares from 1889 plus the shares he had purchased from his brother and Ira Brainard.

Surviving documents at the plant show a pattern of apparent losses from the mid-'20s to the early '40s. The reasons for this are partly external and partly internal.

The external reasons are not hard to understand. In the late nineteenth century many skilled workmen came to this country to better their lot. But the only way this was possible was through greater efficiencies here than in Europe. One of these efficiencies was an economy of scale made possible by America's large internal market. Another was easy access to raw materials and often cheaper fuel. In addition there was a social as well as an economic premium placed on "American ingenuity," which usually meant the elimination of handwork. This was a particular problem, however, for American industries such as glassware, where a premium was placed on the very thing that had to be curtailed. Because of this, American glassware always depended on high tariffs (or foreign wars) for its survival. It is no accident that this industry benefitted in the period immediately following the McKinley Tariff of 1890, the European war of August 1914, the Fordney McCumber Tariff of 1922, the Smoot-Hawley Tariff effective June 1930, and finally, Hitler's conquest of Czechoslovakia in 1938–1939. In the case of the much-maligned Smoot-Hawley Tariff, for example; imports, which accounted for 32 percent of glass and pottery sales in 1929, dropped to 21 percent in 1931 and to 16 percent in 1932 (L 11/43). While the tariff was raised only on blown glass, it was imported blown glass that was competing with American pressed glass. According to one estimate, 150,000 people were employed in Czechoslovakia's glass industry in 1934 (WS 336), and according to Chas West, in 1925 their wages were only a fifth of ours (WC). Largely because of import competition, 1930 may have been the worst year in Westmoreland's long history. With its high proportion of handwork, Westmoreland was particularly vulnerable to imports.

Surviving accounting records show there were internal reasons for Westmoreland's losses as well. In 1923 Westmoreland's main building was extended and a new 16-pot furnace and lehr were installed at a cost in 1995 dollars of a little over $1 million. While the useful life of this construction was between 30 and 40 years and should have been depreciated over this time-span, the company

appears to have written it off in just ten. Some of those loss years would have shown a profit had it not been for the

crippling depreciation. Then too, the company's large number of new moulds made from the '20s on were not capitalized (i.e., placed on the "books" and depreciated), but expensed as they were made. This meant that in heavy mould-making years, there was an artificially high manufacturing cost unrelated to the glass made and sold that year. These irregularities affected Westmoreland's balance sheets as well as their income statements: the company's fixed assets and net worth through this period were both understated. There was nothing wrong with this sort of accounting for tax purposes (assuming it was acceptable — and apparently it was); but it was unacceptable for stockholder reporting. Net worth, or owner's equity, can loosely be defined as, "what's left over after all the bills are paid"; it is the stake the owners have in their business. The most typical complaint made about it is that it generally tends to be too low because it is based on assets valued at historical cost. In the case of Westmoreland, for example, their six-plus acres of land were carried on the books for just $1000.

For 1936 Westmoreland's accounting records show an annual loss of $8000, which pulled the company's net worth down from $77,400 at the end of 1935 to $69,400 at the end of 1936. This last amount, a very respectable $812,000 in 1995 dollars, failed to include as assets the new building addition and thousands of moulds — probably the company's most valuable asset at the time. Nevertheless, in 1937 the Brainards (J.J. was then treasurer, J.H., assistant treasurer) unaccountably

Christmas, 1947. From left: Dorothy Eger, Jessie Ferrante, Gladys DeWalt, Patsy Beckner, Dorothy Kramer, Alfred Petrill, Julie Wallick, Walter M. Brainard, J.H. Brainard, J.J. Brainard, Mildred Myers, Stella Smith (Mrs. J.H.) Brainard, Philip C. Brainard, Leanne Rogers, Dorothy Morman, Dorothy Winterhalter, Sally Stough, Mary Lou Fulgenzio, and Florence Bush.

(factory photo)

lowered December 1936's net worth by 40 percent to $41,300. The file shows evidence this deflated amount was used on their balance sheets for only a few years after which it was restored to its earlier level. Also, a 1954 management consultant study on file used the net worth amounts for these years that would have been in effect had there been no 1937 write-down. But even with this write-down, December 1936's net worth was still close to a half million 1995 dollars.

A short article in a September 1937 trade publication was headed, "Brainard Group Takes Helm at Westmoreland Glass Company" (L 9/37). How did they do it? Why at this time? The first question is easier to answer. The glassware business is on an annual sales cycle similar to the toy business. Finished goods inventories, I understand, start to build in January, reach their peak in August each year, and then drop to their lowest levels at year-end. Every glass company, no matter how profitable, has a need for short term debt to finance their inventories when they approach their peak. Consequently, if these loans were to be called then, any company without an alternate source of cash would be in default. The two Brainards, J.J. and J.H., were responsible for securing these loans, and I believe J.J. and his brother, Edward Heaton, were personally making them to Westmoreland. In August 1937 they evidently called their loans, and neither Charles nor his company was able to pay.

In his account, J.H. Brainard wrote that in 1937 "The West financial interest became worthless." I have no reason to question this statement — in fact, it seems to confirm my impression of what took place then: that when Chas West left Westmoreland, he was not compensated for it. But if the West interest, which was seven-eighths of Westmoreland, was "worthless"; then, so too was the company. There could have been a second write-down of Westmoreland's assets in 1937 that was not recorded, but I think not. I believe the real answer lies beyond economics.

According to company records Chas West had paid himself no dividends from 1929, and possibly before. It is also my understanding he withdrew little or no salary in his last few years. The product cards and the 1932 price list suggest he was attempting to keep his prices low, probably to maintain employment during the depths of the Depression, even though this was an unsound business decision. Westmoreland had minimal fixed costs: Westmoreland needed margin — not volume then. However, I believe Chas West was particularly concerned about the hardship created by the Great Depression, and the story has come down to me he was aghast when he heard that some gift shops in financial distress asked if they could pay their Westmoreland bills with other merchandise.

He underwent a very difficult cataract operation in the mid-'30s that had been postponed for years. In January 1937 he retired as president of the Associated Glass & Pottery Manufacturers "on order of his physicians" (L 2/37). He had no reason to remain at Westmoreland except for his son. After Dan Jenkins, Westmoreland's superintendent, retired at the end of 1935 and was not immediately replaced by Sam Guy; the company, even to alterations in the glass formulas, was being pulled in two directions when Chas West was not there. Chas West was not a confrontational sort of person, and when confronted with a demand for his company and the prospect of a squabble over its "true" net worth; exhausted with the tension, he simply handed it over. Then sadly, the family would never discuss Westmoreland again.

Despite claims of a reorganization, there were no papers filed in Harrisburg, and the accounting continued on the same basis as before. It was simply a change of ownership.

Perhaps we can return to the question posed at the beginning: Was Westmoreland at "a point where it did not seem as if it could possibly survive?" At the first director's meeting held six months after the change of ownership, it was disclosed that Jas Jacob Brainard was receiving a salary of $14,000 (1995: $151,000), Jas Heaton was receiving a salary of $12,500 (1995: $135,000), and Edward Heaton (not employed there) was receiving $1,800 (1995: $19,000) for "part-time duties." In 1995 dollars, the company payouts to these three totaled $305,000: 22 percent of the amount of Westmoreland's 1937 sales, and 19 percent of the amount of Westmoreland's 1938 sales. I believe this answers the question.

Over its 95-year history, there were two different Westmorelands divided almost equally in the middle. The first, the West period, lasted 48 years; whereas the second, the Brainard period, lasted virtually as long. (I am including with the Brainard period the three years following the company's sale in 1981, for there was no break in the type of glassware being made then.)

The West Period, 1889 – 1937

The West period is the more complex of the two, for there is little in the way of glassware the Wests did not make at some point during their period of ownership. In the case of their tableware lines, for example, they made two lines just for Woolworths, but they also made some of America's finest cut glass, much of which was for table use. Nevertheless, when the Heisey Collectors of America reprinted Westmoreland's 1912 catalog in the 1980s they wrote, "This catalog shows that the Westmoreland Specialty Co. produced not only the containers for which they are usually remembered, but several entire pressed glass lines." In other words, even some of America's most knowledgeable glass collectors a decade ago evidently associated West period Westmoreland with their containers and little else.

Just as Sir Arthur Sullivan is remembered today for his "Mikado," and not for his beloved "Ivanhoe," perhaps it is only fair that early Westmoreland is best remembered for its novelties and "packers' goods." After all, that's where the brothers began in 1890, that's what set them apart, and that's where they made the bulk of their money. In early 1916 a trade reporter wrote: "Early last summer Westmoreland transformed the mustard department into the manufacture of tin and combination tin and glass toys of all kinds. The beginning was comparatively small but... today the new department is a formidable toy factory turning out the newest things by the thousands. Some of the articles produced are submarines, wagons, windmills, automobiles, trains, tin dishes, coffee pots and sets, glass dogs, glass watches, glass revolvers... in addition to a full line of novelties in the glassware line..." (L 1/3/16).

Then almost six years later another reporter wrote: "A collection of exceptionally clever novelties in glass... include miniature automobiles, tele-

phone, railroad engine and revolver.... The automobile Jitney has a glass wheel

base with bright red tin wheels and body attractively decorated. A limousine is also treated in the same manner. The cab of the engine is also of brightly colored tin. The telephone and revolver are also gotten up in similar effects. All have spaces for filling with candy..." (J 9/15/21).

But Westmoreland also had another side. A reporter two years later seemed to be referring to an entirely different company when he wrote, "The various products of the Westmoreland Specialty Co. are comprised mostly of hand decorated and cut and etched crystal" (L 11/19/23). Related to this, it is interesting to note that out of 3,120 moulds that survived at the factory in 1991, 439 of them were blow moulds from the West period.

There is one thing that binds most of West period glassware together, and that

1910 House Furnishings Show, Madison Square Garden, NY. The two men pictured are George R. West and the 14-year-old George L. West. While this picture appeared in *Pottery, Glass & Brass Salesman* (8/25/10), the original has come down in George West's family. The decorated opal vessels at the back will prove that these urns and vases, sometimes attributed to Fostoria, were in fact made by Westmoreland. (Avis West)

What is Westmoreland?

Corner of Westmoreland's decorating department in August 1915. Gustav Horn, head decorator, is believed to be the gentleman in the vest with the mustache.

(P.J. Russo)

In 1929 the *Jeannette Dispatch* reported that Westmoreland's glassware was "shipped to all countries of the world." They then added, "It has furnished glassware for the embassies in Japan and Spain" (JD 2/2/29). **This letter from Ambassador Woods to Chas West may explain why. It would be interesting to know just what Westmoreland glassware was used at the two embassies. Unfortunately, Chas West was never able to take his friend up on his invitation.**

is Westmoreland's decorating. From the turn of the century, almost everything of importance at Westmoreland was decorated: souvenir items, mustard containers, early opal, candy containers, art glass, black glass, and even some of the table glass. We know that in 1900 a new foreman was hired (JD 12/28/00), a separate decorating building was erected (L 5/4/00), and by year-end it was found to be inadequate (JD 11/2/00). We know that in 1921 George West was able to describe Westmoreland as, "The largest decorating factory in the United States... the largest decorators of glassware in this country..." (B 1/29/21).

At the turn of the century, Westmoreland turned to decorating to distinguish their glassware from similar glassware made by so many others; a generation later they used it to tailor

their glassware to different markets and to different years. Decorating was key to so much of the freshness they brought to the Pittsburgh Exhibit over the years. While new moulds were expensive, new decorations were cheap. New decorations were another way of creating new glass. In 1936, Chas West's last full year, Westmoreland seems to have introduced 43 new decorations: This, I believe, exceeded the total of all decorations used by Westmoreland in its last 30 years.

This book pictures close to 600 pieces of Westmoreland glass, and it is no accident most of them are decorated. While some are special pieces, the vast majority fairly represents the variety of glassware Westmoreland once made.

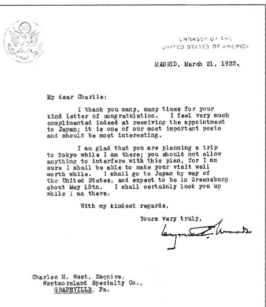

EMBASSY OF THE
UNITED STATES OF AMERICA

MADRID, March 21, 1923.

My dear Charlie:

I thank you many, many times for your kind letter of congratulation. I feel very much complimented indeed at receiving the appointment to Japan; it is one of our most important posts and should be most interesting.

I am glad that you are planning a trip to Tokyo while I am there; you should not allow anything to interfere with this plan, for I am sure I shall be able to make your visit well worth while. I shall go to Japan by way of the United States, and expect to be in Greensburg about May 15th. I shall certainly look you up while I am there.

With my kindest regards,

Yours very truly,

Charles H. West, Esquire,
Westmoreland Specialty Co.,
GRAPEVILLE, Pa.

The Brainard Period — From 1937

In 1944 Ruth Webb Lee wrote: "The Westmoreland Glass Co. is still in operation under entirely different management. They have been intensely active during recent years, in making up reproductions of old time patterns" (LVG 148).

In 1937 when the Brainards took control of Westmoreland, they made a number of changes — all of which made excellent business sense at the time. They gave Westmoreland its first focus and brand identity. They pulled back from direct competition with all the other hand houses and carved out their own special market niche. They promoted their glassware directly to that market and used terms that were mean-

ingful to that market. It may be significant that Fostoria and Westmoreland, two glass companies that went to the expense of advertising directly to the consumer, are two of those that survived into the '80s. This may be because they both cultivated slightly different markets, and because their advertising outlays were not matched by the rest of the industry.

Along with their "demand-pull" promotion, the Brainards increased their prices across the board. While this probably reduced their sales volume and employment initially, it gave the company, with its low break-even point, badly needed margin.

Production changes went hand-in-hand with marketing changes. Using what is known as the "80/20 Principle" — that 20 percent of the goods account for about 80 percent of the sales, they cleared out all slow-moving and hard-to-make glassware. At the same time, they also eliminated all glass colors except for "Antique Blue," their new name for blue milk glass. With these two changes they were able to lengthen their production runs and enjoy many of the cost savings of machine manufacturing, where long production runs are a necessity. Unlike the machine houses, however, they could promote their glassware as "Handmade" — another new term.

It is interesting to examine the evolution of some of their new terms. In a 1939 ad the words "Handmade Reproduction" were used. A year later another ad described Westmoreland's glassware as "Historically Correct." Two years after that the phrase "Faithful Handmade Copy" was used followed by "Authentic Reproduction" in 1943. Finally, in 1944 the Brainards pulled it all together with, "Authentic Handmade Reproduction" — a phrase that would remain unchanged for the next 40 years. Everything from then on was a "Reproduction," but a reproduction of what, was seldom stated.

If the Brainards trimmed the numbers of their offerings from the recent past, they began almost immediately to make copies of older glass. The 1940 price list listed the well known **1943** Urn (with and without the lid) in crystal as well as 14 cup plates (three of which were Westmoreland originals). In milk glass (still called opal in 1940), they listed the Double Hands, the Hand Vase, the **1874** Wedding Bowl, the **1870** Lace Edge Dish, the **'23'** Square-S Plate, and the **1940** line of vases and lamps.

Two years earlier, in July 1938 a "Lacy Dew Drop" sugar and cream was shown on a Westmoreland shelf of milk glass in *American Home* magazine; it was called a "Jewel" pattern. I believe this was one of the first Brainard period reproductions, and it was evidently copied from Cooperative Flint's No. 1902 line of compotes. The **1881 Pan-** eled Grape line that was to be so important to Westmoreland's post-war sales

was first made later in 1950; the similar **1884 Beaded Grape** line was introduced in 1952.

Changes were made to cut back on handwork. Chas West's cutting was abruptly terminated. (This has been confirmed by Robert Jones, who was employed at Westmoreland at the time.) While bottom finishing was continued for a number of years, it seems to have been curtailed in the late '30s. Cameo (raised enamel) decorations were eliminated. While painted floral decorations would continue for decades, this hand work in the Brainard period was all done flat against the glass. Dwight Johnson told me that Gustav Horn, the West's head decorator, was still there when he first came with the company in 1946, but he was no longer Westmoreland's head decorator.

Taken together, these changes seem to have had an immediate payoff. The dollar value of sales in 1938 was up 16 percent from 1937. Reflecting the cutoff of European imports, sales in 1939 were 50 percent above 1938. But more significantly, sales in 1940 were 30 percent above 1939. Milk glass sales surged in the '40s and '50s and Westmoreland was, deservedly, the center of this popularity: their milk glass quality in these years has never been surpassed. Finally, in 1957 all the business decisions made 20 years before were validated. In that year sales peaked at $3.2 million: (in 1995 dollars, an incredible $17.6 million). After-tax earnings were $209,000 (1995: $1.1 million) and employment that year reached a post-war high of 328.

What is Westmoreland?

A Westmoreland department store display from c. 1960. The sign reads, "Be sure to see the special exhibition of lovely old reproductions — featuring first pressings." (company photo)

The 201 line pictured in this ad is an original Westmoreland design dating from 1925.

(*Gift and Art Buyer*, 9/43)

29

What happened next? The Brainards seem to have forgotten, if you put all your eggs in one basket, then you had better watch that basket! Having built a market, they mistakenly confused what they had been promoting to this market with the market itself. An estimated 95 percent of Westmoreland's sales in 1957 were of milk glass, and when milk glass sales peaked and then plummeted, Westmoreland's sales did too. For several years sales fell each year and in 1963 they were at only half of their 1957 level. Over the same period Westmoreland's losses totaled $192,000 (1995: $980,000).

Evidently believing milk glass sales would turn around, the company did essentially nothing for several years. The records show colored glass sales for Fostoria and Imperial were booming, but Westmoreland seemed reluctant to reverse their 1937 decision to abandon color. Decorated glass was the one Westmoreland product in strong demand, but company files show the decorating department was kept understaffed in this period. They did, however, replace their 31-page catalog of 1952 — in 1962.

1964 is the year Westmoreland finally turned the financial corner with the resignation or retirement of several highly paid employees and with the belated return to color in a major way. Later it would be said that Westmoreland's last color period was characterized by a parade of transparent glass colors always too late for their times; nevertheless, sales records from the '60s suggest Westmoreland's colors were well accepted then.

Marks and Labels

Marks

In 1984 Wm Heacock wrote, "There is an unfortunate obsession for signed objects of art…. Value is based strictly on demand, and this demand seems to be entirely 'signature' oriented" (HC II). He then compared this "obsession" to designer labels on clothes, and pointed out that trademarks on glass generally dated only from the early twentieth century.

In 1924 J.B. Kerfoot confronted the opposite problem in pewter. All pewter made in England after 1503 had to be marked. But since this requirement was often relaxed in the Colonies, those who owned unmarked pieces in the '20s were suggesting this was "proof" of their American origin. Kerfoot, writing during Prohibition, poked fun at this assertion with a couple of "silent syllogisms":

This is the probable reason Westmoreland registered their "Keystone-W" mark, which they had been using from 1910 (B1/13/23).

*"All English pewter had to be marked
No American pewter had to be marked
Therefore, all unmarked pewter is American.
Which is about equal to the argument that,*

*No intoxicating beverages may any longer be brought into the United States
No such beverages may any longer be manufactured in the United States
Therefore, all Hooch is Pre-War stuff"* (KP 193).

In 1901 Heisey was the first pressed glasshouse to register a mark — their well-known "Diamond-H." Early that same year Libbey announced they would "stamp" their "copyrighted trademark" (a star within a diamond) on all their blanks sold for cutting (L 3/21/01).

Twenty-two years later Westmoreland registered their "Keystone-W" — a mark they claimed they had been using continuously from July 1910. The reason for their belated action appears to have been an ad for the Willetts Co., a clay pot maker, which used the same mark. It was an obvious copy. The Willetts' keystone contained a "W" and the words "Standard Quality" were written identically to Westmoreland's "Extra Quality." They even managed to "one-up" Westmoreland with an 1887 date! But Westmoreland was using this mark more than a decade before. At the Pittsburgh Exhibit in Janu-

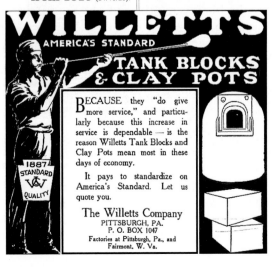

WILLETTS
AMERICA'S STANDARD
TANK BLOCKS & CLAY POTS

BECAUSE they "do give more service," and particularly because this increase in service is dependable — is the reason Willetts Tank Blocks and Clay Pots mean most in these days of economy.

It pays to standardize on America's Standard. Let us quote you.

The Willetts Company
PITTSBURGH, PA.
P. O. BOX 1047
Factories at Pittsburgh, Pa., and Fairmont, W. Va.

1887 STANDARD QUALITY

ary 1911 a trade reporter wrote, "The 'Keystone' tableware lines are the features of the Westmoreland Specialty Co. this year. The '1776 Colonial,' full ground polished bottom is stamped 'Keystone-W' on each piece" (J 1/19/11).

Today, most of the pieces of Westmoreland's six colonial lines will be found marked, but little else. I have found this mark, however, on just one (or so) of the following non-colonial pieces:

1031	Black Bowl Stand
1909	Bowl — 8"
750	Basket
1820	Tray
1908	Bowl — 10"
1865	Bowl — 9½"
1912	Vase, Straight — 6½"
1808	Flower Bowl — 8"
1200	Sugar
1201	Cream
1820	(?) Celery Dish
853	Punch Cup

Except for the mustard mould numbers, the Keystone-W is the only mould mark that will be found on any Westmoreland glassware before the 1950s, but it has survived in some of the colonial pieces that were pressed later. This reissued glass lacks the bottom finishing that will identify the West period originals.

In May 1949, six years after the Brainards renewed the Keystone-W registration, Larry Hamby was hired as Westmoreland's advertising manager. I understand he did not care for the Keystone, and it was apparently he who began the use of the new "WG" mark that is so familiar today. Since Belknap wrote in his milk glass book published in 1949, "I have been informed that Westmoreland intends to mark all future productions of milk glass with either a 'W' or a 'WG'" (BM 269), they had evidently not made up their minds at that time. Presumably, beginning in 1949 or 1950 this mark was first used, but I understand just in certain of the new and replacement moulds. (A mould is usually retired after about 10,000 pressings.) While generally, "WG" marked glass will be newer then otherwise identical unmarked pieces, it is important that future generations not assume all unmarked Westmoreland must have been made in the '40s or even earlier. I have found some of Kerfoot's unmarked pewter collectors alive and well today — and into Westmoreland milk glass!

Marks and Labels

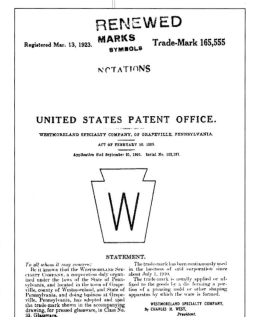

This trademark, granted March 1923, was renewed by the company in 1943.

Labels

A surprising number of pieces of early Brainard period glass have survived with very faded "Little Blue Seals" still on them. We can be certain they were labeled after 1937 because the word "Handmade" appears in the keystone. This term was used from the beginning of the Brainard era, but not before. One of these early labels can be clearly seen in a photograph of a 1939 New York World's Fair cup plate (LCP 130).

It is not clear when paper labels were used in the West period, however. If they had been in general use in the '20s or '30s, some should have survived. Two styles of labels that are shown under Shriners cups of 1906 must have then been in widespread use, for they were designed so that a shop keeper could pencil his price in the center. Because of their whiteness they must have been made of rag-content paper, in contrast to the wood-pulp paper that was used for the square label shown on a 1917 Shriners tumbler.

(P.J. Rosso)

1906

31

What is Westmoreland?

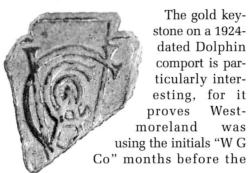

Left, 1924; right, 1917.

The gold keystone on a 1924-dated Dolphin comport is particularly interesting, for it proves Westmoreland was using the initials "W G Co" months before the name change. Notice how similar these stacked letters are to Willetts'. Westmoreland must have been using these letters even before January 1923, when Willetts copied them for their ads.

Patents

The patent for this improbable candy container was the first of three granted to Fred Becker, described by George L. West as a "master mechanic." The other two, granted in 1923 and 1928, were for devices to clamp glass when grinding and polishing. Were any of these whips ever made? If so, have any survived?

Thirty-one patents were assigned to Westmoreland over the years; of these, George West was responsible for 16. The first was the violin bottle described by his son in his short history at the beginning of this book. George West applied for this patent in April 1891, just a year and a half after the company's founding, and then followed this up with an application for his well-known measuring cup five years later.

Earlier in November 1889, however, George M. Irwin received a patent (415868) for his glass screw cap that was used by the Specialty Glass Co. as well as by Westmoreland. This cap can be found on three early Westmoreland screw-top jars: the Brunswick, the Isabel, and the Columbus.

Westmoreland's last patent was granted in April 1929 to Chas West for his **Decagon** or **Cameo Diamond** pressed glass line. While Westmoreland would remain in business for 55 more years, there were evidently no more patents assigned to the company either for glassware or technical invention.

	Patent Date	Patent No.	Years	
G.R. West	01/05/92	21278	14	Violin Bottle
B. Bennett	02/25/96	25194	3½	**Elite** line
G.R. West	08/03/97	27456	14	Measuring Cup
G.R. West	07/02/01	34711	3½	3-Owl Plate
G.R. West	08/26/02	36030	3½	Rabbit Plate
G.R. West	09/08/03	36538	3½	National Plate
G.R. West	02/27/06	37851	3½	Suitcase (Candy)
R. Haley	12/13/10	41034	14	**Floral Colonial** Line
R. Haley	02/14/11	41176	14	**Floral Colonial** Line
G.R. West	03/21/11	41256	14	**1013** Toy Candelabra
R. Haley	04/11/11	41301	14	**1016** Candlestick
R. Haley	04/11/11	41300		Candlestick (never used)
G.R. West	10/15/12	43173	7	Telephone (Candy)
C.H. West	04/22/13	1,059,582		RR Tie & Plate
G.R. West	10/14/13	44741	7	Limousine (Candy)
G.R. West	01/27/16	49252	14	Aquarium
G.R. West	08/15/16	1,194,799		Glass Box
F.C. Becker	09/15/16	49594	7	Whip (Candy)
G.R. West	12/26/16	1,210,121	7	Limousine (Candy)
G.R. West	01/2/17	1,210,572		Glass Polishing Device
G.R. West	05/31/21	58052	14	Ashtray
G.R. West	01/17/22	60281	14	Ashtray
G.R. West	01/17/22	60282	14	Ashtray
F.C. Becker	09/18/23	1,467,992		Clamping Device
C.H. West	01/08/24	63763	3½	Lattice Decoration
G.A. Horn	07/29/24	65338	3½	**Lotus** line
G.A. Horn	12/09/24	1,518,930		"Hammered Metal" Dec
J.J. Brainard	11/03/25	68611		Train (Candy)
C.H. West	05/17/27	72688	7	**1056** Petal Candlestick
F.C. Becker	02/14/28	1,659,074		Clamping Device
C.H. West	04/23/29	78370	3½	**Decagon (Cameo Diamond)** Line

Totals	
George R. West	16
Chas H. West	4
Reuben Haley	4
Fred C. Becker	3
Gustav A. Horn	2
Others	2

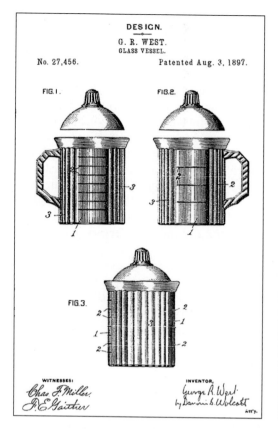

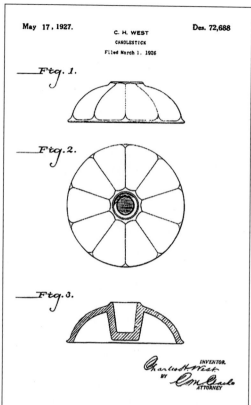

Patents

Left: In Westmoreland's 1901 catalog this was called the Household Measuring Cup Mustard. From 1917 on, after Westmoreland's mustard packaging was discontinued, it was simply called the Household Measuring Cup. It is still being made today in the typical reproduction colors; the original was crystal.

Right: This 1056 candlestick was first shown in the 1926 catalog with several other new candlesticks. Reflecting the latest fashion, six of the nine were low — 3" or under. Some silver candlesticks of the 1730s had "flower petal" bases that may have suggested this design to Chas West.

Westmoreland and the Pittsburgh Exhibit

The Exhibition

It is impossible to exaggerate the importance to American glass of the Pittsburgh Exhibit from the 1890s to the early 1930s. It was the glassware equivalent of the New York Auto Show — the place where everything in glass (and later pottery) was first displayed each January, and fortunately for us today, written up by the trade publications of the time. (For researchers of American glassware of this period, these under-explored show reviews are an excellent resource.)

The Cooperative Flint Glass Co. of nearby Beaver Falls was the pioneer. Displaying their samples in a hotel room in 1883 (1880 was the date later cited), they were soon joined by others. In 1892, despite the folding of many companies into U.S. Glass the year before, 21 glass companies booked rooms in the Monongahela House — the glassmen's hotel. In 1899, despite the similar formation of National Glass in 1898, the exhibitors had grown to 27 glass companies plus two china companies. In addition there were 13 others (including U.S. and National Glass) that had separate dis-

plays nearby. The exhibit continued to grow. Nineteen years later, for example, 40 glass companies along with 20 pottery companies and 32 non-manufacturers (about half, New York importers) took part. This 1918 count excludes ten other glass companies that had permanent showrooms in town.

They were all there in those years — all, that is, with the exception of Fostoria after 1915, and Heisey after 1925 following the death of their exhibitor, C.G. Cassell. He had represented Heisey every year from 1900. Imperial tried to drop out in 1926, but after their "Come to Bellaire" ads proved less than successful, they were back in 1927. In 1937 it was reported that A.J. Bennett, president of Cambridge, had been his company's first exhibitor in 1905, and he was still active 32 years later.

For the glass and pottery manufacturers the exhibit seems to have been as much a social as it was a commercial event. Following the two-week-long exhibit each January, there was an annual banquet sponsored by the Western Glass and Pottery Association. It was originally a dinner followed by entertainment for the manufacturers, but it later became a dinner dance that included their wives. This formal dinner was undoubtedly the grand conclusion to a two week whirl of hospitality by the manufacturers and exhibitors — and of course it would have included the major buyers.

All of the years from the first World War era through the mid-'20s were good exhibition years, but perhaps 1923 should go down in history as the very best. More than 115 companies had displays. Sales then equalled the previous banner year of 1916 — a year when imported glassware from Europe was cut off because of the war. In 1923 there were buyers from all parts of the U.S., Canada, England, and Australia; and visitors included Douglas Stewart, the new director of Pittsburgh's Carnegie Museum and Wm Jennings Bryan. Bryan made the trip from Baltimore where his ailing wife was being treated at Johns Hopkins, to Pittsburgh — possibly just to visit the exhibition. (Presumably the "coin gold" decorated wares were tactfully put away before his visit!)

Pittsburgh

The choice of Pittsburgh for the exhibit in the 1880's was obvious, for at the time Pittsburgh was the undisputed glass capital of America. While Pittsburgh's once-leading glassmaker, Bakewell, Pears, had gone under in 1882, there were still 29 glassware companies in operation within the city in 1888. Together they made 23,000 tons of tableware that year — half of America's output. In addition, there were 29 other Pittsburgh companies making window glass, with a combined tonnage 50 percent greater than the tableware. On top of this, other Pittsburgh glass companies were reported to have made over 42 million lamp chimneys and 85 million bottles that year (J 6/6/89). Ninety-seven years later Wm Heacock would write, "Pittsburgh was the glass capital of the world...I truly feel the wonder of Pittsburgh's rich past every time I drive home from my...office" (HC III).

The choice of the Monongahela House was then just as obvious. Most of Pittsburgh's glass manufacturing was located in the compact area between Mt. Washington and the Monongahela River, just south of the downtown's "Golden Triangle," and from the 1840s the glassmen's hotel and social center had been the Monongahela House, located there along the river. But the Monongahela House was more. In his olympian book, *Pittsburgh Glass 1797 – 1891*, Lowell Inness wrote that six presidents had stayed there, including Lincoln, as well as Jenny Lind, Henry Clay, and the future Edward VII (IL 69).

Beginning in the late '80s, a fundamental change took place in Pittsburgh's glass industry. High transportation and fuel costs, which had so often plagued glassmaking and had earlier caused the glass implosion to Pittsburgh, now turned on Pittsburgh. The city's once natural advantages of cheap river transport and cheap coal for fuel were by then obsolete. Lower taxes, more space, and natural gas discoveries elsewhere made other areas more economical, and rail transport made them just as accessible. The change occurred almost overnight. It is worth noting that when U.S. Glass was formed in 1891, Pittsburgh companies made up seven of its first 15 companies; but when National Glass began just seven years later, there were no Pittsburgh companies numbered among the 19. Nevertheless, the Pittsburgh glass companies that did not go under, or get absorbed into and closed by U.S. Glass, moved out concentrically so that Pittsburgh remained the glass center and the industry's "spiritual home." As a contemporary article explained it, Pittsburghers continued to own and run these companies, and Pittsburgh establishments made the tanks, pots, tools, machinery, and moulds used by these companies (B 5/26/00).

The decline of the Monongahela House was later and more gradual. It continued to be, more or less, the center of the exhibition until 1910, when in the belated triumph of reality over nostalgia, all exhibitors set up in the "Golden Triangle" across the river. From then until the Depression, the new Fort Pitt Hotel became the show's focal point. As late as 1921, however, New Martinsville chose to exhibit their lines back at the Monongahela House — at some distance from everyone else. The Monongahela House was finally razed in 1936 following a severe flood that spring.

Associated Glass & Pottery Manufacturers Inc.

In 1921 Chicago began a determined effort to have the show relocated there. Buyers from the midwest, the far west, and the south, were strongly in favor of the relocation. They complained of the shortage of first-class hotel rooms in Pittsburgh, the poor service, and the lack of things to do. Not mentioned, but no doubt a factor, was the need of travelers from the west to change trains in Chicago. Beginning in February 1922, a month after Pittsburgh, Chicago staged its first "Chicago Exhibit of Glass — Pottery — Lamps & House Furnishings" at the Hotel Morrison. Most of those that set up, however, were dealers and decorators; few manufacturers took part.

The glass and pottery makers were determined to keep the show in Pittsburgh. Pittsburgh was close to almost all the glass companies and less then 35 miles from the pottery center in East Liverpool, Ohio. Pittsburgh was a rail center served by a number of railroads, and shipments could be made from almost all factories without a change of trains. Because of this, Pittsburgh was the only city the manufacturers could ship their barrels to and be assured they would all arrive by a deadline. (What happened when well over 1,000 of these barrels arrived in the city and had to be delivered and unpacked at the same time really stretches the imagination!) From Pittsburgh, buyers could easily tour the plants: In a survey taken in 1921, about 60 percent of those attending the show visited a glass company and about 80 percent visited a pottery (J 5/19/21). Finally, Pittsburgh, the home of so many glass and pottery manufacturers, was the focal point of much of their socializing each January.

In January 1923 the Associated Glass & Pottery Manufacturers Inc. was formed and Chas West was elected its first president. Membership — initially 54 glass companies and 54 pottery companies — was limited to those manufacturing glass and china or else making "allied wares direct from raw materials." This last included H.L. Dixon, the furnace constructor who later that year built Westmoreland's second pot furnace. While the primary purpose of the association was to control the annual show and keep it in Pittsburgh, its purposes extended to other matters of industry interest. Cooperative advertising was agreed to, for example, but there were no advertising or sales restrictions placed on member companies as there would have been had they formed a combine. This means that the chronic over-capacity problem in glass and china was not addressed, even if it was then recognized. Each member company remained fully independent and free to drop out at any time.

This new organization joined together three of Chas West's worlds: Pittsburgh, the glass and pottery industries, and Westmoreland. Two decades earlier Chas West had been active in Pittsburgh's reform movement, and in 1902 he was elected select councilman in a "political landslide" (L 2/22/02). Shortly afterwards he was approached by a group that asked him to run for mayor — an opportunity he had to turn down because of his work. But, he never viewed his work as being bounded by the factory walls. A year after Westmoreland's glass was first exhibited at Pittsburgh's Carnegie Museum, for example, the glass and pottery of other companies was included. And press accounts of Westmoreland's displays at the Pittsburgh Exhibit suggest they were intended as much for the benefit of the city and the industry as for Westmoreland. Perhaps we can turn to these displays.

Westmoreland Displays

Westmoreland first exhibited at the Pittsburgh Show in January 1892. A.C. Brown, who later that year went over to U.S. Glass, represented Westmoreland in Room 147 of the Monongahela House. Four years later Westmoreland again exhibited and received its first major write-up in a trade publication (L 1/15/96). From that time on, except for a one-year gap in 1899, Westmoreland continued to exhibit there every January to the end of the West period.

Beginning in 1903 when Westmoreland booked three hotels rooms, Westmoreland's displays were among the largest at the exhibition; and beginning in 1921, George West's last year, Westmoreland had what the press reported was the

35

Westmoreland and the Pittsburgh Exhibit

largest display there. Clearly both West brothers believed in the importance of this event.

For January 1922, Chas West, just a few months into his presidency, booked the 115 foot long Assembly Room at the Fort Pitt Hotel. With this massive display space, Westmoreland's exhibits began to receive extraordinary press recognition:

1922: "The 'show' of the Pittsburgh Glass and Pottery Exhibition this season is the (Westmoreland) display…" (J 1/19/22).

"Everybody about the hotel was talking about it" (L 1/18/22).

1923: "(Westmoreland's) display this year overtops that of 1922" (L 1/15/23).

"Over 3000 pieces of glassware… the biggest thing of its kind ever assembled in the Pittsburgh market…. 92 barrels of glassware were unpacked… the services of 10 sales people were required" (J 2/8/23).

1924: "Over 100 barrels of glassware in (Westmoreland's) display…" (L 1/14/24).

"Only one or two tables were devoted to lines… shown last year" (B 1/12/24).

"A sales force of nine people… the largest force of sales people ever assembled by one firm for service during the 44 years of the Glass and Pottery Exhibition… over 3000 pieces of ware and no two items were alike… not only attracted all buyers who visited the market, but hundreds of Pittsburgh people, hearing of the show at times simply crowded (Westmoreland's) Assembly room admiring the glass art…" (J 2/7/24).

1925: "The largest force of salesmen on duty… hundreds of 'outsiders' scanned… the display of this company." (J 1/22/25).

1926: "The Display That Had Them All Talking…" (J 2/18/26).

"Like a fairy bower, with green foliage gracefully hanging from the ceiling above… artistic pieces of glassware (were) reflected in the mirrors on all sides…" (J 1/28/26).

"A caleidoscopic [sic] blaze of color" (J 1/18/26).

1927: "(Westmoreland) has maintained its reputation. Startling new decorations vie with new shapes…" (L 1/17/27).

"Between 125 and 150 barrels of glassware…. not only the largest maintained by any single manufacturer, but… the most

From top: Westmoreland's displays in 1922, 1924, and 1926 (L 1/30/22), (L 1/28/24), (L 1/25/26).

varied... almost an exclusive art creation..." (J 1/20/27).

1932: "The largest display in the show...practically everything one can imagine that can be made in glassware" (B 1/16/32).

1933: "The most elaborate exhibit of glassware to be seen..." (B 1/14/33).

1934: "(Westmoreland) has left out nothing that can be made of glass" (B 1/13/34).

Much of the credit for the most breathtaking displays must be given to R.B. Reineck, Westmoreland's "traveling representative" (i.e., sales manager) from 1912 to 1928 — some of the most profitable and creative years in the company's history. He would come to the Fort Pitt a week before the show each year to set up the display, and it was said he would remain in Pittsburgh for days after the close of the exhibit each year just to unwind. He was not a young man. When he was first hired by Westmoreland, he was called "one of the oldest glass salesmen on the job" (he was then 58). After he left Westmoreland in July 1928, he lived just two years longer. A trade reporter wrote of him as "active and alert always, he was an inveterate joker and managed to see the bright things of life

everywhere" (L 7/30). Other companies he represented in his long career were West Virginia Glass, Seneca, Geo. Borgfeldt, and Cooperative Flint.

Because of the major attention Westmoreland received from their displays over the years, we can assign dates to many of their lines, items, colors, decorations, and novelties. The following listing includes what the press saw and reported each January. Bear in mind anything new in January would have been first made in August the preceding year, or even earlier.

Westmoreland and the Pittsburgh Exhibit

Westmoreland's 1927 display (L 3/14/27).

1896 **Sterling** line **Victor** line Amber and ruby staining The "Family Measuring Jar" **1897** **Elite** line **Waverly** line The **300** Condiment Set **1898** **98 Westmoreland** line Green glass **1900** **160** line **1902** **Daisy** line **185** line Opal glass Two lines of lamps Easter novelties Cat and Owl plates **1903** 11 Tableware lines **1904** **400** line St. Louis Fair plates in opal	Barnyard assortment in opal Other opal items **1905** An unnamed tableware line The "Old Oaken Bucket" Opal Easter items w/chickens **1906** Two unnamed tableware lines **1907** An unnamed tableware line Souvenir goods in opal Opal: hats, hatchets, boats, oars, paddles Other opal items A "Colonial line with an engraving" **1908** An unnamed tableware line Colored glass Opal novelties Souvenirs **1909** Dark brown colored ware A straw hat A "Spider containing a freshly fried egg"	**1910** Vases resembling pottery with matt colors **1911** **1776 Colonial** line **Floral Colonial** line "Chippendale" handles The Mission candlestick Carrara Marble One room: Opal glassware One room: "Keystone" lines **1912** **Paul Revere Colonial** line **1700 Colonial** line Candlesticks A rolled edge punch bowl **1913** Cut glass Miniature baskets Reproductions of imported items Imitation Dresden decorated vases The One-piece Bowl and Plate **1914** Shelf supports

1916
Black glassware – matt and bright
Belgian Blue glass
Colored glassware
Colored glass service plates
Floral effects in gold coin
Enameling
The Bulldog Door Stop

1917
"Mahogany" glass
"Tortoise Shell" glass
"Mother-of-Pearl" glass
"White Marble"
Raised enamel rose decoration
Floral decorations
Rock Crystal
Handled candlesticks

1918
Two gold and enameled decorations
Candy jars, cigarette boxes, cigar jars
The "Square Shaped Sugar & Cream"
An invalid tray

1919
Gold encrusted blown stemware

1920
Antique Topaz
Gold encrustations
Line of small vases

1921
Cut crystal
Cracked lustre
Plain lustre
Carrara in 5 colors
"Bowls with Stands and Candlesticks" (first Console Sets)

1922
Copper wheel engraving
Cut crystal plates
Fish bowls with live fish and real water lilies
Japanese aquaria
Iron aquarium and bowl holders
Ruby glass
Antique Canary Yellow
Crackled glass
"Morning Glory" line
"Byzantine" decorated line
"Peach Blow" line with inlaid pearl effect
"Nancy" — "A new color on glass"
Czech-Slovakian enamels

1923
Copper wheel engraving on blown crystal

Diamond cutting and punties
Copper wheel engraving on solid colors — 15th century representations
Fern and Rose engraving
1820 (Flange) line
35 new decorative lines
"Satin Moire" glass
"Greenwich Village" decoration
"Cubist" decoration
A Dresden motif
"Old English" line in crystal
"Mush and Milk Set for Kiddies"

1924
Engraved and cut glass
Black glass
Translucent glass
Mauve glass
Colored glass salad sets
Rainbow effect
Arabian design glass
French decorated glass
"Polish" decoration
"Roseland" line of vases
Two-tone gold raised and encrusted
White gold encrustations

1925
Blown crystal aquaria
New "Prince of Whales" aquaria
Satin black with floral decorations
Solid color tableware with wreath cut edging
Lotus line
555 line
1211 Octagon line
100 decorations on salad plates
60 decorations on cologne bottles
Mould crackle ware
Old Austrian design reproductions
"Mephisto" Red

1926
Copper wheel cutting
Prevalence of color
Reproductions of Sandwich glass
Additions to **555** line
The Dolphin Shell
The **1800** Covered Jar
The Wing Handled Sugar & Cream

1927
"Roselin" glass
Two Spanish designs
"Galle" decorated line
1058 Fruit line
Vases with a checkerboard effect
Leaf plate
Additions to **Lotus** line

A water-filled lamp

1928
A "trompe l'oeil" decanter set

1930
Topaz glass
Black glass
Black glass with enameled flowers
Black glass with silver flowers
Black glass with Godey figures in silver
Crystal with black
All silver and all gold plates
Monogrammed place plates
300 Waterford line
Novel shapes in blown ware
Raised decorations

1931
Belgian Blue glass
Moonstone glass
Amethyst glass
Silver on black glass
'Polka Dot' pattern
Silver stippled line
1706 line
Plates with etched lace doily centers
Bathroom bottles
Perfume bottles
Boudoir lamps in color
Smokers' items

1932
Opal glass
Opal glass combined with black
1932 Wakefield line
"Early American" (555) in crystal and colors
"Uncle Sam's Hat"

1933
Ruby glass
"Milk White" glass with gold eagles
Crystal with light cuttings

1934
1000 Eye line
1933 vases and open twist candlesticks in opal
Zodiac plates
"Victorian Centerpiece on a Glass Plaque"

1936
Ribbed crystal line
Cold and cocktail lunch sets
Etched, cut, and decorated lines

Cutting is surely the most noble of glass decorations. Like woodcarving, it achieves its effect through the removal of material rather than through the addition of something foreign; its beauty springs solely from the material itself. While an artist can paint or gild any number of things, he can cut very little aside from glass. Hand-blocked etching shares these characteristics. But even with this high form of etching, the artist's hand ordinarily creates only a design outline. Unlike most types of etched glass, every piece of cut glass, no matter how simple, was once handled by an artist who created on it the depth and texture as well as the outline of his design. No two cut pieces can ever be precisely alike.

If there is any downside to glass cutting it is this: The finest glass cutting can be compared to the finest carving on London furniture; it exists not to enhance the basic form; it exists independently of it. The cutter's glass "blank" is literally that. His finest blank is usually the most invisible. His artistry is meant to float effulgently on a crystal sea.

Cutting

All glass is cut by holding the glass against a revolving wheel. The most common form of cutting, and the easiest to understand, is stone cutting. In its simplest form it is the bottom "grinding" or "cutting" (both terms have been used) of glassware. For this, a horizontally mounted stone abrasive wheel about four feet in diameter is rotated like a phonograph record while a workman holds the feet of various glass articles against it. This process, followed by polishing, levels their bottoms and confers an aura of quality.

For decorative cutting similar wheels are used, but they are mounted vertically and usually measure from about 2" up to a foot in diameter. (Samuel Hawkes once specified a broader range of 1" up to 3' [JC 10/31].) The glass to be decorated is lowered to the upper edge of these wheels, like tools to be sharpened on a farm grinder, and the glass cutter views his work through the glass. Stone cutting has this in common with reverse painting on glass.

Another form of cutting is known as engraving, a term that is usually synonymous with copper wheel cutting. Because of the unusual talent that is required and the fine detail that can be achieved, there is general agreement that copper wheel engraving is the highest form of cutting there is. Tiny copper wheels are used "from the size of a pinhead" up to about 2" in diameter. Their edges come in a variety of contours and their widths range up to ¼". Joseph Racinger, Westmoreland's head cutter from 1921 to, I believe, August 1937 later said, "Even the simplest design requires some 50 interchangeable copper wheels to arrive at the right shading and sharp outline." He claimed then to have four times that number in his workshop (PG 10/17/60). Since these sculpting wheels have no cutting ability themselves, they must be used with an external abrasive; and because they are made of soft copper, this abrasive must be fine. A slurry of emery or even pumice and linseed oil (the viscosity varying with the wheel width) is employed. Pumice and linseed oil, by the way, is the same abrasive that was once used to rub down varnished furniture. In order to receive this abrasive mixture from above, the wheel must be over the cutting operation, which means the glass has to be brought up to its underside. While the engraver must make continual flicks with his finger to clear the slurry, he is able to view his work directly, rather than through the glass. This means he is able to cut dark or opaque glass.

According to Robert Jones, who worked at Westmoreland from 1924, Westmoreland referred to all this work within the company as "cutting." Nevertheless, from the perspective of a purist, let alone a proud copper wheel engraver, there is a world of difference between this art and "cutting." As Joseph Racinger said, "Anyone can learn glass cutting, but engraving demands years of study and skill" (PG 10/17/60).

There is another form of cutting,

Cut Crystal

properly though seldom called engraving, that is midway between stone and copper wheel work: it uses wheels of iron or steel. Like copper wheels, they require an external abrasive, but unlike them they can withstand a coarser grit without being eroded away. The slurry used with iron wheels is a mixture of sand and water, but because it has to be fed from above, the cutting must take place on the underside of the wheels. One interesting form of iron wheel is called the "gang cutting wheel," which is a wheel with striations around its edge. With it the cutter can create a contrasting texture of fine parallel lines resembling the grooves in a 78-rpm record. Since it apparently dates from about 1913 (CO 14), any glass found with this fine grooving can be assumed to have been cut after this date. I understand the smallest gang cutting wheels are only ⅜" in diameter.

Sometimes more that one type of cutting has to be employed in a particular design. Copper wheel engraving is very shallow owing to the fine abrasive required. While intaglio work, for example, can be finished with copper wheels, its deep cuts have to be started with wheels of stone, or iron and sand. Because of its depth limitation, copper wheel engraving went into an eclipse during the brilliant-cut period, for it could not be used for the deep incisions required. But with the shifting of taste back to "light cutting" in the early twentieth century, copper wheel engraving, with its subtlety, its shading, and its three-dimensional representations, took over from where it had left off decades before. For this reason, much of the finest cut glassware of the 1920s and shortly before, looks remarkably similar to some of the finest cut glassware of the mid-nineteenth century.

Cutting at Westmoreland

For those familiar only with the glass of Westmoreland's last 50 years, it may come as a revelation to learn that Westmoreland was a major glass cutter for the first third of this century. In their 1904 price list, Westmoreland listed nine table tumblers that were available in "cut patterns." Then as late as the 1936 Pittsburgh Exhibit, a reviewer wrote of Westmoreland's "etched, cut and decorated lines" (B 1/18/36). Between these years there were numerous trade references to Westmoreland's cutting.

In the '20s and '30s Westmoreland may have cut more glass than any other glass company in America. At the factory, all cutting operations were performed in front of a long row of large windows that faced south. In 1991 a 53-foot shaft still remained there with 10 take-off pulleys. But there was evidence this shafting once continued another 90 feet for a theoretical total of 28 take-off pulleys, each available for a cutting operation. Dwight Johnson, a Westmoreland chemist and glassmaker who began his employment in 1946, told me he understood there had been "at least 25 cutters employed in the '20s." While few of these men would have been engravers, his estimate does support the impression of major grinding, cutting, and polishing activities that once took place at Westmoreland. Westmoreland's total employment never exceeded 500.

Westmoreland's Brilliant-Cut Glass

There is one type of glassware Westmoreland made in the George West years we may never be able to identify: blown, brilliant-cut glass. In the last paragraph of his story that began this book, George L. West wrote of his fathers' period: "Westmoreland had a special group of skilled artisans, engravers, and cutters who produced the fine pieces of heavy cut glass so much in demand.... Blanks or pieces of glass used in making heavy cut glass had to be handled with care.... They were cooled in special ovens, usually for days...." This is supported by Robert Jones who could recall a "special lehr" just for heavy cut-glass blanks that had been "removed years ago." He told me some pieces were kept in it for weeks.

In the fall of 1941, just before the start of the war, the Chas Wests moved from their 26-room house of almost 30 years to a one-bedroom apartment. I know now this house was full of Westmoreland glass — most of which was tragically scattered at that time. I can still recall tables covered with heavy brilliant-cut crystal at their house sale. I can also recall people observing (and thinking myself) that this glass was very much out of fashion. While there is no reason to believe all this glass had to be Westmoreland's, much of it almost certainly was,

and today, wherever it is, it is just unmarked, orphan glass.

Westmoreland's crystal seems to have been particularly fine in the late George West period; but for one important reason this is hard to understand. After the First World War began in Europe in August 1914, some of America's most esteemed glasshouses ran into trouble because they were cut off from their supply of German potash. But this should have affected Westmoreland too. Sam'l Brainard West, Charles' son and Westmoreland's secretary from 1921, kept a notebook of glass formulations — many of which must have gone back before his time. Of his crystal formulations, half contained potash. Since "Bohemian Flint" is lime-potash glass, some of these potash formulations (some containing lead) would have been the basis for Westmoreland's finest crystal — the sort of crystal that must have been made by Westmoreland in the mid-to-late teen years when I understand potash was all but unavailable.

Westmoreland's Copper Wheel Engraving

Shortly after I began my glass research in the 1980s, I was nearly convinced by a glass authority that no copper wheel engraving could have been done at Westmoreland. It was pointed out to me that fine stone wheel cutting could resemble, and be mistaken for engraving. This is true. But putting aside the direct evidence of much of the glassware shown in this book, there is a great deal of documentary evidence of Westmoreland's copper wheel work.

1. I have found 11 specific references to Westmoreland's "copper wheel engraving" in three trade publications over the six-year period, 1922 – 1927. For the benefit of future researchers they are: (B 1/14/22), (L 1/16/22), (L 1/30/22), (L 1/15/23), (J 2/8/23), (J 4/5/23), (L 6/16/24), (L 1/12/25), (J 7/30/25), (L 1/18/26), (L 3/14/27).

2. Joseph Racinger was hired by Chas West in 1921, and he apparently remained at the company until August 1937. (A surviving cutting of his, on a blown non-Westmoreland blank signed "J Racinger 1938," shows he was on his own that year.) In an article appearing in

a Pittsburgh newspaper in 1960, he discussed his copper wheel apprenticeship and background.

3. In the Westmoreland decorating files from the mid-'30s the term "cherry engraving" can be found. "Cherry" does not refer to a design motif, but to the tiny cutting wheels used in copper wheel work.

4. After H.P. Sinclaire closed in 1928, Westmoreland employed three of their engravers. Clement Nitsche, described as "The most talented and prolific of Sinclaire's designer-engravers"(FS 35), was employed by Westmoreland at an undetermined date (CO 146). Also, Joseph Oveszny and Henry Hauptmann were employed there in 1933 (CO 164). All three men were known copper wheel engravers (FS 42, 43).

According to Robert Jones, there was always a group of several engravers that "spoke German and stuck pretty much to themselves." He could remember Clement Nitsche, but strangely, not Joseph Racinger.

Westmoreland Blanks

These are some of the companies that purchased Westmoreland blanks in the West period to use for their cutting; there are almost certainly others:

Bison Decorating Co.
Didio Bros Cut Glass Co.

Irving Cut Glass Co.
H.P. Sinclaire & Co.
McKanna Glass Co.
Monongahela Valley Cut Glass Co.
Susquehanna Cut Glass Co.

1776 Colonial Half Gallon Jug — Tall
1776 Colonial Tumblers

(c. 1912)

1776 was one of Westmoreland's two original colonial lines; four more were to follow.

Both pieces **"Keystone-W"** marked.

Both ground and polished to pressed circular stars.

A similar tumbler with a serpentine profile was designated, **"1776½."**

1932: Jug available in crystal only; tumbler available in crystal and colors. 1940: Both discontinued. In 1967, however, the jug was reissued in crystal and transparent colors. These reissued jugs will still show the **Keystone-W** mark but not the finished bottoms of the originals.

Jug: 9" h.
Tumbler: 4" h.

1776 Colonial Line introduced Jan. 1911. 1776 Jug and Tumbler first available in 1911. Sunburst cutting available from Jan. 1912.

In 1907 Westmoreland was credited with "A new line of colonial ware (with) an added feature being an engraving" (L 1/5/07). Nevertheless, in later years Westmoreland cited 1910 as the year they had "made the transition to finer glassware." In the second half of 1910 they began to produce two full colonial lines (**1776** and **Floral Colonial**), began to mark these lines, and to ornament them with engraving. For five years beginning in January 1911 they displayed these **"Keystone-W"** marked lines in a separate room at the Pittsburgh Exhibit.

Heisey is usually given credit for leading the pressed glassware industry back to the colonial flute in 1899. In all likelihood they were also the first pressed glass company to mark their tableware glass in 1900. But, I believe Westmoreland was engraving their colonial lines at least four years before Heisey.

The **1776 Jug** seems to be an original Westmoreland design; however, the **1776 Tumbler** appears to be identical to Heisey's No. 300. In 1924 (B 1/-/24), Central, a third maker, advertised a soda fountain glass that appears to be identical to Heisey's and Westmoreland's. What distinguishes these three from others is their interesting capstan profile.

Both the Westmoreland jug and the tumblers are clearly marked and both have bottoms ground and polished to their pressed stars. The glass clarity is exceptional.

1200 Individual Sugar
1201 Individual Cream

**1200/1201 Sugar
and Cream first
available between
1906 and 1912.**

*"(A) pleasing feature
of (Westmoreland's) dis-
play is a fine line with
sunburst cutting, the
shapes being in the main colonial. Modified along these lines the simple but
attractive cutting lends a charm and
individuality to every piece, and places
it in a class by itself"* (L 1/8/12).

At least five other pressed glass companies used this sunburst motif. Possibly
the first was Fostoria, whose sunbursts
may all have had eight rays with five
radial lines between each of the rays.
U.S. Glass' "Six Point Star Design" had
six rays with three lines between each.
Diamond (1914) had a sunburst that
appears identical to Westmoreland's.
Central (1917) had one they also called
"Sunburst" showing eight rays with five
lines between each. Finally, Imperial (c.
1920) had two sunburst designs showing
six and eight rays with three lines
between each.

This sugar and cream, while early and
"Keystone-W" marked, was not part of a
colonial line. Note the "Chippendale"
handles used by Westmoreland from 1907
or shortly before. They will be discussed
in the section on Iridized Glass.

(c. 1912)

1200 and **1201** were item
numbers used just for
this sugar and cream.

Both pieces **"Keystone-
W"** marked.

Despite the rim differ-
ence and the two item
numbers, these were
always sold as a pair.

1932: Both available in
crystal only.
1940: Both discontinued.

Both bowls: 2½" h.

1700 Colonial Match Holders
1700 Colonial Napkin Ring

**Both 1700 items
first available
in 1912.**

*"Rich cut glass in all the staple
pieces is the leading feature of the
exhibit of the Westmore-
land Specialty Com-
pany..."* (J 1/16/13).

Westmoreland used these two
notched-prism motifs from at least 1912.
Fostoria also used one of them in their
early cutting, and in 1914 Diamond pictured the same one in an advertisement
(L 1/12/14). This dash-dot-dot-dash motif
appears in ancient Greek architectural
stone work where it is known today as
"Bead and Reel."

(c. 1912)

1700 was one of the two
colonial lines Westmore-
land introduced in 1912.

Both match holders are
"Keystone-W" marked.

All three items are
ground and polished.

Old English initials were
etched at the factory.

1932: Both available in
crystal only.
1940: Both discontinued.

Match holder: 2³⁄₁₆" h.
Napkin ring: 2" l.

1700 Colonial Vase — 9"

(c. 1912)

Also available in 10".

Both vases originally designated **1700 Colonial.**

Vases redesignated **1602/9"** and **1602/10"** between 1918 and 1924, apparently to avoid the confusion with the **1700/9" Lily Vase** (see Gold & Silver section).

1602 was an item number assigned just to these two vases.

1932: 9" & 10" available in crystal only.
1940: Discontinued.

The cut glass dealer who sold me this vase insisted on keeping one for herself; she referred to it as her "Little Diamond."

This stylized flower resembling a Canada Thistle was widely used by Westmoreland, but also by McKee, Fostoria, and perhaps others.

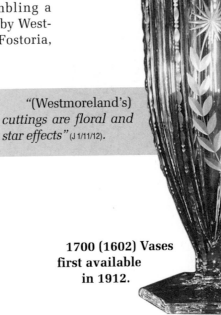

"*(Westmoreland's) cuttings are floral and star effects*" (J 1/11/12).

Height: 9"
Weight: 1⅞ lb. (9")
Weight: 2⅞ lb. (10")

1700 (1602) Vases first available in 1912.

1800 Handled Sandwich Tray — 10", Early

(c. 1916)

1800 was designated a **Plain** line.

Early **1800 Sandwich Tray** discontinued between 1918 and 1922.

Pressed star has 16 rays with gang wheel cuts between them.

Diameter: 9¾"

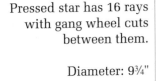

Since Westmoreland replaced this **1800 Sandwich Tray** by another **1800 Sandwich Tray** having an entirely new handle between 1918 and 1922, we know the cutting shown here has to date from before 1922. The petals between the pressed star rays were cut with a gang cutting wheel. Notice how Westmoreland's cutter has contrasted its crisp furrowed texture with gray cutting on the rim.

There are two other handled sandwich trays that resemble Westmoreland's early **1800**. One, I believe by Paden City, has a stubbier, shorter stem with a larger triangular handle. Its stem is round in cross section, whereas Westmoreland's is six-sided. Finally, on the bottom it has a protruding foot ring whereas Westmoreland's is smooth (except for the pressed star). There is also a third similar sandwich tray which is crudely made and has glass webbing that fills the handle ring.

1800 Line introduced between 1913 and 1917. Early 1800 Sandwich Tray first available between 1913 and 1917.

1800 Handled Sandwich Tray — 10", Late

Late 1800 Sandwich Tray first available between 1918 and 1922.

Since this redesigned **1800 Sandwich Tray** was pictured in a 1922 department store ad (Carson, Pirie, Scott of Chicago), we know it had replaced the earlier version by 1922. The cutting design pictured here seems to have been one of those used on some of Westmoreland's cut plates displayed at the 1922 Pittsburgh Exhibit.

While the plates of both sandwich trays show 16-ray pressed stars, the later one was otherwise entirely redesigned. On the early one there is a mould mark that runs from the handle across the sandwich plate showing it had been pressed in one piece in a "joint" mould. While the later handle also shows a mould mark at its base, the plate, itself, is clear. This shows the plate

and handle were pressed together in a compound "shell" mould that left a mould mark only at the plate's outer rim where it was easily fire-polished away.

(c. 1922)

A larger version of the **1800/6" Butterball.**

Pressed star has 16 rays with gang wheel cuts between them.

1932: Available in crystal only.
1940: Discontinued.

Diameter: 9¾"

1800 Butter Ball — 6"

Westmoreland used a loop-shaped handle on their redesigned **1800 Sandwich Tray** and on their **6" Butter Ball.** Heisey and Fenton also made butter balls (sometimes called lemon trays or butter trays) with loop handles; however, both the Heisey and Fenton handles were hexagonal in cross section, whereas Westmoreland's were round. Fenton's item numbers were No. 317 for their sandwich and No. 318 for their butter tray.

I have also seen a third handled sandwich tray with a loop handle, in black glass with a Rockwell silver decoration. The handle, which was round, was quite

coarse and it had a prominent ring or torus on the stem. The tray had no star and it had a protruding foot ring, in contrast to the starred, smooth-bottomed Westmoreland **1800.**

The cross-hatched cutting on this **1800 Butter Ball** is frequently seen in other Westmoreland cutting designs.

An **1800 Butter Ball** is pictured in the Gold & Silver section with a sterling silver rim.

1800 Butter Ball first available between 1918 and 1924.

(c. 1924)

A smaller version of the late **1800/10" Sandwich Tray.**

Pressed star has 28 rays.

1932: Available in crystal only.
1940: Discontinued.

Diameter: 6¼"

752 Basket — 6"

(c. 1921)

Also made 5" & 7".

752 was an item number used just for these striped baskets.

1932: All three sizes available in crystal only. 1940: 7" available in crystal only, then discontinued. In 1978, however, the 5" was reissued in various colors and decorations.

Height: 6"
11" (includes handles)

The **752 Basket** handle halves were pressed together with the baskets and afterwards lifted and joined together in the middle. While Duncan & Miller held a patent on this procedure (they marked their baskets "PAT'D"), Westmoreland must have paid them royalties, found a way around their patent, or waited till the patent expired.

The oval medallions on these **752 Baskets** were intended for decoration. Those from the West period are usually (perhaps always) found with simple cuttings.

752 Baskets probably introduced Jan. 1921.

1820 Five-Part Relish with Cocktail Center — 13"

1820 Line introduced between 1918 and 1924. 1820 5-part Relish first available in 1925. Rim design patented in 1924.

(c. 1925)

Silver decoration #23.

1820 was Westmoreland's **Flange** line.

1932: Available in crystal and colors. 1940: Available in crystal only. Relabeled a **"7-Part Relish."**

Diameter: 13"
Weight: 6 lb.

Less than a month (1/26/25 – 2/23/25) separates two ads (shown on page 24) for Westmoreland's **1820 Five-Part Relish**; the company's name change was effective February 20, 1925.

This relish design seems to have been a popular one. In March 1929 Dunbar advertised a 13" relish tray that seems to resemble Westmoreland's; it was their No. 4033. U.S. Glass made one too. It can be distinguished by the scalloped top on its center cocktail dish. Cambridge also made a similar one. Cambridge's shows two differences, however. The Cambridge pie-slice dishes are dog-legged along their back bottom edges to accommodate a step in the tray. Also, the rim of Cambridge's cocktail center rests directly on the pie-slice dishes, whereas Westmoreland's is much taller and rises up almost an inch. Cambridge's cocktail center also may be marked with Cambridge's "Triangle-C."

The cutting on this pictured relish is on the underside of the tray. Westmoreland's patented "hammered" decoration is discussed in the Gold & Silver section.

1211 Octagon Handled Sandwich Trays — 10"

1211 Line introduced between 1918 and 1924. 1211 Sandwich Tray first available in 1925.

(c. 1930)

1211 was Westmoreland's **Octagon** line.

Left: crystal with black cased handle; Right: crystal.

1932: Available in crystal and colors.
1940: Discontinued.

Width: 10½" (max)

Octagonal plates, so popular in the late '20s, were revivals from an earlier age: they had been popular both in china and silver in the early eighteenth century.

All glassware manufacturers seem to have made octagon handled sandwich trays around 1930. New Martinsville combined an arched handle resembling Westmoreland's **1849** (see the Reverse Painting section) with an octagon plate and assigned it No. 10/2 in their 1926 "Victoria" line. There were at least three other octagon sandwich trays with octagonal outline handles that could be confused with Westmoreland's **1211,** however. Duncan & Miller held a patent (No. 7885 — 3½ years — 1924) on theirs. Their octagonal handle can be distinguished from all others because its flat side is turned to the top. Liberty Works advertised a sandwich tray that resembles Westmoreland's except that its tray has radial ribs (like an open umbrella) while Westmoreland's is smooth. They advertised it as "Octagon Optic — New for 1929" (J 5/29). A third looks identical to Westmoreland's from the top. Both have round rings or toruses on their hexagonal stems, and both have unribbed trays. Underneath, however, the Westmoreland is perfectly smooth while this (and perhaps all others) have a projecting ring. There is also another curious difference. The sides of the Westmoreland handle are smooth while the look-alike is slightly sandy. In addition, the look-alike has two tiny pinholes near the top, evidently from having been held in some manner while still hot.

The gang cutting wheel was extensively used in these two cuttings pictured here. Since I own an aquamarine colored sandwich tray identical to the one on the right above, the cutting must date from 1929 or later: Westmoreland's aquamarine glass was first advertised in December 1928.

Unknown 11" Tray

(c. 1918 – c. 1932)

"Keystone-W" marked.

Ground and polished bottom.

5⅜" x 11¼"

The line designation of this certain Westmoreland tray is unknown. With its flanged edge it might be from the **1820** line; with its flutes it might be from either the **1700** or **1776 Colonial** lines. The **Keystone-W** mark found here is not often seen on non-colonial Westmoreland glassware.

The gray cutting bears some resemblance to several similar designs of the 1920s — in particular, Tuthill's "Fern" design. But, note the similarity of this cutting to that on the early **1800 Sandwich Tray** in this section. This suggests a date of 1921 or before.

1828 Cigarette Box & Cover — 6"

(c. 1930)

1828 was an item number used solely for this cigarette box.

Nominal dimensions: 3½" x 6⅛" x 1¾".

1932: 1828 Cigarette Box available in crystal, colors, and opal; opal cost 44% more than crystal.
1940: Available in crystal and opal; opal cost 58% more than crystal.

Width: 6⅛"
Length: 3⅜"
Height: 1⅞"

1828 Cigarette Box first available between 1918 and 1924.

Westmoreland pictured three rectangular cigarette boxes in their 1924 catalog: two **1800,** and one **1828.** In their 1932 price list the number of **1800** cigarette boxes had risen to seven: five with a single compartment and two with multiple compartments. Fortunately, the dimensions of each cigarette box were penned into my copy of the price list, and this establishes the box pictured as the sole **1828.** (There had been an earlier paneled and footed **1033 Cigarette Box** redesignated a **233 Jewel Box** in 1924; also two cylindrical-shaped boxes were available as cigarette boxes that year.)

This is one of three identically-cut cigarette boxes that have come down in the family. Joseph Racinger was the clearly the cutter (see the Cut Stained and Carnegie sections).

1822 Four-Part Relish — 8"

1822 Relish first available between 1918 and 1924.

(c. 1925)

1822 was an item number used solely for this relish.

1932: Available in crystal and colors.
1940: Discontinued.

Diameter: 8³⁄₁₆"

A form like this one-piece relish would ordinarily be hard to attribute to any maker with certainty. Fortunately, I was able to locate the block mould pictured at the plant and from it verify this one was Westmoreland's **1822 Relish**. This is the first of several pictures in this book of glass photographed in the very moulds from which they were once pressed many years ago.

Given the butterfly's unique charm and its association with flowers, it is surprising not to find it more often in cut glass. Notice the rim of this relish which seems to have been cut with the same

gang cutting wheel used on the **1211 Sandwich Tray** shown in this section.

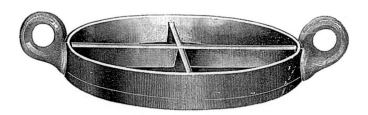

1700 Colonial Vase or Hat Pin Holder — 7"

(c. 1912)

Also available 11" & 12".

1932: 7" available in crystal and colors; 12" available in crystal only.
1940: Discontinued.

Height: 7⅜"

1700/6" Vase first available in 1912. 1700/7" Vase first listed between 1918 and 1924.

"The new '1700' line consisting of vases, candlesticks, lemonade sets, condiment sets and special pieces is shown in Grecian and sunburst cuttings" (J 1/11/12).

Because of the sunburst cutting and the "Grecian" (Bead and Reel) notching, this is clearly an early (c. 1912) vase. In the 1912 and 1917 catalogs it was designated a **1700/6" Vase or Hat Pin Holder,** but from 1924 on it was redesignated a **1700/7" Vase.**

I believe this vase was merely redesignated and not altered. Stated dimensions in glass are usually accurate to +/- ½", and I have sometimes found them off by close to 1". In this case, however, I believe Westmoreland made a catalog error initially.

In 1914 Diamond Glass advertised a vase that resembled this — even to the cutting (L1/12/14). But Diamond's vase had a flat rather than a scalloped top. In that same trade journal, Lancaster advertised a vase identical to Diamonds, but it was pictured without a cutting. New Martinsville's No. 720 is similar, but squatter, has a wide rim, and measures 9½" tall.

Paul Revere Colonial Berry Sugars

**Paul Revere line intro-
duced Jan. 1912. Berry
Sugar first available
in 1912.**

(probably late teens)

Paul Revere was one of the two colonial lines Westmoreland introduced in 1912.

This line can be found only in black glass and crystal.

Both sugars **"Keystone-W"** marked.

1932: 20 pieces in this line available in crystal only.
1940: Discontinued.

Width: 9¼" (at handles)

If the term "Chippendale" is a generation too early for those neo-classical flat-topped handles in widespread use around 1910 (see the Iridized Glass section), the term **Paul Revere** for this Westmoreland line is particularly apt. Paul Revere was a Boston silversmith who lived until 1818. These same jaunty handles were used on silver as well as pewter teapots, well within his lifetime. For example, a surviving pewter (Brittania) teapot that incorporates this handle and

"Chief among (Westmoreland's lines) is the Paul Revere, and the individuality of the famous old Revolutionary war hero is shown in the handsome decoration, for he was refined in his manner, and there is refinement in every line and face of this splendid thing in glass. It is made in a vast variety of shapes and sizes, some of them showing marked individuality and all of them presenting a most attractive appearance..." (L 1/8/12).

er to home (but probably unknown to Westmoreland in 1911), is a surviving silver teapot made by Paul Revere in 1799 that shows a remarkably similar handle. Despite the interest in early silver and pewter at the time, Westmoreland's **Paul Revere Colonial** line seems to be unlike anything made by any other glass company.

The second sugar pictured, showing a sort of eight-petal wild rose, has delicate edge notching around each panel as well as the rim. McKee used a similar wild rose in some of their glass cutting.

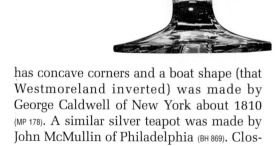

has concave corners and a boat shape (that Westmoreland inverted) was made by George Caldwell of New York about 1810 (MP 178). A similar silver teapot was made by John McMullin of Philadelphia (BH 869). Clos-

51

1700 Colonial High Foot Handled Compotier

(late teens)

Despite its **1700** shape and designation, this piece was given the **Paul Revere** handles.

In 1912 and 1917 Westmoreland referred to this as a "compotier"; later they changed it to "comport." (They were right the first time.)

No visible marking. Yet a similar one in crystal (not pictured) shows a faint **Keystone-W** mark and one in amethyst (see the Iridized Glass section) shows a clear mark.

1932: Available in crystal only.
1940: Discontinued. In 1967, however, it was reissued as a **"1776 Sweetmeat."** It was shown initially in olive green, then in 1973 in other late colors including marble (slag).

Height: 6½" (at handles)

1700 Compotier first available in 1912

With its broad, centered flutes, Westmoreland's **1700** line was inspired by Jefferson's "Chippendale" line introduced five years before. After this huge line of over 400 pieces was sold by Jefferson to Central in December 1918, Central continued to turn it out with its original marking, "Krys-tol," for years.

Westmoreland's high foot handled compotier may be the only **1700** item to have a close counterpart in the "Chippendale" line. There are three differences, however. Westmoreland's compotier is considerably shorter than a similar "Chippendale" compote. It shows a distinct break in the stem just below the bowl, similar to the **Paul Revere Candlestick** (see the Cut Candlestick section). And most important of

all, it was given those swashbuckling **Paul Revere** handles. While Westmoreland's compotier originally came marked, this mark gradually wore down to near-invisibility.

Notice that the wild rose cutting on this compotier is the same as on the preceding **Paul Revere Berry Sugar.** It has the same delicate gang-wheel notching above each flute and between the facets on the stem.

1700 Colonial Individual Celery Holder
1700 Colonial Round Handled Sugar
1700 Cream

**1700 Sugar and Cream first available in 1912.
1700 Celery Holder first available between 1918 and 1924.**

There are no fence straddlers when it comes to this "Round Handled Sugar;" people either love it or hate it. I think it's great! I find it a sort of impish reaction to that staid, flawlessly proportioned cream. I see a baseball pitcher winding up with an umpire looking on. Given the origin of so many of Westmoreland's artists, could we refer to this cream as the Austro-Hungarian Umpire?

An "Individual Celery Holder" was apparently placed in front of every dinner guest for his half-eaten celery, alongside a butter plate for his half-eaten bread. This celery holder shows a very clear **Keystone-W** mark in the top center.

The cutting motif on all three pieces is the same; the flowers and leaves were all cut with a gang cutting wheel.

(c. 1924)

Only the celery holder shows a **Keystone-W** mark.

1932: All three available in crystal only.
1940: All discontinued.

Celery holder: 4½" w.

1700 Colonial Candy Jars — 2 lb. & 3 lb.
1700 Colonial Candy Jar — 3 lb.

Nothing is more closely associated with the classical revival period (1770s on) than the urn — or to be more precise, the urn form body crowned with a cuspate lid. This ancient amphora form may have been first revived as a new shape for silver coffee pots and covered sugars around 1770, but it soon found its way onto everything including balusters, fireplace screens, and even chair backs of the late eighteenth century. The form was just as central to the neo-classical revival which began in the 1890s. Combined with the paneling found on "colonial" glass of the second quarter of the nineteenth century, it became the basis of Westmoreland's **1700 Candy Jar.**

Westmoreland's **1700 Candy Jar** could be confused with Heisey's No. 353, which came in three sizes: ½ lb., 1 lb. and 3 lb. (there was no 2 lb. size). There are two differences, however. Between the foot and the bowl, Heisey's has a high single joint with a ring or torus whereas Westmoreland's has a collar. Also, the underside of Heisey's finial is smooth, whereas Westmoreland's later finials (from c.1920 on) have a break. While I have seen, perhaps, ten times as many Westmoreland **1700s** as Heisey 353s, Heisey sold several very similar candy jars while Westmoreland sold just one.

1700 Candy Jars probably. first available in 1917.

(1920s)

Also made in ½ lb. & 1 lb. sizes.

1932: All four sizes available in crystal only.
1940: 1 lb. size available in crystal only — then discontinued in 1941. In 1973 one size was reissued in etched transparent colors; in 1975 it was also reissued in milk glass.

1 lb: 8" h.
2 lb: 10½" h.
3 lb: 12¾" h.

1707 Candy Jar and Cover — 1 lb., Plain

Also available in ½ lb. size from 1921 and ¼ lb. size from 1926.

1707 was designated an **Optic** line.

1707 Candy Jar usually found in Optic rather than Plain, but occasionally in mixed, Plain and Optic.

1932: All three sizes available in crystal and colors.
1940: Only ½ lb. size available — in crystal only.

½ lb.: 7¾" h.
1 lb.: 9¼" h.

1707 Candy Jars first advertised in 1921.

At least three other companies made candy jars with this conical shape. New Martinsville's No. 149-3 is identical to Westmoreland's except for its round, faceted handle. Westmoreland's **1707**, on the other hand, carries the cone concept right to the top. Counting the conical profile rings, Westmoreland's has a total of nine cone shapes. Fenton's No. 736 is identical to the **1707**, however; even the lids will interchange.

Nevertheless, Berry Wiggins, a glass researcher, has found a way to tell them apart. Beneath their feet they both show a thickening at the edge. But just inside that thickening, Fenton's has a sharp break (possibly a mould mark) while Westmoreland's is perfectly smooth. This observation is typical of Berry Wiggins'

unusual sensitivity to detail. A third company also used this same conical handle on a similar candy jar. Its bowl, however, is taller and its ring profiles are rounded rather than pointed. Its glass is of mediocre quality and there is a prominent mould mark across the top of its thin foot.

The cutting design on the pictured candy jar suggests an early Brainard period painted design shown in a 1943 flyer. All Westmoreland cutting, of course, pre-dates August 1937.

1801 Comport — 8½", Straight

1801 was designated a **Plain** line.

This comport available only with a conical bowl.

1932: Available in crystal and colors.
1940: Discontinued.

Height: 5⅜"
Width: 8"

While this glass comport is certainly Westmoreland's, the cutting may not be. I have seen this same cutting design on a Heisey-marked piece, which suggests it was done by a decorating house.

This **1801 Comport** is one of six I own in several glass colors and decorations.

1801 line introduced between 1918 and 1924. 1801 Comport first available between 1918 and 1924.

As with every West period Westmoreland bowl, there is no mould mark across the bowl, and a very minimal mould mark on the stem. The foot, which was formed in the mould in a cupped shape together with the stem, was worked flat with a wooden "battledore" or paddle.

1209 Sugar & Cream Set

1209 Sugar and Cream set first available in 1918 or before.

1209 was an item number used solely for this square sugar & cream set.

All three sets pictured have finished bottoms; two have bottoms ground and polished to 6- and 8-pointed cut stars.

1932: Available in crystal only.
1940: Discontinued.

In their last catalog of 1932, Fry pictured a square sugar and cream (No.1541) that appears to be identical to Westmoreland's **1209.** After corresponding with the H.C. Fry Glass Society, I have learned that Fry did not purchase Westmoreland's blanks; Fry made their own. The proof is in the handles. While Westmoreland's handles were pressed together with the bowls, Fry's were "stuck" — that is, formed separately and then applied to the bowls while they were over 1400° F. Stuck handles should be

valued because of the handwork involved, but they do have a downside: some have been known to later become "un-stuck."

A Westmoreland **1209 Cream** has been photographed in the same plunger and in the same joint mould where it was once pressed, perhaps 75 years ago. Notice that the spout and handle were both fully formed in the pressing.

Sugar: 3" x 3" (outside)

"Among Westmoreland's special items are... a square shaped sugar and cream..." (J 1/24/18).

Non-Westmoreland Decanter and Wine Glasses

(after 1937)

All six pieces signed "by J.W. Racinger."

Made after 1937 when he was working on his own.

There may have been just one company that supplied his later blanks; the glass is all blown and of good quality. Several large ruby-stained pieces have been found with his signature.

His later work usually shows motifs that are larger and less detailed than those of his Westmoreland years.

So far I have found it difficult to tie his unsigned Westmoreland work to his signed later work — except, perhaps, for his roses.

Decanter: 11⅛" h. (with stopper)

This signed wine set was cut by Joseph Racinger, Westmoreland's head cutter during the Chas West years. The glass is not Westmoreland's.

Most of what we know about Joseph Racinger comes from a *Pittsburgh Post Gazette* article of 10/17/60, written at the time a Pittsburgh jeweler displayed a collection of his cut glass.

Born in 1896 in Bohemia (then a part of Austria), he began a four-year apprenticeship in his uncle's glass shop at the age of twelve. He claimed that for four years he worked 72 hours a week with no pay. In 1912 when he was 16, he migrated to America and apparently continued his apprenticeship in this country.

Racinger apparently was one of the group of Bohemian-trained artists and cutters hired by Chas West in 1921. There is a bowl signed by Racinger and dated 1921 that I believe was Racinger's presentation piece, engraved when he first came to Westmoreland (see the Carnegie section). The 1960 jewelry store display of more than one hundred of his pieces included this bowl.

When he left Westmoreland, probably in 1937, Racinger moved to the Rochester (Beaver County, Pa.) area where he con-

tinued to cut on his own and for the Myers Company (a local jeweler). In contrast to his Westmoreland period glass, I believe most of his later work is signed. Some of his later glass has also come down to us with a paper label he used, still attached. Paul Mortimer, a Racinger collector, told me he was supposed to have been a difficult man to get to know. Yet, I understand that Racinger attended and gave each six-year-old a monogrammed glass at a birthday party held at his daughter's house in the early '60s. Tom Srembo, another collector of his glass, told me he died in 1969.

The *Post Gazette* reporter, blindly reflecting the "Less is More" movement of the preceding 20 years, wrote that Racinger had witnessed a "Change in taste... from the overcrowded design to the more simple, outstanding type." She quoted Racinger as saying: "Twenty or 30 years ago the engraver couldn't get enough designs crowded on a piece of glass. Today the simple designs are more effective and it takes two days rather than two weeks to do them." Clearly, the *Post Gazette* reporter, and strangely, Racinger too, saw these earlier designs as being made up of detached elements and failed to recognize their interplay. It is as if the composer, J.S. Bach, had been condemned to live twenty-five years longer, been made to adapt to the new "Sensitive" style embraced by his youngest son, and then been forced to dismiss his earlier compositions as so much cacophony.

1828 Cigarette Box Cover — 6"

(April 1930)

A wedding present to Helen West Wilson from Westmoreland's employees.

Racinger was just one of, perhaps, half a dozen e n g r a v e r s employed at Westmoreland at any one time.

Since Racinger's Westmoreland work was unsigned, identification can be made only on the basis of his style, technique, and skill. The roses and leaves on this cigarette box lid, while simple, suggest Racinger's work.

Free-Blown Hanging Vase or "Stalactite"

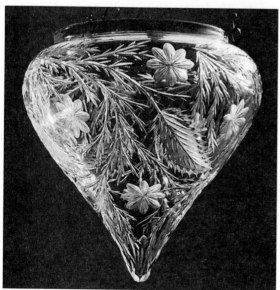

just above the tip probably cover marks left by a snap used to help support the shapeless glass as it was being worked into a vase (the pontil scar is less than ½" wide).

The design seems to be based on elements of two ferns: the hartford and the clubmoss. That dazzling leaf with its tiny spores seems to be taken from a fertile clubmoss leaf with a large central spore case.

The cutting itself is polished except for the hartford leaflets and the clubmoss leaves. Since both of these show intaglio cutting of considerable depth, this vase can best be appreciated by handling it.

One of my earliest memories is of this vase hanging in a window of my grandparents' music room. I have seen it over the years — always in a window, and always with some sort of vine hanging from it. Because of this, I was faced with a major restoration of the inside of the glass when I acquired it. When I wrote a friend and told him about the hours of work I had done on it, he wrote back, calling it a "labor of love." With that I wrote to assure him no one would ever again use it as a vase —"that way, Love's Labour's Last!"

(Date unknown)

Cutting designed by Helen (Mrs. Chas) West.

A family piece owned by Charles and Helen West.

Height: 7"

This is one of four important pieces of Westmoreland glassware Charles and Helen West took with them when they moved to a one-bedroom apartment in 1941. Beginning in 1948 it was passed along to various relatives; I am the fourth in line. I understand the vase was cut at the factory from a design of Helen West's. In its obituary the *National Glass Budget* referred to her as a "painter and botanist" (B 6/12/48).

The vase itself is free-blown. The exterior is irregular and there is a pontil scar at the tip. The four deep mitre cuts

Cut Crystal Candlesticks

1932/2 — 11" Bowl with Elephant Candleholders. A one-piece Console Set dating from 1932, it was originally available in crystal and colors. It is being reproduced today in cobalt blue and black.

I believe Westmoreland once made a greater variety of candlesticks than any other glass company.

In the early twentieth century candlesticks and kerosene lamps sold to entirely different markets. Candles were not then meant to be practical. Just as open fireplaces were cherished by those with central heating, candles were cherished by those with electricity. Before electricity, lamps, not candles, were the rule.

Reflecting this, Westmoreland's 1904 price list showed 26 kerosene lamps but no candlesticks. Eight years later the situation was reversed: the 1912 catalog pictured 16 candlesticks and no lamps. In 1924 the company offered 45 candlesticks, and two years later, 51. By 1932, the number had grown to 82 candlesticks — or 99, if different sizes are counted separately.

Westmoreland's 1940 price list, however, recorded only 22 candlesticks, and

of these just 14 were holdovers from the early Depression and before. Part of the explanation is the thinning of Westmoreland's product offerings that began in 1937, but another part of the explanation is the post-Depression mood of practicality so pervasive at the time. With the near-universal use of electricity, the electric lamp, rather than the anachronistic candlestick, was what America wanted, and Westmoreland positioned itself to satisfy this demand. (See the Miscellaneous section.)

Because most of Westmoreland's West period candlesticks were decorated, they can be found in various sections of this book. Of the 82 candlestick varieties available in 1932, nine of them are pictured in this section in cut crystal, while 19 others (plus two not available in 1932) are pictured elsewhere. Some of Westmoreland's most inspired and complex decorations from this period can be found on their candlesticks.

Here is a list of all 99 candlesticks recorded in the 1932 price list together with the authentic company names used for them.

Westmoreland Candlesticks available in 1932

	Candlestick No.	Size (")	Westmoreland Name		Candlestick No.	Size (")	Westmoreland Name
	1000	9½			1034	8, 9, 11	Solid Bottom
*	1001	Low			1035		Crucifix
	1002	6½, 8			1036	9	
	1004	4½	Birthday		1038	9, 12	Spiral
	1005	4	Birthday		1039		Hld Birthday
	1006	7			1040		Candle Adapter
	1007	7			1041	9	
	1008	7		*	1042	6½, 9	
	1009	6, 7			1043	8	Hollow Bottom
	1010	7			1044	8	
	1011	4½, 5½		*	1045	8	
	1012	7, 8			1046		Ash Tray
*	1013	5	Candelabra		1048		Candle & Cigarette Holder
	1015	7	Mission	*#	1049	4, 9	Dolphin
	1016	7, 8			1050	9	Ball Stem
	1017	8	Mt. Vernon		1051	Low	
	1018	4, 6½			1052		Handled
	1019	8		*	1053	4, 9	Diamond Foot
	1021	7		*	1054	3	Low
	1022	8		*	1056	Low	
	1023	7, 9, 12		*	1057	Low	Octagon Foot
	1027	8		*	1059	7	Candle Ashtray
	1028			*	1060	5	
*	1032			*	1061	2	
	1033						

Westmoreland Candlesticks available in 1932 (Cont.)

Candlestick No.	Size (")	Westmoreland Name	Candlestick No.	Size (")	Westmoreland Name
* 1062	3		* 23	7	
* 1063		Star Fish	24	8	
* 1064	4		1211		Birthday
* 1066	3½	3 Handled	* 1930	3	
* 1067		3 Balls	* 1932/2	11	Bowl w/Elephant Candleholders
* 1068	3				
* 1070	Low		# 1933	7	

Tied to Tableware Lines

Candlestick No.	Size (")	Westmoreland Name	Candlestick No.	Size (")	Westmoreland Name
* 77	5	Hobnail	* 1211	4	Octagon – 2 Hld
250	3½	Rings – optic	* 1211/1	3	Octagon
* 300	6	Waterford Sq. Foot	* 1211/2	3	Octagon
* 555	3½, 9	Early American	* 1706	5	Optic – Fancy Edge
*# 555	6	Candelabra	* 1707	4	Optic – 3 footed
* 555/1		Early American	* 1710	3, 8	Spiral
* 555/2	5½	Early American Sq. Foot	* 1909	4	
700	4½	Modernistic	*# 1921	Low, 9	Lotus
1020	9	Paul Revere	* 1928	4½	
* 1058	4	Fruit Design	1932	6	Wakefield

* Candlesticks available in color in 1932

\# Candlesticks available in opal (milk glass) in 1932

1019 Candlestick — 8"

The **1019** was, perhaps, Westmoreland's most patrician candlestick. Its lip suggests it may have been adapted from a silver design of the period, which in turn could have come from a Queen Anne period (c. 1710) design in brass.

Every crystal **1019** I have seen was flawlessly made and rich in spectral fire. This probably reflects the era when they were made: the teen years and just before — the era of Westmoreland's finest quality crystal.

The cutting on this candlestick is in one of Westmoreland's two Grecian ("Bead and Reel") styles.

> *"An endless variety of (Westmoreland's) candlesticks shows to excellent advantage... some of these may be found in the old original brass in more than one famous mansion of colonial days..."* (L 1/8/12).

1019 available in 1911 or before.

(c. 1912)

Numbers **1000** to **1070** were used for Westmoreland's candlesticks.

Ground and polished top and punty.

1932: Available in crystal only.
1940: Discontinued.

Height: 8⅝"
Weight: 1⅝ lb.

Paul Revere Colonial Candlestick — 9"
Reuben Haley's 1016 Candlestick — 7"

(c. 1912)

Paul Revere was one of Westmoreland's six colonial lines.

Paul Revere Candlestick ground and polished punty.

1016 also available 8".

1016 ground and polished top and punty.

Patent 41301 granted to Reuben Haley on 4/11/11 for 14 years.

1932: **Paul Revere** and **1016** (both sizes) available in crystal only.
1940: Both discontinued.

Paul Revere: 8¾" h.
1016: 7": 7½" h.
8": 8¼" h.

Paul Revere first available in 1912. 1016 first available in 1911.

"(Westmoreland's) new colonial candlesticks have won much favor…" (P 1/12/11).

Suggesting a Chippendale chair flanked by two Queen Anne chairs, these handled candlesticks are two of the most arresting that Westmoreland ever made.

"In the 'Paul Revere' are some candlesticks in unique effects and lemonade sets both showing very attractive light cuttings" (P 2/15/12).

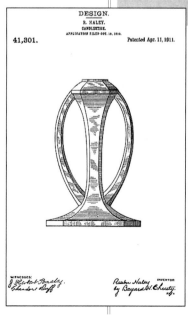

The **Paul Revere Candlestick** will be pictured again and discussed at the end of the section.

Reuben Haley, designer of Westmoreland's patented **Floral Colonial** line, patented the **1016 Candlestick** several months later. By taking Westmoreland's prestigious **1019 Candlestick** and attaching these arms, he managed to create an Art Nouveau triumph. Art Nouveau, never as popular in America as in Europe, was based on the curved line. It was sinuous, botanic, and often floral.

On this **1016 Candlestick,** notice how Haley's arms seem to grow naturally and organically out of the splayed foot. Notice how they highlight the curvature of the stem by complementing it. Notice how they taper as they rise and then disappear gently into the lip. But then look down from the top and see Haley's surprise: he has contrasted all these curves in one plane with hexagons in the other!

Although based on the **1019 Candlestick,** the **1016** required an entirely separate mould. For this reason there is a 7" **1016** but no corresponding 7" for the **1019.**

This cut flower design, resembling a Canada thistle, is the most frequently seen early Westmoreland cutting. But since it was also used by McKee, Fostoria, and possibly others, it should not be considered as anything more than a possible indicator of a Westmoreland piece.

60

1015 Mission Candlestick — 7"

1015 Mission first available in 1911.

"The Mission candlestick is perfect in design and highly finished" (L1/16/11).

(c. 1920)

Consistently measures 6½" or less.

1932: Available in crystal only.
1940: Discontinued.

Height: 6⅜"

I have seen a number of these **Mission Candlesticks,** but this is the only one I have seen decorated in any manner. Decoration runs counter to the Mission aesthetic. While Mission furniture is closely associated with Gustav Stickley's well-known Craftsman movement (1898 – 1916), Mission seems to have been an umbrella term of the period covering the furniture of McHugh, "Fra" Hubbard, Frank Lloyd Wright, the Stickleys, and others. It was austere, straight-lined, square-cut, unvarnished, and unadorned: in short, everything the contemporary Art Nouveau was not. These Westmoreland candlesticks were well-named for they suggest the tall, narrow backs of Mission side chairs.

The **Mission** stem and base appear to be identical to those used on Westmoreland's novelty **1015 S Candlestick** (1910 or earlier) available in 4" and 6" sizes. The **1015 S** had two "Chippendale" handles and was probably copied from a Jefferson/Central design. Jefferson/Central's look-alike was available with handles in 4½", 7½", and 9" sizes, and without handles in both 7" and 9" sizes. All five of these should be found marked "Krys-tol" near the base of the stem. The five item numbers assigned were respectively, T: 314, 317, 318, 325, and 328.

Reuben Haley, who patented Westmoreland's **1016 Candlestick,** also patented a second candlestick. While it looks as though it could have been the basis of the **Mission Candlestick,** the **Mission** preceded his design by more than a year. I believe Haley was trying to do the impossible: combine his Art Nouveau **1016** with the **Mission** — two styles that were immiscible. His hybrid design, while assigned to Westmoreland, was never used.

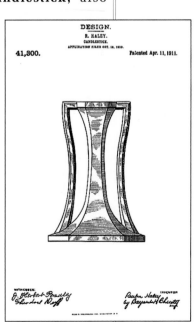

61

1012 Candlesticks — 7" and 8"
1012 Candlestick — 7"

(1915 – 1925)

Ground and polished
punties.

1932: Both sizes available
in crystal only.
1940: Discontinued.

7 Inch: 7⁷⁄₁₆" h.
8 Inch: 8½" h.

1012 first available in 1912 or before.

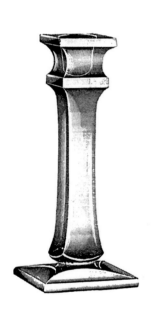

Until recently, I believed Westmoreland's **1012 Candlestick** was derived from what I had assumed was a brilliant-period cut glass prototype pictured in Dorothy Daniel's cut glass book (DD 156). Then I acquired a Westmoreland 8" **1012** with the strawberry diamond cutting shown in her book. The bottom of this candlestick (not pictured) is ground and polished all the way across, and the top is ground and polished leaving no mould mark except at the base of the stem. The glass quality is exceptional, and even though pressed, it would not disappoint a brilliant-cut collector. I now believe the Daniel candlesticks are Westmoreland's 7"

1012s, and the **1012** design is original.

The two photographs show three different ways Westmoreland's flower or thistle can be found. The flower sprig on the taller 8" candlestick is most commonly seen; it was available two or four sprigs to a candlestick stem. The cutting on the single candlestick is exceptionally beautiful because the floral wreath was actually cut on the underside of the foot.

The **1012 Candlestick** is also pictured in black glass in the Black Glass section.

1041 Candlestick — 9"

1041 first available between 1918 and 1924.

H.P. Sinclaire's "Diamonds and Silver Threads" cutting design was patented in 1913 and used by them until about 1920. Here it appears on Westmoreland's **1041 Candlestick** with the diamonds and the hexagonal vintage motif, but without the silver threads or the deep mitre cuts of the original diamonds.

Westmoreland was a supplier of blanks to Sinclaire. These candlesticks could have been sold to Sinclaire, who then did this cutting. But I think there is a more likely explanation. After Sinclaire closed in 1928, three Sinclaire engravers found employment at Westmoreland at various times: Clement Nitsche, Joseph Oveszny, and Henry Hauptmann. Clearly, the stock-in-trade of these artists was the design work they knew and felt comfortable with, and they certainly would have been encouraged to continue where they left off when they came to Westmoreland.

While we may never know who was responsible for the beautiful polished grape leaves on this **1041 Candlestick,** I feel it must have been one of these three Sinclaire engravers.

Ironically, Chas Reisenstein, a Pittsburgh jeweler, was able to obtain a patent (512100) on this design in 1921. I have also run across it on the rim of a china plate in an ad of the late '20s. The design is of Oriental derivation.

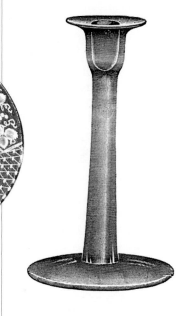

(c. 1930)

1932: Available in crystal only.
1940: Discontinued.

Height: 8⅝"

1027 Candlesticks — 8"

1027 first available between 1918 and 1924.

The **1027** was another of Westmoreland's Art Nouveau candlesticks; notice the similarity of the **1027** to a rose bud on its slender stem.

Both of these pairs have notched stems. A third pair I have seen showed Westmoreland's Grecian cutting. Because these stems are six-sided, a great many individual passes against the cutting wheel were required. Three, six-pointed stars and a single eight-pointed star were cut on the bottoms of the feet.

Evidently, the specifications were fairly loose for some of these cuttings, and Westmoreland's cutters were not closely monitored.

(c. 1924)

Ground and polished tops.

6- and 8-pointed cut stars.

1932: Available in crystal only.
1940: Discontinued.

Height: 8"

63

1023 Candlesticks — 7"

(1915 to 1925)

Also available 9" (hollow) and 12" (solid) from 1924 or before.

There is a similarity between this candlestick and the **1025 Card Holder** (see the Miscellaneous section) first made in 1913.

1932: 7", 9" & 12" available in crystal only. 1940: Discontinued. However, the **1023** may have been reissued in the late Brainard period in etched colored glass.

Height: 7⅜"

1023 first available between 1913 and 1917. A similar 1009 available in 1912 or before.

The **1023** was Westmoreland's lowest priced 7" candlestick — in 1932, just $2 a dozen wholesale. Because of its low price and its popular Craftsman design, it is the one most commonly seen today — ordinarily without decoration. While it was introduced in the teen years, it shared the design of the **1009**, introduced in 1912 or earlier.

There are four competitors' candlesticks which could be confused with this one. New Martinsville's No. 169 came in a 7" size only. While almost identical to Westmoreland's, its plunger came up to just under the candleholder, and its exterior corners were slightly chamfered. U.S. Glass' No. 63 — 7½" also looks almost identical but has a slightly greater space between its two ridges. (The ridges on Westmoreland's 7" **1023** are exactly 1⅛" apart measured from the center of each.)

Jeannette made an almost exact copy of the **1023.** However, Jeannette's glass is noticeably cruder, and there is a sharp mould mark at the side of Jeannette's top ridge. (Both of Westmoreland's ridges are squared off and perfectly smooth.) Jeannette's shaft is slightly thicker — 1" versus ⅞" — and its total height is exactly 7". (Westmoreland's is 7⅜".) Finally, Cambridge appears to have made a near lookalike, but with rounded corners on the base.

Westmoreland used two plungers in making its **1023** and evidently used them at the same time. One of them was pointed, and the other was blunt. The pointed cavity will measure 2⅞" up from the base whereas the blunt cavity will vary from 3⅜ to 3⅝". There is no measurable difference in the outsides of these Westmoreland candlesticks.

1019 Candlestick — 8"

If this simple cutting had been done on anything but the venerable **1019 Candlestick**, it would have been less effective. The early glass, bursting with refractive energy, was fire-polished to total smoothness. Then the top and the punty were both ground and polished. When the cutter added his six palmettoes to the bottom of the foot, he cut them around the edge of the punty so they appeared to be growing out of the punty ring. From above, the thickness of the crystal acts as a magnifier. The domed punty captures and directs the light, and the facets bring the palmettoes in and out of view depending on the angle.

(c. 1912)

Ground and polished top and punty.

Height: 8⅝"
Weight: 1⅝ lb.

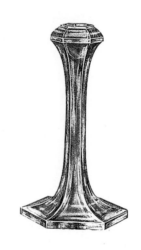

1021 Candlestick — 7"

This **1021 Candlestick** was cut in the more commonly seen of Westmoreland's two Grecian cutting patterns.

Heisey made a candlestick similar to Westmoreland's **1021**, but Heisey's design is eight-sided. Jeannette's No. 5132 could be confused with Westmoreland's. However, the most obvious difference between them is the plunger cavity. While Jeannette's stops half way up and ends in a point, Westmoreland's is blunt and rises to about ½" from the bottom of the candleholder. Jeannette's total height is exactly 7" whereas Westmoreland's is about 7⅜". At the top rim, Jeannette's has a sharp mould mark whereas Westmoreland's is perfectly smooth.

Berry Wiggins, a glass researcher, has discovered a very subtle difference at the neck: Westmoreland's neck has a slightly tighter curve than Jeannette's. This difference, however, can be seen only in a side-by-side comparison.

I believe there was also a third company using this design, but with a shorter plunger height — more like Jeannette's.

1021 first available between 1913 and 1917.

(c. 1915)

1932: Available in crystal only.
1940: Discontinued.

Height: 7⅜"

Paul Revere Colonial Candlestick — 9"

Paul Revere Colonial line introduced Jan. 1912. Paul Revere Candlestick first available in 1912.

(c. 1912)

This line, originally not numbered, was assigned the number **1020** in the 1920s.

This candlestick is possible Westmoreland's first to be tied to a tableware line.

Ground and polished punty.

1932: Available in crystal only.
1940: Discontinued.

Height: 8¾"
Weight: 1¾ lb.

"The keystone lines of Plain Colonial and Art Glassware displayed by L. E. Smith are far more extensive than shown in 1911." (L.E. Smith, having left the firm that still bears his name, apparently worked as Westmoreland's sales manager for a year before relocating to Chicago.) *"An imitation rock crystal and cut is called the 'Paul Revere.' The cuttings are floral and star effects"* (J 1/11/12).

The spirited shape of these **Paul Revere** handles comes from ebony teapot handles of the Federal period (see the Cut Crystal section). But then these teapot handles seem to be derived from those enduring mid-eighteenth century "cupid's bow" crestrails of Chippendale chairs, which in turn appear to have drawn their inspiration from the ancient pagoda roofs of China. I believe this shape in glass, however, can be found only on Westmoreland's **Paul Revere** handled pieces.

> *"Colored glass was the child of the engraving art for it was soon obvious that if engraving on crystal was beautiful, it was infinitely more so when cut through a color. Such was the status of the glass industry at the time of the 1876 Centennial Exposition . . ."* (DD 144).

It may be the America was introduced to stained cut-to-clear glassware as late as the 1870s as Dorothy Daniel suggested in 1940. But if so, America was decades behind Europe. According to Wm Heacock (HC III), the process for amber staining, presumably as a substitute for the casing or flashing used earlier, was registered in 1818, and then within a few years was used throughout Europe. Today, however, it is usually associated with Bohemian engraving of the 1840s and 1850s.

While the more traditional casing or flashing is a glass coating on a glass blank (flashing is thinner than casing), staining is a chemical coating similar to iridizing. The yellow-amber color is typically produced by the application of silver chloride (some sources say silver nitrate) to glass. After the coating is applied, the blank is fired in a "muffle" furnace to about 1000° F to create the color and to bond the coating to the glass. In two respects, the staining process differs from iridizing, however: with iridizing, the metallic salts are sprayed onto the hot blank immediately after it is removed from the muffle, and in quality iridizing there are several such sprays.

Westmoreland's Staining

Westmoreland was staining in amber and ruby glass colors at least from the beginning of 1896 (L1/15/96). But in that early era Westmoreland's staining seems to have been chiefly used as decorative work in its tableware lines. A few years later, around 1910, Westmoreland was amber-staining crystal. But this alternative to amber glass (which Westmoreland also made at about this time) was largely confined to their iridized pieces. Westmoreland's staining as a background for cutting seems to date from 1921, coinciding with Chas West's hiring of Joseph Racinger and perhaps other central European engravers. The **1820 Bowl** pictured in the Carnegie section of this book, dated 1921, confirms this initial date, whereas the **1900 Bowl** shown near the end of this section suggests this staining was used to the end of Westmoreland's cutting 16 years later. While some of Westmoreland's translucent cased colors from 1927 on (red, blue, green, violet, and lemon yellow) could be, and have been, confused with stains, Westmoreland's only stain color used with cutting in the 16-year period was amber (actually a range of hues from medium yellow to amber — the difference possibly resulting from temperature variations in the muffle). Most of Westmoreland's most important cutting from those years seems to be found on their amber-stained blanks.

1708 Covered Sweetmeat

(late 1920s)

1708 was designated an **Optic** line.

Originally designated **1211,** this sweetmeat was renumbered in 1925 when **1211** became the exclusive designation for Westmoreland's growing **Octagon** line.

Available either with a cover or belled without a cover. The cover added a third to the cost.

1932: Available in crystal and colors.
1940: Discontinued.

Height: 9"
Width: 4½"

Optics is to glass what vibrato is to singing. Both are intended to convey excitement and mask imperfection, but both can bring about undulant fever. In the case of glassware, however, optics is often pleasingly subtle. Many Westmoreland pieces of the '20s were offered "plain or optic" — a choice made possible with a simple change of plunger; but this sweetmeat was one of the pieces not available plain.

Economy Tumbler made was appears to be an identical "compote and cover," their No. 7556, in the mid-'20s. For iden-tification purposes, there are sixteen optic rays in the Westmoreland cover; Economy's will probably prove to be plain or else have a different count.

Notice how the cutter was indifferent to the optic rays on the lid and the bowl sides. Notice also his three sets of ovals — on the foot, at the edge of the bowl, and at the edge of the cover. Finally, notice his circle of leaves, which rotates in a clockwise direction around the cover.

WESTMORELAND SPECIALTY CO.

GRAPEVILLE, PA.

Manufacturers of High Grade Glass Ware. Plain, Cut and Decorated— for Gift Shops, Florists and Table Use.

*No. 1211
Covered
Sweetmeat*

(L 5/28/23)

1826 Mayonnaise — 6"
1800 Mayo Ladle

(late 1920s)

1826 Mayonnaise also available with a rolled edge (same mould).

1826 was an item number assigned just to these two bowls.

This **6" Mayonnaise** was redesignated a **5" Mayo Bell** in 1932.

The 1926 catalog erroneously lists this ladle as number **1837**; **1837** was actually a smaller, hemispheric jelly ladle.

1932: Bowls and ladle available in crystal and colors.
1940: Bowls discontinued; ladle available in crystal only.

Width: 5⅝"
Stem/bowl: 1⅞"

Since this cutting motif of flowers and leaves on vertical gang-wheel-cut stripes can be found on non-Westmoreland glass, it cannot be used for identification. While I have found it on more Westmoreland pieces than on all others combined, it is likely this unpatented motif was used by various cutting houses in the '20s at the time when there was so much borrowing. Notice in this cutting how the leaves frame each of the flowers in contrast to the preced-ing piece; this variation is more commonly seen. The "eyebrows" over each of the flowers are probably not unique to Westmoreland (or perhaps to Racinger), but they seem to be almost a Westmoreland signature-mark. The cut ovals on the unstained foot are identical to those on the preceding piece. Notice the cutting on the stained ladle; this, too, seems to be almost a signature-mark.

Westmoreland's **1826 Mayonnaise** can be seen with a 14" platter elsewhere in this section. The critical stem-to-bowl dimension confirms both bowls are the same.

1820 Footed Honey — 6"

1820 line introduced between 1918 and 1924. 1820 Footed Honey first available between 1918 and 1924

(1920s)

1820 was Westmoreland's **Flange** line.

1932: Available in crystal only.
1940: Discontinued.

Width: 6½"

I recall this cutting from my childhood; it was on some of my grandfather's glass that was sold off in 1941. That basket with its big, bulging eyes is just the sort of thing that can make an indelible impression on a young imagination. When, after so many years, I saw and acquired this little piece, it was a homecoming.

I have seen this cutting several times recently and each time it was on a stained cut-to-clear crystal blank. One blank, however, was a handled sandwich tray not made by Westmoreland. Since then I have noticed occasional pieces of Westmoreland cutting or other Westmoreland decorating done on non-Westmoreland blanks; most of it appeared to date from the '30s. Surviving records show a few instances of Westmoreland purchases of glass blanks from other companies: for example, Bryce stemware. Whether this was done primarily to complement an assortment, to finish an order, or just to keep Westmoreland's cutters and decorators busy, it was in fact done, and we should not be surprised to see examples of it.

1840 Vase — 10"

(1920s)

Also available 6" and 8".

1840 was an item number assigned just to these three vases.

1932: 6", 8" & 10" available in crystal and colors. The 10" cost three times as much as the 6".
1940: All three sizes discontinued.

Height: 7"
Width: 9⅞"
Weight: 3⅛ lb.

In the '20s, U.S. Glass made a very similar vase to this — their No. 15179 (Factory G). Since they supplied it in 5½" and 10" sizes, these two sizes could easily be confused with Westmoreland's. None of these vases show any mould seams, all show a circumferential joint mark just above the ankle, and all of them show a similarly worked foot. However, Westmoreland's small 6" vase is squatter. While U.S. Glass' is 5" tall, Westmoreland's is only 4¼" tall. There are three important differences in the 10" vases. While U.S. Glass' rim is about 10½" across, Westmoreland's averages 9¾". Also, while Westmoreland's foot is close to 5" across, U.S. Glass' is about 4½" — less than half the diameter of the rim. Finally, weighing more than 3½ lb., U.S. Glass' 10" vase is about a half pound heavier than Westmoreland's.

8" and 10" first available between 1918 and 1924. 6" first available in 1925.

Blown "Egyptian" Vase

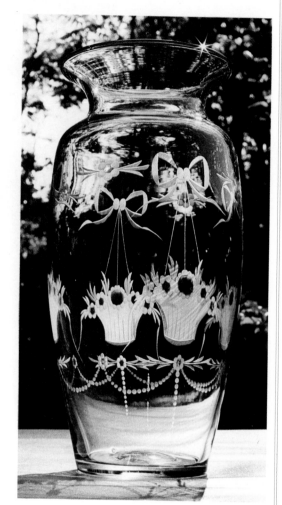

(c. 1930)

Vase blown in the same shape as Westmoreland's blown **"Egyptian"** jars from the turn of the century

Height: 13"
Width: 5½"
Base: 3¾" d.

The festoons of graduated pearls combined with the basket motif suggests a date of about 1930 for the cutting.

The vase, not shown in the catalogs, is pictured with three Westmoreland decorations in this book; two of them are shown in the Cased Glass section. Aside from differences in the neck, the shape of these vases is identical to the **"Egyptian"** jars made by Westmoreland at the turn of the century. Their uniform diameter and precise angle at the base suggests they were blown in one of these jar moulds. On the other hand, their large, ground punties and their lack of concentric marks (showing they had been turned in a blow mould) sug-

gests they could have been free-blown.

But free-blown or "off-hand" glass is not simply glass blown into the air; it has to be formed with various tools and fixtures. There is a "block," for example, resembling half a blow mould that free-blown glass is rolled in to give it its shape. Because of such tooling, needed on all free-blown and most mould-blown glass, the dividing line between them is a hazy one. Westmoreland once made a great deal of mould-blown glass. In 1991 there were 439 blow moulds that still survived at the Westmoreland factory even after the mould scrappings of 1924 and 1946.

1840 "Flower Center" Vase — 10"

(1925)

Fort Dearborn called this vase a "Flower Center."

Fort Dearborn's "Graceful Scroll" cutting.

Height: 7"
Width: 9¾"
Weight: 3⅛ lb.

Fort Dearborn was a wholesale distributor that sold to jewelry stores and gift shops through their catalog, which they called a "Gift Book."

On page two of their Gift Book for 1925, they pictured a group of 16 cut pieces — 15 of which were Westmoreland's. The design, centered around a Bohemian rococo shell, was described as a "Graceful Scroll Motif combined with Floral Sprays in White Relief against Amber background."

Because these top-of-the-line Westmoreland pieces can still be found by persevering Westmoreland or Racinger collectors, let me list them here:

1820 L F Comport — 11"
1042 Candlesticks — 9" (paired with
1820 Comport)
1820 Cheese and Cracker
1840 Vase — 10"
1815 Cupped Bowl — 10"
1820 Footed Honey — 6"
1801 H F Ball Stem Sweetmeat — 8"
1820 Mayonnaise
1800 Ladle
1909/1 Bowl — 11"
1031 Bowl Stand
1820 Bowl Flared — 9"
1926 Mayonnaise
1801 Platter — 14"
1820 H F Sweetmeat — 6"
U.S. Glass No. 15319 Compote — 7"

We can be certain Westmoreland did this cutting because of the number of design elements shared with other Westmoreland cuttings. The symmetrical shells and the leaves all point to Racinger; the cutting quality is up to his standard.

Fort Dearborn's wholesale price for the Flower Center was $15 in 1925 ($132 in 1995 dollars).

1820 Low Foot Comport — 11"
1042 Candlesticks — 9"

1820 Comports first available between 1918 and 1924. 1042 Candlesticks first available between 1918 and 1924.

As the dining room sideboard, or "console," came into more widespread use after World War I, so did the need for something to place on it. For many it was a glass bowl filled with fruit, framed by two candlesticks.

In 1921 these bowls and candlesticks were apparently not yet sold together, for a reporter saw this combination as something new: "(At Westmoreland's display at the Pittsburgh Exhibit) each bowl has a stand and two candlesticks to match, making an effective set. There are three shapes to select from" (L 1/10/21). Was Westmoreland the originator of the console set?

Three years later, at the 1924 Pittsburgh Exhibit, the press noted, Westmoreland's console sets were "The largest shown in Pittsburgh by any firm... and the demand was pronounced just as active as the line was attractive" (J 2/7/24).

A year after that, Fort Dearborn's wholesale price for this **1820 Bowl** with two **1042 Candlesticks** with "Graceful Scroll" cuttings was $24 (1995: $211).

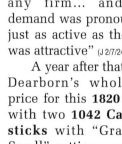
(L 1/28/24)

(1925)

1820 LF Comport also available 9".

1042 Candlesticks also available 6½".

Fort Dearborn's "Graceful Scroll" cutting.

1932: Both available in crystal and colors.
1940: Both discontinued.

Comport: 11⅝" w.
Candlesticks: 9⅛" h.

1042 Candlesticks — 9"

(1925)

Fort Dearborn's "White Rose" cutting.

Height: 9⅛"

On another page of their 1925 Gift Book, Fort Dearborn pictured these same 16 pieces with a different cutting which they described as a "Rose Design — Glass engraved in White Rose, Dewdrop Center with highly polished Crystal Leaves in beautiful contrast against Amber Casing."

There seems to have been some confusion, for the "White Rose" pattern, which was patented by the Irving Cut Glass Co. in 1916, has a rose with gray cut petals (RA 305). The rose used by Westmoreland here was patented by the McKanna Cut Glass Co. that same year and they apparently called it "Rose Bud" (RA 312). It had gang-wheel, striated petals, and a bright "Harvard" star in the center as it does here. Both of these roses seem to have been copied by several cutting houses in the '20s.

There are two differences between the McKanna and the Westmoreland rose, however. McKanna's is circular, whereas Westmoreland's has seven distinct outer lobes. Also, at the center McKanna's has a true hobstar creating a smooth-topped English hobnail, whereas Westmoreland's is busy with hobstar crossings. While Westmoreland was a supplier of glass blanks to McKanna (RA 312), there is no reason to believe McKanna cut these Westmoreland pieces for Fort Dearborn. Nevertheless, if this rose design was cut by Joseph Racinger, it is the only design I am aware of where he used a gang cutting wheel.

Fort Dearborn's wholesale price for a pair of these **1042 Candlesticks** with the "White Rose" cutting was $10.50 in 1925 (1995: $92).

Three Piece Salad Set:
1801 Serving Platter — 14"
1826 Mayonnaise — 6"
1800 Mayo Ladle

(c. 1926)

Fort Dearborn called this a "Three-Piece Salad Set."

Fort Dearborn's "Design No. 229."

Platter: 14" d.
Foot: 8" o.d.

There was a third Fort Dearborn cutting available in 1925; it was called simply "Design No. 229." While the items offered were yellow-amber stained just as they were in the other two decorations, the staining was separated from the somewhat simpler cutting that was done around the unstained rims.

Except for the ring used to position the bowl, this platter is identical to the known **1801 Platter** shown in the Cased Glass section. To create this ring, a plunger had to be altered. Neither the salad set nor the altered platter was listed in the 1932 price list.

The "Three Piece Salad Set" was not available in "Design No. 229" in 1925. However, the wholesale price of this set in the "Graceful Scroll" cutting that year was $22.50 (1995: $198).

1801 Plate — 9"

(c. 1926)

1801 was designated a **Plain** line.

1801 Plates ranged from 6" to 21".

Ground and polished bottom.

1932: **1801 Plates** 6" to 14" available in crystal and colors; 14" also available in opal; 21" available in crystal only.
1940: Seven sizes available in crystal; four also available in opal.

Diameter: 8⅞"
Foot: 5⅛" o.d.

1801 Plates first available between 1918 and 1922. 1801 — 9" Plate first available in 1926.

This salad plate was designed and cut by Joseph Racinger; it needs no signature. Notice the dental rim suggesting the serrated edge of a gold coin. Notice the C's used as arches with corbel supports. Notice the nearly symmetrical rococo shells in five different styles, the foliage, and the terrain with its diagonal slashes and projecting tufts of grass. Notice the Racinger animals (here, does and bucks) with their expressive mouths, their big round eyes, and their muscles and wrinkled skin. Finally, notice the Racinger castle with its A-shaped entrance and its oval windows with short horizontal lines above and below each, a domed roof capping every bay, and minarets over select roofs. While some other Bohemian cuttings will include a few of these features, taken together they point to Racinger. Compare this plate to the blue bowl in the Cased Glass section, and compare both of these to the Racinger-cut salon vases in the Carnegie section.

Cutting identification must be based on a complex of characteristics — not just one. For example, we must never chase Racinger from piece to piece solely on the basis of his dental evidence. There is, after all, a name for such inductive leaps: they are known as "transendental."

1800 Rose Jar and Cover

1800 line first available between 1913 and 1917. 1800 Rose Jar first available in 1926.

"Among the more interesting new items (in Westmoreland's display at the Pittsburgh Exhibit) *are a rose jar and cover in shape like the famous Portland Vase"* (L1/18/26).

(late 1920s)

1800 was designated a **Plain** line.

Except for three dresser sets and a 9" x 15" tray, the rose jar was the most expensive **1800** item in 1932.

The rose jar's 6¾" rim width is necessary to accommodate the cover.

A family piece owned by Charles and Helen West.

1932: Available in crystal and colors.
1940: Discontinued.

Width: 6¾"
Height: 13" (w/lid)
Weight: 3⅜ lb.

This rose jar and cover was one of the four important pieces of Westmoreland the Wests took with them when they moved to a one-bedroom apartment in 1941. Chas West valued this and clearly saw nothing incongruous about cutting of this quality on a stained (as against a cased or flashed) blank. Cutting on a stained blank has one very significant advantage: Since the staining is thin, the cutting through it has crisp edges as the close-up picture will show. Cutting is always a little ragged when done through casing or even flashing.

When talking to a reporter of the local paper in 1923, Chas West used the phrase "The spur of high wages for paramount designs of great beauty" (JD 1/16/23). Here he was referring to the success of the Pittsburgh area in general and Westmoreland in particular in attracting Bohemian talent. He continued with what may be an indicator of his thinking at the time: "(The Bohemians) hand down their secrets from generation to generation. Each generation is to guard the secrets of decorating and is directed by the elders to improve on older designs. Initiative is taught." Chas West's rose jar certainly shows "initiative." Its engraved design is an Americanization of the central European hunt cutting. Instead of a castle, a watch tower, and a deer, it employs a pointer and a pheasant.

77

1800 Footed Vase — 10"

1800 Footed Vase first available in 1926.

(late 1920s)

The **1800 Vase** is ⅝" narrower at the rim than the rose jar.

1932: Available in crystal and colors. As a vase it was priced 20% below the rose jar.
1940: Discontinued.

Width: 6⅛"
Height: 9¾"
Weight: 2¼ lb.

This **1800 Vase** is even more stunning than the preceding rose jar. Without the lid, more light can get behind the cutting, and the cutting here, is if possible, even finer.

While this vase is not as spectacular as the blue lamp in the Cased Glass section or the stained **1820 Bowl** in the Carnegie section, in its detail it is fully equal to both of them. Notice every muscle, every feather, every hair is as carefully delineated as if it were part of an engraving on a stock certificate. Except for minor differences such as the pheasant's tail feathers, the design on this vase and the rose jar is the same. Because the close-up pictures were taken from inside the jar and the vase, there is a pronounced arching of the dog and the pheasant. Notice how symmetrical Racinger's shells tend to be; this seems to be a Racinger characteristic.

Compare these with a close-up of the cover of the cigarette box pictured on page 48. Notice the similarities between the setter on the cigarette box and the pointer: the pose, obviously, but also the eye and the nose. Notice also, the similarity of the grassy terrain. Knowing Racinger was the cutter of the rose jar and the vase, we can safely assume he was the cutter of the cigarette box with all its arabesques and crisscrossings not seen on the other two. Similar arabesques can be found on the signed **1820 Bowl** in the Carnegie section.

Where did he get the idea of substituting these dogs for the scholastic deer of his early years? It may be only a coincidence, but Chas West's shotgun (a Parker "D" of 1895) has a pointer engraved on one side of the breech block and a setter on the other. Both animals are posed just as they are here, and the ground beneath them has tufts of grass remarkably similar to Racinger's.

1900/2 Bell Bowl — 12"

1900/1 Bowls first available between 1918 and 1924. 1900/2 Bowls first available in 1926.

The feel of this cut bowl suggests the late '30s or even the '40s. It is in the *Directoire* or French Directory style that was coming into vogue at this time. It shows that Westmoreland was still using its yellow-amber staining in the mid-to-late '30s, and it also shows the direction Westmoreland's cutting might have continued to take had it not been terminated in 1937.

The design and execution both seem to point to Racinger, and if so, we can assume he was there till the end. But whether or not the cutting was Racinger's, we can be sure it was Westmoreland's. The design's crisscross lines can be seen on a number of earlier Westmoreland cuttings. There is nothing unique about these lines, but they tend to be commonly seen on Westmoreland cuttings. The design's stylized fern or palm branches can be seen on the small **1841 Comport** in the Iridized section; they

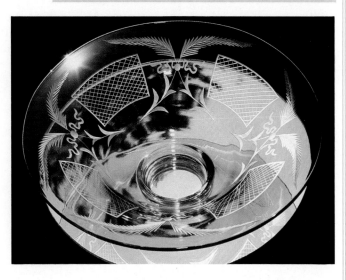

were employed there to frame three neo-classical urns.

Notice how the artist has managed to update some of Westmoreland's traditional design elements. He has transformed its leaves into arrowheads, its vine stems into arrow shafts, its palm branches into arrow feathers, and its grape vines into ribbons. It is important to remember this design was conceived in an era when any design at all was beginning to be frowned upon. But this design could then, and could now, hold its own with the very best of any era.

(1930s)

1900 was designated a **Plain** line.

1900 Bowls had peg bottoms that allowed them to slip out of simple block moulds.

1900/2 Bowls also available rolled edge and flared (same mould).

Three comparable **1900/1 Bowls** were 2" narrower at the rims and ¼" smaller at the peg feet.

Foot ground and polished.

1932: All **1900 Bowls** available in crystal and colors.
1940: Discontinued.

Bowl: 11¾" d.
Foot: 3¼" d.

? — 1900 Bell Bowl
? — 1032/0 Flower Bowl Stand

Is this bowl and stand Westmoreland's? The color is right. Staining was used by few companies in the '20s and '30s, and fewer still were using this yellow-to-amber color. The shapes of both bowl and stand are, I believe, unique to Westmoreland. The bowl with its cylindrical (pegged) foot and the stand with its covered sides were both made as Westmoreland would have made them with no visible mould marks. Nevertheless, both sizes are wrong.

Westmoreland could conceivably have come out with bowls and stands in new sizes after the 1932 price list. But in 1991 I found moulds for all the flower bowl stands that were available in 1932 at the factory, but among them there were no additional

sizes. Also, while I have seen this same cutting design on a Westmoreland **857 Jelly**, I have also seen it on a Duncan & Miller compote and a Heisey-marked piece, suggesting it was done by a cutting house. This stand without the bowl is pictured in the Miscellaneous section.

(c. 1930)

Ground and polished bowl foot and stand top.

Bowl: 8½" d.
Foot: 2⅝" d.

79

Cut Colored Glass

Cut colored glass is rare before the 1920s. Since an important purpose of polished cutting is to bring out the fire in fine crystal, and the ideal of rough cutting is to appear suspended in air, it is a wonder cutting was ever done on colored blanks. Most colors just seem to compete with cutting.

In the '20s, however, glasshouses — particularly Westmoreland — combined cutting with their trendy new colors, and trade reporters wrote about it warmly, if a little less than enthusiastically. The first trade reference to Westmoreland's cutting on colored blanks was in early 1923:

"(Westmoreland's) solid color copper wheel engraved line was representative of the Fifteenth century period" (J 2/8/23). Unfortunately, the glass color was not given. A year later a Pittsburgh Show reviewer wrote, "There was also a very good line of (Westmoreland's) cut colored glass which we would like to describe in detail" (L 1/14/24). Unfortunately, though, he didn't.

Because cutting is suppressed by colors, I have found that next only to iridized Westmoreland, cut colored Westmoreland has been the most difficult glass I have had to photograph.

1801 Plate — 9" (Green)

(c. 1926)

1801 was designated a **Plain** line.

1801 Plates ranged from 6" to 21".

Ground and polished bottom. Cut star. Gang-wheel-cut rim.

1932: Plates 6" to 14" available in crystal and colors; 14" also available in opal; 21" available in crystal only.
1940: Seven sizes available in crystal; four also available in opal.

Diameter: 8⅞"
Foot: 5" o.d.

"Among the new things Westmoreland has brought out for 1925 is a line of solid color tableware with a cut edge.... The colors are attractive, notable among them being green. The cutting on the edge, which takes the form of a wreath effect, gives a pleasing finishing touch" (P 1/29/25).

1801 Plates first available between 1918 and 1924. 1801 — 9" Plate first available in 1926. Green glass first advertised Sept. 1924.

Three years before, Westmoreland had introduced the "most extensive display of cut plates at the (Pittsburgh) exhibit." They were then all crystal and all had star bottoms. They were offered in ten different cutting patterns and ranged in price from $7.50 to $36 a dozen wholesale (1995: $67 − $320) (L 1/16 & 1/30/22).

I have seen this same wreath cutting on a Westmoreland console set. Notice how its festoons and tassels have been executed solely with gang cutting wheels.

Like most Westmoreland plates, the foot ring on this one shows gradual curves with no sharp breaks between the rim and the foot and between the center and the foot. It also shows a characteristic indented ring on the top just above the foot. Also, like most Westmoreland plates, this one shows faint rotation marks in the center that prove the plate was pressed "regular" (i.e., in a bowl shape) and then worked out flat. Because of this handwork, stacked Westmoreland plates will show some variation in rim angle.

1901 Fan Vase 9½" (Green)

1901 Fan Vase first available in 1927.

(c. 1928)

The **1901** mini-line was designated **Regular Scallop**.

This fan vase was made in just one size.

1932: Available in crystal and colors.
1940: Discontinued.

Height: 9½"

Fan vases had a burst of popularity in the late '20s. After they were pressed, they were removed from their moulds with conical shapes that were then flattened. Because of this, they should all be adaptations of something else such as the bottoms of covered comports that used the unworked shape. Nevertheless, I have never seen this scalloped fan vase unflattened.

Everything but the stems in this simple cutting was executed with gang cutting wheels; the flower seems to be a freely-interpreted clematis.

1820 Dolphin Comport — 11" (Green)

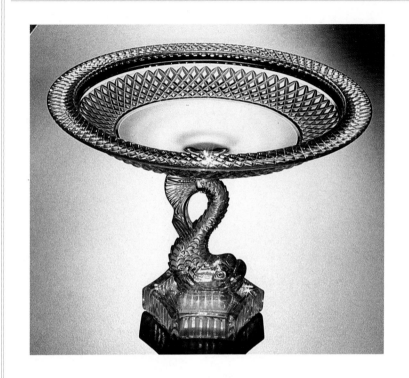

(c. 1927)

Also available 7".

1820 was Westmoreland's **Flange** line.

1849 was the number assigned to all **Dolphin** items except for these two comports and a **1211 Handled Sandwich.**

"Rock Crystal" (polished) mitre cutting.

1932: All **Dolphin** items available in crystal, colors, and opal. Both **1820 Comports** available in combinations of black (casing) and white opal glass. 1940: All **Dolphin** items discontinued in 1940 except the candlesticks and the 8" shell.

Height: 8¼"
Diameter: 11"
Weight: 3¼ lb.

"New Dolphin console sets... the outstanding feature of this line (is) that in each item the stem is in the shape of a dolphin. There are three numbers in clear, solid colors, deep blue, emerald green, and amber, undecorated. There is one in robin's egg blue with silver bands and a silver dolphin, one in peach blow with black dolphin and black line decorations, one in emerald green with hammered silver band, one in blue with black decorations" (J 10/9/24)

Despite its appearance, the design on this comport was not pressed; it was first deep-mitre cut and then polished — probably with acid. The mitres were cut with a V-shaped stone or iron wheel, and the same cutting wheel seems to have been used above the rim, beneath the bowl, and on the side of the foot. It is ironic that Westmoreland was now making cuttings that resembled pressings, when just 15 years before, it was trying to make pressings that resembled cuttings. However, in the late '20s, polished cutting was very much in fashion, and it was referred to as "rock crystal" by the industry.

(L 1/19/25)

1708 Fan Vase — 8" (Amber)

1708 — 8" Fan Vase first available in 1927. Amber glass first advertised Sept. 1924.

(late 1920s — early 1930s)

1708 was designated an **Optic** line.

1708 Fan Vases available 6" & 9" from 1926 plus 4" & 8" from 1927.

1932: **1708 Fan Vases** 4", 6", 8", 9" & 12" available in crystal and colors. 1940: Discontinued.

Height: 8¼"

"(Shown at Horace C. Gray's Westmoreland display in New York City) *a copper wheel engraving in ship design*" (J 7/30/25).

While at first glance, the sails and the keel appear to be etched, the grain across them proves they were executed by hand with a cutting wheel. Not visible in the photograph are the scribed lines around the sails, and the planks and portholes in the keel.

While the **1708 Fan Vase** was first available in 1926, the 8" size was first available in 1927 with an optional, fitted flower block. The stem design may have been suggested by one used on a frequently-seen fan vase of Steuben's from the '20s.

1042 Candlesticks — 9" (Amber)

1042 Candlesticks first available between 1918 and 1924.

(late 1920s)

Also available 6½".

1803 is the number of this same candlestick with mould crackle.

1932: Available in crystal and colors.
1940: Discontinued.

Height: 9¼"

Between 1830 and 1860, simple-lined, broad-surfaced Empire furniture was employed as "canvas" for the rich mahogany veneers which were so popular at the time. Eighty years later, simple-lined, broad, surfaced **1042 Candlesticks** were similarly employed as canvas for Westmoreland's rich artwork. Today, more varied Westmoreland handwork can be found on these **1042 Candlesticks** than on any other glass Westmoreland made. This is why they can be found in eight sections of this book.

There is a problem with 9" **1042**s that defies any easy explanation, and it is just the sort of problem that makes glass research so fascinating. You will notice that the surviving mould, photographed at the plant, shows a well defined lower ring, or torus, just under the baluster. Of the 50 **1042**s I own, however, only 17 show a prominent ring. Seven show just an embryonic ring, while the remaining 26 — about half — show no lower ring at all. I found that the ring's absence was unrelated to the "paddling" of the feet (the **1042** feet began "regular," or cup-shaped, like Westmoreland plates, and like them had to be flattened). Rather, I found it resulted from a swollen stem. When I measured all 50, I found the stems of the third, ringless, group were more than 1/16" wider on average than those of the first group. Then, when I weighed them, I found those of the third group averaged 2½ oz. (12%) more. In both weight and measure, I found those in the second group were midway between the other two.

Now, ordinarily this is just the sort of difference that proves there was more than one maker involved. But in all three of these **1042** groups there are candlesticks that can be positively identified as Westmoreland's — not just by their decoration (Westmoreland sometimes decorated purchased blanks) but by the conclusive evidence of their glass colors.

Berry Wiggins, a glass researcher who has shared my interest in this dilemma, came up with a theory that almost ties all the loose ends together. In 1925 Westmoreland introduced a **"Mould Crackle"** line of seven pieces. These had "crackle" lines in the

moulds that left a sort of a crackle caricature in the glass. Few **Mould Crackle** pieces seem to have been sold; but each one, and that includes the **1042 Candlesticks** required a separate mould. Given the popularity of the **1042 Candlesticks** Berry has speculated Westmoreland cleaned out the crackle from this mould (which began just below the top ring) and then used it as a second **1042** mould. Beautiful! But while his theory almost washes, we are still left, as it were, with a couple of odd-colored socks without mates. The earliest this metal removal could have taken place was in late 1926, and some of the decorations on these "group 3" candlesticks seem to predate this. Also, how can you account for those seven "group 2s" — the candlesticks with the embryonic rings?

Paden City and Lancaster both made candlesticks that resemble the **1042**. Paden City's No. 116, however, could scarcely be confused with Westmoreland's. Its top ring looks as though it had slipped down about 3/16" below the candleholder/stem juncture, and its stem, instead of being serpentine in profile, had a straight taper. Lancaster's No. 853, on the other hand, could pose more of a problem. While it resembles Westmoreland's ringless "group 3" candlestick, its candleholder is slightly less bulbous. Also, it has a very faint upper ring with a very prominent mould scar across it. All **1042**s, in contrast, have very strongly defined upper rings showing little or no mould marks.

The four **1042 Candlesticks** pictured are all "group 3s" that show no lower ring. The cuttings on these are variations of the first two cuttings shown in the Cut Stained section. Notice how much less visible these cuttings are here, particularly on the stems, because the cutting does not break the color.

1801 High Foot, Ball Stem Sweetmeat — 8" (Amber)

For some of those familiar with Pairpoint's B366 comport, this Westmoreland copy may be a letdown. Westmoreland's stem, after all, was pressed as a single unit, and since Westmoreland never made a bubble ball, the ball on Westmoreland's stem served merely as a stabilizing device. I included this sweetmeat for two reasons. First, while West period Westmoreland tended not to copy comparable glass, they were influenced by, and sometimes copied, better glass, and this comport is an excellent example. Second, with its rich depth of color combined with the sparkle of its "rock crystal" polished mitre cuts, this piece surely deserves its own place in the sun. Mitre cutting such as this, had been used for decades in brilliant-cut designs. It was used alone in the '20s by Pairpoint, who called it their "Monroe" cut, and in the '30s by Hunt, who called it their "Reproduction of old Waterford." T. G. Hawkes also used it in this 1925 – 35 period and named it their "Delft Diamond Waterford" cutting. This was the era, after all, when all chairs were "Chippendale," all silver was "Paul Revere," and all glass not "Sandwich" had to be "Waterford!"

1801 Sweetmeat first available in 1925.

(late 1920s)

"Rock Crystal" (polished) mitre cutting.

1932: Available in crystal and colors.
1940: Discontinued.

Height: 7¼"
Width: 8¼"

1211 Octagon Ice Tub with Metal Handle — 5x6 (Roselin)

Westmoreland's ice buckets are frequently found with their original tongs. They were supplied by M.W. Carr of West Somerville, Mass., and they came either nickel- or silver-plated.

These "Moderne"-looking chevrons were cut entirely with a gang cutting wheel. While this appears to be the simplest cutting in the book, there may be more here than meets the eye. How did the cutter bring his wheel to a vertical line at the center of each panel and leave no overlapping marks?

There is another ice bucket almost identical to the **1211** that can be distinguished by its raised isosceles triangles at the top of every panel; I do not know the maker.

1211 line first available between 1918 and 1924. 1211 Ice Tub first available in 1927. Roselin glass first advertised July 1926.

(c. 1930)

1211 was Westmoreland's **Octagon** line.

1932: Available in crystal and color.
1940: Discontinued.

Height: 6"
Width: 5¼" (max)

1820 Dolphin Comport — 11" (Roselin)

(c. 1929)

Height: 8¼"
Diameter: 10⅞"
Weight: 3⅜ lb.

This Westmoreland cutting design seems to be a mutation of a Bohemian rococo shell. The orderly carousel-like design border is taken from the convoluted edge of a shell. Also, the same double radial lines within the border can be found crisscrossed within some of these shells. To me the design suggests one of these irregular shells, placed in balance on a dolphin's tail, and then spun so fast that the shell has stretched itself out into a circle. This cutting design seems to have been made just for this comport: the bowl suggests a body in an endless pirouette.

Both the roses and the oval plaques point to Racinger as the "spin doctor." The design is totally cut; none of it is etched. There are 33 scallops, and each one has 18 serrations at its outer edge. That means close to 600 separate passes had to be made against the cutting wheel on just this part alone. The gang cutting wheel was not used. How could Chas West have paid American wages and made any money on this sort of engraving? Given Westmoreland's atavistic accounting, he had no way of knowing the true cost of such work; but if he had known, I am not sure he would have cared.

"2" Salt & Pepper — 8-Sided (Aquamarine)

"2" Salt & Pepper first available in late 1932 or 1933. Aquamarine glass first advertised December 1928.

(c. 1934)

"2" was a single-item number.

1932: Typed entry indicates crystal only; colors clearly became available, however.
1940: Available in crystal only.

Height: 6⅝"

Since this salt and pepper set was typed into my copy of the 1932 price list, we can assume late 1932 or 1933 was the time of its introduction. It was Westmoreland's most expensive salt and pepper at that time, and it sold for fully a third more than the next most expensive pair.

Even if the maker were not known, three things would point to Westmoreland: the ring at the ankle, the Gothic top, and the nearly colorless aquamarine color. The color, the fire of the transparent glass, and the presence of the cutting, would all point to the mid-'30s or before.

The tops of this pair are sterling silver. Westmoreland typically used two similar top shapes for their salts and peppers in this era: this one with a silver finial and another where the dome itself rises to a point. Those with finials are always sterling silver or silver-plated on brass. (Check these closely — the mark is a third of the way up from the threads.) The others are always plated — silver or nickel on brass, though occasionally gold over nickel. Chromium-plated tops all date from the Brainard period, and chromium-plated pot metal (zinc die-

cast) tops date from the late Brainard period. Chromium, which first appeared on cars in 1928 – 29, is a protective plating over nickel — but one that imparts a cold, bluish, less reflective surface. Nickel on the other hand resembles polished silver when new. Although two tableware line salts and peppers, **555** and **77 Hobnail**, were priced identically with the same tops, I have seen only sterling tops on **77 Hobnail Salts and Peppers,** and I have never seen a sterling top on a **555 Salt and Pepper.** Since these lines were sold together in the late '20s and early '30s (sometimes referred to by the trade as "round and square hobnail"), I have no explanation for this curious difference.

This cutting motif, resembling a pearl necklace with its graduated beads, seems to have been widely used around 1930. It can be found, for example, on some of T. G. Hawkes' glassware of the period.

1820 Low Foot Comport — 11"
1042 Candlesticks — 9" (Belgian Blue)

1820 Low Foot Comports first available between 1918 and 1924. 1042 Candlesticks first available between 1918 and 1924. Late Belgian Blue glass available from January 1931.

(c. 1932)

Bowl: 11½" d.
Candlesticks: 8¾" h.

Compare this butterfly with the one in the Cut Crystal section. Here, three wheels were used: a gang cutting wheel, a V-shaped wheel, and a small U-shaped wheel with a width of about a quarter of an inch and a diameter of several inches. The gang cutting wheel was not really a device to enable the fast cutting of parallel lines; it was more. Its tight serrations would hardly have been possible before its invention around 1913. Notice in this design how these serrations have given the outer portion of the butterflies' wings their texture. The effect of edge feathering was achieved by a second pass against the wheel; for this, the serrations had to be perfectly aligned. Cutting is not as simple as it appears.

Since there is no cutting on the candlesticks, these three pieces do not really constitute a console set.

Like cutting, etching involves the material removal of glass. But unlike cutting, which grinds into the glass with a revolving wheel, etching erodes it by sandblasting, or more typically corrodes it with the chemical action of flourides. Chemical etching was apparently first used in Germany about 1670, but strangely it was not used in this country until 200 years later. By the early 1870s, however, it was being widely used for a contrasting texture on the pressed pictorial glassware that had become so popular after the Civil War. (See Westmoreland's **1058 Fruit Design** in the Tableware section and the George Washington plates in the Miscellaneous section.) I understand Gillinder called their etching room the "Pioneer room" because of the large quantity of Pioneer pattern ("Westward-Ho") glass that was being etched there. In this era, etching was used for its matt texture; the "needle-etched" designs that mimic engraving came later.

Depending on the acids used, etching can be bright as well as matt. Westmoreland used bright etching to create its "engine turned" etched glass (shown in this section) and to polish its "rock crystal" cuttings (see the Cut Colored Glass section). But Westmoreland's etching was, for the most part, "matt" (Westmoreland's term). In its earliest examples from the 1890s, Westmoreland's etched glass was matt-etched all over. But some of Westmoreland's most outstanding later glassware was hand-blocked and relief-etched. This was glass, coated with a wax "resist" that was selectively applied by hand, leaving parts of the glass unprotected. An early use of this technique was Westmoreland's "Carrara Marble Filigree" — described in the 1910 Butler Brothers catalog as, "Glass body etched finish, relief crystal, filigree deposit design." In other words, it differed from Westmoreland's usual silver or gold filigree (see the Gold & Silver section) in having an etched finish. In a Westmoreland ad of 1910, it was similarly described as, "crystal glass silver satin finish, with the raised work 'cut out' in polished effect." In January 1911, this Carrara marble etching was being sold on opal (milk glass) blanks. Still later, the etching was being done on crystal that was then cased in various colors (see the Cased Glass section). But over the years, the term "Carrara" was always applied to Westmoreland's etched glass. Westmoreland was not alone, though. In November 1910, Jefferson introduced their "Corona" — an apparent imitation. They described it as "a marbled effect in glass . . . one which so closely resembles Italian marble as to puzzle any layman."

There is another form of etching, called plate etching, that is found beneath Westmoreland's gold bands. A design was first engraved, or etched, onto a metal plate which was then coated with wax. Then, just as with a monochrome transfer, the plate design (in wax rather than paint) was transferred by a tissue to the glass. After the glass was submerged in acid, the design appeared in relief. I understand this process was patented in 1859 by James Napier of Scotland.

Finally, there is another form of etching: needle, or pantograph etching, that Westmoreland did not do. Nevertheless, it was very popular in the glassware industry in the late '20s and '30s as an inexpensive substitute for cutting. With this process, a number of glass objects — goblets, usually — could be decorated mechanically and simultaneously through the use of "needles" being guided by a design on a steel plate. After the wax coating was scratched through by the needles and the glass acid-dipped, the design would appear. Pantograph designs are often fussy and suggest the ornate work used on silver plate of the time. Some of them seem to have been deliberately calculated to give Good Taste a bad name. I have seen well over 1,000 decorated Westmoreland pieces of this era, and have seen just one of them decorated in this manner. Because of this, I attribute this isolated piece to a decorating house.

George West's "6" Owl Plates — 7" (Crystal)

"6" Owl Plate first available in 1901.

(c. 1902)

"6" was a sequential number assigned just to this plate.

"Pat'd July 2, 1901" marked inside foot of both plates.

Patent 34711 granted to George West for 3½ years.

Etched all over; etched crystal apparently preceded opaque glass.

Gold decoration with painted, "Merry Christmas" and "Easter Greetings" in Westmoreland's typical gold, back-sloping souvenir lettering.

1904: Available as an "Opal Novelty" only.
1932: Available in opal only.
1940: Available in opal only.

Width: 7⅜"

"To their line of cat plates... (West-moreland) have added a line of owl plates tastefully decorated in floral and land-scape decorations. The owl plate is so radically different in design from anything heretofore produced that the firm have had it patented" (L 1/11/02).

Period owl plates can be identified in two ways. First, whether they were made of opaque glass or etched crystal, they all apparently came decorated. Today, they should still show traces of this early cold decoration. Second, period plates will bear a patent inscription on the back. This was later removed when it dated the design.

While George West's owl plate may have been made in opaque glass continuously for over 50 years, in etched-crystal form it had a comparatively short life: by 1904 it was available only in opal glass.

DESIGN.

No. 34.711.

Patented July 2, 1901.

G. R. WEST.
PLATE.
(Application filed June 1, 1901.)

WITNESSES:
Herbert Bradley
Florence M. Dapper

INVENTOR
George R. West
by Darwin S. Wolcott Att'y.

"4" Stamp Plate — 7"
"227" Sleigh — No Cover (Crystal)

"4" Stamp Plate first available in 1901 or before. "227" Sleigh first available in 1904 or before.

(Plate 1901; sleigh c. 1901)

"4" and **"227"** were both single-item numbers.

Both etched all over; etched crystal apparently preceded opaque glass.

"K. T. Conclave 1901 — Reading, Pa." on plate.

1904: Both available as "Opal Novelties" only.
1932: Both discontinued.
1940: Both available in opal only.

Plate: 7⅜" d (max)
Foot: 4¼" o.d.
Sleight: 5½" l. (at rim)

Although the "1901" on this etched plate predates George West's patented **"National Plate"** by two years (see the Opaque section), the fleurs-de-lis on both plates are identical. Westmoreland also used the fleur-de-lis device at the turn of the century on the **'155' Tumbler**. But Westmoreland was not alone. New Martinsville also used it in the '20s, and probably earlier, on a plate almost identical to Westmoreland's. They called theirs a No. 10 Souvenir plate. While both plates have 16 fleurs-de-lis making up the open rim, New Martinsville's appear to be proportionally taller and their centers more pointed. I believe the white plates shown in Millard (MS 15), Belknap (BM 10E/251e), and Ferson (FF 647) are all Westmoreland's. By 1904 the plate was available in opal, but no longer available in etched crystal.

Two sleighs were recorded in the 1904 price list under "Opal Novelties": the **227** without a cover, and the **231** with an egg cover (see the Opaque section). This suggests that the frequently seen, and far more logical, sleigh with a robed Santa may be recent. By 1904 neither Westmoreland sleigh was still available in etched crystal.

Because the 1932 price list recorded neither the plate nor the sleigh, there was probably a 25- or 30-year hiatus for both. The 1940 price list, however, recorded the **"4" — 7"** plate again, and understandably called it the **"Fleur-De-Lis"** plate. It also recorded a sleigh which was given the number **1872**.

In January 1941 the company advertised this sleigh in the *Crockery and Glass Journal*. Then a month later they carried it direct to the consumer with an ad in *House and Garden*, which is reprinted here.

They described it as "An Exciting Revival... after an absence of 50 years... for over 50 years the Sleigh Bowl mold has been lying in our mold bin and only recently been uncovered...."

An Exciting Revival

...after an absence of 50 years. Westmoreland presents the graceful, beautiful SLEIGH BOWL in Milk Glass... Made from the original mold.

For over fifty years, the Sleigh Bowl mold has been lying in our mold bins and only recently been uncovered. The Sleigh Bowl was one of our first designs and in its reproduction it retains the charm and sparkle of the original. • As a gift or for your home, its quaint design will be extremely attractive... it is especially suited to the Victorian revival in decoration. • The Sleigh Bowl has various uses—for fruit, nuts, candy, or for flowers. See it at the better stores in your community.

Westmoreland Glass Co., Grapeville, Pa.
Manufacturers of Quality Handmade Glassware

91

1820 Flared Bowl — 9"

1820 Line introduced between 1918 and 1924. This 1820 Bowl first available between 1918 and 1924.

(c. 1924)

1820 was Westmoreland's **Flange** line.

Ground and polished bottom.

"CME" (crystal, matt etched).

1932: Available in crystal only.
1940: Discontinued.

Diameter: 9⅜"

"(Westmoreland's 'King Tut' line is) *a new novelty in fancy glassware which we are confident will catch the flood tide of popular favor. For not only does it embrace the peculiar mystic appeal... of the ancient craftsman... it also is a vigorous and original decoration. In choosing the sacred vulture with outstretched wings, the design has happily selected one of the most decorative forms found in ancient Egyptian art*" (J 6/14/23).

Westmoreland certainly caught the "flood tide of popular favor" in the timelines of so many of their Egyptian-inspired designs. The Egyptian craze began in 1922 with the discovery of King Tutankhamen's 3,300 year old tomb, continued the following year with the opening of the sepulchral chamber, and climaxed in February 1924 with the opening of the sarcophagus.

The design on this pictured bowl is a Westmoreland representation of an Egyptian representation of four papyrus umbrels. The green "leaves" are highly stylized calyxes, and the red blazes represent the papyri rays. Both of these devices can be found in the same red and green colors in ancient Egyptian designs. Westmoreland's design was a modification of the #110 decoration (not shown) which represented a lotus blossom.

1847 Toast & Cover (#470 Decoration)

1847 Toast & Cover first available in 1925.

(c. 1925)

1847 was an item number assigned to two relishes plus this toast & cover.

Ground and polished bottom.

1932: Available in crystal only.
1940: Discontinued.

Diameter: 10½"
Height: 5½"
Weight: 4¼ lb.

I believe this decoration, Westmoreland's #470, was what a reported described as, "Cubist decorations on an etched body" (L 1/15/23). It was available in 1924, and presumably a year or so on either side of that date. It is, perhaps, the most vigorous decoration Westmoreland ever placed on any of its glass.

Since the cover was intended to be placed over warm toast, there is an interesting vent hole in the middle of the handle.

462 Breakfast Set (#470 Decoration)

Four Stacking Sets first available in 1914. #470 Decoration available in 1924.

(c. 1924)

462 was the item number assigned to four combinations of these stacking sets.

Eight-pointed pressed stars on the three square bottoms.

Length: 5⅜"

The original stacking set had a bottom that was ground and polished to the pressed star, and Britannia (thin pewter) shaker tops. This one from c. 1924 does not have a finished bottom and has nickel-plated brass tops. Any with chromium-plated tops will date from the Brainard period.

"(Westmoreland's) latest addition… and one that is really novel, is a set that is made of glass and that consists in a little sugar bowl, with on either side a salt and pepper shaker supported by little arms or handles projecting from the bowl. The cover for the sugar bowl is a cream pitcher, which in turn is covered by a butter plate…. It will retail at a good profit at 50 cents (1995: $7.65) and should also prove an excellent item for the hotel trade. A condiment set of somewhat similar nature is now in course of preparation. The bottom portion of this is similar to the breakfast set with a mustard taking the place of the cream pitcher" (P 9/17/14).

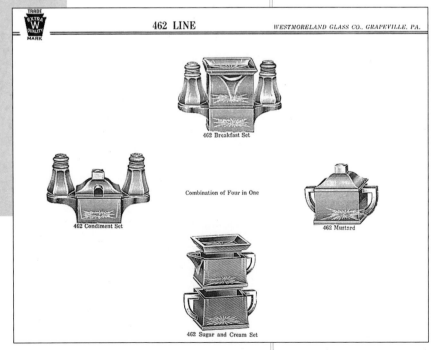

Gustav Horn's 1921 Lotus Mayo & Plate

1921 Lotus line introduced June 1924.

(c. 1925)

1921 was the number for Westmoreland's **Lotus** line.

This line grew from eight items in 1925 to 17 items in 1926.

Patent 65338 granted 7/29/24 to gustav Horn for 3½ years.

1932: 36 Lotus items available in crystal and colors; most Lotus items also available in opal.
1940: 24 Lotus items available in crystal only. Low candlesticks and individual salt also available in opal.

Bowl: 5" d.
Plate: 8½" d. (max)

Following several Egyptian designs from their decorating department, Westmoreland launched their **Lotus** line, designed by Gustav Horn, Westmoreland's head decorator. The timing was perfect: the first **Lotus** ad (L 6/2/24) appeared less than four months after the opening of the Tutankhamen sarcophagus. Nothing Westmoreland ever did before or would ever do later would cause such excitement: "The patented lotus flower design, which was shown in bowls and flat pieces, which was offered in green and also alabaster glass, was sold to practically every buyer who visited the display" (J 1/22/25).

"The latest product of the Westmoreland Specialty Co... is a line of lotus flower bowls and plates in a number of color combinations. As might be imagined from the name, these bowls and plates resemble the beautiful lotus flower with its pointed petals. The bowls are in ivory tone with yellow center; some show the petals dipped in color — orchid or maroon. Both are pleasing tones and are well set off by the ivory body color and the yellow center. The plates are also made in matt green to represent green leaves" (P 7/2/24).

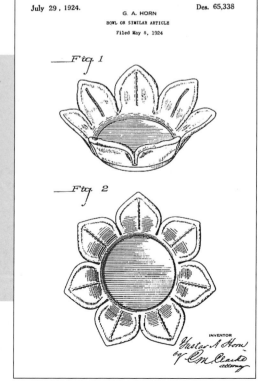

1921 Lotus Cupped Bowl — 9" (Roselin)
? — 1709 Candlesticks

9" Cupped Bowl among the first eight Lotus items available in June 1924. Roselin glass first advertised July 1926.

(c. 1920s)

1932: Bowl available in crystal, colors, and opal; opal cost 88% more than crystal.
1940: Bowl available in crystal only.

Bowl: 9" d. (max)
Candlesticks: 5⅞" h.

The accolades continued: *"The patented lotus flower design is given and deserves the central position.... This glassware in bowls and accompanying plates is shaped like the flower for which it is named. The body is etched all over and is delicate white while the floral tips are in choice of blue, red, and green. The ware also is made in alabaster glass and also in green, blue, and amber etched glass"* (L 1/12/25).

Although the candlesticks in this console set are unknown, they share the bowl's Roselin color and bear a striking resemblance to a **1709** cologne often shown paired with the **Lotus** cologne.

"1" Shell Nappy — 6"

"1" Shell Nappy first available between 1902 and 1904.

(c. 1936)

"1" was a single item number.

Designated a "Shell Nappy" to the 1940s.

No ground and polished punty between the three feet.

Also shown in Iridized and Opal sections.

1904: Available under both "Misc. Ware" (crystal and possibly colors) and "Opal Novelties."
1932: Available in crystal, color, and opal.
1940: Available in crystal and opal (however, opal was lined out in 1941).
The 1952 catalog pictures it again in milk glass.

Width: 5½"
Length: 6⅜"

This shell nappy is the last piece in this section to be uniformly etched all over — either by being dipped in acid or being subjected to acid fumes. It dates from the very end of the West period.

Company records show these shells were sold to Rockwell Silver Co., in November 1934 in crystal, and in November 1935 in "crystal matt etched." The etched shells cost Rockwell 8½ percent more than the plain crystal.

Reuben Haley's Floral Colonial Round Nappy — 9"

(c. 1911)

Floral Colonial was one of Westmoreland's two original colonial lines.

Large **Keystone-W** mark.

Patents 41034 (1910) and 41176 (1911) granted to Reuben Haley for 14 years.

Diameter: 9"
Height: 3⅜"

Floral Colonial line introduced January 1911.

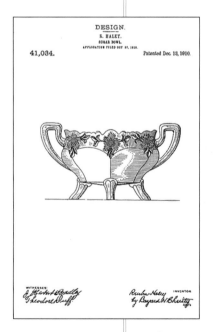

In order to better simulate cutting, Westmoreland etched this pressed design with either sand or acid. The result looks remarkably like gray or "satin" cutting. And the glass quality, the color, and the weight, are just what one would expect in a cut piece of the period. The effect of this etching, strangely enough, would be reversed 15 or 20 years later when real cutting was acid polished to a pressed-glass-looking shine (see the Cut Colored Glass section).

In 1913 U.S. Glass advertised their new "Athenia" line. While its decoration is more geometric than Westmoreland's, the two could be confused: the Athenia bud vase bears a particular resemblance to the **Floral Colonial 10" Handled Vase.**

Sometime between 1918 and 1924 Westmoreland's **Floral Colonial** moulds were machined out to create a plainer, more up-to-date design. The new line, which substituted blank panels for the **Floral Colonial's** flowers and leaves, was

called the **76 Colonial** (see the Tableware section). But the grinding removed only the decoration. Because the forms themselves were seen as holdover from another era, few of these hybrids were ever sold. The grinding was carried out on all moulds, and therefore all surviving **Floral Colonial** glass has to pre-date the early '20s. All of these moulds appear to have been scrapped.

(P 2/16/11)

1042 Candlestick — 9"

Fort Dearborn was a wholesaler that sold to jewelry stores and gift shops through their catalog which they called a "Gift Book." This candlestick is part of the Fort Dearborn console set shown in the Cut Stained Glass section; Fort Dearborn called the cutting design the "Graceful Scroll." This candlestick is included here because of its curious mixture of etching and cutting. While other parts of the design have been cut, the scalloping has been sandblasted. For some reason Westmoreland resorted to this shortcut on these candlesticks, and yet used a cutting wheel to create a frosted effect on all the other items of this assortment I have seen. The photo-

graph highlights the etching here; it is actually hard to detect without a magnifying glass.

1042 Candlesticks first available between 1918 and 1924.

(1925)

1042 also available 6½".

Fort Dearborn's "Graceful Scroll" cutting.

1932: Available in crystal and colors.
1940: Discontinued.

1708 Three-Footed Plate — 8"
(#C542 Cutting Design) (Aquamarine)

Notice how the simple etching on the underside of this trivet has articulated the center ring and turned each foot into a three-dimensional quatrefoil. Because the aquamarine color is so light, the polished mitre cuts appear to have been cut on a crystal band. The gray or "satin" cuts as well as the etching seem to concentrate the blue color, however.

1708 3-footed Plate first available in 1925. Aquamarine glass first advertised Dec. 1928. #C542 cutting available in the 1930s.

(early to mid-1930s)

1708 was designated an **Optic** line.

Optic is on the underside.

1932: Available in crystal and colors.
1940: Discontinued.

Diameter: 8⅜"

1801 Comport — 8½" (Roselin)

1801 line first available between 1918 and 1924. 1801 Comport first available between 1918 and 1924.

(c. 1930)

1801 was designated a **Plain** line.

1932: Available in crystal and colors.
1940: Discontinued.

Diameter: 8"
Stem/bowl: 1⅞" d.

rosive action of acid. This process was widely used by Westmoreland, usually in combination with enameling, as it has been here.

First, the underside of the bowl was relief-etched to create a delicate floral design in the clear Roselin glass. Black and white enamels were then used as well as lines of "coin gold" to give the design definition. ("Coin gold" was the industry term for the matt gold used by Westmoreland and others between the two world wars.)

This is the first of Westmoreland's hand-blocked relief etchings shown in this section. Hand blocking is the process of hand painting a wax resist onto select portions of glass to shield them from the cor-

1905 Bell High Footed Bowl — 9"

1905 Comports first available in 1927.

(c. 1928)

1905 was an item number assigned to three comports sharing the same stem (common mould).

1932: Available in crystal and colors.
1940: Discontinued.

Height: 6½"
Diameter: 9"
Stem/bowl: 3¾" d.

This high-footed bowl, or comport, was first stained all over and then the fern design was hand-blocked. Afterwards the comport was submerged in acid, which selectively cut through the stain.

Westmoreland's "Engine Turned" Motif

The following four Westmoreland pieces all share a common double-etched design pattern — the same pattern used by Wedgewood around 1780. Wedgewood used it exclusively on what they called their "black basalt," which was, evidently, a black homogeneous china made from volcanic rock. The name they gave their design, "engine turned," shows they created their stripes with a cutting wheel. (Today, we use this same term for decorative fish scaling on polished metal.) I have not yet found this design on any Westmoreland black glass, and despite all of Westmoreland's innovative cutting, this design was etched by Westmoreland and not cut.

Westmoreland's "engine turned" effect was achieved by first etching the entire glass bowl with a solution of hydrofluoric acid and fluoride salts, which gave the glass an overall matt appearance. Next, a wax resist was applied by hand to all parts that were to remain matt, and following that the glass was treated with hydrofluoric acid alone. This was the acid that was apparently used to create a bright "rock crystal" effect on glass after gray cutting, and here it brightened the alternate stripes that had been left unprotected. A minor thickness of glass was removed with each successive etching confirming this sequence. Also, slight irregularity in the lines shows they had been hand-blocked.

This "engine turned" motif was particularly effective on curved — concave or convex — surfaces.

1700 Colonial Candy Jar — 2 lb.

1700 Candy Jars probably first available in 1917.

(1920s)

1700 was one of the two colonial lines Westmoreland introduced in 1912.

Also made in ½, 1 & 3 lb. sizes.

1932: All four sizes available in crystal only.
1940: 1 lb. size available in crystal only, then discontinued in 1941.

1 lb: 8" h.
2 lb: 10½" h.
3 lb: 12¾" h.

1800 Roll Edge Frappe — 10"

1800 was designated a **Plain** line.

1932: Available in crystal only.
1940: Discontinued.

Diameter: 10"
Foot: 5⅜" d.
Weight: 3¼ lb.

1800 line first available between 1913 and 1917. 1800 Frappe first available between 1918 and 1924.

1816 Covered Urn

Without the lid, it was designated an **1816 Flower Vase**.

1816 was an item number used just for the urn and vase.

1932: Discontinued.
1940: Discontinued.

Width: 10"
Height: 10"
Weight: 4 lb.

1816 Urn first available between 1918 and 1924.

1820 Low Foot Comport — 9"

Also available 11".

1932: Available in crystal and colors.
1940: Discontinued.

Height: 4¼"
Diameter: 9⅜"

1820 Comports first available between 1918 and 1924. This blue color available from 1924 to 1929.

1049 Dolphin Shell — 12" (Roselin)

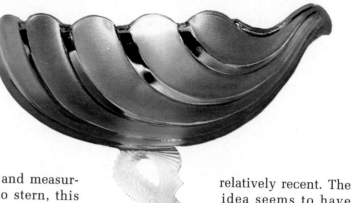

The first Dolphin items introduced in 1924. Both Dolphin shells first available in 1926.

Weighing nearly 6 lbs. and measuring nearly 13" from bow to stern, this dolphin shell is truly imposing: the marine equivalent of Atlas and the heavens.

Westmoreland's new **Dolphin** line was first mentioned in a press release of October 1924 (J 10/9/24). In January 1926 at the Pittsburgh Show, four **Dolphin** pieces, including this shell, were added to the five already in the line. In his review a trade reporter wrote, "The Dolphin shell compote is a truly remarkable production…" (L 1/18/26). Later that year another reported described it as: "The large epergne with a mammoth-sized shell as

the bowl with a dolphin as the standard emerging from the sea of glass…. The shell is alternately bright and satin finish…. The fish is mat or satin finish which enhances its beauty considerably" (JC 9/15/26).

Neither the dolphin nor the shell forms are of recent origin. The dolphin was employed in early Christian art, and the scallop shell in classical architecture. But the combination of the two in glass is relatively recent. The idea seems to have originated — not with a littoral glasshouse, but with Pittsburgh's Bakewell Pears, who patented their design about 1870. Their design consisted of a dolphin mounted on a hemispheric base supporting a small shell bowl.

While the concept of the dolphin shell may have been Bakewell Pears', the form of this mid-'20s piece was entirely Westmoreland's. The etched decoration of the time conveyed motion to the shell and vigor to that put-upon dolphin. By enhancing the form with this inspired decoration, Westmoreland fashioned one of the treasures of its innovative years.

(c. 1927)

1049 was the number assigned to seven of the ten **Dolphin** items.

1049 Dolphin Shell also available 8".

1932: All **Dolphin** items available in crystal, colors, and opal.
1940: All **Dolphin** items discontinued in 1940 except the candlesticks, the 7" comport, and the 8" shell (available in opal only). By 1952 the 12" shell was reissued (milk glass only).

Height: 9¾" (max)
Length: 12¾"
Weight: 5¾ lb.

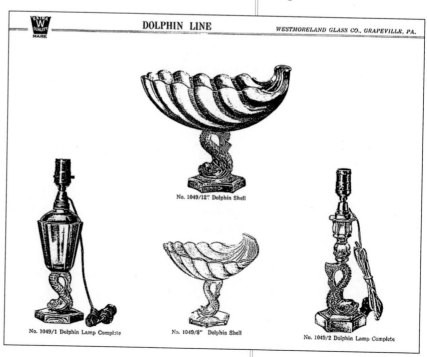

DOLPHIN LINE   WESTMORELAND GLASS CO., GRAPEVILLE, PA.

No. 1049/12" Dolphin Shell

No. 1049/1 Dolphin Lamp Complete

No. 1049/8" Dolphin Shell

No. 1049/2 Dolphin Lamp Complete

Cased Glass

Just three and a half months before he left Westmoreland, George R. West said in an interview, *"We are the largest decorators of glassware in the country, and manufacture 25 different varieties. We are producing case lustre ware by an entirely new process, our own invention, which enables us to far undersell foreign concerns"* (B 1/29/21).

By "Case Lustre," George West was referring to Westmoreland's sprayed opaque (and later translucent) glass coatings that were used from 1910 or shortly before, through the 1930s. George West was right, of course, in pointing out the cost savings of this sprayed glass over dipped casing or overlay. But what is most significant is that he was claiming Westmoreland was the originator of the spray technique.

Westmoreland always referred to their glass sprays as "Case Lustre" or simply "Casing." While this may seem to be stretching things a bit, consider: if cased glass is the encasement of glass of one color by the glass of another, this is precisely what the Westmoreland's casing is — only the spray application sets it apart. The term "Case Lustre" distinguished it from another color treatment used by Westmoreland at the time, "Lustre Stain," which was a brushed metallic salt that was also followed by a high temperature firing. Unfortunately, Westmoreland's casing has often been confused with paint — a confusion fed by the necessary and historically proper use of the term, "enameling" for Westmoreland's brushed decorations. Chemically, Westmoreland's casing and enameling are the same. Both are made of glass dust or "frit" mixed with an abnormal amount of lead to reduce the melting point, tin to contribute opacity, and metallic oxides to give it color.

Westmoreland's cased enamel was applied in one of two ways. Either the combined powders were mixed with oils, and this mix was then sprayed onto the blank, or else the blank was first brushed with oils and then the combined powders were air-brushed against the oil coating. Whichever way the casing was applied, the blank was heated to a temperature of about 1000° F; this was high enough to burn off the oils and melt and fuse the glass permanently to the blank.

To put this 1000° F in perspective, molten glass in a pot furnace is about 2500° F. A glass blank is about 1400° F when it is placed into a lehr for stress relieving and gradual cooling. 1000° – 1200° F is considered the highest temperature range a blank can be reheated to without risking deformation or settling.

A turn-of-the-century writer noted the close glass/enamel relationship: "All enamels, whether white or colored, are practically glass since the basis of all of them is silica (sand), while the coloring oxides used in glass making are also used in the composition of enamels. The solvents (fluxes) are also the same, the only difference between glass and enamels being the larger proportion of solvents used in enamels at a point below the temperature in which the metal (glass blank) to be coated shall oxidize, distort, or melt" (B 12/1/00).

According to Berry Wiggins, a glass researcher; in addition to several decorating houses, there were at least four other glass companies that used similar colored sprays in the '20s: Central, Diamond, Lancaster, and U.S. Glass. However, their coatings may have been ceramic rather than glass. Westmoreland's sprayed coating seems to be smoother than any other, it is more easily cleaned and restored than any other, and Westmoreland's colors cannot be dislodged with any abrasive (including steel wool) I have experimented with. Westmoreland's sprayed coating is not paint; it is glass.

Pottery Effects on Glass

Also sold in Butler Brother's 1910 catalog, but only in brown casing and with monochrome transfers.

Mugs: 4⅝" h.
Pitcher: 15" h.
Pitcher: 3⅝ lb.

In August 1910, Westmoreland advertised this tankard set as "Pottery Effects on Glass." The ad establishes the fact that Westmoreland was using their sprayed casing as far back as 1910 — 14 years before cars were first spray-painted.

Pottery Effects on Glass

Among our Holiday Novelties meeting with great success this season the Tankard set illustrated above is a leader - they all buy it. Pottery effects are simulated with exactitude for the first time in glass. Popular priced—big show for little money. Complete sets to be had in any of the three subjects—Drinking Scenes, Elks and Mottoes. See them without fail.

Complete 7-Piece Sets in Mottoes, Elks or Drinking Scenes.

Carrara Ware

This is the name we've given to the daintiest line of novelties in glass brought out in years. It is crystal glass silver satin finish, with the raised work "cut out" in polished effect. We also add pretty miniature flowers, making a distinct line. Twenty-five articles embracing novelties for the dressing table, desk and den and some few table pieces. Each piece wrapped in white tissue and packed in pasteboard boxes. You want this line. Send for price list.

5c and 10c Novelties

We manufacture the largest and best line of novelties in glass to retail at 5c and 10c each in the market.

See them at the Household Show, Madison Square Garden, this week or in our New York showrooms.

No. 1015S 4-in. Retails at 5 cts. each.
No. 1015S 6-in. Retails at 10 cts. each.

No. 1012S 5-in. Retails at 10 cts. each.

WESTMORELAND SPECIALTY CO., Grapeville, Penn.
NEW YORK OFFICE: DEMOREST & CO., 46 MURRAY STREET

These sets were available in the cased colors of brown, green, purple, and perhaps blue. Because Westmoreland's tankard set was also available through the Butler Brothers catalog, and brown was the only color available through them, brown is the color most commonly seen today. Purple, shown here, is the rarest of the colors used.

Westmoreland offered three decorations in their ad: "elks," "mottoes," and "drinking scenes." Through Butler Brothers they offered the "stag," "monk," and "merry maker group." Of these, I believe only the merry maker group was sold both ways.

While most decorations on these tankard sets were monochrome transfers, the elk decoration on this purple set was hand-painted. For a discussion of the monochrome transfer process, the Fostoria claim, and more pictures of Westmoreland's "Pottery Effects on Glass," see the Opaque Glass section.

Butler Brothers was a wholesale catalog house that sold glassware and china in barrel and case lots to retail stores.

1019 Candlestick — 8" (Mahogany Glass)

1019 Candlestick first available in 1911 or before.

(1916)

Ground and polished top and punty.

Mahogany Glass patent applied for, but apparently not granted.

1932: Available in crystal only.
1940: Discontinued.

Height: 8⅝"
Weight: 1⅝ lb.

The previous owner of these candlesticks told me he had tried unsuccessfully to remove the "paint" with paint remover and steel wool. The red-brown casing was sprayed and the wood grain was brushed. It is, of course, fused glass, and cannot be removed.

"The latest addition to the list of surprises handed out by (Westmoreland) is a line of glass lily bowls, flower bowls, flower holders, candlesticks... that resemble highly polished mahogany in a fashion so true to nature as to be almost startling.... Nothing of a similar nature has ever before been attempted in glass manufacture.... The color of mahogany is perfectly copied, but it is the secret process of imitating the grain that makes these articles so wonderfully attractive" (P 5/18/16).

(P 5/25/16)

1832 Handled Nut Bowl — 9" (Green Carrara)

(1920s)

Also available as a 10" fruit bowl and an 11" sandwich tray (same mould).

1832 was an item number assigned just to these three items.

1932: Available in crystal only.
1940: Discontinued.

Width: 9"

"Carrara Marble" was a term first used by Westmoreland in 1910 for their etched crystal. The following year the term "White Carrara Marble" was applied to their etched opal, or milk glass. In 1921 "Carrara" was expanded to include five colors, and in 1924 to six: blue, green, yellow, pink, lavender, and orange. These colors were Westmoreland's cased colors sprayed onto etched glass. This Carrara nut bowl was etched on the outside and then sprayed in green.

Although this nut bowl seems to have no look-alike, McKee used this handle on their No. 151 — 10½" handled sandwich tray. Westmoreland's handle has a ring or torus, whereas McKee's does not.

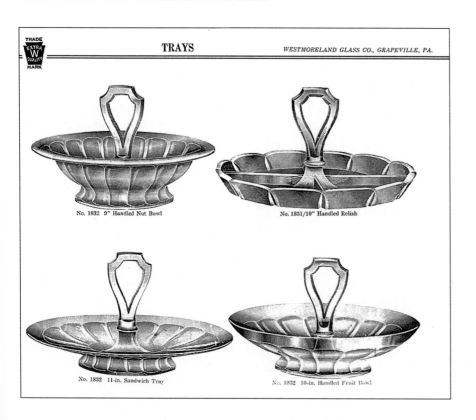

TRADE MARK

TRAYS   WESTMORELAND GLASS CO., GRAPEVILLE, PA.

No. 1832 9" Handled Nut Bowl

No. 1831/10" Handled Relish

No. 1832 11-in. Sandwich Tray

No. 1832 10-in. Handled Fruit Bowl

Gustav Horn's 1921 Lotus: Low Candlestick — 2½" Tall Candlestick — 9"

Both Lotus Candlesticks first available in 1925.

(c. 1926)

Lotus patent (65338) granted 7/29/24 to Gustav Horn for 3½ years.

Casing color is lilac.

1932: Both candlesticks available in crystal, colors, and opal.
1940: The low candlestick and a three-light candelabra both available in crystal; the low also available in opal. The tall was discontinued.

Low: 2½" h.
5⅝" w. (max.)

"A new shape (in the patented Lotus flower design) *is a very attractive candlestick with twisted stem and floral top and bottom, hand made"* (L 1/12/25).

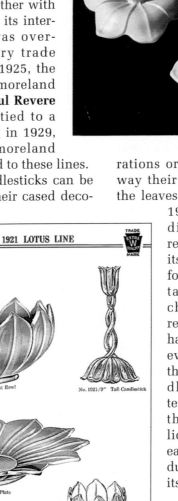

Since the **Low Lotus Candlestick** was introduced together with the more striking 9" with its interesting twist stem, it was overlooked by contemporary trade reporters. Introduced in 1925, the two were the first Westmoreland candlesticks since the **Paul Revere Colonial** in 1912 to be tied to a tableware line. Beginning in 1929, however, all new Westmoreland candlesticks would be tied to these lines.

Early **Low Lotus** candlesticks can be recognized not only by their cased decorations or glass colors, but also by the way their candleholders are nestled in the leaves. Sometime between 1940 and 1952, the 2½" candlestick was discontinued. Then when it reappeared in the 1962 catalog, its leaves formed an arched platform resembling the base of the tall candlestick. With this change, the candlestick was redesignated, "3½"." There may have been a third version, however. The 1926 catalog pictures this 2½" candlestick with its candleholder mounted on a flattened bed of lotus leaves. While this could have been artistic license, it may represent a still earlier version. Fenton is reproducing this candlestick today in its late, 3½" form.

The **Tall Lotus Candlestick** was discontinued by 1940 and was apparently never reissued.

WESTMORELAND GLASS CO., GRAPEVILLE, PA.   1921 LOTUS LINE

No. 1921 Low Candlestick

No. 1921 Ftd. Mayo Fld.

No. 1921/9" Lotus Cupped Bowl

No. 1921/9" Tall Candlestick

No. 1921/13" Flared Plate

No. 1921/4" 7 Canned Lotus Flower and Plate

No. 1221 Ind. Salt

No. 1921/5. 8½" Lotus Mayonnaise and Plate

750 Basket — 6"

750 Baskets probably
first available January 1921.

"(In Westmoreland's display at the Pittsburgh Exhibit) *there are baskets of every description from plain crystal through a range of colors to black. There are three to four sizes for each variety of basket... Carrara and others. The Carrara comes in five colors with crystal handles"* (L 1/10/21).

(1920s)

Also available 3", 4", 5", 7" & 8".

750 was an item number used just for these six baskets.

1932: 3" to 6" available in crystal and colors. 7" & 8" available in crystal only. 1940: 3" to 6" available in crystal only (an opal option for the 6" was handwritten in — then lined out). It was offered again with ruby staining and a painted or decal decoration in 1977.

Basket: 6⅜" h.
With handle: 12½" h.

By this date "Carrara" had expanded to cased, etched crystal in a variety of sprayed colors. Since this basket was not etched, however, it is not Carrara.

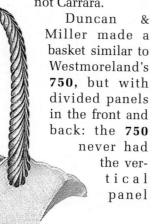

Duncan & Miller made a basket similar to Westmoreland's **750**, but with divided panels in the front and back: the **750** never had the vertical panel dividers below the handles found on all of Duncan & Miller's. Nevertheless, both companies made their baskets the same way with handle halves pressed with the baskets. After the basket was removed from the mould, they were pulled up with "tweezers" and joined in the middle.

For some reason, Westmoreland's black trim lines were not composed of glass, and are, therefore, vulnerable to abrasion. While they were applied with a brush, other enameled decorations which were brushed are as indestructible as Westmoreland's sprayed casing.

The **750 Basket** is also shown in the Iridized & Crackled and the Gold & Silver sections.

1840 Vase — 10" (#1 Decoration)

8" & 10" first available between 1918 and 1924. 6" first available in 1925.

(c. 1924)

Also available 6" & 8".

1840 was an item number assigned just to these three vases.

1932: 6", 8" & 10" available in crystal and colors.
1940: Discontinued.

Height: 7¾"
Width: 9⅛"
Weight: 3⅛ lb.

"(In Westmoreland's display at the Pittsburgh Exhibit) *particularly striking is a number designated as Decoration No. 1 in Mephisto red, with a deep scallop in gold and with a dotted line border in blue and white"* (J 1/31/24).

The gold arcs in this design suggest the interlaced semicircles found on furniture inlays and in door transoms of the late Federal period of the early nineteenth century.

The Mephisto red casing was sprayed below the rim; the green, the gold, and the blue and white dots were all brushed on above the rim. ("Mephisto" was the devil in Goethe's *Faust*.)

U.S. Glass made a broad-rimmed vase that could be confused with this. While the Westmoreland foot measures about 5" across, the U.S. Glass foot is about

4½" — less than half the diameter of its rim. (See the detailed comparison in the Cut Stained section).

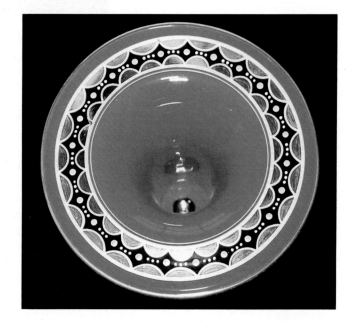

1211 Octagon Sugar & Cream Set

1211 line first available between 1918 and 1924. 1211 Sugar & Cream Set first available in 1927.

(c. 1936)

1211 was Westmoreland's **Octagon** line.

1932: Available in crystal and colors.
1940: Discontinued.

Height: 4⅝" (at sugar handles)

In this decoration the white casing was sprayed inside the feet and the bowls. The boats and the water were brushed on the outside.

The silver trim is a bright silver lustre, which suggests this decoration dates from the mid- or late-'30s.

In 1927 U.S. Glass launched their No. 337 Octagon Service line. While their sugar and cream resemble Westmoreland's, they are not likely to be confused: the U.S. Glass proportions are far broader, and each panel has a scalloped top.

1854/2 Chocolate Box & Cover
1707 Candy Jar & Cover — 1 Lb. — Optic
1777 Colonial Grapefruit — 7"

(c. 1925)

1854 also available in a smaller size: **1854/1.**

1707 also available in ½ lb. size from 1921 and ¼ lb. size from 1926.

1707 also available plain (not optic).

1777 was the fifth of Westmoreland's six colonial lines.

1854 and **1777** have ground and polished bottoms.

1932: **1854/2** available in crystal only (**1854/1** available in crystal and colors). **1707** — all three sizes available in crystal and colors. **1777** — available in crystal. 1940: **1707** — ½ lb. size available in crystal only.

1854: 7½" d.
1707: 9¼" h.
1777: 8" d.

1777 Grapefruit first available between 1912 and 1917. 1707 Candy Jars first advertised in 1921. 1854 Chocolate Boxes first available between 1918 and 1921.

It is interesting that both the chocolate box and the grapefruit bowl came with pressed stars, and yet these stars were enhanced in two different ways: while the star on the grapefruit bowl was cut, the star on the chocolate box was etched. Star enhancement with a cutting wheel was often done by Westmoreland, but I know of only one other instance of etching used to enhance a pressing (see the **Floral Colonial Bowl** in the Etched Glass section).

Heisey's No. 353 grapefruit is similar to Westmoreland's **1777**, but Heisey's is taller and has less taper in the sides. Also, while Heisey's has eight facets, Westmoreland's has ten.

I have seen this same radial gold-line design with a pale-green and pale-red background. In all cases the cased color was on the backside of the glass.

WESTMORELAND GLASS CO., GRAPEVILLE, PA.   1777 LINE

1777/7" Grapefruit

1777/8" Nappy

1777/9" Nappy

1777 Butter Tub

1777/5½" Ice Tub Star Bottom

1777/4½" Nappy

1777 Marmalade and Cover

1777/6½" Plate. Also made in 7½"

1707 Candy Jar & Cover — ½ Lb. — Optic
1800 Mayo or Comport — 7"

1800 Mayo first available between 1913 and 1917.

(c. 1930)

1800 Mayo also available 6" belled (same mould).

1800 was designated a **Plain** line.

1932: **1800 Mayo** available in crystal, colors, and opal.
1940: **1800 Mayo** discontinued.

1707: 7¾" h.
1800: 6½" d.

This is a variant of the radial gold-line design shown in the preceding picture; I believe this one is later.

The candy jar could be confused with Fenton's No. 736. However, Fenton's has a sharp break (probably a mould mark) beneath the foot, while Westmoreland's is perfectly smooth. (See the detailed comparison in the Cut Crystal section.)

Every company made a small mayonnaise bowl in the '20s similar to Westmoreland's **1800,** but except for U.S. Glass' No. 16161 "whip cream," Westmoreland's is alone in having a sharp angle between the bowl and the extended ankle. U.S. Glass' bowl can be distinguished by its straighter bowl sides. Westmoreland's bowl has a more bulbous shape.

111

1900 Footed Tumblers — 8½ Oz. — Plain
1801 Plates — 8½"
1802 Plates — 10½"
1801 Serving Platter — 14"

(c. 1930)

All three lines were designated **Plain**.

Platter and plates have ground and polished bottoms.

1801 Plates ranged from 6" to 21".

1802 Plates available, 7½", 8" & 10½".

A family set.

1932: **1900** (listed as both a "Footed Tumbler" and a "Goblet") available in crystal, colors, and opal. **1801 Plates** 6" to 14", available in crystal and colors. 14" also available in opal. 21" available in crystal only. **1802** 7½" and 10½" available in crystal and colors; 10½" also available in black. 8" available in crystal only. 1940: **1900** "Goblet" available in opal only. **1801** All sizes available in crystal; 6", 8", 8½" & 14". Also available in opal. **1802** 10½" available in crystal only.

Plates:
8⅜" d. foot: 5" o.d.
11" d. foot: 7⁷⁄₁₆" o.d.
14⅜" d. foot: 8" o.d.
Tumbler: 5¼" h.

This luncheon set was owned by Charles and Helen West, and then by my father. It was particularly valued by him, and I cannot recall ever seeing it used. The backs of the plates were spray-cased as well as the footed tumblers up to the point where the feet were attached to the bowls. The black foliage appears to have been transfer-printed after which the three colors were used. The grapes and leaves are in raised enamel, and the grape colors show an interesting shading not visible in the photograph. Two things about the design deserve mention: First, the grapes in the design were combined with very ungrape-like leaves. And second, this high-style Art Nouveau design was about a generation out of date. The story that has come down to me from an unreliable source is that Helen West designed and painted this set. While she could have designed the transfer master, I see no reason to believe she also painted

**1900 Footed Tumblers first available in 1927.
1801/1802 Plates first available between 1918 and 1922.**

the glass as well. This set must date from about 1930, and this late use of a turn-of-the-century design suggests the work of the Bohemian artists working at Westmoreland at the time (see the Carnegie section). If I am correct, other Westmoreland pieces can be found in this design.

As impractical as it may seem, all pieces were trimmed with gold, and the black as well as the raised enameling was applied to the top. There is an interesting explanation for the unevenness of these stacked plates. They were all pressed in a "regular" bowl shape and then were worked out by hand into a plate form.

1820 Bowl — 13½"

"Another new number of unusual richness is in raised enamel. The motif is a graceful fruit decoration in natural colors..." (J 6/14/23).

With its yellow casing beneath the glass, and its monochrome transfer and raised-enamel fruits above the glass, this bowl has much in common with the preceding luncheon set. And like the luncheon set, its fruited festoons and pendants seem to have been inspired by throw-back design — in this case, Beaux Arts architectural ornament popular a couple of decades before.

Notice how Westmoreland's decorators cleverly worked the **1820** flange rim into their design. In their hands the plain rim of burnt or oxidized gold became an early gilded picture frame surrounding a still-life painting.

1820 line introduced between 1918 and 1924. 1820 Bowl first available between 1918 and 1924.

(c. 1924)

1820 was Westmoreland's **Flange** line.

Ground and polished bottom.

1932: Bowl available in crystal only.
1940: Discontinued.

Width: 13⅝"
Weight: 4 lb.

1707 Candy Jar & Cover — ½ Lb. — Optic

This is the first of several pictures showing Westmoreland's translucent cased colors. These translucent colors may have been used solely in the late '20s, and I believe the "Transparent Rose" that was introduced in the fall of 1927 (J 9/8/27) is what is shown in the photograph.

A closed, colored glass blank is a poor candidate for glass cutting, for only reduced light can get behind it; and the deep red of this candy jar only compounds the problem. Cutting, however, may have been the only embellishment used by Westmoreland on their translucent colored glass. On open pieces such as plates and bowls, it was successful; but on closed, and even two-sided pieces, it looks turbid.

(c. 1929)

Height: 7¾"

1865 Bowl — 9½"
1031/0 Flower Bowl Stand — 2¾"
1042 Candlesticks — 9"

1865 Bowls first available between 1918 and 1921. **1031 Stands** first available between 1913 and 1917. **1042 Candlesticks** first available between 1918 and 1924.

(c. 1929)

1865 Bowl also available 10½" — straight sided.

1031 Stand also available in six larger sizes (early 1920s on).

1042 Candlestick also available 6½".

1865 and **1031** were item numbers.

1932: Bowl, stand, and candlesticks all available in crystal and colors. 1940: All discontinued.

Bowl: 9⅜" w.
Foot: 2⅜" d.

This is the same translucent cased color found on the preceding candy jar. Notice how brilliantly it has brought out the cutting on the open bowl, and yet made almost invisible the cutting on the candlestick stems. I can recall this cutting design from my childhood on some of my grandfather's glass; as a four-year-old I found it very sinister. It is almost certainly Racinger's. Notice the precision of his dental edging and cross-hatching. Notice, too, how his grinning incubus has evolved awesomely from that formal rococo shell pictured on page 116. A great deal of thought, work, and skill went into the cutting on this bowl. Since Racinger did only copper wheel engraving, establishing any cutting as Racinger's confirms it is copper wheel engraving, also.

There is evidence Westmoreland made two different **1865** — 9½" bowls which differed only in their feet. One bowl has a knobbed foot with a short indented ankle. This foot is never found ground and polished. The other has a foot that was ground and polished almost up to the bowl bottom. Because its foot was not extended, this otherwise identical bowl sits ¼" lower. A compound shell mould was required to make the first bowl, but a simpler block mould, the type used for the plates and the early mustard lids, was used for the second. Two plungers, also, were used. The evidence for this is the presence of a **Keystone-W** which will be found in every one of the first style bowls, but in none of the second. The feet on both bowls measure the same, small, 2⅜" across.

This is just the sort of difference that ordinarily points to two makers. But the Carnegie bowl, this bowl, and others I own all share the knobbed foot, while two others shown in this book share the ground foot with the **Keystone-W** mark. A surviving decorating catalog supplies photographic evidence both bowls were being made concurrently in the mid-'20s, and both were designated **1865**.

Blown "Egyptian" Vase — 13"
High Foot Sweetmeat — 6"

(c. 1930)

Vase blown in the same shape as Westmoreland's blown **"Egyptian" Jars** available at the turn of the century.

Sweetmeat stem and base made in the same mould as Westmoreland's **1800 6½" High Foot Sweetmeat.**

1932: **1800 Sweetmeat** available in crystal only.
1940: **1800 Sweetmeat** discontinued.

Vase: 3" h.
Base: 3¾" d.
Sweetmeat: 6" h.
Stem/bowl: 1¾" d.

I believe the "Transparent Green" that was introduced in the fall of 1927 (J 9/8/27) is what is shown in the photograph. If so, it confirms Westmoreland was still cutting the same "Graceful Scroll" design for Fort Dearborn around 1928 (see the Cut Stained section).

Neither of the pieces pictured is shown in the catalogs, but both appear to be Westmoreland's. The vase is pictured twice in this section and also in the Cut Stained section. The sweetmeat is pictured three times in this section with Westmoreland's cased and engraved decorations.

The vase is blown — possible free-blown, for there is a ground punty on the bottom showing a pontil rod had been used to hold the vase when the neck was formed. Also, the sides do not show the distinct circumferential marks that would show it had been turned inside a blow mould. The shape of this high-shouldered vase seems to date back to Westmoreland's blown **"Egyptian" Jars** from the turn-of-the-century; only the hand-formed necks differ.

I have seen one of these "Egyptian" vases in Westmoreland's distinctive Belgian blue glass with an engraved decoration and a Hawkes acid mark. This establishes two things: the vase was, indeed, made by Westmoreland, and if the mark is genuine, Westmoreland was a supplier of blanks to Hawkes.

The sweetmeat has the same stem and foot as the **1800 Sweetmeat** (see the Gold & Silver section). Most important of all, the critical stem-to-bowl measurement is the same on both. While the foot and lower stem may differ slightly from piece to piece because they have been hand-shaped, the stem attachment area is unaltered after it leaves the mould; it will never vary.

115

1820 Low Foot Comport — 9"

1820 Comports first available between 1918 and 1924.

(c. 1929)

Also available 11".

1932: Both comports available in crystal and colors.
1940: Discontinued.

Height: 4¼"
Diameter: 9⅜"

In 1960 Joseph Racinger referred to an old design of his apprentice days which he called "The Deer Hunt" (PG 10/17/60). This bowl, the plate pictured in the Cut Stained section, and the vases pic-

tured in the Carnegie section, are tied to this design. Compare the design on these four pieces, then refer to the detailed comparison in the Cut Stained section.

The Complete Cut and Engraved Glass of Corning shows a "Blue-stained bowl designed and engraved by Joseph Ovenzny ca 1940. Diam 21.3 cm (8¼")." The blank used was Westmoreland's **1809 — 8" Cupped Bowl** — not made after

1937. This bowl may bear a **Keystone-W** mark on the inside. The stain would be Westmoreland's translucent-blue casing pictured here, which would date the bowl to the late '20s or possible the early '30s. The dentals, the C's, the corbels, the foliage, the stag, and the shells all appear to be identical to those pictured on this **1820 Bowl**. Since the date was in error, it would not be unreasonable to conclude the attribution was in error, too. But on the same page Joseph Oveszny was said to have worked at Westmoreland sometime after his employment at H.P. Sinclaire. Racinger and Oveszny were both originally from Bohemia. Could these men have served their apprenticeships together?

1848 Bell Bowl — 13"

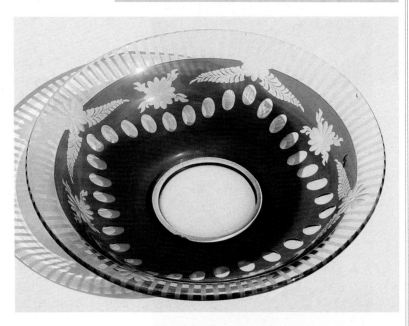

1848 items first available between 1918 and 1923.

This bowl shows a fourth translucent color used by Westmoreland. A fifth translucent color (not shown) was a lemon yellow.

Although the ovals were cut and polished, the remainder of the design was left gray- or satin-cut. These polished ovals, each forming a diminishing lens through the cased glass, may have been suggested by similar cuttings from the mid-nineteenth century (RN 188).

The **1848 Bell Bowl** can also be seen in etched black glass in the Carnegie section.

(c. 1929)

1848 also available as 12" cupped, 12" round, 13" roll edge, 13" flared bowls, and as a 14" plate (same mould).

1848 was an item number for the five bowls and plate.

Ground and polished bottom.

1932: **1848** items available in crystal and colors.
1940: Discontinued.

Diameter: 12¾"

High Foot Sweetmeat — 6"

This is the first of three pictures showing the same decoration of the early '30s on different blanks. It is the second of three pictures showing this uncataloged sweetmeat with a certain Westmoreland stem.

The decoration consists of cutting, etching, amber staining, and sprayed casing. Since these four operations took place in different areas of the plant, the logistics must have been formidable. Both the artificial complexity of this simple design and the fact I have seen it on several inferior non-Westmoreland blanks supports my belief that Chas West was doing everything he could during the Depression to keep his cutters and decorators working.

(c. 1933)

Height: 6"
Stem/Bowl: 1¾" d.

1800 Footed Vase — 10"

1800 Footed Vase first available in 1926.

(c. 1933)

1932: Available in crystal and colors.
1940: Discontinued.

Height: 9¾"
Width: 6⅛"

While Pairpoint made a vase (No. A1083) with a shape related to this in the '20s, the two could never be confused. The Pairpoint stem was half the total height of their vase, and the Pairpoint ball, one element of a three-element stem, was always cut or bubbled. Westmoreland's ball was there for stability, and on stained pieces it was rarely left unstained. (Pairpoint's magnificent ball probably had its origin in late nineteenth century vases with "paperweight" bases.)

Compare this vase to the **1800 Vase** in the Cut Stained section. Notice the difference the decoration makes to the otherwise identical blank.

Blown Egyptian Vase — 13"
1820 Low Foot Comport — 11"

1820 Low Foot Comports first available between 1918 and 1924.

(c. 1933)

1820 Low Foot Comport also available 9".

Vase: 13½" h.
Bowl: 13¼" w.

This "festoon" or "string-of-pearls" motif was used by several companies in the early '30s. Hawkes used it from 1932 to World War II in a pattern they called "Saphire Blue." Also, U.S. Glass used it in their cutting #437 of 1932. If we knew its origin was English, would we be justified in calling it the "Venerable Bead?"

High Foot Sweetmeat — 6"

This is the third photograph in this section showing the same Westmoreland uncataloged sweetmeat. The top of the foot was stained as was the underside of the bowl, and the stem was spray-cased. The blank was entirely crystal.

(c. 1931)

Height: 6"
Stem/bowl: 1¾" d.

1840 Vase — 10"

than five years later. Notice, however, the similarities in the two cuttings: the ovals on the feet, the small flowers, and most of all the leaves. If Racinger was the cutter of that Fort Dearborn design, then he was the cutter here — and both cuttings are up to his standard. He has cut his foliage on the top through the stain so that it shows up white. Then he has cut the beading and the small flowers from below so they appear amber. The stain was applied to the foot, the ankle, and the top of the vase; the casing was applied to the neck and the outside of the trunk down to the ankle.

The synergistic effect of the cutting, staining, and black casing is almost overpowering.

(c. 1931)

Height: 7¾"
Diam: 9¾"
Weight: 3¼ lb.

Compare this **1840 Vase** with the **1840 Vase**, or "Flower Center" in the Cut Stained section. The latter was cut in the Fort Dearborn "Graceful Scroll" design in 1925 and this, I believe, was cut more

1211 Octagon Ice Tub with Metal handle — 5 x 6

1211 Ice Tub first available in 1927.

(c. 1930)

Height: 6"
Width: 5¼" (max)

At first glance, this ice tub appears to have been cut with an abrasive (stone) cutting wheel; yet, it cannot have been. In stone cutting the cutter must be able to hold the work above his wheel and see through the glass he is cutting. Here, with this opaque-black casing this would have been impossible. This cutting had to have been done beneath a metal wheel — either iron or copper — with a slurry of sand or emery fed from above. Since this ice tub is a mate to one that has come down in our family, we can be certain of the Westmoreland cutting.

Westmoreland's **1211 Ice Tub** was shown in a Lotus decorating catalog in black glass with Lotus' silver decoration. We know Westmoreland was the maker, for Lotus used Westmoreland's **1211** for its designating number. Lotus, together with most decorating companies, retained the glass companies' line or item numbers.

1902 Low Foot Comport — 8"

1902 line first available in 1927. 1902 Low Foot Comport first available in 1927.

(c. 1930)

1902 was designated a **Plain** line.

1932: Available in crystal and colors.
1940: Discontinued.

Diameter: 7⅝"
Stem/bowl: 2⅝" d.

This comport is crystal with black-sprayed casing; the black is particularly smooth.

The cutting shows a carnation with carnation buds and foliage. The flowers and the buds are part-polished. Around the rim there are about 190 "nicks" created with a cutting wheel — each about ⅛" wide. Because of the opaque color, all of this cutting had to have been done with a metal wheel.

The **1902 Low Foot Comport** can also be seen in crystal with etching and applied silver in the Gold & Silver section.

98 Vase — 13" (Lamp)

97, 98, 99 Vases first available between 1918 and 1924.

(1924)

Also available 11" (No. **97**) and 15" (No. **99**).

97, **98**, and **99** were single-item numbers.

A family piece.

1932: All three sizes available in crystal and colors.
1940: Discontinued.

In their review of Westmoreland's 1924 display at the Pittsburgh Exhibit, *National Glass Budget* wrote of *"The skillfully designed and carefully and exquisitely hand decorated lamp that required days to make and would run up into three figures to own"* (B 1/12/24). (A Ford in the mid-'20s could have been bought for $400.)

China, Glass & Lamps wrote, *"An extremely beautiful lamp…. Shows crystal glass painted blue, and given Czecho-slovakian cutting, the pattern is unburnished except for the high spots in the design, and looks like the Old English cased glass that collectors pay such fabulous prices for"* (L 1/14/24).

This lamp was one of four important pieces of Westmoreland that Charles and Helen West took with them when they moved to a one-bedroom apartment in 1941. As a child living in my grandparents' house, I loved this lamp because of its deep blue color. But because of its location in their dark living room, I never really saw the cutting. Since light can get behind the cutting only through the cutting, the lamp's impact is lost if it is not placed in front of a window.

It was only recently I was able to confirm this family lamp was Westmoreland's. In the late 1980s, a glass authority questioned how such a thing could have been made by Westmoreland. Earlier, my mother had simply referred to it as her "blue lamp." But the blank and its blue casing both clearly establish it as a Westmoreland piece. The blank is the same **98 — 13" Vase** pictured in the Black Glass

section, and the blue casing is Westmoreland's sprayed glass. Of perhaps equal significance, we can clearly establish Racinger was the lamp's cutter by comparing it to the signed **1820 Bowl** in the Carnegie section. And from the many design elements on these two pieces, we can identify other Westmoreland pieces that were cut by him.

The lamp actually has four cut faces and not three. The most elaborate face, the one that ties this cutting directly to the signed Carnegie bowl, is repeated. When Racinger later said, "Twenty or thirty years ago the engraver couldn't get enough design crowded on a piece of glass" (PG 10/17/60), he must have had this lamp in mind.

121

Chas West's Decoration

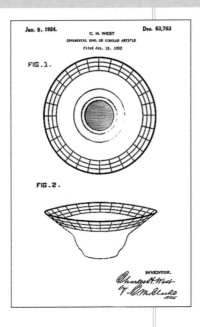

Chas West's patented lattice decoration warrants its own special section here — not just because it is so striking, but because it was Westmoreland's most frequently used decoration in the '20s.

While very simple, it seems to have a chameleon-like ability to be transformed by the various glass shapes it is found on. It suggests a number of different things. It looks Oriental, yet Craftsman. It would not seem out of place with Frank Lloyd Wright's contemporary architecture. On some glass it suggests a cobweb; on others, a trellis. A reviewer in the '20s called it "latticework." Today, some call it "deco." It was designed to allow the background — the table or tablecloth usually — to become part of the design; it was also intended to show off the transparency of the glass.

This bizarre but beautiful decoration well deserved its popularity, but its very popularity may have hastened its decline. I believe it was no longer being used in the Depression years of the early '30s when its dramatic squares would have seemed as dated as those octagons that were so strongly associated with the prior age.

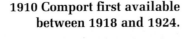

1910 Tall Comport — 9"

(c. 1922)

There was a **1910** mini-line of five pieces, but this comport was not included with them.

This **1910** was a single-item number.

1932: Available in crystal and colors.
1940: Discontinued.

Height: 8¾"

1910 Comport first available between 1918 and 1924.

"A patented design (of Westmoreland's) *that has had great success has... an inch and a half crystal border crossed with gold lines to form squares. They have had great success with it for two years and are continuing it"* (L 1/14/24). Despite this contemporary trade report, I have seen Chas West's lattice decoration only with black or silver lines.

The **1910 Comport** with a central European decoration is pictured in the Carnegie section. Notice its rim has alternating wide and narrow scallops.

1034 Candlestick — 9"

1034 candlesticks first available between 1918 and 1922.

"*(At Westmoreland's display at the Pittsburgh Exhibit) a line of tableware can be had in colorful combinations of French gray and black, yellow and black, orange and black, and green and black. This shape also can be had yellow with lattice work border in black lines*" (L 1/16/22).

For a discussion of this candlestick design, see the Iridized and Miscellaneous sections.

(c. 1922)

Also available 8" & 11".

Ground and polished punty.

1932: The three **1034** sizes available in crystal only. 1940: 9" and 11" available in crystal only, then discontinued. The 8" with a reassigned **1776** number was pictured in the 1967 catalog in olive green, and again in 1980 as a crystal reproduction. In 1981 it was redesignated 9" and pictured in all the 1981 colors.

Height: 9⅝"

1038 Candlestick — 9"

1038 candlesticks first available in 1922.

(c. 1922)

In 1924 also available 11" & 12".

1932: 9" & 12" available in crystal only.
1940: Discontinued.

Height: 9⅜"

Westmoreland's **1038** can be distinguished by the faceting on the sides of their candleholders and on the tops of their flat feet, and also by the rings at both ends of their "barley-twist" stems.

The blue candlestick pictured in the middle is decorated in "Carrara," which in the '20s was sprayed casing on etched glass.

The **1038 Candlestick** was introduced in 1922 — the same year as Chas West's lattice design. Responding to the contemporary interest in Spanish Baroque furniture and architecture, several glass companies made similar candlesticks in the early to mid-'20s.

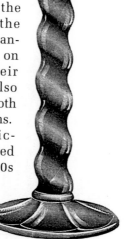

123

1909/1 Bowl Rolled Edge — 11"
1042 Candlesticks — 9"
1031/2 Bowl Stand — 5"

(c. 1924)

In 1924 four plain **1909 Bowls** are available (same mould).

In 1927 Westmoreland introduced a new **1909** line with no connection to the four bowls. The bowls were redesignated **1901/1**.

Bowl has a ground and polished bottom.

1932: Bowls, stands, and candlesticks all available in crystal and colors. 1940: Discontinued.

Bowl: 11⅜" d.

For a comparison of the Westmoreland **1031** and a similar Fenton bowl stand, see the Miscellaneous section.

1909/1 Bowls first available between 1918 and 1924. 1031 Stands first available between 1913 and 1917. 1042 candlesticks first available between 1918 and 1924.

"(Westmoreland's) *flower and fruit bowls… are fascinating. Black glass stands are made to go with these bowls and there are also companion candlesticks"* (L 1/10/21).

In January 1921 Westmoreland seems to have pioneered the concept of the console set. Three years later a reviewer wrote, *"The variety of* (Westmoreland's) *console sets was the largest shown in Pittsburgh by any firm — and the demand was pronounced just as active as the line was attractive"* (J 2/7/24).

1848 Bell Bowl — 13"
1002 Candlesticks — 8"

(c. 1924)

1848 also available 12" cupped, 12" round, 13" belled, 13" flared, and a 14" plate (same mould).

1848 was an item number for these five bowls and the plate.

Bowl has a ground and polished bottom.

1932: Six **1848** items in crystal and colors; **1002** available in crystal only. 1940: All discontinued.

Candlestick: 8" h.
Bowl: 12½" d.
Foot: 4¼" d.

1848 Bowls first available between 1918 and 1924. 1002 Candlesticks first available between 1918 and 1924.

The **1002 Candlestick** suggests a Doric column with its lip forming the cornice and its rings forming toruses at the capital and base. While it was made in two sizes, 6½" and 8", the beading shown in the catalog woodcut can be found only on the smaller 6½" size.

1820 Cheese & Cracker — 10" (#381 Dec.)

1820 line introduced between 1918 and 1924. #381 Decoration available in 1924.

(c. 1924)

1820 was designated Westmoreland's **Flange** line.

Plate has a ground and polished bottom.

1932: **1820 Cheese & Cracke**r available in crystal only.
1940: Discontinued.

Cheese: 4⅞" d.
Foot: 3¼" d.
Plate: 9⅞" d.
Foot: 5" o.d.

Westmoreland's **1820** line was characterized by a heavy flange at the rim of each piece. Its broad, flat surface was often used for ornamental work. Here, Westmoreland treated it as a heavy bronze ring, much like the rim of a balance wheel in a watch. To me this is the most interesting form of Chas West's decoration because it is so deceptive: the sense of substance that is there in the center vanishes — only to reappear in triumphal vigor at the rim.

Chas West seems to have preferred his design in glass rather than steel, however. When my mother bought her first car in 1929 (a Model "A" roadster), I understand he insisted on her getting it with disk, instead of wire wheels for safety reasons. It was a very interesting looking Ford!

In his design's usual form, with the lattice work on the outside, Westmoreland's decorating number is 314. Here, though, where the lattice-work is bounded by an external rim, Westmoreland used the decorating number 381.

1002 Candlesticks — 8"
1865 Flower Bowl — 9½"
Ornamental Iron Stand

1865 Bowls first available between 1918 and 1921. 1865 Bowl & Stand available in 1921.

(c. 1922)

Bowl also available 10½" — straight sided (same mould).

1865 was an item number assigned just to these two bowls.

"Keystone-W" marked.

Ground and polished punty.

1932: Both bowls available in crystal and colors. Stand discontinued.
1940: Discontinued.

Bowl: 9⅜" w.
Foot: 2⅜" d.
Candlestick: 8" h.

"Among the most attractive sets shown (in Westmoreland's display at the Pittsburgh Exhibit) *was that termed 'Orange Ware' taking its name from the color of oranges. It is trimmed with black bands and supported on various colored iron stands and bases. It takes an expert to distinguish this glassware from the finest ever imported"* (B 1/29/21).

Later that same year another reporter wrote, *"One of the many delightful things in* (Westmoreland's) *novelty glassware… is their No. 1865 Flower Bowl with wrought iron stand. This may be had in a variety of different colors such as orange and black, green, peach blow, gray crackled lustres, in blue, orange, champagne, burgundy, also the same colors in plain lustres"* (J 7/28/21).

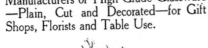

Westmoreland Specialty Co.
Grapeville, Pa.
Manufacturers of High Grade Glassware —Plain, Cut and Decorated—for Gift Shops, Florists and Table Use.

No. 1865 Flower Bowl and Ornamental Iron Stand with Flower Blocks. Made in Crystal, Fancy Decorations and Colors.

REPRESENTATIVES:
New York—H. C. Gray Co., 310 Fifth Ave., Bldg.
Philadelphia—Peacock & Roop, 1007 Filbert Street.
Boston—H. P. & H. F. Hunt, 41 Pearl Street.
San Francisco—Himmelstern Bros., 718 Mission St.

According to Robert Jones, who was first employed at Westmoreland in 1924, Westmoreland made all their bowl stands and aquaria supports on the premises. For those readers familiar with the plant, in the 1920s Westmoreland's blacksmith shop was located in the old boiler room where moulds were stored in the 1980s.

The ring in the photographed stand has a particularly neat scarf joint. Westmoreland's blacksmith shop was capable of doing first-class work.

(L 7/18/21)

1800 Cracker & Cheese Plate — 10"

1800 Cracker & Cheese Plate first available in 1917.

(c. 1929)

In 1932, **1800 Cracker & Cheese Plate** also available 11".

1800 was designated a **Plain** line.

Plate has ground and polished bottom.

1932: **1800 Cracker & Cheese** plate available in crystal, colors, and opal. 1940: Discontinued.

Cheese: 7⅞" d.
Foot: 3¼" d.
Plate: 9¾" d.
Foot: 5⅛" o.d.

In 1910 Wm Krebs obtained a patent on a double dish for cheese and crackers. In 1917, the year Krebs' patent expired, Westmoreland introduced their first and most generic cracker and cheese — their **1800** shown here. Shortly afterwards, all glass companies were making their own. Since most are very similar, we have a problem today distinguishing between them. Westmoreland's **1820** (pictured in this section) and **1211 Octagon** (pictured in the Black Glass section) pose no problem for they are like no other. Westmoreland's **1800,** though, could prove confusing. Central's No. T1103 and Fenton's No. 316 closely resemble the **1800.** And except for a stubbier cheese dish stem, U.S. Glass' No. 15320 does, too. Westmoreland's cracker plate has a gentle rise up to the projecting ring that holds the cheese dish in place. Also, Westmoreland's cheese dish has a flared rim with a particularly tight curvature.

In this late (c.1929) decoration, the lattice design is used as a rose trellis. However, the trellis was painted beneath the rim while the roses were painted on top. The glass is crystal that has been etched, and then spray-cased.

Enameled Flowers

From the very earliest days of Westmoreland's decorating, flowers were a part of their decorations. Enameled flowers deserve their own section here because they were so widely used and because they were so extraordinarily varied.

The flower decoration most commonly seen and the one most closely associated with Westmoreland is the rose spray, which includes rather generic leaves and often a single forget-me-not. This spray was used as early as 1906 on the Shriners Los Angeles plate, and it was still in use at the end of the West period 31 years later. Beginning in the teen years, the roses in the spray were executed in raised enamel. This was a two-step process that involved, first, painting a white or a light gray foundation on the glass blank, and then covering it with colored enamel. Two separate firings may have been required.

Westmoreland was not the only American company to use these Bohemian-inspired roses, but it may be possible to distinguish Westmoreland's by their smooth, shiny surfaces. Many of those of other companies seem to be duller or show a pocked surface.

While only some of the flowers were executed in raised enamel during the West period, all of the roses were (from the teen years on). No flowers in raised enamel seem to date from even the earliest of the Brainard years, and any roses found painted in thin paint directly against the glass will date, I believe, from this later period.

1007 Candlestick — 7"

(c. 1912)

Erroneously listed as 12" in the 1924 catalog.

1007 is a candlestick number.

1932: Available in crystal only.
1940: Discontinued.

Height: 7"

1007 Candlestick first available between 1905 and 1912.

The **1007** was one of Westmoreland's earliest candlesticks, first made shortly after 1905. The three-flower decoration, repeated three times on the faceted foot and three times on the stem, was cold-decorated.

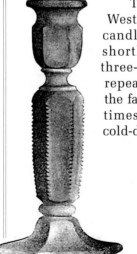

1208 Cream

(c. 1925)

1208 was an item number used for two sugar & cream sets.

Ground and polished bottom — no pressed star.

1932: Available in crystal and colors.
1940: Available in crystal only.

Sugar (foot): 2" d.
Cream (foot): 1⅞" d.

Westmoreland offered their **1208 Sugar & Cream Set** with and without a star bottom; the cream pictured does not have the star. Both cream moulds survived at the factory in 1991, and both were designated **1208.** Ordinarily, this is the sort of difference that confirms a second maker, but in this case there were at least six other makers of this design (see the Gold & Silver section).

The only way to be sure of a **1208 Sugar** or **Cream** is to find one with a known Westmoreland decoration, and then compare its handles to others in question. Since the bottoms were always ground and the tops were formed after pressing, the bowls will vary from piece to piece. But as the handles were all pressed in the mould (i.e. not "stuck"), they will allow a precise comparison.

1708 Fan Vase — 9" — Optic

(c. 1932)

1708 was designated an **Optic** line.

In 1926 available 6" & 9"; in 1927 also available 4" & 8".

In 1927 a specially fitted Flower Block was available.

1932: 4", 6", 8", 9" & 12" available in crystal and colors.
1940: Discontinued.

Height: 8¾"

"There has been a revival in the fan vases, so called, which were quite popular in days long gone.... Westmoreland's fan vases are in green, blue, amber, Roselin, and crystal. On all the colors are a great variety of decorations... gold lines, gold festoons, cuttings, etchings, and engravings. There are also treatments in colors on crystal.... These vases offer a new way to display flowers, especially the smaller ones and those with short stems. There is also a flower holder to fit in the top of the vase...."

(L 7/12/26).

1708 Fan Vases first available in 1926.

1707 Candy Jar & Cover — ½ Lb. — Optic

(c. 1925)

Also available in 1 lb. size from 1921 and ¼ lb. size from 1926.

Also available plain (not optic).

1707 was designated an **Optic** line.

1932: All three sizes available in crystal and colors.
1940: Only ½ lb. size available — in crystal only.

½ lb: 7½" h.

The **1707 Candy Jar** resembles Westmoreland's **1713 Candy Jar** (not pictured) first available between 1918 and 1924. Like the **1707** it was also available either plain or optic, but it came in just the 1 lb. size. While the lids on both appear to be the same, the **1713** had a 1" vertical band above the conical bowl that was intended for decorating. It was available in crystal in 1932, but discontinued by 1940.

For a comparison of Westmoreland's **1707** and Fenton's No. 736 candy jars, see the Cut Crystal section.

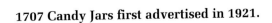

1707 Candy Jars first advertised in 1921.

1800 Mayo or Comport — 7"
1849 Butter Ball — 6"

1800 Mayo first available between 1912 and 1917. 1849 Butter Ball first available between 1918 and 1924.

Both of these pieces share the same decoration: four narrow gold rings just beyond the sprayed casing, and red, white, and blue forget-me-nots — all with yellow centers. The red on the mayonnaise bowl is Mephisto red.

A comparison of Westmoreland's **1849 Butter Ball** and Fenton's No. 318

lemon tray can be found near the end of this section.

(c. 1925)

1800 Mayo also available 8" & 10".

1800 was designated a **Plain** line.

1849 was an item number for this, a 10" handled sandwich, and a 4½" lemon tray.

1932: Both available in crystal and colors.
1940: Discontinued.

Butter Ball: 6½" d.
Mayo: 6½" d.

1820 Sandwich Tray — 10"

1820 line introduced between 1918 and 1924.

(c. 1925)

1820 was Westmoreland's **Flange** line.

1932: Available in crystal only.
1940: Discontinued.

Diameter: 10"

Westmoreland used this same tray handle on its **1849 Handled Sandwich** (see the Reverse Painting section) and on its **1849 Butterball** (pictured in this section). New Martinsville and Fenton also used the same handle design. Fenton's can be identified, however, by the absence of faceting below its stem ring.

Though all glass in Westmoreland's **1820** line will have a flanged rim, the flange on this sandwich plate has been scaled back so that it does not compromise the tray's usefulness.

1707 Candy Jar & Cover — 1 Lb. — Optic
1708 Covered Sweetmeat

1708 Sweetmeat first available in 1918 and 1923.

(c. 1924)

Sweetmeat originally designated **1211,** but renumbered in 1925 when **1211** became the exclusive designation for the **Octagon** line.

1707 and **1708** both designated **Optic** lines.

1932: **1708** — available with the cover, or crimped or belled without the cover. All three available in crystal and colors. 1940: **1708** — discontinued.

1707: 9¼" h.
1708: 9" h.
4½" w.

Westmoreland's **1708 Sweetmeat** could be confused with Economy Tumbler's No. 7556. Also, Westmoreland's **1707 Candy Jar** could be confused with Fenton's No. 736. For a comparison of the sweetmeats, see the Cut Stained section; for a comparison of the candy jars, see the Cut Crystal section.

Notice the minor variation between the decoration on the two glass pieces and that in the close-up. West-moreland in the West period used its decorations not only to tailor its glass to different markets, but to tailor it to different years. Because of this, we might be able to assign precise dates to many of Westmoreland's decorated pieces if we could date some of the minor yearly changes. For example, we know the close-up shows Westmoreland's decoration #303, which was available in 1924. That means the variation with its gold cross-hatching probably dates from a year or two on either side of 1924. But which side?

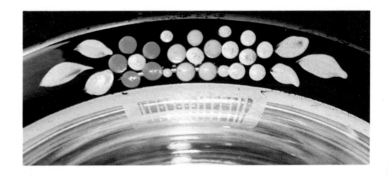

Bohemian Vase

This free-blown vase is Bohemian, and it probably dates from 1914 or before. Westmoreland and Bohemian roses were both painted in raised enamel and look much the same — understandable, given the Bohemian origin of so many of Westmoreland's decorators. Raised enameling gives roses a warm, three-dimensional appearance that will be apparent from the close-up photographs that follow.

The foliage festoons pictured on the vase may be solely European, for I have never seen them used with Westmoreland or American enameled roses.

1700 Colonial Candy Jar — 3 Lb.

Westmoreland often juxtaposed decorative devices from various past periods; this candy jar is an excellent example. Its urn shape is neo-classical, its imitation-cut flutes or facets date from a half century later, and its Bohemian roses date from a half century after that. But then notice how nicely it is all brought together with Westmoreland's "little criss-cross lines."

"Gold plays a very considerable part in (Westmoreland's) new line... the gold is applied in a rather novel fashion. Delicate little criss-cross lines give the general effect of a spider web. Pretty enamel treatments complete the decoration" (P 2/6/19).

If I were into naming these things, I might want to call this decoration the "Wm Jennings Bryan" because of its Crosses of Gold!

(c. 1919)

Also made in ½, 1, and 2 lb. sizes.

1700 was one of the two colonial lines Westmoreland introduced in 1912.

1932: Four sizes available in crystal only.
1940: 1 lb. size available in crystal only. Discontinued in 1941. In 1973 one size was reissued in transparent colors, and in milk glass in 1975.

1 lb: 8" h.
2 lb: 10½" h.
3 lb: 12¾" h.

1700 Candy Jars probably first available in 1917.

133

1820 Lowfoot Comport — 11"
1060 Candlesticks — 5" (Roselin)

1060 Candlestick first available in 1927. Roselin glass first advertised July 1926.

(c. 1928)

1820: 11½" d.
1060: 5" h.

Westmoreland used their Bohemian rose decoration extensively in the five-year period beginning in 1917, and then again from about 1927 on. While the triple forget-me-not was (or remained) in use in the first five years of the Chas West period (1921 – 37), the rose seems to have been put aside in favor of numerous contemporary designs that were used then.

The Roselin color and the **1060 Candlestick** both confirm this rose decoration is from the later period. The casing sprayed on the backside of the Roselin glass is actually white. Roselin was the last of Westmoreland's five late pre-Depression colors that consisted of amber, blue, Roselin, and two greens.

The **1060 Candlestick** was one of a group of low candlesticks introduced in 1927 — one of the last not to be tied to a tableware line. It was one of two with a sort of mushroom top that was so popular at the time. There is a Paden City candlestick that could be confused with Westmoreland's **1060,** but Paden City seems to have taken Westmoreland's **1060** stem and inverted it.

1849 Butter Ball — 6"

(1920s)

Diameter: 6½"

For this small diameter handled tray, Westmoreland reduced its usual three forget-me-nots to two, clearly subordinating it to the rose spray.

1900/2 Rolled Edge Bowl
1042 Candlesticks — 9"

1042 Candlesticks first available between 1918 and 1924. 1900/1 Bowls first available between 1918 and 1924. 1900/2 Bowls first available in 1926.

(c. 1928)

1900/2 Bowl also available belled and flared (same mould).

Three comparable **1900/1 Bowls** were 2" smaller at the rim and ¼" smaller at the peg base.

1900 was designated a **Plain** line.

1042 Candlesticks also available 6½".

1932: Bowl and candlesticks available in crystal and colors.
1940: Both discontinued.

Bowl: 12" d.
Foot: 3¼" d.

Since the preceding console set dates from 1927 or later, this one with the same rose decoration must, too. This is not the first lilac- or lavender-cased Westmoreland I have seen with its gold in nearly original condition. I suspect the color was considered difficult, and so these glass gifts were simply taken up to the attic along with the equally difficult neckties and never used. Notice that while the casing was applied to the tops of the candlesticks, it was applied to the underside of the bowl — the part not normally seen.

Notice, too, the red center in the Westmoreland rose. Unfortunately, this is not helpful in identification, for the centers of many Westmoreland roses, particularly those from the '30s, show concentric rings instead. While many of Westmoreland's red-centered roses can be found framed with "eyebrows," these may be the artistic flourishes of particular decorators.

For some reason each one of the 22 dots that make up all of Westmoreland's triple forget-me-nots are perfectly round. Nevertheless, the variation in their spacing shows these dots were painted individually.

857 Honey & Cover
1503 Covered Sugar or Bonbon

(1920s)

An **857 Jelly**, identical to the honey, had a cut-out for a ladle.

A **1503 Cream** to go with the covered sugar was available in the 1920s.

857 and **1503** were item numbers.

1932: **857 Honey** and **Jelly** both available in crystal and colors. **1503 Bonbon** available in crystal and colors. Cream discontinued. 1940: **857** and **1503** discontinued.

857 & 1503 first available between 1918 and 1924.

857: 4¼" d.
1503: 4⅝" d.

These two pieces share Westmoreland's paired forget-me-nots with a single-rose spray. Notice the difference between the two rose sprays, however.

The **857 Jelly** was also available with a cut decoration on colored glass.

1700 Colonial Candy Jar — 2 Lb.

(c. 1929)

Height: 10½"

Because this rose decoration can be tied to the decoration on the late **1211 Octagon Jelly Bowl** in the Black Glass section, we can be fairly certain it is from the period of 1927 or later. Notice that while the jelly bowl's roses have red centers, the roses on this candy jar have concentric rings.

This is the only **1700 Colonial Candy Jar** I have seen where the gold was applied to nearly the entire finial; usually it was confined to the top half. It is also unusual in that the red-cased band above the facets was not edged with gold.

1835 Comport — 7" (Yellow Carrara)

1835 Comport first available between 1918 and 1924.

This is a certain Westmoreland decoration because of its #GE-2 (gold, etched) band. The bottom of the bowl, the stem, and the foot are in Westmoreland's yellow "Carrara."

A great many steps were required to decorate this little comport. First, the outside was etched, and then spray-cased, and then fired. Then the rim was etched, the gold was applied, and the comport was fired again. Next the white foundation for the raised enamel was applied, and the comport was probably fired for a third time. Finally, when the enamels were applied to the white backing, the comport was fired for the final time.

Bakewell Pears made a footed bowl similar to Westmoreland's **1835** around 1875. They called it a "flared bowl" and it came in 8", 10", and 12" sizes. U.S. Glass' No. 15151 also looks similar, but it was, apparently, 7" tall. While Westmoreland's **1835** was almost 7" wide, it was only 6" tall.

(c. 1927)

In 1924 this Comport was designated 6". From 1926 on it was redesignated 7". (Apparently the 1924 measurement was the height and the 1926 measurement was the diameter.)

1835 was an item number used solely for this comport.

1932: Available in crystal and colors.
1940: Discontinued.

Width: 6¾"
Height: 6"

1033 Candlestick

"(At the Pittsburgh Exhibit, Westmoreland's) enameled and gold encrusted lines are the largest shown here this season" (J 1/24/18).

Teapot handles identical to this were made in the late Federal period by Samuel Williamson, a Philadelphia silversmith, but the gadrooning and the hexagonal lip and drip-tray suggest silver candlestick designs of more than 100 years earlier. Here, as it did so often, Westmoreland's eclecticism triumphed!

1033 candlestick first available between 1913 and 1917.

(c. 1918)

1932: Available in crystal only.
1940: Discontinued.

1841 High Foot Comport — 6½"

(late 1920s)

In 1924 available 5½" & 8". From 1926 available 5½", 6½" & 9".

1841 was an item number used just for these comports.

1932: All sizes available in crystal only.
1940: Discontinued.

Height: 6½"
Diameter: 5¼"
Stem/bowl: 1⅝" d.

1841 Comports first available between 1918 and 1924. 6½" size available from 1926.

This decoration may not be Westmoreland's, for I do not recognize the etched pattern under the gold. If Westmoreland did not apply the gold band, then they were not responsible for the roses either.

This etched design with its two "pinwheels" seems to have been used by several different companies. Because there are several very similar designs, be careful in using it for identification.

Rim of 1906 Syria Shriners Saucer

(1906)

Entire saucer with cup pictured in Syria Shriners section.

Diameter: 6"

Up to this point, the roses pictured have all been single roses, usually combined with the triple forget-me-nots that began this section. The next eight pictures, however, will show the roses in groupings of two and three.

The importance of this 1906-dated rose painting is that it preceded by 11 years the first press announcement of Westmoreland's roses: "(The) newest creation in floral decorated glassware. A dainty decoration of pink roses with green leaves in rich heavy enamels..." (P 1/11/17). The spray pictured looks remarkably similar to Westmoreland's later raised-enamel double-rose sprays. Nevertheless, it was applied with thin, flat paint rather than the "rich heavy enamels" mentioned in the press announcement.

1700 Colonial Candy Jar — 2 Lb.

"Solid color bands embellish the underside of the (Westmoreland decorated) *glass"* (P 1/11/17).

This black backing, which seems to date from 1920 or shortly before, is invariably brushed. While fired, it seems to be as fragile as the gold.

In this design the numerous forget-me-nots overwhelm the roses.

(c. 1920)

Height: 10½"

1800 Mayo or Comport — 7"
1800 Mayo ladle
1800 Cracker & Cheese Plate — 10"

"(A Westmoreland decoration shows) *the background color based in a dark tone applied to the inside or lower side of the article while the main decoration is on the obverse. This background is almost invariably in blue or black"* (P 2/6/19).

Notice the enameled decoration on the ladle; ladle decorating was a common Westmoreland practice.

Several companies made cracker & cheese plates that were almost indistinguishable from Westmoreland's **1800.** You will find Westmoreland's **1800 Cheese Dishes** have a particularly tight rim curvature.

(c. 1920)

The 1926 catalog erroneously lists this ladle as **1837.**

In 1932 the cracker plate also available 11".

Plate has ground and polished bottom and a cut (from the flat) star.

1932: All items available in crystal and colors. Comport also available in opal. 1940: Ladle available in crystal only. Rest discontinued.

Mayo: 6½" d.
Plate: 9⅞" d.
Cheese: 4⅞" d.

1800 Mayo and Cracker & Cheese first available between 1913 and 1917.

139

1800 Syrups — 8 Oz.

1800 Syrups first available between 1918 and 1922.

(c. 1921)
(c. 1927)

Also available in four-ounce size.

Plate bottoms ground and polished to the 20-point pressed stars.

1932: Discontinued.
1940: Discontinued.

Jug: 5¼" h.
Plate: 5" d.

Strangely, Westmoreland's syrup is pictured in all catalogs and ads only with a metal lid. Yet, both of these syrups pictured have glass lids, and the mould for the glass lid survived at the factory in 1991. Notice the tiny enameled rose on the top of one of the lid finials.

New Martinsville's No. 190-0 "molasses jug, cover, and plate" could be confused with this Westmoreland syrup. However, the New Martinsville proportions are squatter, and its lid finial is rounded and very wide.

Since Westmoreland's syrups were blown and their handles "stuck," they will show no mould marks. The term "stuck" means the hand-formed handle was attached to the jug after it was removed from the mould.

(L 12/25/22)

Non-Westmoreland Rose Spray

These American non-Westmoreland flowers are included here to show that not all raised-enamel rose sprays on pressed blanks are Westmoreland's. Nevertheless, this paired rose combined with a single rose and forget-me-not is a decoration we would normally associate with Westmoreland. But Westmoreland's raised enameling seems to be free from the sort of pitting or cratering shown here, and Westmoreland's leaves all seem to be shaded rather than articulated as they have been here.

1800 Cracker & Cheese Plate — 10" (Aquamarine)

Aquamarine glass first advertised Dec. 1928.

(c. 1932)

Plate has ground and polished bottom.

Plate: 10¼" d.
Foot: 5⅛" o.d.
Cheese: 4¾" d.
Foot: 3⅜" d.

This is one of Westmoreland's 1930s decorations which has combined cutting, etching, "coin gold," and two-step raised enameling. It was made during the Depression when Chas West was evidently trying to keep as many of his decorators working as possible.

The alternating double-rose motif is virtually the same as that shown on the **1800 Cracker & Cheese** in the C. West Decoration section.

Because the aquamarine blue is so light, the unetched rim that displays the beautiful cutting appears to be crystal.

141

(1920s)

1700 Colonial Candy Jar — 2 Lb.

This candy jar has a silver cover which could have been sold with it originally, and a design showing a bouquet of three roses. I have seen this same design on another **1700 Candy Jar** with its solid black band intact. While fired, the band pictured has largely been worn away.

Westmoreland's **1700 Candy Jar** could be confused with Heisey's No. 353. For a comparison, see the Cut Crystal section.

"23" Bowl — 10"

"23" — 8½" **Bowl first available between 1913 and 1917. "23"** — 10" **Bowl first available between 1928 and 1932.**

(c. 1932)

"23" was a single item number.

1932: **"23"** — 10" **Bowl** available in crystal and colors.
1940: Discontinued.

Bowl: 9¾" d.
Foot: 4½" d.

3¼" height and 4½" foot diameter, the more prominent groove and the concave base on the 10" bowl required a new or at least reworked mould.

Jeannette's No. 5164-10 may look almost identical, but Westmoreland's **"23"** will show faint rotational marks on the bottom and no mould mark across the bowl.

Since I have seen this same decoration on two **1707 Candy Jars,** I accept it as Westmoreland's. The black-sprayed casing was applied to the underside of the bowl, but not to the foot.

Through 1927 the **"23" Bowl** was available only in the 8½" size. Then sometime between 1928 and 1932 it was replaced by the 10" size pictured. While both of these **"23"** bowls share the same

1849 Butter Ball — 6" (Roselin)

Although this decoration is on a Roselin color Westmoreland blank, I believe it is by a decorating house. The decoration seems to suggest several I have seen on Cambridge pieces from the '20s.

Fenton's No. 318 is nearly identical to this **1849 Butter Ball**; however, Fenton's slightly taller handle is not faceted below the ring, whereas Westmoreland's is. Also, in common with other Westmoreland butter balls (lemon trays) and handled sandwich trays, Westmoreland's has a smooth bottom, rather than a projecting circular foot ring. Westmoreland also made a nearly identical 10" handled sandwich tray (see the Reverse Painting and Gold & Silver sections).

Roselin glass first advertised July 1926.

(c. 1928)

Diameter: 6½"

1827 Straight Edge Honey — 6½"

1827 Honey first available between 1918 and 1924.

We can attribute this decoration to Westmoreland on the basis of the leaves. Notice how they resemble those on the **1211 Candlestick** pictured in the Reverse Painting section.

(late 1920s)

Also available as a 6" rolled edge comport (same mould).

1827 was an item number assigned just to these two pieces.

1932: Available in crystal and colors.
1940: Discontinued.

Diameter: 6½"
Stem/bowl: 1¾" d.

143

1211 Octagon Footed Sweetmeat SE (Straight Edge)

1211 Line first available between 1918 and 1924. 1211 Sweetmeats first available in 1927.

(c. 1929)

Also available "RE" (rolled edge) from the same mould.

1932: Available in crystal and colors.
1940: Discontinued.

Width: 7⅝" (max.)

While the leaves here appear almost life-like, the lilies appear to be caricatures: three explosive spots of bold, undifferentiated white! They could have been more painstakingly painted, but if they had been, would be design have had the same thrust?

It is a simple decoration consisting of just four things: the lilies, the stems, and the leaves in two forms. Notice that the decoration is only one part of the overall design; the other part is the glass form, so rarely considered in glass decoration. The happy result hints of the majestic surge of three swimming dolphins.

1211/1 Octagon Bowl — 13" SE (Straight Edge)

1211/1 Bowls first available in 1927.

(c. 1928)

Also available as a 10½" crimped bowl (see colored glass section), an 11" bell bowl, and an 11" cupped bowl (same mould).

Ground and polished foot.

1932: All four bowls available in crystal and colors. The SE bowl also available in opal.
1940: The SE bowl available in opal only.

Width: 12½" (max.)
Foot: 3½" (max.)

This is one of two brilliant Cubist floral decorations pictured in this book; the other appears on the **1820 Comport** in the Reverse Painting section. There is nothing subtle about this decoration, and there is no doubt in my mind that it is Westmoreland's.

I made a return trip of 200 miles just to buy this bowl. I bought it with a chip and paid triple what I thought I should have been charged just to own it. The bowl's ground and polished bottom is unusual, for **1211 Octagon Bowl** bottoms are ordinarily unfinished.

Fenton's No. 1676 bowl of c.1933 could be confused with this; both bowls measure about 12½" at the

widest point. But notice the very prominent groove around Westmoreland's tall octagonal foot: Westmoreland's bowl was not intended to be used with a bowl stand. Heisey made a bowl similar to Fenton's with a short, protruding foot; however, Heisey's bowls should all be marked with "Diamond-H" in the top center.

The **1211/1 SE Bowl** can also be seen in the Black Glass and Colored Glass sections.

1042 Candlestick — 9"

This enameled decoration is Westmoreland's and it dates from the 1930s. I have seen a very similar decoration on some Westmoreland bath bottles from the same decade. In the West years, when Westmoreland's decorators were plumbing every conceivable source for their ideas (one hand-painted decoration was even called "Henry VIII and his Six Wives"!), it was inevitable these Bohemian-trained artists would turn to the rococo. In this style, popular in the south German area in the mid-eighteenth century, decorative lines flow in free, asymmetrical curves.

I believe the rococo curves of this candlestick and the interesting trellis work were taken directly from interior architecture rather than from other glass. The red and white raised enamel flowers, the dots, the foliage, and the beautiful blue, however, are pure Westmoreland.

(1930 – 1937)

Height: 9⅜"

1700/2 Colonial Urn — Crimped
1038 Spiral Candlesticks — 9"

Surely, this is Westmoreland eclecticism at its very best.

The spiral candlesticks suggest Spanish Baroque architecture or possible Dutch or English furniture of the late seventeenth century. The urn, the base of Westmoreland's 2 lb. **1700 Candy Jar** with a crimped rim, is neo-classical with flutes or facets suggesting cut glass of half a century later. The flared three-point husks or bellflowers suggest Baltimore furniture inlays of the Federal (c. 1800) period, and Westmoreland's use of

light green and yellow colors suggesting dyed inlays strengthens this allusion. Finally, the iridizing that appears on the bright yellow lustre stain, hints of the excavated glass of ancient civilizations.

I have included this set in the Flower section because of its major design element, the bellflower, and because of the blue flower included in the decoration. Notice the common decorative elements on this set and on the **1910 Comport** in the Carnegie section. Notice also the alternating etched panels on the urn and on the faceted candlestick bases. The decoration is repeated on each of the etched panels, and each panel is trimmed in gold.

This set is also pictured in the Iridized section, but these photographs fail to do it justice. In a room of mine crowded with glass, this set is what everyone is drawn to.

1700 Urns probably first available in 1917. 1038 Candlesticks first available in 1922.

(c. 1923)

Set also shown in Iridized section.

Urn is Westmoreland's **1700 Candy Jar** with a crimped edge. All four sizes available as urns.

In 1924 the **1038 Candlestick** also available 11" & 12".

1932: Urn discontinued. 9" and 12" candlesticks available in crystal only.
1940: Both discontinued.

1038: 9⅜" h.
Urn: 7¼" h.

Reverse Painting

While reverse painting on glass was evidently first practiced close to 2,000 years ago, it seems to have been particularly popular in Europe between the sixteenth and the nineteenth centuries. Its chief justification was its freshly-painted look with the paint protected by glass; but its inherent weakness was the fragility of the cold (unfired) paints that were traditionally used. Surviving early nineteenth century eglomise clock panels and Westmoreland's turn-of-the-century cold decorations both show the long-term instability of paint on glass. But fired glass enamels, unlike paints, will not lift; and even though unprotected, they will always appear fresh.

Because of this, what sets Westmoreland's reverse painting apart from its exposed enameling is not so much its appearance, as its mode of application. In reverse painting, either the artist faces the top of the glass while bringing up his brush to the backside, or else he paints from above with the glass inverted. Whichever way he does it, the painting order is reversed: the colors or shading that would ordinarily go on last go on first. Unfortunately, Westmoreland's ubiquitous and fragile gold was always applied to the upper side of its glassware. And so, while Westmoreland's reverse painting will remain forever young, the worn gold will show its age.

1900 Flange Bowl — 14"
1054 Low Candlestick — 3"
1707 Candy Jar & Cover — ½ Lb. — Optic

(1927)

In 1932, the **1900 Flange Bowl** also available 10½" & 16".

Bowl has ground and polished bottom.

1054 was one of Westmoreland's first candlesticks in the new, low style.

1707 Candy Jar also available in 1 lb. size from 1921 and ¼ lb. size from 1926.

1932: **1900 Bowls** available in crystal and colors. **1054 Candlesticks** available in crystal and colors. **1707 Candy Jars** available in crystal and colors. 1940: Bowls and candlesticks discontinued. **1707 ½ lb. Candy Jars** available in crystal only.

Bowl: 13" d.
Foot: 3¾" o.d.
1054: 3¼" h.
1707: 7½" h.

1900 Flange Bowls and 1054 Candlesticks first available in 1926. 1707 Candy Jars first advertised in 1921.

"Spanish influence in glassware decoration reached an artistic height in new creations of the Westmoreland Glass Co.... In one decoration... there is a wide border of flowers in orange on a background of beige.... Another Spanish floral has larger flowers of alternating dull red and purple with gold lines and edges" (L 1/17/27).

This second Spanish decoration has been reverse-painted on all pieces of the console set and the lid of the candy jar. The outside of the candleholders and the underside of the candy jar foot were sprayed with an opaque-white casing.

The 14" **1900 Bowl** was one of the glass blanks Westmoreland sold to H.P. Sinclaire of Corning for their cutting and decorating (FS 76).

146

1211/1 Octagon Candlestick — 3"

1211 line first available between 1918 and 1924. 1211 Candlesticks first available in 1927.

While these leaves are palmate, red, and reverse-painted, notice how closely they resemble those shown on the **1827 Honey** in the Flower section. The gold veining, which suggests crackled glass, was applied to the top of the base.

Two **1211 Octagon Candlesticks** were introduced in 1927. Confusingly, Westmoreland introduced two other low octagonal candlesticks at the same time, but designated these as **1608** and **1057**. None of the four survived into the Brainard period.

(c. 1928)

1211 was Westmoreland's **Octagon** line.

Two **1211 Octogon Candlesticks** were joined by a third (**1211/2 – 3"**) by 1932.

1932: All three 1211 **Candlesticks** available in crystal and colors. The **1211/2** also available in opal. 1940: All three discontinued.

Height: 3¼"

1054 Low Candlestick — 3"

This is the same **1054 Candlestick** form pictured with a Spanish decoration and a cased candleholder at the beginning of this section. The palmate leaves are similar to those on the preceding **1211 Octagon Candlestick.**

In the late '20s every glassware company seems to have made a variant of the **1054 Candlestick.** Because of this, some of its key dimensions will prove useful. The **1054** foot is 4½" in diameter. Since it was worked to a wedged, but flat form, it will show rotational marks on the bottom, but no mould seams. Its total height is 3¼". The distance between its two candleholder ridges is exactly 1¹⁄₁₆". The top ridge (the rim) measures 2³⁄₁₆" across and the lower ridge is ⅜" narrower. Its ring or knop is located just above its wedged foot. Finally, it is unique in having fingernail-catching breaks or fillets on the underside of the candleholders as well as on the top of the knop creating a collar in the concave stem.

Fostoria's No. 2324 candlestick could be confused with Westmoreland's. In January 1926 Fostoria applied for a patent for theirs (16021) which was granted for 14 years. Fostoria's lower ridge though, extends out slightly beyond its rim.

Then in March 1926 Paden City applied for a patent on their No. 119 candlestick, which is nearly identical to Westmoreland's. This patent (16784) also was granted — but for only seven years. At the time Paden City filed, Westmoreland had been making their **1054** for half a year or more, and it was clearly pictured in their 1926 catalog. Paden City's look-alike will show a mould seam on the top and the foot, no break below the candleholder, and a 1⅛" distance between the lower ridge and rim.

There were several other companies with similar designs including Cambridge (No. 628), McKee (No. 100), and L. E. Smith.

(c. 1927)

Height: 3¼"

147

1909/1 Belled Bowl — 11"

1909/1 Bowls first available between 1918 and 1924.

(c. 1924)

Ground and polished bottom.

In 1924, four **1909 Bowls** were available (same mould). In 1927 Westmoreland introduced a new **1909** line with no connection to these bowls. At that time the bowls were redesignated **1909/1**.

1932: **1909/1 Bowls** available in crystal and colors. 1940: All four discontinued.

"Another interesting item (in Westmoreland's display at the Pittsburgh Exhibit) *was of translucent glass with long sprays of fruit and leaves painted underneath the glass, the veiling of glass giving to the painted sprays a blurred outline that was most attractive. These pieces were finished with a gold line, put on top of the glass, which served to enhance the blurred effect of the sprays"* (L 1/14/24).

Notice the use of the same monochrome transfer that was employed on the yellow **1820 Bowl** pictured in the Cased Glass section. Six months before the Pittsburgh Exhibit write-up, another reviewer wrote: "Employing a similar fruit motif (to the yellow cased **1820 Bowl**) is another new line, in bright but soft colorings, giving the mellow effect of stained glass, or an underglazed print on the finest china. The fruit clusters are framed in gold bands" (J 6/14/23).

The "veiling," the "blurred outline," the "soft colorings" were created by etching the topside of the bowl from the double gold bands out to the edge, and then reverse painting the fruit on the backside. Afterwards, the entire backside of the bowl was spray-cased.

1211 Octagon Handled Sandwich —10"

(late 1920s)

1932: Available in crystal and colors.
1940: Discontinued.

Width 10½" (max.)

While this decoration feels Central European, I believe its ultimate origins lie in the Orient. Note the similarity of Westmoreland's design to the carved Chinese pheasants in a peony bush on this Ch'ing Dynasty Chinese temple screen.

The design delineation seems to have been provided by a monochrome transfer after which the bright colors were added. Then when the entire bottom side was spray-cased, the handle was left in a contrasting crystal.

Other octagonal sandwich trays can be found in the Cut Crystal section.

1849 Handled Sandwich — 10"

1849 Handled Sandwich first available between 1918 and 1924.

(c. 1927)

1849 was an item number for this, a 6" handled butter ball, and a 4½" lemon tray.

1932: All three available in crystal and colors.
1940: Discontinued.

Diameter: 9⅝"

I have seen this same friendly decoration on three other Westmoreland pieces. Notice the colors employed: They are identical to those used in the Spanish decoration at the beginning of this section. While the art work seems to suggest Pennsylvania Dutch design, this may just reflect their common German origin. All parts of Westmoreland's decoration appear to have been freehand-painted.

In 1925 New Martinsville advertised their No. 10 Sandwich Tray (L 2/16/25), that from the top-side appears to be identical to Westmoreland's **1849**, even to the facets below the stem ring. But underneath the New Martinsville's, there is a projecting foot ring in contrast to Westmoreland's, whose base is perfectly smooth. Fenton also used this design, but I believe only on their No. 318–7" butter ball. Fenton's butter ball lacks the faceting below the stem ring, and has, I believe, a projecting foot ring.

1820 Low Foot Comport — 9"

1820 line first available between 1918 and 1924.

(c. 1924)

Also available 11".

1820 was designated Westmoreland's **Flange** line.

1932: Available in crystal and colors.
1940: Discontinued.

Diameter: 9¼"

While the oxidized silver was applied to the top of the foot and the flanged rim, the cubist flowers were painted on the underside of the bowl. This decoration seems to have been one of several where Westmoreland used a monochrome transfer showing flowers or fruit growing out of a black ring. Their consistency and uniformity of spacing shows the black lines were not painted freehand.

This high-spirited memento of the "Roaring '20s" was Westmoreland's #41 decoration, and it was available from early in the decade. The bowl was photographed on a mirror in order to show the enameled side.

1801 Plates — 8"

**1801 Plates first
available in 1922
or earlier.**

(c. 1930)

1801 was designated a
Plain line.

Bottoms ground and
polished.

1932: Plates 6" to 14" available in crystal and colors;
14" also available in opal;
21" available in crystal
only.
1940: Seven sizes available
in crystal; four also available in opal.

Diameter: 8"
Foot: 5" o.d.

These reverse-painted fruits were designed and painted by Helen (Mrs. Chas) West. She painted them at home with special enamels supplied by the company. Afterwards, the plates were returned to the factory, sprayed with two cased colors each (the rim color, and then the white), gold-lined, and fired (probably more than once). The gold lining was the only part of the decoration not applied to the backside of the glass.

At one time several of us were each given two of these plates. But the importance of Helen West's painting goes beyond her family's interest. Her conception proved to be the basis of Westmoreland's #64 decoration — the only decoration that carried over into the post-World War II period. It seems also to have been the basis of a MacBeth Evans (division of Corning) decoration of the late '40s (WE 253).

(L 9/14/25)

Zodiac Plate — 9"

(1940s)

Also available 15".

1940: Both sizes available in crystal. 15" also available in opal for 76% more than crystal.

Small: 9" d.
Large: 14⅝" d.

Zodiac Plates introduced January 1934.

Westmoreland's **Zodiac Plates** (9" and 15") were first advertised in December 1933 and were then introduced at the Pittsburgh Exhibit a month later. Originally, they were all crystal and were all decorated from the backside in two of Westmoreland's lustre colors of champagne and steel blue. The plate pictured is the particularly rare 9" size, and because of its red center, it dates from the Brainard period. This red or ruby stain was used by Westmoreland in the early twentieth century, and then again from the 1940s on. While the plate pictured is unmarked, later Brainard period **Zodiac Plates** will bear a **WG** mark in the top center.

Robert Rupp, Westmore-land's general manager for many years, told me that few of these **Zodiac Plates** were made because the company could not sell them for enough to cover their decorating cost. Company records bear him out. In 1962, the same year Westmoreland sold 17,000 **Beaded Grape Milk Glass Honeys,** they sold just 107 — **15" Zodiac Plates,** and only 87 of them were decorated. Since the decorating cost was as high for the 9" as for the 15" plate, there is no record of a **9" Zodiac Plate** produced in the early 1960s.

While the mould for the 15" plate still survived at the factory in 1991, collectors may be pleased to know it was frozen fast with rust caused by a roof leak.

(L 12/33)

"Look up carnival glass, or taffeta glass in your antique book when it comes. I gather that it is prized by collectors and hard to find because it was a cheap grade of glass when made in the 1900 to 1925 period, given away as prizes in carnivals, with no pride-of-ownership connected with it. But the secret of its iridescence is said to have been lost and no one presently in the glass business can reproduce it. This is just the talk I overheard."

This paragraph is taken from a letter written in March 1964 by a Westmoreland manufacturer's representative to J.H. Brainard, Westmoreland's president at the time. What neither of these men realized was that Westmoreland had been a pioneer and a leading producer of this glass, which we now call "carnival," almost 60 years before.

In 1982 Wm Heacock wrote: *"For many years carnival glass collectors have considered most of this glass to have originated by the BIG FOUR — Northwood, Fenton, Imperial, and Millersburg.... It now appears we are dealing with the BIG SIX when it comes to carnival glass.... Dugan/Diamond... was clearly responsible for as much carnival glass production as each of the big four.... It appears conclu-sive that the Westmoreland Specialty Company... was ALSO a major manufacturer... with more than 35 patterns and novelties to their credit.... Other companies such as Cambridge, U.S. Glass, Indiana Glass, and Consolidated made limited contributions to the field, but nothing near the West-moreland total.... There has never really been any serious question that Westmore-land made carnival glass. The big surprise is that they made so much"* (HE).

Heacock then pointed out: *"A 1908 (Butler Bros., Westmoreland) assortment... shows an 'antique iridescent' group of items described as 'something entirely different.' Indeed this is the very FIRST example of car-nival glass to ever appear in ANY of the BB catalogues on record"* (HE). Two things are important here: First, if this glass was available in 1908, it had to have been first made no later than late 1907, after the summer break. And second, while several companies were selling their carnival through Butler Brothers by 1910, Westmore-land was the only one in 1908.

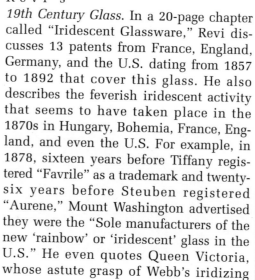

Edward G. Minnemeyer was Westmoreland's sales manager at about this time. Since he was the brother of Walter G., one of the founders of Dugan, Heacock has suggested Dugan could have influenced Westmoreland's carnival glass. Perhaps so. But while Edward did leave Westmoreland at the end of 1911 to team up with his broth at Dugan, he had worked for Gillinder in Philadelphia just before joining Westmoreland at the end of 1908. At the time he came, Westmoreland had already been making this glass for over a year. I think it is much more likely Dugan's carnival in 1912 was influenced by Westmoreland's carnival of 1911 and before, rather than the other way around.

If carnival — pressed iridized glass — is considered to date from 1907 (and I understand from researcher Berry Wiggins this date may be pushed back), blown iridized glass actually predates it by a full half-century. For those interest-ed in its fascinating history, I strongly recom-mend A.C. Revi's *19th Century Glass.* In a 20-page chapter called "Iridescent Glassware," Revi discusses 13 patents from France, England, Germany, and the U.S. dating from 1857 to 1892 that cover this glass. He also describes the feverish iridescent activity that seems to have taken place in the 1870s in Hungary, Bohemia, France, England, and even the U.S. For example, in 1878, sixteen years before Tiffany registered "Favrile" as a trademark and twenty-six years before Steuben registered "Aurene," Mount Washington advertised they were the "Sole manufacturers of the new 'rainbow' or 'iridescent' glass in the U.S." He even quotes Queen Victoria, whose astute grasp of Webb's iridizing treatments that same year should cause us to question our impression of her as the two-dimensional monarch portrayed by Lytton Strachey. The queen proved she could not be outglassed!

Revi's iridescent chapter points out two things that are important to us here. First, there are actually two forms of iridescence that have been seen on classical glass. There is incandescence, the one we usually think of, which was caused by surface deterioration over time. But there is also another, a "metal sheen" that was actually applied by the Romans to their glass. Several of Westmoreland's sprays have a metallic sheen, and though I understand it is not highly valued by carnival collectors, it certainly has a respectable pedigree. The second thing relevant to us is this: The iridescence seen in "Aurene" and various nineteenth century glasses is not something within the "metal" (molten glass) that is drawn out by heat, but is a metallic vapor or spray not unlike the sprayed coatings used by the carnival glassmakers about 1910. The conclusion I have drawn is, the difference between all of these glasses is only one of degree — not of kind. I have a particular fondness for one of the early matt finishes Westmoreland used, because out of all the carnival sprays I have seen, it seems to most closely resemble "Favrile." Perhaps the explanation is that both resulted from carefully applied, multiple sprayings, and the use of acid rather than alcohol as a vehicle. A further explanation has to be that these sprays were similar chemically.

From 1912 on, Westmoreland never again sold their iridized glassware in Butler Brothers, but Westmoreland continued to make this glass at least through 1927. Most of their late iridescence is extremely subtle and very hard to photograph. In 1916 a trade reporter wrote of Westmoreland's "'Rainbow,' a richly colored iridescent black glass" (J 8/13/16). Five months later, two trade publications mentioned Westmoreland's "Mother-of-Pearl," which was iridized opal (milk glass). While Westmoreland had iridized their opal earlier, the earlier iridescence is heavy and tends to hide the glass. Mother-of-Pearl, in contrast, is so light it is almost invisible at certain angles. When Westmoreland began to make and sell carnival again in 1976, their first revival glass resembled Mother-of-Pearl; in fact, it was given the name. But within a year of two, this name was being used for all of Westmoreland's neo-carnival — not just their iridized milk glass.

Westmoreland's iridized glass was mentioned by a reviewer of Westmoreland's display at the Pittsburgh Exhibit in 1924. Almost four years later another trade reporter wrote: "Then there is (Westmoreland's) iridescent tangerine line. This is quite as attractive as their... diamond optic.... There is also to be seen a range of pieces in iridescent French green (in addition to 'Rose Velva'). A number of items in these two lines are also featured with black glass bases" (J 9/8/27). In the '20s some of Westmoreland's finest glassware was iridized.

294 Sugar — 295 Cream (Crystal)

(c. 1910)

This antique-bronze treatment was described by Butler Brothers in 1910 as a "Verde green metallic finish — (an) exact copy of the high grade metallic. An art special...."

The sugar and cream set looks for all the world as if it had been made of metal; the outside suggests both the bronze statuary and the bronze door-lock escutcheons that were so popular at the time. Green, however, the color of well-oxidized copper, is an interesting element. The rich, uncorroded-looking gold-bronze of the bowls shows through the glass, for the sprayings were applied only to the outside. This finish may be an imitation of some of the bronze iridized glass of the 1880s.

This set was sold originally as a souvenir item from Effort, Pa. (1990 population, 800).

Filigree Sugar & Cream (Crystal)

Filigree line first made between 1905 and 1907.

(c. 1909)

Filigree was Westmoreland's original name for this line.

In addition to the name, Westmoreland also assigned numbers — but a different number for each item.

1904: Not listed.
1932: The lone survivor of this line was the **10 Filigree Tobacco Jar** available in crystal, color, and opal.
1940: Discontinued.

Sugar: 2½" h.

Butler Brothers was a catalog wholesaler that sold assortments of glass and china in barrel and case lots to retail stores. In Butler Brothers' 1908 catalog, this pictured sugar and cream set was included in Westmoreland's, "Filigree gold and silver decorated novelty assortment." Although shown there in crystal, this set was not one of the four or five **Filigree** items included in the important Westmoreland assortment of iridized glass in the same 1908 catalog, and therefore in its iridized form, it must date from 1909 or later.

Westmoreland's **Filigree** was a spirited parody of the real thing, which could be defined as a delicate tracery of gold or silver wires. This explains why Westmoreland's earliest **Filigree** pieces are most often found in crystal with the raised, filigreed patterns highlighted in gold or silver lustre. The form of this sugar and cream set is taken from a late nineteenth century china design, and I believe it is of Oriental derivation.

I have seen an almost identical pair of these photographed **Filigree Sugars** and **Creams,** also souvenir items, but with opalescent (white) rims. Press reports of January 1907 and January 1908 mention Westmoreland's souvenir items at the Pittsburgh Exhibit.

294 Sugar — 295 Cream (Amethyst)

294 Sugar — 295 Cream first available between 1905 and 1907.

(c. 1908)

294 and **295** were the original item numbers assigned to this sugar and cream.

1904: Not listed.
1932: By 1932 both sugar and cream were assigned the single number, **295**; they were available in crystal only.
1940: Discontinued.

Height: 2⅝"
Cream: 3" d.
Sugar: 3¼" d.
Feet: 1⅜" d.

This appears to have been Westmoreland's first sugar and cream set that was not part of a tableware line. It was one of the first of Westmoreland's items to use the "Chippendale" handle, and it was one of its first examples of iridized glass from late 1907.

Cooperative Flint made a sugar and cream similar to this: their No. 500. Cooperative Flint's proportions, though were substantially broader; their sugar was twice as wide as it was high. Later, around 1919 U.S. Glass made a sugar and cream that could be mistaken for Cooper-

ative Flint's, but with coarser handles.

In the 1908 Butler Bros. catalog, Westmoreland's **294/295 Sugar** and **Cream** was featured alone as an "Egyptian iridescent sugar & cream set. Egyptian design, gold lining, beautiful iridescent lustre surface." Unfortunately, the glass color was not mentioned. This set also made up two of the dozen items of the Westmoreland assortment in the same catalog described as "Antique Iridescent... something entirely different... a new departure in decorated crystal." In 1982 WM Heacock singled out this set as

"The first example of today's collectible carnival glass to appear in a 1908 Butler Brothers Catalogue" (HE).

The gold and silver iridescence in these bowls may have been an imitation of a decoration actually applied to glass by the Romans and not an imitation of surface deterioration over time. In the sugar and cream pictured, the color difference (one is silver; the other gold) was the result of a temperature difference in the glass. While both the sugar and cream were about 1,000° F when sprayed, the temperature of the gold sugar was slightly cooler than the silver cream.

"EGYPTIAN IRIDESCENT" SUGAR AND CREAM SET.

1C815—Diam. 3¼, ht. 3, double side handles Egyptian design, gold lining, beautiful iridescent luster surface. 3 sets in box.
Set, 18c

294 Sugar — 295 Cream (Crystal)

Benjamin Jacobs applied for a patent on an "ornamental glass dish" in January 1907, and his patent was granted a month later. However, it is not clear just what it was he had patented. His "glass dish" was a sugar bowl with six broad flutes or panels and square-topped handles. Simple, paneled glassware had been made off and on by a number of companies for about 75 years, and at that time it was referred to as "colonial." (Westmoreland, for example, had made a colonial-style tumbler in the 1890s: their **No. 6 Flute Soda**). As for the handle, Lenox China had been using that shape, which it had borrowed from silver, from at least 1902. In silver, the design, in wide-spread use by 1907, had been revived in the 1890s from silver of the neo-classical period of 100 years before.

Jacobs had been associated with Ohio Flint Glass in 1906, and with Jefferson Glass, evidently as early as 1907, for his "glass dish" became the basis of a new Jefferson tableware line that year. This line, which numbered over 400 pieces when it was sold to Central Glass in 1919, used both the square-topped handle and the broad panels pictured in the Jacobs patent. Whether Jefferson was the first company to use these handles in glass is less important than the fact that their 1907 line, which they called "the Chippendale," popularized them. Within a few years these handles were being used by every glass tableware maker in America, and throughout the industry they were known as "Chippendale" handles.

Westmoreland's first use of the handle could have been on this **294/295 Sugar** and **Cream**. It was first made by them in 1907 — or possibly even earlier. The sugar and cream set pictured, appears to be the one that was described in the 1908 Butler Brothers catalog as having a "gold lining" and an "iridescent lustre surface."

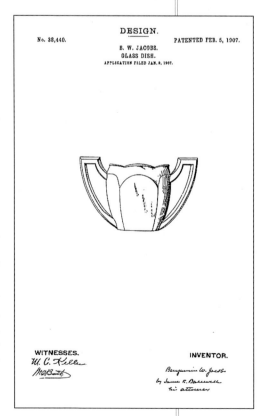

DESIGN.

No. 38,440.   PATENTED FEB. 5, 1907.

B. W. JACOBS.
GLASS DISH.
APPLICATION FILED JAN. 9, 1907.

WITNESSES.

INVENTOR.

Paneled Pattern Salad or Fruit Dish
Paneled Pattern Rose Bowl
(Turquoise)

Dish and Rose Bowl first made in 1910 or before.

(c. 1910)

"Paneled Pattern" was Butler Brothers' original description of this design.

Dish: 8¼" d.
Rose Bowl: 4" h.

Two pieces of evidence point to Westmoreland as the maker of this dish and rose bowl: glass color and inclusion of the dish in a Butler Brothers Westmoreland assortment. Let us look at each of these:

Color. In 1898 Westmoreland, along with much of the glassware industry, made a green glass that is often found decorated with gold lustre. Sometime before 1905, however, Westmoreland apparently discontinued that color. Around 1910 Westmoreland was making glass in a light blue color, but apparently only for its opalescent (opaque white-trimmed) glassware. This Westmoreland opalescent blue appears indistinguishable from the opalescent blues made by Northwood, Fenton, and perhaps others at the time. Westmoreland chose not to offer their iridized non-opalescent glass in the medium blue and green colors used by other companies, however. Instead, Westmoreland split the difference and came up with a blue-green, or turquoise color.

It was unusual, and the reason for its unusualness is not hard to understand: it was precisely this color that glassmakers were trying to get away from because it resembled glass made with iron impurities in the sand (see the **104 Pickle Jar** in the Colored Glass section). Dan Jenkins, Westmoreland's superintendent, must have put up with a lot of kidding from his counterparts in other companies when Westmoreland marketed this color. To my knowledge it was used around

1910 only by Westmoreland, used for only a few years, and used only for their iridized pieces. Westmoreland's iridized glass in this color often shows a particular depth and vitality.

Butler Brothers sold glassware and china in barrel and case lots, and each lot consisted of one or more complete assortments that were pictured in their catalogs. Since all lot shipments were made directly from a china or glass company, we know each assortment had to have been made by a single manufacturer. Today, this means we can be certain about an entire assortment if we can be certain about any single item in the assortment. In the case of Butler Brothers' Iridescent Salad or Fruit Dish Assortment, we can tie the Paneled Pattern dish to Westmoreland on the basis of both glass color and mould marks (discussed elsewhere in this section) found on several of the items in the assortment.

With the Paneled Pattern dish the foliage design is on the outside, in contrast to four of the other dishes in the assortment. This means the design was in the mould, not the plunger; and therefore, while this three-footed dish may be found in a variety of shapes, it will always have the same design.

The rose bowl pictured was made from the same mould as the Butler Brothers dish. Notice how the same 18 scallops around the rim of the Butler Brothers dish are shown compressed around the small 2⅛" opening of the rose bowl. While the lower portion and the three swirled feet are identical in both, notice how the compressed vine stems form arched panels in the upper half of the rose bowl. Notice how the sinuous design echoes the swirls of the feet. As the vine rises from the lower half of the rose bowl, the foliage becomes smoother and less detailed. The iridizing dramatizes this effect by changing from a complex and somber mix of colors to simple, light metallic gold toward the top. On the Butler Brothers dish, the silvery iridescence is on the inside — the smooth side.

Polka Dot Bowls — Crimped (Amber) (Amethyst)

Iridized & Crackled Glass

Polka Dot Bowls first made in 1909 or before.

(c. 1910)

"Polka Dot" was Butler Brothers' original name for this pattern.

Diameter: 8½" (max.)
Foot: 3" d.

In the preceding Butler Brothers assortment, two of the six bowls have a Polka Dot design. The difference is that one is crimped like the two photographed while the other is plain. Of the six assortment bowls, those with the Polka Dot design are the only ones I have not seen in Westmoreland's turquoise glass; the two photographed bowls are amber and amethyst. While the amber bowl shows a silver iridescence, the amethyst bowl shows combined gold and spectral treatments similar to those on the preceding rose bowl.

Fenton made two bowls that are similar. The name later given to these Fenton bowls, "Coin Dot," seems highly appropriate, for Fenton's dots are dull and flat-topped in contrast to Westmoreland's, which are domed and very shiny towards the center of the bowl. Though the more commonly seen of Fenton's two has a stippled surface, the other is smooth. The Fenton bowls have five or six circles of dots beyond the seven dots in the center whereas the Westmoreland bowl has seven.

There is just one part of these bowls that remains unworked after the glass is taken from the mould: the foot and the indented "ankle." Because of this, they are critical in identification. Both the Westmoreland Polka Dot bowl and the Fenton Coin Dot bowls share a nearly identical foot and ankle. But Fenton's foot measures 3⅛" across whereas Westmore-

land's measures 3". Also, while both show circumferential mould marks, or rings, around the outside of the feet, Fenton's bowls show two major vertical mould marks that come down to, and possibly past this ring, whereas Westmoreland's bowl shows five vertical mould marks in the ankle that end at the ring.

Today, it is always assumed that when several similar pieces of glass are found, Westmoreland must have been the imitator. Unfortunately, this is the high price all of Westmoreland has been made to pay for its later "Authentic Handmade Reproduction" era. George R. West was competitive; he had a particularly inventive mind. In his statements, his ads, and in family lore, he took almost fanatical pride in being an innovator. I believe for all West period glass, George West glass in particular, care should be taken before embracing some of these names ending in "variant" that have been assigned to Westmoreland's glassware.

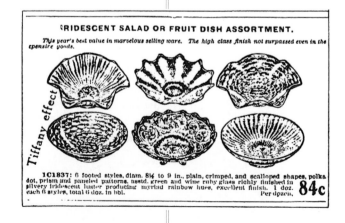

Polka Dot Bowl — Plain (Amethyst)
Peacock Optic Bowl — Scalloped (Opalescent)

**Peacock Optic first made
in 1908 or before.**

(c. 1909)

Peacock Optic was Westmoreland's original name for this pattern.

1932: The lone survivor of the **Peacock Optic** pattern was the **1801 Peacock Optic Plate** — 7½". Available in crystal and colors.
1940: Discontinued.

Polka Dot: 8⅜" d.
Peacock Optic: 8⅝" d.
Feet: 3" d.

This amethyst Polka Dot bowl differs from the preceding two in having a plain, rather than a crimped form, and in showing a third iridescent treatment: silver to gold; shiny to satin. Notice the deep, contrasting chromatic iridescence around the seven polka dots in the center. Four iridescent tones or treatments were used in this bowl.

The "scaling" on Westmoreland's **Peacock Optic Bowl** was in use more than a quarter of a century earlier. In 1874 a Wm Kirchner, assignor to Atterbury, patented a twin-compartment handled dish that pictured this pattern. While it was evidently the handled dish that was patented and not the pattern, the pattern was, in fact, in the original mould. Kirchner's scaling was flat — neither convex like Westmoreland's nor concave.

Notice the 24 identifying scallops around the rim of the **Peacock Optic Bowl.** With a simple substitution of plunger, this same bowl was sold with a wholly different design. This design (not shown) shares the same Art Nouveau feather motif of Westmoreland's **228** line of c.1902 and its **550** line of c.1910 (see the Tableware section). Unfortunately, this beautiful Westmoreland conception has been tagged with the "variant" suffix,

implying another maker's similar design came first. I believe there is no evidence to support this.

Both the **Peacock Optic** and the Art Nouveau feather-design bowls also share the same feet and mould marks. If a third bowl showing a different plunger design is found with these characteristics: 24 scallops on the rim, two vertical mould marks in the ankle, and a 3" diameter foot, then it was made from this same Westmoreland mould.

The **Peacock Optic Bowl** was made of opalescent (white-rimmed) glass. Opalescent glass was made in the same manner as traditional "opal," or milk glass, from a formulation containing bone ash or calcium phosphate. If a batch was super-saturated with phosphate, a rather gray and brittle opal resulted. (One of the early names for the opal was "bone glass.") If the amount of phosphate was reduced, a sort of "clam broth" glass resulted. But as Dwight Johnson, Westmoreland's glassmaker from 1965, pointed out, "phosphates follow heat." So, if a glass bowl with reduced phosphate was reheated in a "glory hole," the phosphate was drawn to the heat, creating a white rim leaving the rest of the bowl transparent. This was possible because the phosphate did not mix particularly well with the molten glass. I realize this theory contradicts numerous sources that refer to the change of color created by high temperature, but the proof of Dwight Johnson's assertion is this: the temperature in the glory hole is no greater than in the tank or furnace the opalescent glass first came from, and yet after selective reheating, this glass is transparent except for its opalescent portion. The phosphate did not change color; it was drawn to the heat.

Peacock Optic Finger Bowl & Plate (Amethyst)

In their 1909 catalog, Butler Brothers showed this **Peacock Optic Bowl** and **Plate** in a grouping which included Westmoreland's **"1" Shell Nappy** and their **252 Low Foot Comport,** both of which are pictured in this section. The bowl was described as, "IC 830, Finger Bowl — 4¾", deep shape, ground and polished bottom, green and wine ruby colors, rich reflecting optic design — facsimile of the hammered brass effects." The plate was described as, "IC 831 Plate — 6½", flat shape. Matches and can be used with IC 830 Finger Bowl." Wholesale price for the bowl was 84¢/dozen and for the plate 72¢/dozen. (1995: $13.50 and $11.60)

Despite Butler Brothers' mention of "green" (Westmoreland's turquoise), I have seen these pieces only in amethyst. The plates are less frequently seen today than the bowls.

(c. 1909)

Bowl and plate have ground and polished bottoms.

Bowl and plate were made from the same mould.

Finger Bowl: 4¾" d.
Plate: 6³⁄₁₆" d.
Feet: 2¼" o.d.

Daisy Bowl (Opal)

This Daisy Bowl was made from the same mould as the following Peach Bowl. Its blue opal color can be seen on some of the plates and mustard containers made in the pre-World War I period (see the Opaque Glass section). While it was not crimped, the rim appears to have been shaped giving it a slightly hexagonal shape.

This Daisy Bowl shares with the Peach Bowl a foot showing a peripheral mould mark at the outer edge. There are just two vertical mould marks in the ankle that stop at this mark. The foot measures 3" across, and the ankle, centered ⅜" above the bottom, measures 2⅝" across. If any bowl in question — new or old — shares these marks, measurements, and rim characteristics, consider it made from the same Westmoreland mould.

(c. 1910)

Diam: 8¼" (max.)

Peach Bowl — Crimped (Opal)
Peacock Optic Bowl — Crimped (Opalescent)

**Peach Bowl first made in
1909 or before.**

(c. 1910)

Peacock Optic: 8½" d.
(max.)
Peach Bowl: 9" d. (max.)
Feet: 3" d.

The Peach Bowl

In 1910 Butler Bros. included this bowl in a Westmoreland assortment describing it as a "Floral Design." We can be more specific, however: the design consists of peach blossoms and peach leaves. Westmoreland probably chose this glass and decoration to help carry out its peach (or peaches and cream) theme.

The Peach bowl was made of opal, or milk glass. Because of the bone ash that was used as a whitener then, the early formulation appears thin and slightly gray. Westmoreland seems to have been one of very few glassmakers that iridized milk glass, and they did this for a number of years. This bowl's iridized treatment predates Westmoreland's "Mother-of-Pearl" that is pictured in this section.

Notice the nine scallops on each of the six crimps separated by smooth sections of about 1⅛". While Fenton used a similar scalloped rim, Fenton's scalloping was continuous and not broken. Because of their rim divisions these Westmoreland bowls will seldom be found without six crimps. The crimping was not in the mould; it was done either free-hand, or in a press shortly before the

bowl was placed in the lehr for annealing and cooling.

There are at least five, and possibly six or more iridized bowls seen today that share this particular Westmoreland outer rim. Since the peach design in the pictured bowl is in the plunger, a new bowl design could be made up by merely making a new plunger or altering an old one.

The Peacock Optic Bowl

The **Peacock Optic Bowl** was supplied plain, or crimped as pictured here. Notice that a scallop was centered at each of the crimps. For this, the crimping had to be as precisely done as it was on the Peach Bowl.

Westmoreland did a great deal of early iridizing on opalescent blanks — usually crystal, but sometimes colored glass. I have seen this same bowl in a blue opalescent (a light-blue transparent glass with a white rim). Only the underside differed, for when viewed from the top, the blue did not show through the iridizing. The quality of the iridizing on this and on the preceding **Peacock Optic Bowl** would in my view allow them to be placed alongside almost anything in iridized glass.

252 Low Foot Comport — 6" (Turquoise)
Ribbed "Swung" Vases (Amethyst) (Turquoise)

**252 line introduced
between 1902 and 1904.
Ribbed design first available after 1904.**

(c. 1910)

252 was an original Westmoreland line designation.

1904: Westmoreland listed
15 items in their **252** line.
Westmoreland also listed
three swung vases, but this
ribbed design was not one
of them.

252: 6" d. (max.)
Left Vase: 8¾" h.
Right Vase: 9" h.

The 6" low foot comport in the center of the photograph is from Westmoreland's **252** line (see the Tableware
section); this comport may be the only
item in this line that was ever iridized.
Despite this comport's rich turquoise
color, the iridizing on this one is particularly inelegant. The **252** foot design suggests the "Egg and Dart" pattern found in
classical Greek architectural ornament.

The vases on the right and the left are
both certain Westmoreland because of the
turquoise color shown on the one. Both
were pressed from the same mould, and
both were called "swung" vases. They
were given this wonderfully descriptive
name because they were grabbed by their
bases while semi-molten, and swung in
an arc to lengthen them. In 1904 one of
Westmoreland's swung vases was offered
in lengths varying from 6" to 27". Though
the amount of glass used was evidently
the same, the longest cost nine times as
much as the shortest, reflecting the higher scrappage rates on the longer vases.

Both of the swung vases pictured
here have 3⅛" diameter feet. There are
three vertical mould marks visible in the
ankles that end at the peripheral mould
marks on the outside of the feet. What is
most important for identification is this:
there are twelve ribs or teardrops, alternately thick and thin, that begin just
above the ankle and protrude through the
top. The base is plain and sunken; there
is no star.

There is another swung vase that
could be confused with Westmoreland's,
but it has nine ribs all equal in size, and
the webbing between the ribs is expanded out. A third also bears a resemblance
to Westmoreland's, but this one has a
pressed star within its 3⅜" diameter foot.
I have seen a number of Westmoreland
vases shaped like the one on the left. All
but one was amethyst and the remaining
one was turquoise. All shared the same
interesting metallic iridizing — deep, and
yet glossy. The somber amethyst color
seems to do it particular justice.

Ribbed Flat Spoon (Amber)

(c. 1910)

Width: 9" (max.)

Early in the century Westmoreland used the terms "banana stands," "fruit stands," and "fruit baskets" for its folded bowls, but they were all on pedestals. Westmoreland used the terms "ovals," "oblongs," "pickles," and "flat celeries" for its folded bowls, not on pedestals, but with raised ends. I found only one example of a simple folded bowl not on a pedestal in several early catalogs, and Westmoreland referred to it as a "flat spoon."

While several similar folded bowls were made by other manufacturers, this is a certain Westmoreland piece. It was pressed in the same mould as the preceding two vases, but unlike them it was not swung. It shares the same 3⅛" foot, the same three vertical mould marks in the ankle, and the same 12 teardrops that are alternately thick and thin.

Reeded Crimped Bowl (Turquoise)

(c. 1910)

This bowl shows the importance of iridizing. It would be identical to the bowl pictured on the next page, except that it was treated with a silver iridescence instead of the more common chromatic iridescence used on that bowl.

Another very similar reeded-ray design can be found as one alternative to the peach design on the scalloped-edge bowl shown earlier in this section. This design change was achieved through the substitution of a plunger with a reeded design for the one with the peach motif. But this plunger was not the same as the one used here. There are 54 reeded rays (rather than 48) in the design of the scalloped-edge bowl, and its reeding softens as it approaches the center.

Reeded Crimped Bowl (Turquoise)

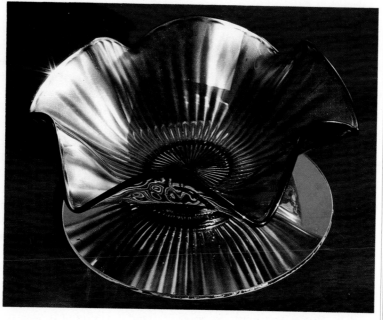

Reeded Bowls first made in 1909 or before.

(c. 1910)

Made from same mould as the Polka Dot Bowls.

Diameter 8¾" (max.)

In their "Special Iridescent Glassware Ass't" of 1910, Butler Bros. showed two Westmoreland Polka Dot bowls and two Westmoreland reeded bowls. One of each was plain and the other was crimped. Most important, all four were made from the same mould. All four shared a 3" diameter foot, ringed with a mould mark around the outside, and five vertical mould marks in the ankle just above this mark. While these bowls were available in two very different designs, the design was in the plunger — not the mould, and so a simple change of plunger made possible this entirely new design.

Several companies made reeded bowls that look almost the same. The photographed bowl can be positively identified as Westmoreland's, however, because of its turquoise color and the detail of its foot and ankle. This reeded bowl has a smooth rim that extends just ⅛" beyond the reeding. There are exactly 48 reeded rays and they seem to sharpen as they come together at the center of the bowl.

There is a bowl in a conventional green color that is very similar to this. Its foot resembles Westmoreland's, but it measures 3³⁄₁₆" across. It has just two vertical mould marks and they begin under the foot and extend up into the bowl area. The side of its foot is smooth, showing it was made very differently with a joint mould rather than a shell mould. There are 53 reeded rays, and the rim beyond

them is about ¼" wide. While the glass itself is rather crude, the iridescence is exceptional. Without such a detailed examination, this bowl (its color aside) could be mistaken for Westmoreland's. I know — I bought one by mistake.

SPECIAL IRIDESCENT GLASSWARE ASST.

This new special price means a saving of about 33⅓% to you. You can't duplicate elsewhere.

1C1597: Asstd. shapes, allover golden and silvered iridescent blends, rib, prism and floral designs.
4 doz. salads, average 8 in.
1 doz. 5¾ in. footed jelly dishes.
1 doz. 6½ in. high comports.
6 doz. in bbl.

78c

Doz.

Footed Jelly Dish (Amethyst)

Iridized stem pieces first made in 1909 or before.

(c. 1910)

"Footed jelly dish" appears to be Butler Brothers' original designation of this stemmed piece.

Height: 5¼"
Width: 5½" (max.)
Foot: 3⅛" d.

The Butler Brothers "Special Iridized Glassware Ass't" of 1910 showed four iridized Westmoreland stemmed pieces.

While the one pictured was treated with a silver iridescence, another I own is chromatic. I prefer the one pictured, for against the somber amethyst glass, the silver iridescence has more vitality. Both show a beautiful satin finish at the outer edge.

The interesting flared and paneled stem was probably borrowed from fine, cut stemware of the nineteenth century. While it is simply a baluster shape with faceting, I have not found an antecedent for it so far. Westmoreland used this faceted stem on seven of its goblets and wine glasses from the turn of the century; the shape was also suggested on Westmoreland's **1012 Candlestick** shaft (see the Cut Candlestick section). I do not believe it was used by any other pressed glassmaker in this period.

Footed Jelly Dish (Opalescent)

(c. 1910)

"Footed jelly dish" appears to be Butler Brothers' original designation of this stemmed piece.

Height: 5"
Width: 5¼" (max.)
Foot: 3⅛" d.

This Polka Dot pattern jelly dish is crystal, opalescent, with a silvery-amber iridescence. Notice that it combines a six-pointed star with a conventional six-sided stem.

This is one of the four Westmoreland stemmed pieces shown by Butler Brothers in their 1910 "Special Iridized Glassware Ass't."

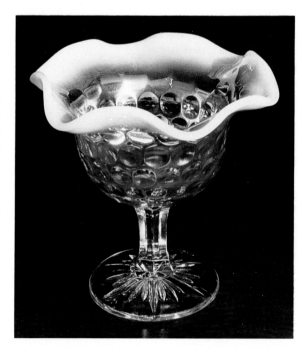

High Comport (Amber)

I have seen this comport in turquoise and amethyst as well as amber; my first choice is the amber because of the way it seems to suggest a volcanic fire. The silver iridescence has the depth and the satiny look I have come to associate with early multiple spraying.

There are a great many early stemmed carnival pieces, and I have found very few are Westmoreland's. Three of the four Westmoreland stemmed pieces in Butler Brothers' nine-piece assortment have six-pointed pressed stars, and the fourth has a faceted bulbous stem. Westmoreland may have been the only maker to use either of these devices on their iridized stemmed pieces, and if so, the presence of one or the other can serve as a Westmoreland indicator.

The sides of this comport show interesting pressed swirls with six short and six tall leaves around the outside. I believe the leaves are those of the prickly acanthus, so frequently portrayed by the ancient Greeks and Romans. Was this

part of Westmoreland's effort to build a connection between this little iridized dish and the glass of the ancients? I sense the presence of George West here just as I do with the "peaches and cream"-decorated Peach Bowl in this section.

(c. 1910)

"High comport" appears to be Butler Brothers' original designation of this piece.

Height: 5½"
Width: 6¼" (max.)
Foot: 3¼" d.

"1" Shell Nappy — 6" Shell — 4" (Turquoise)

These two turquoise shells were decorated with the same underwhelming iridescence that was used in the **252 Bowl** shown earlier; their turquoise color ties them to the c. 1910 period.

Since the 6" Shell Nappy was made continuously from the turn-of-the-

century, it is far more frequently seen than the 4" Shell. Early 6" Shell Nappies can be distinguished by the 1¼" ground "punties" located between their three tapered feet. These flat areas were eliminated when a new mould was made in the '30s, or possibly before. For some reason the c. 1910 4" Shell does not show this flat spot. In common with so many Westmoreland carnival pieces from around 1910, the 4" Shell is neither listed in any of my price lists nor shown in any of my catalogs.

"1" 6" Shell Nappy first available between 1902 and 1904. 4" Shell available only c. 1910.

(c. 1910)

"1" was an item number assigned to the 6" Shell Nappy, and perhaps to the 4" size as well.

1904: 6" Shell Nappy listed under both "Misc. Ware" and "Opal Novelties" (i.e., available in crystal and opal, and possible in colors).
1932: 6" Shell Nappy available in crystal, colors, and opal. 1940: 6" Shell Nappy available in crystal and opal. Opal was lined out in 1941. In 1952 the 6" Shell was available in milk glass.

6": 5¾" w.
4": 3⅞" w.

167

"1" Shell Nappy — 6"
1001 Candlesticks (Crystal)

1932: **1001 Candlestick**
available in crystal and
colors.
1940: **1001 Candlestick**
discontinued.

Shell: 5¾" w.
1001: 1½" h.
3⅞" d.

1001 Candlestick first available between 1918 and 1924.

This is not a console set. The pieces were photographed together because they show the same iridizing; and what is equally important, they are all amber-stained crystal. On a stained piece there is usually some portion through which you can sight and see clear glass.

At least seven other glass companies made low spool-shaped candlesticks in the mid- to late-'20s, and it may be next to impossible to tell them apart. Fortunately, Westmoreland's **1001** was one of the decorated pieces shown in an Irving Cut Glass catalog of the '20s. It can be identified because Irving retained Westmoreland's number.

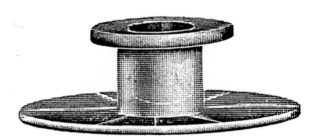

Basketweave Mustard Cream
Basketweave Tub

Mustard Cream pre-dates mid-1915.

(c. 1912)

Tub: 8½" h.

"Three new colors have just been created by the technical department of the Westmoreland factory. These are known as burgundy, champagne, and steel blue. The first is a rich red. The second, as might be imagined a pale straw color with an iridescent lustre; while the third likewise suggests its name" (P 6/20/18).

The color on these two pictured crystal pieces is not amber, but Westmoreland's "champagne lustre." We are faced with two difficulties here. First, the tub, vase, or lidless cookie jar should be part of a line, and yet such a line was never shown in any Westmoreland catalog. And second, while the cream on the left appears to be a lidless Westmoreland mustard cream, Westmoreland had shut down its mustard operations three years prior to this press announcement. My tentative conclusion is that the tub was one of several pieces in a short-lived Westmoreland mini-line (BM 108B), and not connected to Indiana/Greentown's "Cat in a Basket"

(FF 45), despite the similar triangular rim of Westmoreland's cream. The cream, which is Westmoreland's, was, I believe, a mustard cream stained and iridized in 1915 or before. Despite the press report quoted, there are simply too many instances where press reports heralded something as "new" that had been in prior use. More than likely "new" meant only, exhibited for the first time at the Pittsburgh Show where few mustard containers would have been displayed. More Westmoreland lustre-stained glass can be found in the Miscellaneous section. For a discussion of Westmoreland's basketweave pattern, see the Opaque Glass section.

Four Iridized Mustard Creams:

"6" Peacock (Amethyst)

Victor (Turquoise)

Basketweave (Crystal with Champagne or Smoke Lustre)

Mustard Creams and Sugars all predate mid-1915.

(c. 1912)

"6" is the number the company used for their reissued **Peacock Sugars** and **Creams.**

Victor was an original Westmoreland name.

1932: Not listed.
1940: **"6" Peacock Sugar** and **Cream** available in opal only.

"Down-Easters" notwithstanding, **Victor** is an original Westmoreland design that appears to date from 1893 (see the Tableware section). In the 1890s, the **Victor** crystal sugar and cream plus a covered spoon and a covered butter were used for mustard packaging (LVG 236); they were among Westmoreland's first mustard containers. Later, the sugar and cream were made in transparent colors and iridized; the lids, however, were rarely, if ever, iridized. The turquoise color pictured, suggests a date close to 1910 for the **Victor Cream.**

Two of these mustard creams were made of colored glass: amethyst and turquoise, and two were lustre-stained: champagne and a smoke color I will not try to identify. The two stained creams are certain Westmoreland because of the basket crosses on their bottoms, and because of that frustrating finial on the surviving lid. This finial or knob was shaped the way it was so the lid would slip out of a simple block mould as easily as it later would out of a diner's fingers. There were two styles of these slippery knobs: one was smooth and tapered, and the other, shown here, was reeded on the sides and crowned on the top.

Victor

The turquoise cream on the right is from Westmoreland's **Victor** line. The claims of the Canadians and the

Peacock

Even if the maker of that amethyst Peacock Cream on the left were unknown, the evidence would point to Westmoreland. The top rim was taken from that row of "eyeballs" on Westmoreland's **Victor Cream.** The reeded spout, the ankle paneling, and the stippling were all borrowed from the **Victor** line as well.

In their 1953 Reproductions catalog, the Brainards pictured this set in milk glass and wrote, "Originally made in the 1890s. Made only in limited editions." But this sugar and cream had been listed in their 1940 price list and shown in their comprehensive 1952 catalog. The Chippendale handle establishes a probable introductory date of 1907 or later. This Peacock Sugar and Cream has been reproduced in modern carnival, possibly as early as the late 1970s.

Benj. Bennett's Elite Bowl (Wisteria)

Elite line patent filed Oct. 1895. Wisteria glass available in 1916.

(unknown.)

Elite was the original Westmoreland name for this line.

Patent 25194 granted 2/25/96 to Benj. Bennett for 3½ years.

1904: 52 **Elite** pieces listed
1932: Discontinued.
1940: Discontinued.

Diameter: 8" (max.)

"The new Elite, a complete line containing the pattern of the handsome jug and tumblers of the name put upon the market last year, has now grown to a set of 106 pieces and embodies the star and rounded bead line or pillar, modified or pinched in so as to encompass the star and reflect the light in the pattern very strongly. The fan shaped, radiating incuts finish off the figure and make it one that will remain in favor a long time... " (L 1/13/97).

Apparently so, for fully eight years later Fostoria introduced their 1333 line (named "Sydney" in 1906) that could be confused with this. Fostoria's diamond figure is broken into smaller diamonds, and these are in turn further subdivided.

This bowl appears to have been made from the **Elite Sugar Bowl** mould. The sugar bowl was one of the few **Elite** pieces with just five rays rather than the usual seven or nine. It was also one of the few with a plain area above the rays, and the only one of these to have a lid ledge and no handle. (There were two **Elite Sugars,** and both probably shared the same mould.)

Westmoreland's **77 Hobnail** line as well as one of Westmoreland's Wool-

worth lines had bowls with lazy, undulating outer rims and sharp breaks just in from these rims. Both of these lines, however, dated from the late '20s. This carnival bowl shares these same two characteristics, but here they resulted from necessity — not style: The bowl's decorative sharp break is the lid ledge of the **Elite Sugar Bowl.**

Wisteria is a very pale amethyst color.

1776 Colonial Tall Sweetmeat — Roll Edge
1700 Colonial High Foot Handled Compotier
(Amethyst)

**1776 line introduced Jan.
1911. 1776 Sweetmeat first
available between 1913
and 1917. 1700 line introduced Jan. 1912. 1700
Compotier first available
in 1912.**

(c. 1914)

1776 and **1700** were two of
Westmoreland's six colo-
nial lines.

Both pieces **"Keystone-W"**
marked.

1776: 7" h.
1700: 6½" h. (at handles)

Both of these stemmed pieces were made shortly after Westmoreland's Butler Brothers carnival period that ended in 1912. Both were made of the same deep amethyst glass, and both were iridized with the same thin spectral spray. While they are both marked colonial pieces, they are from two different colonial lines.

The **1700 Compotier** pictured is the very one pictured by Heacock in 1982 (HI). He wrote it had been shown at an ACGA convention, and he pointed out its Westmoreland mark, claiming it was "The only trade marked example of Westmoreland carnival known." This was no doubt true in 1982.

The compotier is pictured in crystal in the Cut Crystal section. There, the relationship between Westmoreland's **1700 Colonial** line and Jefferson's Chippendale line is discussed as well as the use of Westmoreland's **Paul Revere Colonial** handles on this compotier.

The **1776 Sweetmeat** is pictured again in the Colored Glass section. There, the amethyst color and its replacement with Wisteria in 1916 is discussed.

1865 Bowl — 9½" (Crystal)

1865 Bowls first available between 1918 and 1921.

"(Westmoreland's) *latest creation is a most artistic showing of fancy glassware in French gray finish. This being accomplished by a hand process* (i.e., spraying) *which makes it very much softer and more pleasing in appearance than a sand blast…. It is further ornamented by the application of gold and enamels*" (P 3/21/18).

(1918)

1865 Bowl also available 10½" — straight sided.

1865 was the item number assigned just to these two bowls.

"Keystone – W" marked.

Ground and polished bottom.

1932: Available in crystal and colors.
1940: Discontinued.

Diameter: 9⅜"
Foot: 2⅜" d.

While the gray-sprayed cased lustre was applied to the bottom of the bowl, the iridizing was applied to the top. The edge was etched before the gold was applied, and the gold was applied both to the top and to the underside (as it usually was in Westmoreland's gold-decorated glass) to allow for wear. The particular etched and "coin gold"-covered band is a Westmoreland design, used during the World War I period.

1867 Urn & Cover (Crystal)

1867 Urn probably first available in 1918.

This covered urn shares the same "coin gold" etched band design with the preceding **1865 Bowl**; this dates it to the World War I era. It was spray-cased (a fused glass coating) in green under the foot and lid and inside the urn. Unfortunately, the subtle iridizing applied to the outside is not really visible in the photograph.

This same lid was used on the **1800 Rose Jar & Cover** (see the Cut Stained section) and on the **1823 Comport & Cover** (see the Gold & Silver section).

(c. 1918)

1867 was an item number used solely for this urn.

1932: Available in crystal only.
1940: Discontinued.

Urn & Cover: 11" h.

173

1700 Colonial Candy Jar — 1 Lb. (Opal)

1700 Candy Jar probably first available in 1917. "Mother-of-Pearl" introduced Jan. 1917.

(1917)

Also available in ½, 2 & 3 lb. sizes.

1932: All four sizes available in crystal only. 1940: 1 lb. size available in crystal only, then discontinued. In 1975 reissued in milk glass.

Height: 8"

"(Westmoreland's) principal feature is the 'mother-of-pearl' line, which is shown plain and in gold and silver raised decorations, the burnished gold treatment being a distinct novelty" (J 1/11/17).

"(Westmoreland's) latest novelty… is a striking decoration in a solid color covering the glassware, giving an almost perfect effect of a pearl oyster shell. The brilliant pearly iridescent coloring has been produced in all its natural beauty and richness. The new color is certainly the finest ever brought out by the concern" (P 1/11/17).

Westmoreland's "Mother-of-Pearl" followed by one year their "Tortoise Shell" and their "Rainbow" — "a richly colored iridescent black glass." While

Westmoreland, Fenton, and perhaps others had iridized opal glass for some years (see the Peach Bowl in this section), this may be the first use of a light iridescence directly on a white opal blank. Later, in the early '20s, Fostoria used this same term for some or all of their iridized glass. Much later, in 1975 Westmoreland used it again for the modern carnival they brought out that year.

The Geo. Borgfeldt ad of February 1917 shows a Westmoreland **23 Bowl**, a Westmoreland **1031 Bowl Stand**, a Westmoreland **1850 Flower Block**, and a Westmoreland bird. Westmoreland and Borgfeldt seemed to have had a long-standing relationship during the West period; Westmoreland made candy containers for Borgfeldt using Borgfeldt's moulds. R.B. Reineck, Westmoreland's sales manager from 1912 to 1928, had earlier been employed at Borgfeldt.

(P 2/8/17)

1023 Candlestick — 7" (Crystal)

1023 Candlesticks first available between 1913 and 1917.

This **1023 Candlestick** was amber-stained, and then iridized. I have seen a number of pieces of Westmoreland's that were amber-stained in the period just before late 1924 when amber glass was brought back. In the case of Westmoreland's engraved glass, however, amber and amber-yellow staining continued to the end of the West period.

While the candlestick pictured is Westmoreland's **1023,** there are four others that could be confused with this one. For a detailed comparison, see the Cut Candlestick section.

For a detailed comparison, see the Cut Candlestick section.

Iridized & Crackled Glass

(early 1920s)

Also available 9" (hollow) & 12" (solid) in 1924 or before.

Resembles the **1025 Card Holder,** first made in 1913.

A similar **1009 Candlestick** first available in 1912 or before.

1932: 7", 9" & 12" available in crystal only. **1023** was Westmoreland's lowest-priced 7" candlestick in 1932.
1940: Discontinued. However, the 7" was evidently reissued in the late Brainard period in etched, colored glass.

Height: 7¼"

? – 1043 Candlestick — 8" — Hollow Bottom

Is this candlestick Westmoreland's **1043** (hollow bottom) candlestick or Fenton's No. 449? They were both based on a silver design of the period. Note the indent that would have been a soldered joint in the silver original. While the feeling is neo-classical, I believe the silver prototype was actually an early twentieth century design that combined elements of two earlier periods.

While the blue color in the pictured candlestick could be Fenton's, it is an exact match for the blue used by West-moreland from late 1924 to 1929. The iridizing could be by either company. The faceting, carried down to the "solder connection," suggests Westmoreland because it remains sharp right to the break as it does in known Westmoreland solid bottom candlesticks. This faceting seems to become rounded about an inch above the break in Fenton's No. 449 candlesticks. At the time of this writing, however, I am prepared to concede the candlestick to Fenton for one reason: Westmoreland's 1932 price list shows that the **1043** candlestick was available only in crystal that year. It is possible, but unlikely, that this candlestick was available in colors in the late '20s — but not in 1932.

Northwood's No. 696 has often been compared to this candlestick. But Northwood's shows a very pronounced knob just above the break, and it has somewhat huskier proportions. Indiana and Lancaster also made candlesticks along these lines, but their candlesticks had raised hollow bases.

1043 Candlestick first available between 1918 and 1924.

(1924 – 1929)

1043 available 8" only.

1034 is almost identical, but had a solid base and came 8", 9" & 11".

1932: **1043** available in crystal only.
1940: Discontinued.

Height: 8¾"

1700/2 Colonial Urn — Crimped
1038 Spiral Candlesticks — 9"

(c. 1923)

1038 Candlestick also available 11" & 12".

1700 Urn available in four sizes.

1932: Urn discontinued. 9" and 12" candlesticks available in crystal only. 1940: Both discontinued.

1038: 9⅜" h.
Urn: 7¼" h.

1700 Urns probably first available 1917. 1038 Candlesticks first advertised in 1922.

This magnificent set has almost everything: etching, gilding, staining, enameling, and — what is important to us here — iridizing on the stained amber surfaces. Because of its decoration, the set is also pictured in the Flower section.

Westmoreland's **1700 Urns** were made from the paneled urn bases of the **1700 Candy Jars.** Their rims were flared and crimped.

1841 High Foot Comport — 6½" (Crystal)

1841 Comports first available between 1918 and 1924.

(late 1920s)

In 1924 available 5½" and 8".

From 1926, available 5½", 6½", and 9".

1841 was an item number assigned just to these comports.

Height: 6⅝"
Diameter: 5⅛"
Stem/bowl: 1⅝" d.

In the art world there is no such thing as "Handsome is as handsome does." Reasonable or not, an object's aesthetic worth ascends as its utility declines. (Even among classic car enthusiasts, *Ultima Thule* is when the driver is seated directly over the axle — the rear axle!) Given that, this little comport, sold to me as Steuben, has to be taken very seriously, indeed: It is totally useless.

Besides its Westmoreland iridescence, it has Westmoreland's "Transparent Rose" sprayed casing of 1927, and there is that tell-tale mould mark on the stem. Because the foot was formed with a paddle, or "battledore," this mould mark veers off before ending at the top of the foot. This is typical of Westmoreland's stem pieces.

Notice the similarity of the engraved urn to the **1705 Candy Jar** in the Gold & Silver section. Notice the similarity of the fern or palm leaves to those on the **1900 Bell Bowl** at the end of the Cut Stained section.

300 Square Foot Vase — 10" (Crystal)

(c. 1929)

Also available 8".

Also available with lids as 12" & 15" covered urns in 1932.

The vase and the urn minus its lid are identical (unlike the **1800 Vase** and **Rose Jar**).

Waterford was the original Westmoreland name of the **300** tableware line.

1932: Both vases and both urns available in crystal and colors. The 10" vase and the 15" urn also available in opal.
1940: The 10" vase and the 15" urn available in crystal and opal. Opal costs just 14% more than crystal. In 1952 both vases and urns available in crystal, crystal trimmed with ruby, and milk glass.

Height: 10"
Weight: 3½ lb.

300 Covered Jar first available in 1927.

"The name 'Waterford,' when applied to glass, immediately brings to mind the beauty and charm found in wares of this kind… (Westmoreland's Waterford) *line is offered in combinations of crystal and amber and crystal and black, and may be had in rose, green, or plain crystal"* (L 9/30).

"All pieces (of the Waterford line) *have the square foot which has been quite popular"* (L 1/31).

Before launching their **300 Waterford** line in 1930, Westmoreland offered just their **300 Covered Jar** and this **300 Vase** (the same thing without the lid) three years before. In January 1927 (JC 1/14/27), a New York importer advertised a very similar jar which it called a "Waterford Sweetmeat Jar." It would be interesting to learn who made this jar, for Waterford had been out of business since 1851. But "Waterford" was one of those magical names that were "in the air" then — like "Chippendale," "Colonial," and "Sandwich."

The stain on the **Waterford Vase** pictured is not amber, but Westmoreland's champagne lustre.

"23" Bowl — 8½"
1031/2 Stand — 5"

"23" Bowl — 8½" first available between 1913 and 1917. 1031 Stands first available between 1913 and 1917.

(1920s)

"23" was an item number assigned just to this bowl.

Ground and polished bottom, cut stem.

1932: **"23" Bowl:** 8½" discontinued. 10" available in crystal and colors. **1031 Stands** available in crystal and colors.
1940: All discontinued.

Bowl: 8" d.

The worn iridizing, not visible in the photograph, is on the upper-side of the pictured bowl. The decorative cased lines on the underside may be Westmoreland's "Cloisonné" described by the contemporary press as being a Mosaic pattern (P 6/28/23) (J 6/14/23). Notice the immense cut star — free-cut, and not cut on a pressed outline.

The 8½" **"23" Bowl** pictured is identical to the 8½" **1808 Flower Bowl** except for the lower groove in the **"23"**. Both measure 8" across the top, 4½" across the base, and both are 3¼" tall. This is the

sort of difference that ordinarily points to two makers, for the two bowls required two entirely different moulds. While the plain **1808 Flower Bowl** was made in a simple block mould, the grooved **"23" Bowl** would have required a compound shell mould. The 1917 Borgfeldt "Mother-of-Pearl" ad shown earlier in this section pictures this **"23" Flower Bowl** (with a groove). Through 1927 the **"23" Bowl** was available only in the 8½" size; however, by 1932 it had been replaced by a 10" **"23" Bowl** (see the Flower section).

1900/1 Bell Bowl — 9½"

(late 1920s)

1900 was designated a **Plain** line.

1900/1 also available as a 10" roll edge bowl & a 10½" flared bowl.

The **1900/1 Bell Bowl — 9½"** is nearly identical to the **1865 Bell Bowl — 9½"** — but it has a wider, deeper foot.

Three comparable **1900/2 Bowls** had a 2" wider rim and a ¼" wider foot.

1932: All **1900 Bowls** available in crystal and colors. 1940: Discontinued.

Diameter: 9⅞"
Foot: 3" d.

1900/1 Bowls first available between 1918 and 1924.

The iridizing on the underside of this Westmoreland bowl can be clearly seen; the etching is on the top. Westmoreland was one of comparatively few that iridized their most important glass in the '20s and perhaps even the '30s, and this seems to be a Westmoreland iridized treatment.

The purpose of the "hockey-puck" foot was to enable the bowl to slip out of a simple block mould. With this mould there is no visible mould mark.

The only mark was left at the rim of the bowl where it was fire-polished away.

1865 Bowl — 9½" (Dark Green)

(c. 1922)

"Keystone – W" marked.

Ground and polished bottom.

Diameter: 9⅛"
Foot: 2⅜" d.

1865 Bowls first available between 1918 and 1921. Dark green glass introduced January 1922.

Dark green and ruby are two of the three colors Westmoreland introduced at the Pittsburgh Exhibit in January 1922.

(L 9/19/21)

"Another new offering (from Westmoreland) *is crackled lustre flower bowls… "* (L 1/10/21).

"(In Westmoreland's display) *in solid colorings there is an attractive ruby, including bowls, plates, and candlesticks in attractive shapes and sizes. There is also a dark green line of bowls, plates, and candlesticks"* (L 1/16/22).

750 Basket — 5" (Crystal)

750 Baskets probably first available January 1921. Crackle introduced January 1921. Champagne lustre introduced June 1918.

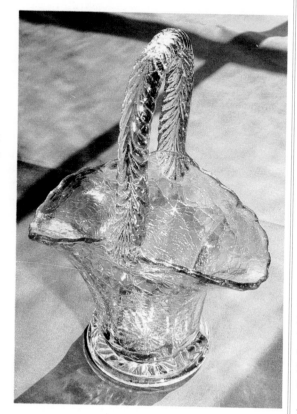

"(In Westmoreland's display) *There are three to four sizes for each variety of basket — of crackled lustre, covered etching, plain lustre, Carrara, and others"* (L 1/10/21).

(c. 1922)

Also available 3", 4", 6", 7" & 8".

750 was an item number assigned just to these six baskets.

1932: 3" to 6" available in crystal and colors. 7" & 8" available in crystal only. 1940: 3" to 6" available in crystal only (an opal option for the 6" was written in then lined out). It was offered again in 1977 with ruby staining and a painted or decal decoration.

Basket: 5" h.
With handle: 8¾" h.

Crackled glass is included here, because like iridized glass it is related to what we call "stretch." In his book *Stretch in Color,* Berry Wiggins wrote, "Stretch is the iridescence that has come apart at the edges, or sometimes all over the piece... " Similarly, crackled glass, or "crizzled" as Westmoreland's workmen used to call it, is glass whose outer surface has come apart — "all over the piece." Robert Jones, first employed at Westmoreland in 1924, told me it was made by quickly and violently water-quenching hot glass. The surface of the glass, contracted by the water, shrank and opened up tiny fissures that were then joined by reheating. Westmoreland made crackled glass at least from late 1920 to late 1924, when it was superseded by "Mould Crackle," first advertised in September 1924 (L 9/22/24).

The crystal basket pictured was decorated with champagne iridescent lustre.

For a comparison between this basket and a similar one by Duncan & Miller, see the Cased Glass section.

181

A great deal of silver and gold was used on Westmoreland glass during the West period. While gold was largely restricted to ornamental accents much like the striping on cars of the period, silver usually played a major part — sometimes the only part — in the decoration. Let us examine these two decorative metals separately.

Encrusted Gold

Gold encrustation was usually referred to as "coin gold" — apparently not so much because of the cachet of "coin silver," but because of the alleged practice of glass and pottery makers of throwing gold coins into *aqua regia*. Aqua regia was a combination of acids that was capable of dissolving gold and turning it into a brown precipitate that settled at the bottom of the tank. The gold, or more precisely gold oxide, was combined with mercury, mixed with a flux and oil, and then painted onto a glass blank. It was typically applied to the top and backside of a rim that had been plate-etched beforehand (see the Etched Glass section). The gilded glass was then heated to about 1,000° F in a muffle (a small decorating kiln) that fused the gold and burned off the oil and mercury. In 1900 the press reported that two kilns for burning gold onto glassware had recently been installed at Westmoreland (JD 12/28/00).

The term "coin gold" was restricted to the matt-finish gold used throughout the industry from about 1915 to the late '30s and beyond. The bright, shiny metallic gold used prior to 1915 and again from the late '30s on, was known as "lustre gold."

Gold on china is overglaze, and therefore equally unprotected from wear; nevertheless, it is far more durable than gold on glass. I believe this is because of the greater porosity of china.

Silver Deposit

Glassware has been "mounted" with silver for centuries, but from the 1880s on, most of glassware's decorative silver has been "silver deposit" — that is, electroplated silver. The plating was prepared by first painting a fluxed-silver precipitate onto a glass blank and then firing the blank. This process was identical to the process of fusing coin gold to glass, and the matt appearance of the coated silver can be said to resemble matt gold as well. In a few cases, Westmoreland's silver decorations stopped at this stage, but in the vast majority of cases this process was only the first step in electroplating. In order for the glass to be plated, a wire connected to an electrical terminal had to be attached to the fused-silver coating, after which the glass was suspended in a plating tank containing silver cyanide. When an electric current was passed between the glass and a silver bar, also suspended in this solution, atoms of silver were transferred through this silver cyanide to the coated portion of the glass. A similar procedure is used today whenever plastic, a non-conductor like glass, is chrome plated.

The term "Sterling" that was sometimes used for the plated silver is a misnomer. "Sterling" was a term first used by Tiffany in the 1850s to indicate their solid silverware was 92.5 percent pure — the same as English currency. This was considered a step up from the 90 percent pure coin silver then used for American and other currencies of the time. In silver plating, however, only pure 100 percent silver can be transferred through electrolytic action. This rules out "Sterling" as well as "999/1000 Fine" — a term used by Fostoria in their advertising in 1913!

Unlike gold, plated silver can withstand frequent handling; but unlike gold, it requires constant polishing. In July 1931 Lotus advertised a "Non-Tarnish Sterling Silver Deposit" which they claimed was "a new patented process" (L 7/31). Nevertheless, earlier that year, trade reporters wrote of this breakthrough as being industry-wide. It consisted of a protective coating of rhodium, plated over silver — a process comparable to the plating of chromium over nickel that began about two years before. Unlike the protective chromium, however, the rhodium was fragile, and silver deposit from '30s seems to be just as prone to tarnishing today as the unprotected silver used earlier.

While I have not come across anything that specifically mentioned the existence of silver plating tanks at Westmoreland, the large quantity of surviving silver-plated Westmoreland suggests they had this capability. Nevertheless, ads and surviving records show the following decorators (and no doubt others) bought Westmoreland blanks at various times and then sold them with their own silver decorations:

Edmondson Warrin Inc.
Lotus Glass Co.
Silver City Glass Co.
Sterling Glass Co.
Rockwell Silver Co.
National Silver Deposit Ware Co.
Weidlick Sterling Spoon Co.

"98" Westmoreland — Four-Piece Set

"98" Westmoreland line introduced Jan. 1898.

(c. 1898)

"98" Westmoreland was the original Westmoreland designation for this line.

1904: 56 pieces listed.

"The Westmoreland line is listed as (Westmoreland's) newest creation for 1898, in clear and green with or without gold" (L 1/12/98).

"(Westmoreland's) new 98 line, the Westmoreland, presents a rather striking appearance in heavy imitation cut pattern, and shows up well in green decorated with gold, and with crystal with gold stem decors" (J 1/13/98).

These two Pittsburgh Exhibit write-ups show Westmoreland was decorating in gold lustre, at least from late 1897.

Puritan 4-Oz. Mug
Filigree Puff Box

Puritan items first available in the 1890s. Filigree items first made between 1905 and 1907.

(c. 1907)

Puritan and **Filigree** were both original Westmoreland names.

Both of these pictured pieces were souvenir items.

Press reports of Jan. 1907 and Jan. 1908 mention Westmoreland's souvenir items.

1904: **Puritan** — five items listed. **Filigree** — Not listed. 1932: **Puritan** — Discontinued. **"10" Filigree Tobacco Jar** available in crystal, colors, and opal. 1940: Both discontinued.

Puritan Mug

The 1904 price list has an interesting entry that reads, "Puritan Mug, Ribboned and Boxed, Decorated in Gold or Lettered." This is the pictured 4-oz. mug — apparently the only **Puritan** item sold in any way other than as a lidded container. I have seen this **Puritan Mug** with gold decoration on green glass (used throughout the industry in 1898), and Wm Heacock has pictured it in cobalt blue (HCI 82) and amethyst (HCIII 46). Westmoreland's **Puritan** line consisted of just five pieces: a wine glass, 4-, 6-, and 8-oz. mugs, and a handled egg cup. In 1904 all five of them were sold tin-covered as "packers' goods" (which means Westmoreland may have used them for this purpose, too), and all of them except for the 6- and 8-oz. mugs were also available in opal (milk glass) with lids, at the same price.

In 1984, Heacock wrote that he believed the "beaded swirl" motif shown on this line originated in the 1880s with the Leerdam glassworks of Holland (HCI 81–4). He pointed out Leerdam's design was evidently first copied by Geo. Duncan & Sons in 1889 or 1890 followed by six or seven other American companies, one of which, of course, was Westmoreland. I believe Westmoreland's five **Puritan** pieces, however, should be considered Westmoreland's only glass made using this design.

Filigree Puff Box

Filigree was Westmoreland's unifying name for a group of items sharing the same design, but all having different sequential numbers. The **Filigree** name may or may not have been first used by Westmoreland (I understand Dugan used it in 1907 for a very different gold application) but I have no doubt the design is original. Who else but the ever-whimsical George West could have conceived of gilding a cascade of soap bubbles and calling it **Filigree**! It was a Yankee Doodle update.

Twelve **Filigree** items made up a glassware assortment shown in a late 1907 Butler Brothers catalog. Assuming these items were introduced at that time, they would have been first made no later than early 1907 from moulds made the year before. "Carrara Marble" Filigree apparently dates from 1910. The Butler Brothers catalog for that year described it as "Satin etched finish, relief crystal, filigree deposit design." A six-piece Westmoreland bureau set Butler Brothers pictured was available in a choice of "Pearl, delicate pink, or nile green." Twenty-two years later, a lone survivor, a **"10" Filigree Tobacco Jar** was still available.

"69" Orange Sherbet
Footed Orange Sherbet

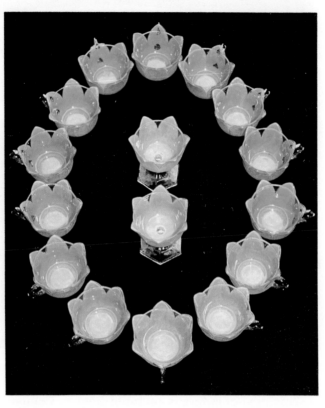

69 Sherbet first available in 1906.

(c. 1910)

The handled sherbet was used in 1906 (with some modification) as a Syria Shriners Souvenir.

"69" was Westmoreland's original item number.

1904: Not listed.
1932: Discontinued.
1940: Discontinued.

These pictured sherbets were both offered in the Butler Brothers catalog where they were described as "Realistic as nature. Nothing more unique in art glassware." While the bowls were the same and both were treated to the same fired "Natural Color" decoration, one came with a "gold decorated rustic stem handle" and the other was on a "high colonial crystal foot."

The handled cup was evidently made two ways. The first, sold with a punch bowl and intended for drinking, had a rim that came up to the tips of the orange peels. These cups may have been sold only with the punch bowl and may have been available

only with iridizing. In their catalog for 1909, Butler Brothers offered Westmoreland's "Golden Iridescent Punch Set," a 12½" orange-design bowl on a separate colonial stand and twelve rustic-handled cups. While the bowl had protruding orange peels, the cups were smooth-rimmed.

The second handled cup, pictured here, could not be used for drinking. Its rim was ⅜" below the tips of the orange peels, and it was sold as a sherbet. Westmoreland could have made both types of cup without making a new mould by use of an 1874 Benjamin Bakewell patent (IL 414). This patent made possible the pressing of two different types of glass in a single complex mould using two plungers. By simply substituting plungers, Westmoreland could have changed the height of the cup rim.

I believe that the sherbet was initially sold only with orange decoration and it was not then available iridized. If there is a question, check the foot ring: If it is not ground and polished, the cup is later.

185

1820 Dolphin Comport — 11" (Opal)

Dolphin: 11" comport, 9" candlestick, and handled sandwich first available in 1924.

(late 1930s)

Also available 7".

1820 was Westmoreland's **Flange** line.

1849 was the number assigned to all **Dolphin** items except for these two comports and a **1212 Handled Sandwich.**

1932: All **Dolphin** items available in crystal, colors, and opal. Both **1820 Comports** available in combinations of black (casing) and white opal glass.
1940: All **Dolphin** items discontinued in 1940 except the candlestick and the 8" shell.

Diameter: 11"
Weight: 3⅝ lb.

This opal comport is pictured here because it shows a very early reuse of lustre gold after a break of more than 20 years. Since Westmoreland's **1820 Dolphin Comports** were discontinued following three price increases in 1940, this one had to have been made either at the very end of the West period or the very beginning of the Brainard period. The dull, thin painting directly on the glass suggests the latter.

Because of the milk glass tendency to set up quickly, Westmoreland had to use a "wafer" between the bowl and the dolphin (the two parts were made separately); in transparent glass this was unnecessary. Also, to extend the workability of the milk glass, lead was added to the batch. Because of this lead, the comport pictured weighs about 11 percent more than the same comport in transparent glass. Two **1820**

Comports in transparent glass are shown in the Cut Colored Glass section and another is shown in the Carnegie section.

The leaves, buds, twigs, and purple or blue berries seem to be a representation of the purple chokeberry. The foliage garland suggests one by Hodgetts, Richardson & Son of about 1880 (RN 92).

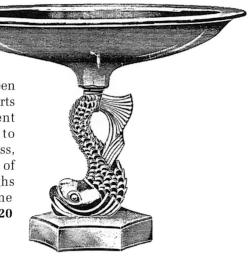

1835 Comport — 7", 1810 Flower Bowl
1823 Comport & Cover
1800 Mayo or Comport — 7", 1800 Mayo Ladle
GE-2 Dec.

1835 and 1823 first available between 1918 and 1924. 1810 and 1800 Mayo first available between 1913 and 1917. GE-2" Dec. first available in 1921 or before.

(c. 1922)

1835 was an item number used solely for this 7" comport.

1823 was an item number used solely for this covered comport.

1800 was designated a **Plain** line.

1800 Mayo also available 8" & 10".

1932: The **1810** was discontinued; the others, however, were all available in crystal and colors. The mayo was also available in opal.
1940: The ladle was available in crystal only. The rest were discontinued.

1835: 6½" w. 6¼" h.
1810: 7⅝" w. 7⅛" h.
1823: 6½" w. 9" h.
Mayo: 6¾" d.

These four pieces show Westmoreland's "GE-2" decoration. The "GE" stands for gold-etched, so called because the rim design was etched into the glass before the gold was applied. GE-2 is the most commonly found Westmoreland gold-band decoration. I have seen it on a number of Westmoreland pieces dating from about 1920 to the mid-'30s.

The **1823 Comport** used the same lid as the **1800 Rose Jar & Cover** shown in the Cut Stained section. In 1971 the company reissued this piece with a stem modification as a **1902 Covered Compote**. It was available in milk glass and in partly-etched transparent green.

1810 Flower Bowl
GE-2 Dec.

1810 Flower Bowl first available between 1913 and 1917.

(c. 1927)

Before 1926, only 6½" available. In 1926, 4", 5", 6", 7" & 8" available.

1810 was an item number assigned just to these flower bowls.

1932: Discontinued.
1940: Discontinued.

Height: 7¼"
Diameter: 7⅝"

This is the same **1810 Flower Bowl** shown in the preceding picture. It is not clear from the actual measurements whether this is the 7" or the 8" bowl.

If "optic" is ordinarily comparable to a soprano's vibrato, the optic in this vase would have to be her trill! Because this vase was blown and made without a plunger, the optic appears on the outside — the mould side. Because of this, the vase could not be rotated in the mould.

Cambridge also made a thistle-shaped vase that could be confused with this, but the rim of the Cambridge vase was rolled — that is, it juts out at right angles from the side of the vase.

1705 Handled Candy Jar — 1 Lb.
GE-2 Dec.

1705 Candy Jar first available between 1918 and 1924.

(c. 1922)

1705 was an item number used solely for this candy jar.

This candy jar shares the lid with the 3 lb. **1700 Colonial Candy Jar** (h: 4¾"; d: 5½").

1932: Available in crystal only.
1940: Discontinued.

Height: 10¾"
Weight: 8⅜" (max.)

This candy jar should be shown draped in a toga! Notice how the gold GE-2 decoration has been inverted so that it resembles a classical Greek anthemion or palmette band.

With the willow behind it, this jar suggests the amphora-shaped urns placed on plinth bases in memorial pictures of about 1800. They were always shown with weeping willows — and widows.

Notice the remarkable similarity of this neo-classical jar to the three cut urns on the **1841 Comport** pictured in the Iridized section.

1700 Colonial Four-Part Relish & Comport
GE-2 Dec.

1700 Relish & Comport first available between 1918 and 1924.

Notice how the etched bands and the gold overlay had to be arched to respond to the rim-scalloping on the relish dish. Notice, too, how the four bands had to be worked between the compartment dividers. In this type of plate etching, a wax impression is ordinarily carried by tissue paper from a metal plate to the glass intended to be etched. Here, there had to be a tissue, strong yet sufficiently flexible to allow the design to be bent.

Another company made a relish dish almost identical to Westmoreland's. It too has twelve scallops, and radial lines, four compartments around a circular center,

and it measures just ¼" wider than Westmoreland's. However, there is one important difference: while Westmoreland's twelve radial lines, or pie-cuts, are indented at the outside edge, these same pie-cuts on the look-alike protrude.

Heisey and Pairpoint also made similar relish trays with 16 scallops. Heisey's 1170 Spice Tray – 10" is not likely to be confused with Westmoreland's, for it has a pressed pinwheel star, no pie-cuts, and four broad panels of vertical reeding on the outside edge. Westmoreland's **1700** may have been the only one to be offered with a center dish.

(c. 1922)

1700 was one of the two colonial lines Westmoreland introduced in 1912.

A larger **1700 Six-Part Relish & Comport** also available.

The four-part relish dish also available without the comport.

The comport was the same as the **1800 Cheese & Cracker** cheese dish.

This relish dish has a cut star.

1932: The four-part relish & comport available in crystal and colors. The six-part relish & comport available in crystal only. 1940: Both discontinued.

Relish: 10⅜" d.

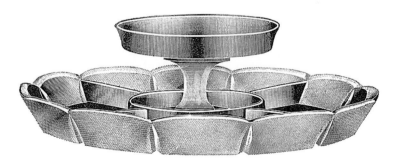

1800 Mayo or Comport — 7"

(late 1920s)

Width: 6⅜"

The pebbled surface on the outside of the bowl was not etched, but sprayed and fired; it resembles the decoration found on the **"23" Bowl** in the Iridized section. The etched backing for the gold band on the rim appears to be a variation of Westmoreland's GE-2 design; I have not seen it elsewhere.

Although this is a probable Westmoreland decoration, it is on a certain Westmoreland blank. Notice the characteristic sharp bend where the bowl joins the extended ankle. Westmoreland's **1800 Mayo** and **1800 Ladle** are among

the blanks shown in an Irving Cut Glass catalog of the '20s.

Blown Glasses

Are these two glasses examples of the "gold encrusted blown and stem ware… shown in a full line" by Westmoreland at the Pittsburgh Exhibit in 1919? (J 1/23/19)

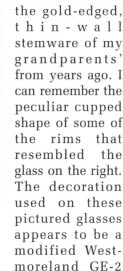

(c. 1919)

I can recall the gold-edged, thin-wall stemware of my grandparents' from years ago. I can remember the peculiar cupped shape of some of the rims that resembled the glass on the right. The decoration used on these pictured glasses appears to be a modified Westmoreland GE-2 band. All this suggests these glasses could have been made by Westmoreland.

On the other hand, a much simpler explanation is that Westmoreland merely decorated the stemware of other glass companies — particularly Bryce Bros. There seems to have been a close association between Westmoreland and Bryce

Bros. of nearby Mt. Pleasant. For more than ten years Westmoreland and Bryce Bros. set up their Pittsburgh Exhibit displays in adjoining areas of the Fort Pitt Hotel. There are surviving photographs of Chas West at Kirk Bryce's golf outings. Finally, there is a record of a Westmoreland purchase of Bryce stemware, presumably for decorating, in the '30s, suggesting there had been purchases made on other occasions.

I have been asked, "Why didn't Westmoreland make thin, blown stemware? Why did they leave that important bridal market to everybody else?" My answer is that at one time they may have made such glass, but in the late '20s and '30s it would have meant going head-to-head with imports plus almost all of the rest of the American glassware industry. Blown glass is where the most acute competition was — particularly from abroad. Out of more than a score of American companies that had tried to make money with blown stemware, almost all had fallen by the wayside by the 1960s, and only Bryce survives today — as Lenox Crystal. The question really should be turned around: "Why did so many glass companies make blown, thin-walled stemware?"

C. 1918 Westmoreland Gold Border

This broad rim design seems to have been used on some of Westmoreland's World War I era pieces (1916 – 1918); it was apparently not used later.

"The finest grade of gold decorated crystal is encrusted with 22 karat coin gold. This coin gold... is fired under a temperature of 1,200 degrees practically fusing the metal with its glass background and making it an integral part of an exceptionally exquisite whole" (JC 2/4/20).

The writer must have penned this on his return trip from Parnassus! Gold and silver do not take kindly to glass' lack of porosity, and they are much more easily abraded away than are enamels, which do fuse to glass when subjected to extreme heat.

GE-6 Gold Border

This etched band was first available in 1924 or before. It was still in use in 1933 or later.

Cambridge used an etched band with an eight-petal flower that could be confused with this. But the Cambridge flower is flatter, broader, and more prominent. Also, it lacks the strange tongue or tassel that hangs from the center of each Westmoreland flower.

1820 Sugar & Cream Set

1820 Sugar & Cream set first available in 1925.

(c. 1929)

1820 was Westmoreland's **Flange** line.

This Rocaille gold-band design has also been seen on another Westmoreland piece.

1932: Available in crystal and colors.
1940: Discontinued.

The interesting curved rim of this **1820 Cream** can also be found on the **1820 Quart Jug** (pitcher) and the **1820 Mint Boat** (sauce boat) (neither pictured).

The foundation for this Rocaille gold was not added to the glass. It appears not to have been etched either, but cut in some manner with a wheel. Notice the varying depth and curvature of each incision. Since there is no pattern, it must have been done free-hand.

1820 Five-Part Diamond Relish — 11½" (Roselin)

1820 Diamond Relish first available in 1927. Roselin glass first advertised July 1926.

(c. 1927)

1932: Available in crystal and colors.
1940: Available in crystal only.

Diameter: 11½"

This five-part relish was one of the four most expensive items in the **1820** line in 1932. It consisted of six separate pieces that required four moulds to make.

I have seen this cheerful design of birds and flowers only on another **1820 Diamond Relish**.

1207 Sugar & Cream Set

1207 Sugar & Cream Set first available between 1913 and 1917.

(c. 1929)

1207 was an item number used solely for this sugar & cream set.

Round pressed star. Ankle groove just above the bottom.

Optic on the inside (plunger side).

1932: Available in crystal only.
1940: Discontinued.

In the 1925 Butler Brothers catalog, these Westmoreland **1207 Sugar and Cream Sets** were sold in crystal with two styles of simple "Floral and Leaf Spray cuttings" for $3.95 and $5.40 a dozen (1995: $34.75 and $47.50). These seem to have been Westmoreland's "bread-and-butter" sugars and creams, for they are never found with ground and polished bottoms nor with outstanding cuttings.

I have seen a **1707 Salt & Pepper** with this same gold-etched design, suggesting it was Westmoreland's.

Foot: 2¾" d

193

1854/2 Chocolate Box & Cover

(1920s)

Also available in a smaller size: **1854/1.**

1854 was an item number assigned just to these two chocolate boxes.

Lid is optic.

Ground and polished bottom.

1932: **1854/1** available in crystal and colors; **1854/2** available in crystal only. 1940: Discontinued.

Diameter: 7½"

1854 Chocolate Boxes first available between 1918 and 1921.

The pressed, round star was enriched by being etched rather than cut; this is the only instance of etching I have found on a Westmoreland pressed star.

With gold on the top of the lid and spray casing below it, this chocolate box is decorated in a manner similar to the one shown in the Carnegie section. Both show raised detail work beneath the gold on the lid glass.

1042 Candlesticks — 9"

1042 Candlesticks first available between 1918 and 1924.

(c. 1930)

Also available 6½".

1042 was a candlestick number.

The blue casing on these candlestick shafts was ended at the gold rings; it was then sprayed on the underside of the feet. This gave the upper side of the feet, the gilded side, greater brilliance.

The gilded decoration resembling gold leaf feels Bohemian to me; but it can be tied to Westmoreland because of the black-veining on the gold. It resembles similar veining on Westmoreland's "Silver Rose" decoration of

1932: Available in crystal and colors.
1940: Discontinued.

about 1930 — so named because it was inspired by the short-lived **1706 Silver Rose** tableware line of 1929. Items in this line shared a single pressed rose in cameo.

1042 Candlesticks — 9"
GE-88 Dec.

This GE-88 decoration is a combined band of silver and gold applied to an etched surface. The silver was evidently unprotected, and today it will always appear black; nevertheless, it can be polished. This design was available in 1924, and probably for several years around that date.

(c. 1924)

1042 Candlesticks — 9"

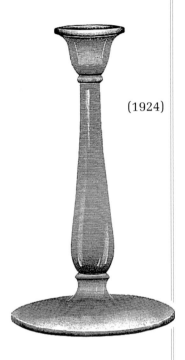

(1924)

This silver design was inspired by, or perhaps directly copied from, an hour hand on an early eighteenth century tall case clock (NW 484).

I regret that I cannot claim it for Westmoreland. It is by Edmondson Warrin, a New York decorator, and his timely decoration can also be found on some of Westmoreland's black glass that he advertised in 1924 (L 11/3/24).

199 Colonial Mustard

(before 1921)

199 was an item number assigned just to this colonial mustard.

It was not from one of Westmoreland's six colonial lines.

1932: Available in crystal only.

1940: Available in crystal only.

Height: 3¾" (with lid)

"There is also a splendid line of glassware for silver deposit, and of this the Westmoreland people have made a specialty for some time" (P 2/15/12).

199 Mustard first available between 1906 and 1912.

Because of the frequent appearance of this sort of silver decoration on known Westmoreland forms from before 1912, I can only conclude the silver was Westmoreland's. If so, Westmoreland must have had a silver-plating facility then, for this silver was built up with plating after the foundation was brushed on and then fired.

1840 Vase — 10"

8" & 10" first available between 1918 and 1924. 6" first available in 1925.

(c. 1928)

Also available 6" & 8".

1840 was an item number assigned just to these three vases.

1932: 6", 8" & 10" available in crystal and colors.
1940: All three sizes discontinued.

Height: 7⅛"
Width: 9¾"
Weight: 3⅛ lb.

This is the same translucent blue casing shown in the **1820 Comport** in the Cased section, but here it has been sprayed onto an etched surface. While this cased color is Westmoreland's, there is no assurance the silver decoration is, too.

For a detailed comparison of Westmoreland's **1840** and U.S. Glass' 15179 vases, see the Cut Stained section.

1800 High Foot Sweetmeat — 6½"

The sprayed yellow and blue casing that suggests Venetian glass is almost certainly Westmoreland's, but the silver decoration was applied by another company. In 1924 a trade publication pictured nine glass items sharing this same silver decoration; but of the nine, only one, or possible two, were on Westmoreland's blanks (JC 6/18/24).

That same year this Westmoreland sweetmeat was included in an unrelated grouping of glass decorated by the Wheeling Decorating Co. This is the shape that is shown in various catalogs of the '20s. There is another comport, however, with a very shallow, gently curved bowl that is not shown in these catalogs. Three of them, pictured in the Cased Glass section, have known Westmoreland decorations. Because their stems, feet, and stem/bowl measurements are identical to those on this sweetmeat, they had to have been made by Westmoreland, too.

1800 Sweetmeat first available between 1918 and 1924.

(c. 1924)

1932: Available in crystal only.
1940: Discontinued.

Height: 6⅝"
Width: 6"
Stem/bowl: 1¾" d.

1042 Candlestick — 9"
U.S. Glass Three-Footed Bowl

(c. 1924)

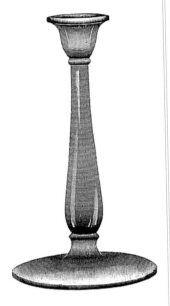

Since the silver decoration is not Westmoreland's and the bowl is by U.S. Glass, I would suspect this entire decoration has been done by a decorating house. The sprayed casing color seems to be close to one used by Westmoreland, but the quality of the spraying is not up to Westmoreland's standard. Notice that the **1042 Candlesticks** were sprayed down through their lower rings, and then beneath their feet.

1849 Handled Sandwich — 10" (Roselin)

1849/10" Handled Sandwich first available between 1918 and 1924.

1849 was an item number for this, a 6" butter ball, and a 4½" lemon tray.

1932: Available in crystal and colors.
1940: Discontinued.

Diameter: 9¾"

I believe this silver decoration is by Lotus, based on its similarity to other known Lotus silver designs. In a Lotus catalog of c. 1930, a Westmoreland **1849 Handled Sandwich** was pictured in black glass; it had Westmoreland's **1849** item number designation.

For a comparison of Westmoreland's **1849** and New Martinsville's No. 10 Sandwich trays, see the Reverse Painting section.

1820 Oval Relish — 7½" x 9½"

1820 Oval Relish first available in 1926.

Although the silver may have been applied by another company, the cutting is almost certainly Westmoreland's. Notice the delicate notching around the inner edges of the two set-in dishes. I have seen identical edge notching on three other Westmoreland relish sets. Two also were trimmed with silver while the third was decorated only with cutting. That spectacular cut star pictured was not cut on the lower tray but on the two set-in dishes.

(late 1920s)

Ground and polished tray bottom.

1932: **1820 Oval Relish** available in crystal only.
1940: Discontinued.

7¾" x 9¾"

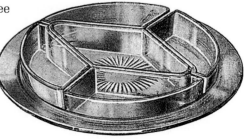

1820 Five-Part Diamond Relish — 11½" (Roselin)

Compare this diamond relish with the identical relish trimmed in gold shown earlier in this section. Notice that while gold is prone to wear, plated silver can lose its adhesion. Just as a "cold solder joint" in an early radio may not show up for decades, a tenuous silver connection to glass may not show up for some time either. Originally, the silver foundation on this relish tray was fired onto the glass, and this then became the cathode for silver plating. A film of wax, perhaps, or maybe just a variation in the temperature was all it took to cause the eventual problem you can see at the backside of the rim.

(c. 1927)

Diameter: 11½"

199

1902 Low Foot Comport — 8"

(c. 1928)

1902 was designated a **Plain** line.

1932: Available in crystal and colors.
1940: Discontinued.

Diameter: 7⅝"
Stem/bowl: 2⅝" d.

1902 line introduced in 1927. 1902 Low Foot Comport first available in 1927.

This decoration combines silver deposit and etching in a very precise way. While Westmoreland could have supplied these part-etched comports to a silver decorating house, it seems highly likely that the two activities were done not far apart. Westmoreland could have done both. Another **1902 Low Foot Comport** is pictured in the Cased Glass section.

Unknown Covered Bowl

(c. 1925)

Ground and polished bottom; pressed star.

Diameter: 6" (max.)

This glass blank is not shown in any of my catalogs, but since this is the second one I have seen with a known Westmoreland decoration, it was probably made by Westmoreland. The round finial appears to have the same design that was used for lids of dresser sets a few years later.

To protect against wear, the back side of the gold band was also treated with gold — as it usually was on Westmoreland's gold-trimmed glass.

Gustav Horn's
1820 Five-Part Relish with Cocktail Center — 13"

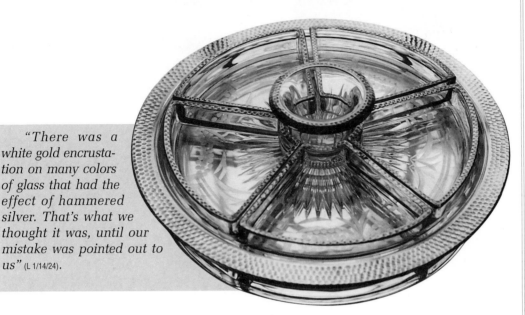

"There was a white gold encrustation on many colors of glass that had the effect of hammered silver. That's what we thought it was, until our mistake was pointed out to us" (L 1/14/24).

1820 5-Part Relish first available in 1925.

(c. 1925)

#23 decoration.

Patent 1.518.930 granted to Gustav Horn 12/9/24.

1932: Relish available in crystal and colors.
1940: Available in crystal only. Relabeled a "7-part relish."

Diameter: 13"
Weight: 6 lb.

This remarkable design technique seems to have been introduced at the Pittsburgh Exhibit in January 1924. Three months later, Gustav Horn, Westmoreland's head decorator, applied for a patent for it which was granted at the end of the year.

This was a very labor-intensive substitute for inexpensive plate etching, but Gustav Horn was evidently not concerned about cost. Not only did each of his "hammer blows" require a separate pass against the cutting wheel, but also in his patent drawing he showed the cutting wheel striations at different angles, which would have required the glass to be constantly turned. This glass is never found cut this way.

The 5-part relish pictured has a total of 1,790 "hammer blows" on the seven dishes, created by 1,790 separate passes against the cutting wheel. Afterwards, the cut areas were brushed with silver, fired, and then plated with more silver. The rims on the tray and the small dish in the center were backed with silver to protect them against wear.

Because of its outstanding cutting, this same **1820 Relish** is pictured in the Cut Crystal section. For a comparison between Westmoreland's relish and two others that are similar, refer to that section.

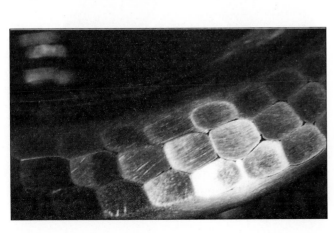

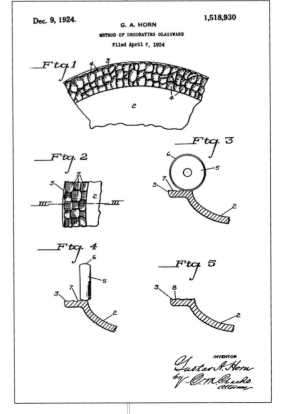

Dec. 9, 1924.   1,518,930
G. A. HORN
METHOD OF DECORATING GLASSWARE
Filed April 7, 1924

INVENTOR
Gustav A. Horn
by O. M. Clark
attorney

1208 Cream

(c. 1925)

1208 was an item number used for two sugar & cream sets.

1932: Available in crystal and colors.
1940: Available in crystal only.

Because Gustav Horn's decorative band was cut and not etched, and was used with silver as well as gold, it was designated simply 23 rather than GE-23.

Westmoreland offered the **1208 Sugar & Cream Set** with and without a pressed star. The one pictured, showing a pressed star, has huskier handles than the Westmoreland set with a plain bottom.

Both cream moulds survived at the factory in 1991, proving Westmoreland made these sugars and creams both ways. **1208** was the number assigned to both of them.

A number of companies made similar sugars

and creams with and without pressed stars. Here are some that could be mistaken for Westmoreland's **1208:**

Central — High sugar handles, and no dip in the rim of the cream.
Fenton No. 145 — The sugar rim shares the dip of the cream.
Fostoria No. 1480 — No bottom star.
McKee No. 9 — Pressed star.
Pairpoint No. 1230
U.S. Glass "R Simplicity" cream; "R No. 3" sugar — no bottom star.

1841 Tall Comport — 9"

(late 1920s)

In 1924 available 5½" & 8".

In 1926 available 5½", 6½" & 9".

1841 was an item number assigned just to these comports.

1932: Three sizes available in crystal only.
1940: Discontinued.

Height: 9¼"
Stem/bowl: 2½" d.

This shows an **1841 Comport** and a close-up of its rim. Because the coin gold application was thin, we can see the marks from the cutting. Notice that the comport rim was held at right angles to the revolving cutting wheel, and the wheel was probably about 2" in diameter and about ³⁄₁₆" wide. Notice too, every inner cut comes to exactly the same distance from the inscribed line. Not a single cut penetrates, or even touches it.

At least one other company used a similar "hammered" design under silver plating. But the marks were either in the mould or else etched, for they appear smooth and shiny. Only Westmoreland's seems to have been used with gold, and only Westmoreland's will show the roughness or striations caused by the cutting wheel.

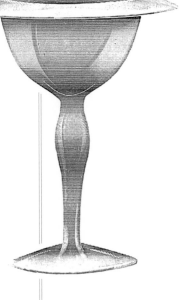

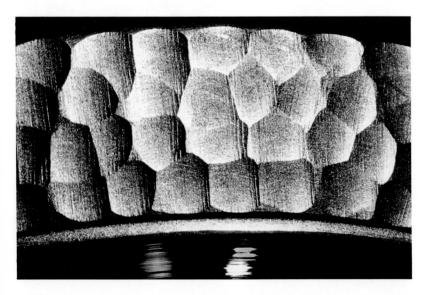

750 Basket — 5"

(1920s)

Also available 3", 4", 6", 7" & 8" sizes.

750 was an item number assigned just to these six baskets.

"Keystone-W" marked.

1932: 3" to 6" available in crystal and colors; 7" & 8" sizes available in crystal only.
1940: 3" to 6" available in crystal only (an opal option for the 6" was written in, then lined out). It was offered again in 1977 with ruby staining and a painted or decal decoration.

Basket: 5⅛" h.
With handle: 10" h.

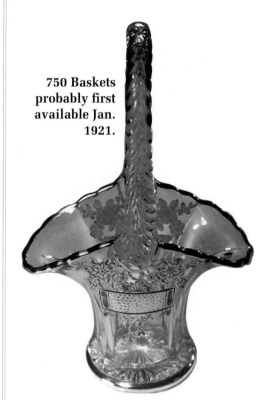

750 Baskets probably first available Jan. 1921.

The **Keystone-W** mark, unexpected in this **750 Basket,** suggests Westmoreland was responsible for the silver decoration. Westmoreland rarely used this mark on anything but their colonial lines, and I have noticed decorating houses often ground and polished away manufacturers' marks from their purchased blanks.

The decoration also supports this conclusion. The "hammer blows," the tall ovals, and the incised border of the plaques were all cut into the glass before the silver was applied. The surface decoration on the silver was engraved, but it was not the "bright-cut" type of engraving so often found on silver.

For a comparison between this basket and a similar one by Duncan & Miller, see the Cased Glass section.

1700 Colonial Lily Vase — 6"

(c. 1915)

From 1912, **1700 Lily Vases** available 6" & 9".

1932: 6" available in crystal and colors; 9" available in crystal only. The 9" cost 2½ times as much as the 6".
1940: Discontinued. However, in 1967 it was reissued as a **1776 Vase/Candle** in three colors and in crystal with a ruby-stained stem.

Height: 6⅜"

Despite this catalog drawing, the lips of all Westmoreland's lily vases should ordinarily have six lobes. This is because of the greater glass thickness at the location of each of the six panel dividers. This same effect can be seen on the ribbed pieces pictured in the Iridized section. The well-known Tiffany "Jack-in-the-Pulpit" vase has a smooth lip, reflecting its smooth-sided conical stem.

This lily vase was made from the same mould as the **1700 Vase or Hatpin holder — 7"**. See the Cut Crystal section.

1700 Lily Vases first available in 1912.

1800 Butter Ball — 6"

1800 loop-handled pieces first available between 1918 and 1922.

(1920s)

Marked "Sterling 8093" plus hollow ware mark of Watson Co. Attleboro, Mass.

1932: Available in crystal only.
1940: Discontinued.

Width: 6¼" (glass)
7½" (total)

For centuries, silver makers combined their silver with glass. This enabled the precious metal to go farther, and besides, glass combined with silver offered more visual excitement than glass or silver could alone.

This is one of three identical Westmoreland butter balls I found less than nine months apart. The glass displays a Westmoreland cutting — the same cutting design that can be seen on a **1209 Sugar & Cream** in the Cut Crystal section. Crimped around the glass is a sterling band bearing the hollow ware mark of the Watson Co. of Attleboro, Mass. This "sword-within-a-wreath" mark was used by them from 1905 — 1929.

The glass-to-silver fit had to be precise. Did Westmoreland sell these butter balls to Watson after cutting, or did they buy the bands from Watson to crimp themselves?

Opaque Glass

The Post War Years

Today, when most people think of Westmoreland, they think of milk glass. Beginning in the 1940s, the company began to spend a great deal of money on consumer advertising (over 4 percent of sales in the late '50s), and for years most of this advertising focused on milk glass. But this money was well spent. In 1957 Westmoreland's sales climbed to $3.2 million ($17.6 million in 1995 dollars), and milk glass accounted for virtually all of it.

According to Robert Rupp, Westmoreland's general manager from 1965, Westmoreland made and sold 75,000 No. 757 milk glass pansy baskets in 1957. Even if Westmoreland had made these baskets in every one of the year's 365 days, they would have had to turn out over 200 of them each day to arrive at this total by year-end. Nevertheless, based on its selling price, sales of this little basket seem to have been less than three percent of Westmoreland's milk glass sales that year.

After peaking in 1957, however, Westmoreland's milk glass sales plummeted. In fact, three successive losses in the early '60s, resulting from this decline, almost put Westmoreland under. Because milk glass was "hot" in the '40s and '50s, other companies were drawn to it, and eventually the market simply became engorged with all the milk glass that had been produced. While Westmoreland continued to make and promote milk glass in all subsequent years, this glass never again came close to regaining its earlier importance. According to Dwight Johnson, Westmoreland's glassmaker from 1965, the proportion of milk glass in Westmoreland's sales, declined from about 90% in the '50s down to about 50% (of a much reduced sales volume) by the '70s. Company records bear him out. Nevertheless, over the years, Westmoreland probably made more of this glass than any other maker and they almost certainly made it for a longer, unbroken span of time.

Opal vs. Milk Glass

Throughout this book I have used the term "opal" for Westmoreland's milk glass prior to World War II. This is partly a desire to stick to authentic terminology and partly an attempt to blend my writing in with the various contemporary passages I have quoted. "Opal" was the only term used by Westmoreland before the war, and according to Robert Jones, a Westmoreland employee from 1924, it was the only term used by the older glass men right up to the time of the company's closing. (Like "Carnegie," "Vallerysthal," and "Steuben," "opal" is accented on the second syllable.) An interesting 1943 ad managed to work in three terms: "opal," "milk glass," and "milk-white glass," but after that, "milk glass" because standard in all Westmoreland's ads and company correspondence. While "opal" is admittedly a perplexing word, its use allows us to separate Westmoreland's early, primarily original glass from its later, primarily reproduction glass.

The Starting Date

Westmoreland had been making opal glass continuously for decades before the 1950s, but the later claim that Westmoreland had been making it "from the 1890s" appears to be in error. Perhaps we can examine some of the early evidence.

Westmoreland first exhibited their glassware at the Pittsburgh Show in January 1892, and their exhibits of 1896, '97, '98, and 1902 were briefly reviewed by several trade journals. While these reviews focused primarily on the tableware lines, they also mentioned decoration and glass color. Nevertheless, I have found no mention of Westmoreland's opaque glass in any reviews of the '90s. In a January 1902 review, however, a reporter wrote of Westmoreland's molasses cans (pitchers) and salts and peppers in "white opal" (L 1/11/02). He noted that Westmoreland's opal was available either "fire decorated" or "cold decorated," implying this glass was all sold decorated. While something not reported hardly constitutes proof, these reviews would at least suggest an 1898 – 1902 time span for Westmoreland's first opal.

In what was, perhaps, Westmoreland's first ad, in December 1897 the company called itself "Manufacturers of Novelties, Fine Pressed and Blown Glassware" — but there was no mention of opal. In what was, perhaps, Westmoreland's second ad, though, in February 1901 the company now called itself "Manufacturers of Fine Crystal and Opal Glassware." This suggests we can narrow our time span by a year to 1898 – 1901.

On August 1, 1900, Westmoreland reopened after the usual four-week summer break. Three months later, in November, the press reported that at Westmoreland, "Another tank was started this week on opal goods" (JD 11/2/00). Then, six months after that, in May 1901 a trade journal wrote, "Their four months (i.e. dating from the 1901 Pittsburgh Show) business in both crystal and opal has been gratifying" (J 5/9/01). With these accounts our span can finally be narrowed to the second half of 1900.

Let us consider some of Westmoreland's tableware lines. The **Elite** line was introduced in January 1896, the **Waverly** in January 1897, and the **98 Westmoreland** in January 1898. While these were very popular lines at the time consisting of more than 50 items each, none of them, I believe, can be found today in opal. But two early twentieth century lines, the **Star** and the **Daisy** (Jan. 1902) can be. These two are pictured in opal in Belknap (BM 131) and Ferson (FF 289, 290, 291).

Consider Westmoreland's earliest mustards. We know that at least from the beginning of 1891 Westmoreland was making containers for mustard. But it appears that in the '90s only transparent tableware glass was being used for that purpose. Westmoreland's containers made expressly for mustard seem to date back no earlier than the beginning of the opal period. In December 1900 the press reported: "Something new in (Westmoreland's) line of glassware for the year 1901 is the mustard sets. Moulds for these are being made and they are expected to be good sellers" (JD 12/28/00). Then in March 1902 a trade publication mentioned a couple of new Westmoreland sets, the "Swan" and the "Fruit" (L 3/29/02). Since these were both reissued after World War II, they are familiar to us today.

Did Westmoreland make opal glass in the 1890s? The answer has to be no. Did Westmoreland, however, make opal glass in the nineteenth century? The answer has to be yes — but just by the skin of their milk-white teeth! As 2000 will be the final year of the twentieth century, 1900 was the final year of the nineteenth. (Just wait till this issue heats up again!) And so any opal glass Westmoreland made in 1900 has to be considered nineteenth century — and properly Victorian, too. But again, only just. At the century's close, Queen Victoria's reign had only three short weeks remaining; the Queen died January 22, 1901.

Opaque Chemistry

As most milk glass collectors already know, opaque-white glass is believed to have originated in Europe (in sixteenth century Venice according to most accounts) as one of several substitutes for expensive Chinese porcelain. In its early years it apparently consisted of crystal glass with the addition of china clay (kaolin) and bone ash (ground, calcined bones) for opacity. Since it later shared these ingredients with bone china, and in its translucency resembled bone china, it was sometimes referred to as "bone glass."

Apparently, there were two shortcomings to this simple mix. First depending on its source, the bone ash (often referred to as "phosphate" or "phosphates") would impart inconsistent coloring, and this coloring would usually veer towards a cold gray. And second, if the batch was super-saturated with bone ash and clay, the glass was fragile; if it was not, the glass was thin and opalescent. I am not clear whether the early, thin white glass of Sandwich was intended to be an imitation of pottery, but certainly the porcelain-white opal glass of Pittsburgh from the late nineteenth century was (despite the universal use of this curious name).

Nineteenth century American glassmakers were apparently the first to add flourine to the batch. This was first in the form of fluorspar — and then kryolite, a mineral brought over "From Greenland's Icy Mountains." With flourides, glassmakers were able to achieve their goal of a dense, opaque white of a predictable hue. But this new whitening agent also had its faults. First, regardless of whether tanks or pats were used for the molten glass, the flourides would attack them. Over the years, many technical articles were written addressing this problem without really solving it. Second, the flourides created an even more brittle glass with minimal worka-

Opaque Glass

bility. Glassmakers found that by adding feldspar and lead to their batch they could extend the working time and soften the glass. But once again they were confronted with new problems. Feldspar, related to kaolin, and actually used as early as the sixteenth century, was said to aggravate the tank-burnout problem. Lead was expensive, and for its cost it endowed opal with none of its aural and visual traits so cherished in crystal. Nevertheless, it managed to carry over to opal one of its failings: a hypersensitivity to heat and cold. The high lead content of Westmoreland's later milk glass may explain the breakage problems collectors have complained about over the years. That, plus the natural tendency of people to treat like china anything that looks like china!

It seems there has never been any one best formulation for opaque glass. All formulations are apparently compromises, and glassmakers have always had to make tough choices.

George West's "7" Rabbit Plate — 7"

(c. 1902)

"7" was a sequential number assigned just to this plate.

6" rabbit also available as a plaque (FF 73).

Patent 36030 granted 8/26/02 to George West for 3½ years.

Cold decoration.

1904: Available as an "Opal Novelty."
1932: Available in opal only.
1940: Available in opal only.

Plate: 7¼" w.
Rabbit: 5⅞" w.

"7" Rabbit plate patent filed Feb. 1902.

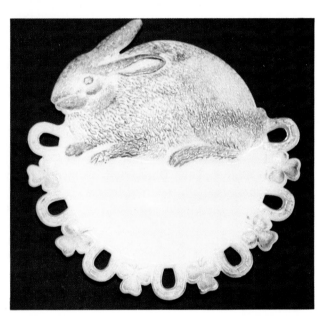

With its prominent rabbit's feet, clovers, and upturned horseshoes, this plate must have been George West's special salute to the new century. When he patented it in 1902, the twentieth century's second year, the world was still full of hope and belief in the inevitability of progress. George West's keen allegorical sense can be found in other Westmoreland pieces of the time — particularly the Shriners glass from 1903 on.

Millard (MS 43) and Belknap (BM 7a) claim this plate can be found in blue and white.

This particular plate is marked "PAT. APPL'D FOR" inside the foot.

"5" Cat Plate — 7"

5 Cat Plate first available in 1901 or before.

(c. 1901)

Also available 8".

"5" was a sequential number assigned just to this plate.

Cold decoration.

1904: Both sizes available as "Opal Novelties."
1932: Both sizes available in opal only.
1940: 8" available in opal only. 7" discontinued. By 1952 both sizes were being made again.

Width: 7¼"

A very yellowed label on the back of this cat plate reads, "For Bertie Epperman." Bertie Epperman, I understand, inherited this plate and left it to her grandson at her death. Her grandson then sold it to the dealer who sold it to me. It is certainly a tribute to the plate that it can have been so cherished by two successive owners.

This plate can be found pictured in Belknap (BM 10c), Millard (MS 16), and Ferson (FF 477/647). Millard claims it can be found in blue and white.

George West's "6" Owl Plate

"To their line of cat plates, which proved to be one of the greatest novelties ever placed on the market, (Westmoreland) have added a line of owl plates... the owl plate is so radically different... that the firm have had it patented" (L 1/11/02).

This plate can be found in Belknap (BM 10c), Millard (MS 21), and Ferson (FF 500/646). It is also pictured in the Etched Glass section.

"6" Owl Plate patent filed June 1901.

1904: Available as an "Opal Novelty."
1932: Available in opal only.
1940: Available in opal only.

Width: 7⅜"

(1909)

"6" was a sequential number assigned just to this plate.

"Pat'd July 2, 1901" marked inside foot ring.

Patent 34711 granted to George West for 3½ years.

Cold decoration with painted "Souvenir Grangers Picnic 1909."

George West's "15" National Plate — 7"

"15" was a sequential number assigned just to this plate.

"Pat. Sept 8. 03 36538" marked underneath, behind flag.

Patent granted to George West for 3½ years.

Cold decoration with painted, "Souvenir Oswego, NY."

1904: Available as an "Opal Novelty."
1932: Available in opal only.
1940: Available in opal only.

Plate: 7⅜" (max.)
Foot: 4¼" o.d.

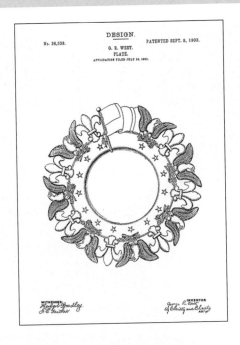

"15" National Plate patent filed July 1903.

The **"15" National Plate** was the third of the three plates George West patented from 1901 to 1903. It was the basis of Westmoreland's Wyoming Monument plate (FF 418), the Roger Williams Memorial plate (FF 639), and several 1904 St. Louis Exposition plates (L 1/16/04).

In their 1952 catalog the Brainards referred to this as "An authentic Westmoreland reproduction of a very old popular 7" souvenir plate of the late Victorian period." However, George West's patent on this plate was granted almost three years after Queen Victoria's death.

"8" Cupid Plate — 7"
"14" Easter Chick Plate — 7"

"8" and "14" were sequential numbers assigned just to these plates.

These are two of a set of five plates with identical rims.

The first period plates were apparently always decorated.

Millard (MS 22) claims the **Easter Chick Plate** was available both in white and blue.

Belknap (BM 6b) claims the **Cupid Plate** was available in white only.

1904: All five available as "Opal Novelties."
1932: "8" and "9" available in opal only. Rest discontinued.
1940: "9" and "17" available in opal only. Rest discontinued. By 1952, the five were combined with eight others into a group generally known today as the "Bakers Dozen."

Plate: 7⅜" (max.)
Foot: 4¼" o.d.

The Five-Plate Set first available between 1900 and 1904.

These are two of a set of five Westmoreland plates sharing identical rims. The other three are the **"9" Niagara Falls Plate**, the **"12" Garfield Memorial Plate**, and the **"17" Donkey Plate**. These are the original Westmoreland names and numbers.

On the basis of style, Belknap referred to the **Cupid Plate** as an "Excellent example... of the '80s" (BM 6b); nevertheless, the five must date from some time after 1891. While Garfield was shot in 1881, an architectural contest for his monument was not held until nine years later, and construction did not begin until the following year. Because of the assassination date, this is the plate that had once pushed back the apparent period of origin of all five.

Westmoreland could have acquired the moulds from another glass company around 1900 when they began to make opal glass. But if so, there should be surviving plates with decorations painted by an earlier company. At this time, I believe the plates are original to Westmoreland, which made one mould with this interesting border of two interpenetrating squares and then made five different plungers to go with it.

Blue Rope Edge Basket

(c. 1905)

No mould numbers.

Length: 5⅜" (overall)

This is the first of several pictures in this section showing Westmoreland's early baskets. Atterbury patented a basketweave and rope design in 1874. However, while Atterbury's roped handle and rim are similar to Westmoreland's, Atterbury's basketweave shows a double-strand warp in contrast to the single strand used on all of Westmoreland's. But this single strand was not unique to Westmoreland. Bellaire Goblet (a U.S. Glass Company) and Indiana/Greentown (a National Glass Company) also used this same weave.

There is one thing that will often make a positive Westmoreland identification possible: the mould numbers which appear on most (though not all) of Westmoreland's opal mustard containers. They appear in a bold, block style, are always centered (if possible), and ordinarily range from 2 through 6, 2 and 3 being the most common. They range in size from ¼" to ⅜", but are usually ⁵⁄₁₆" tall. Since they always appear forward, the numbers of the special die sets had to be typographically backward. The absence of a mould number on a lid or a base is not proof an item is not by Westmoreland, but the presence of one always seems to indicate that it is. Since these stamped numbers were originally very deep, they can often be found on Brainard period reissues — sometimes next to late "WG" marks. Other early opal pieces can be found with numbers in italics or script that are two or three digits long; they are light and some appear almost to have been penned. While the presence of one of these numbers is an indicator of age, it is also proof that the glass is *not* Westmoreland's.

The purpose of Westmoreland's numbers seems to have been to identify the particular mould used on these early mass-produced mustards. The reason it is sometimes found on the plunger side, however, escapes me. In a normal production run, two or even three identical moulds would have been used together with a single plunger. Incidentally, the lid numbers will seldom agree with the bowl numbers.

The cream pictured bears no mould numbers, but it is in a Westmoreland blue opal color, has a Westmoreland single filament warp, has a Westmoreland basket-cross on the bottom, has a Westmoreland peg finial, and it shows traces of early paint on its Westmoreland-type rope border.

"1" Bushel Basket Sugar
257 Peep Cover For No. 1 Basket

"1" Sugar/257 Cover first available between 1900 and 1904.

(c. 1904)

Numbers and designations taken from the 1904 price list.

No mould numbers.

1904: Basket and cover available separately as "opal novelties."
1932: Discontinued.
1940: Discontinued.

Basket: 3¾" d.

This Westmoreland basket has a rope border, a single-filament warp, and a basket cross on the bottom; but neither the lid nor the base shows a mould number. Westmoreland made this sugar with no matching cream.

While the plaque displays a monochrome-transfer decoration, an artist has hand-painted the four chicks yellow and an egg (barely visible on the bottom) a bright red. The presence of the plaque shows this basket was always supplied with a decoration. Millard (MS 150/323) and Belknap (BM 142b) have both either photographed the backside of this basket or else their baskets were pressed in another mould without the plaque.

The color of this early mass-produced opal glass lacks the dense creamy-white color collectors associate with Westmoreland's later and more serious pieces. There is a faint, greenish cast to the white of this basket, which shows that the iron in the sand was not sufficiently neutralized by manganese.

"2" Flower Basket Spoon

(c. 1904)

Number and designation taken from the 1904 price list.

Egg cover is interchangeable with the one used on the egg-covered sleigh (this section).

No mould numbers.

1904: Available as an "Opal Novelty."
1932: A **"2 Basket with a Chicken Cover"** was available in opal.
1940: Also available with a decorated comb and eyes. In the 1952 catalog it was pictured and described as a **"#2 Hen on a Handled Basket."**

Width: 5"
Height: 4⅜" (total)

This cheerful egg-covered basket still bears its red Westmoreland label proving it was first sold as a mustard container. With an egg cover and no plaque, this may have been the first available version of the basket, for it was pictured this way in a c.1902 catalog page reproduced in Ferson (FF 640). It was on a page showing six of Westmoreland's "Opal Novelties."

From an early date, however, the basket also came with a round plaque on the side intended for decorating. It was also available from an early date with a hen mounted on the lid. We can be sure the hen version was also in early use, because Millard (MS 323) has pictured one with some of its early cold decoration remaining.

Notice that in contrast to the **"1" Bushel Basket,** the rope motif continues on the inside of this basket; in fact, it totally surrounds the two handles.

There is a basket cross on the bottom which is covered by the original paper label.

"2" Basket first available between 1900 and 1904.

Hen
Duck

The Hen

> "(At Westmoreland's display at the Pittsburgh Exhibit) *Let me not forget the Barnyard Assortment, two whole carloads of which were sold to a single house"* (L 1/16/04).
>
> "*S.Q. Hamilton* (Westmoreland's sales manager, 1902 – 1906) *is showing enough chickens in his Easter decorations to arouse suspicion as to his being a chicken fancier by avocation"* (L 1/14/05).
>
> "*The largest number of five inch covered hens made in this country were manufactured by the Westmoreland specialty company.... Its founder and president, Mr. Charles H. West, assured me that the prosperity of his concern was due to the very large sales of these little dishes in the old days filled with prepared mustard, which sold in carload lots"* (LPG 610).
>
> "*I have found one of the hen dishes with the name of the Westmoreland Specialty Co. Grapeville, Pa., still on it. These were very common in milk-white (both hens and roosters) but were more scarce in white with blue heads, in opaque blue with white heads, and in any other color would be considered a rarity"* (LVG 306).

If Westmoreland was the largest hen producer in this country, they were far from being the only one — or even the first. There were possibly four or five others including Indiana/Greentown, Challinor Taylor, and possibly New England Glass. Indiana/Greentown's hen is remarkably similar to Westmoreland's. But while Indiana/Greentown's hen has large, round eyes, Westmoreland's appears to be half open. Also, Westmoreland's tail feathers end in a smooth curve whereas Indiana/Greentown's are scalloped at the back. Finally, Westmoreland's can be distinguished by the mustard mould numbers that appear on the inside of most of Westmoreland's 5" hens. I have seen these hen numbers ranging from 1 through 6, which means there were at least six numbered plungers used with the same, or a greater number of moulds.

Westmoreland's early catalog picture of a hen on a basket seems to be inaccurate, for all Westmoreland's hens faced the left, and their tail feathers were clearly separated from their back feathers. While any Westmoreland hens or other animal containers found in transparent, iridized glass are recent, some remarkable early animal containers can be found with transparent colors and even black, combined with white. One of these Westmoreland black and white hens is currently on exhibit at the Philadelphia Museum of Art.

The Basket
These hens and the duck are on the first of three period baskets Westmoreland used for their animal-covered containers. Frank Chiarenza, a glass

First available between 1900 and 1904.

(c. 1905)

A mould number appears only on **Duck** basket.

1904: The **Hen, large size,** the **Hen, small size,** and the **Duck** were three of the ten animal-covered containers available as "Opal Novelties."
1932: Not listed.
1940: Not listed. By 1952, however, a **"#1 Large Hen"** and a **"#2 Medium Hen"** were both available. The **#1 Hen** was also available in blue ("antique blue") and combinations of blue and white.

Basket: 4¼" x 5½" o.d.

213

Opaque Glass

authority, has referred to this basket as Westmoreland's "Diamond Basketweave." Like the rope and basketweave baskets in the three preceding photographs, it has a large basketweave cross on the bottom.

But this Westmoreland basket is nearly identical to one made by Indiana/Greentown; in fact there is only one clear way I have found to tell them apart. If you turn both baskets over, you will see that the Westmoreland basket weaving is as detailed on the bottom as it is on the sides, whereas Indiana/Greentown's is softer and almost seems to vanish towards the center cross. Of course, only the Westmoreland

basket will show mould numbers.

I believe this style basket was used originally by Westmoreland with the **Hen,** the **Duck** (FF 75), and the "Closed-Neck" **Swan** (BM 155b).

Rabbit

(c. 1905)

Rabbit and basket both have mould numbers.

1904: The **Rabbit,** the **Lamb,** and the **Lion** were three of the ten animal-covered containers available as "Opal Novelties."
1932: Not available.
1940: A **"#5 Rabbit"** was available in opal only. In 1952, it was called a **"Mule Eared Rabbit"** and it was available with or without pink eyes and ears (BM 274).

Basket: 3⅝" x 5⅜" o.d.

The Rabbit is on the second of three period baskets Westmoreland used for their animal-covered containers. The Fersons have called it a "Picket Base" (FF 85); Belknap, an "Octagon Base" (BM 165a). This

base was shared with Westmoreland's **Lamb** (MS 316), (BM 165a) (FF 87) and its **Lion** (MS 305) (FF 89). Fortunately, these animals cannot be switched to other bases because the octagonal shape is unique.

First available between 1900 and 1904.

214

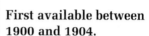

Cat
Dog
Rooster

First available between 1900 and 1904.

All covers and baskets pictured have mould numbers.

1904: The **Cat**, the **Dog**, and the **Rooster** were three of the ten animal-covered containers available as "Opal Novelties."
1932: Not listed.
1940: Not listed.

Basket: 4" x 5⅜" o.d.

This was the third of three period baskets Westmoreland used for their animal-covered containers. The Fersons have called it a "Wide Ribbed Base" (FF 16). Notice that Westmoreland's ribbing is wide, smooth, and continuous, in contrast to narrower, broken ribbing found on similar baskets made by McKee. I believe this style basket was used originally by Westmoreland with the **Cat** (BM 174c), the **Dog** (MS 318) (BM 174c), and the **Rooster** (FF 11).

Despite the remains of cold decoration, the Cat pictured in modern. The glass color and uniformity resembles the fine milk glass of the '50s rather than the early mustard-container opal of about 1905. Also, there are no fine crack lines. It still bears its mustard mould numbers, however.

Since the Dog was apparently never reissued, it is seldom seen today. Notice the black delineation around the eyes.

The blue and white Rooster pictured should probably have a transparent blue basket. Evidently, the unusual combinations of transparent blue, transparent amber, and black with white opal heads

were made in the mustard era. A variety of mould numbers can be seen in them today, and I understand a black and white Hen has come down to us with the remains of mustard still in it.

? — Dolphin Mustard Container

Cold decoration.

1904: Not listed.

Length: 7½"

Indiana/Greentown is believed to have made three variations of this Dolphin. One has an oval mouth ending in a smooth, continuous lip. Another has a similar mouth ending in a serrated lip (like the edge of a coin). The third has an irregular mouth with smooth lips and sawtooth sides. The first two share the same, small anal fin, while the third has a prominent, swept-back fin that, never-theless, clears the table by a quarter inch. All lids seem to interchange.

The Dolphin pictured has an irregular mouth combined with a small fin. In contrast to the three attributed to Indiana/Greentown, all areas of the interior of this one can be easily reached with a large spoon. Because of the particular colors used to decorate this Dolphin, I believe it was made by Westmoreland as a mustard container. There are no mould marks, however.

One of the Indiana/Greentown designs has been made recently in blue milk glass. I saw one with an irregular mouth, a large anal fin, and a pointed interior cavity. It bore the "V-in-a-circle" mark of Summit Glass.

Square Shaped Mustard Sugar and Cream

(c. 1905)

Both lids and the sugar bowl have mould numbers.

Both: 5" h.

These square sugars and creams are among the most frequently seen of West-moreland's early mustards; they seem to be as common in blue opal as in white. Note the scalloping on the rims and the lids. The creams and the sugars have different lids; they will not inter-change.

These lids with their "hog-scraper" tops suggest the chimneyed roofs of Westmoreland's Log Cabin and Stone House mustard banks — both shown in this section.

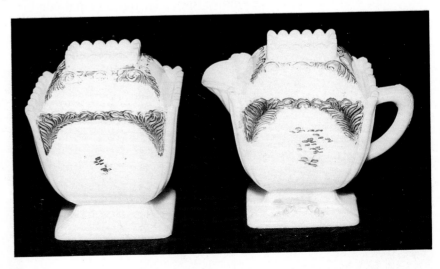

Mustard Sugars

The motif on the shell mustard sugar seems to have been derived from the Geneva pattern which originated with Northwood (probably) or McKee (possibly) around 1900 (HMW 143).

I have seen eight or ten cornucopia sugars, but I have never found a Westmoreland mustard mould number on one — nor in the lid of one. Nevertheless, I understand one has been found with its original red label, confirming both its Westmoreland and its mustard origin. There was also a companion cream for this sugar — a single cornucopia with a

stemmed gourd or cucumber for a lid. Bear in mind, there is no reason why any Westmoreland mustard sugar should be found with a cream, since they were originally sold separately.

(c. 1905)

Shell lid has a mould number.

Shell: 6¼" h.
Cornucopia: 4⅞" h.

Tall Mustard Cream and Sugar

Westmoreland made and packaged mustard to mid-1915 when the factory space was turned over to toy making and candy packaging. We can be certain about the timing of this important change, because it was reported in the trade press at the time (L 1/3/16). For the last fifteen years of Westmoreland's mustard activity, opal sugars and creams were widely used as mustard containers, and the designs for these opal mustards tended to differ from the designs for transparent glass.

This is the only example I have seen of a period mustard container, normally seen in opal, made entirely of transparent glass. It is also the only example I have seen of a transparent colored mustard container without iridizing. The Belgian blue color dates this sugar to the very end of the mustard era: 1915. Both the containers pictured share identical cold-gold decoration. Both show mustard mould numbers. Both tops will interchange. The cream still bears its original Westmoreland mustard sticker covering the mould number; presumably the sugar once came with one too.

Belgian blue glass first available in 1915.

(c. 1915)

The cream is blue opal. The sugar is early Belgian blue.

Both lids and containers have mould numbers.

Cream: 6¼" h.
Sugar: 6½" h.

Swan Mustard Cream

"Back in 1897, after a final turn, the molds for Westmoreland's Swan, covered milk glass cream and sugar were carefully cleaned and stored away in the Westmoreland vaults.... We are bringing them out again — after half a century of repose — in a 'limited edition'."

Swan Set first available 1902.

(c. 1905)

Swan and lid both have mould numbers.

Width: 5⅜"

(J 12/47)

The back-dating in this 1947 ad is at variance with an early trade report which reads, "The Westmoreland Glass Specialty Co. of Grapeville, Pa., are having a good run on their two new mustard sets, the 'Swan' and the 'Fruit'" (L 3/29/02). The swan set mentioned is this pictured cream and its companion sugar — not the "closed neck" swan on the "diamond basketweave" basket. The "Fruit" is probably the sugar and cream later called, **No. 108 Cherry and Grape.** This fruit set is perhaps the most commonly seen of the early opal mustards, and its successful reissue in the '40s may have been responsible for Westmoreland's similar looking **Beaded Grape** line (taken directly from U.S. Glass' "California" line) introduced in 1952.

While Westmoreland's 1901 catalog shows no swan items, the 1905 catalog shows the swan toothpick — related to this sugar and cream, but unlike these, not a mustard item. In 1984 Wm Heacock attributed Westmoreland's swan design to an English Sowerby design of the 1880s (HCI 46) and pictured a vase he said was made by them. This Sowerby design could very well be the inspiration for Westmoreland's initial design. But as incredible as it may seem, the sugar and cream set shown in the 1947 ad may have been made from later moulds taken directly from this Sowerby prototype. The wings on these swans are short and straight and there is an almost neoplastic protuberance beneath each of the swan's necks just as on Heacock's Sowerby vase. The differences between the two creams are obvious, but I have an early sugar (not pictured) that shows major differences with the sugar in this 1947 ad as well. Westmoreland used several sets of moulds for most of their mustards, and there is no reason why they might not have used two or more similar designs around 1905. But if the design shown in the 1947 ad is old, then we should be able to find an early example or else a mould number in the modern repressing that will confirm this.

The photographed cream and its lid both bear mould numbers. Lids for the sugar and cream on the original design almost interchange, but not quite: the sugar lid is about ⅛" longer and wider. I do not know if the lids of the reissued design will fit the early swans.

The Fersons (FF 174) have pictured the original Westmoreland mustard cream. Millard (MS 215) has pictured the original sugar. However, Belknap (BM 280) has pictured the two reissues in a late Westmoreland publicity photograph.

Swan Mustard Creams
Mustard Steins

(c. 1905)

Lids missing on all four
containers.

Both swans and steins
have mould numbers.

1904: **Steins 8-oz.** are listed under "Opal Novelties."
1932: Discontinued.
1940: Discontinued. Just
before Westmoreland's closing in the early 1980s, two
steins were reissued in
iridized ruby glass, however.

Lidless steins: 4⅞" h

The purpose of this grouping is to show four of the opal colors sometimes found on Westmoreland's early mustard containers: a thin white, a light blue, a darker blue, and a green. The dark blue is rarer than the light blue, and the green is particularly rare. It is usually seen on these steins where it has been confused with Indiana/Greentown's slightly yellower Nile green. These steins also came in a deep powder-blue color, and possibly also a chocolate brown. Out of about two dozen period Westmoreland steins I have seen, all were made of opal glass. Any steins found today iridized or in transparent colors are recent repressings.

Dwight Johnson, Westmoreland's glassmaker from 1965, told me he used either red copper oxide or black copper oxide to make his blue milk, and potassium bichromate to make his green milk. In S. Brainard West's notebook of pre-1938 formulations, however, "Blue Opal" was made from powdered blue (dilute cobalt) and copper scales, while "Green Opal" was made from iron scales. There were two blue opal formulations, but only a single green one in his notebook.

I have seen three different designs used on Westmoreland's 8-oz. steins, and I understand there may be more. Of the three I have seen, two had three scenes and the third had four. Two had trellis-work around each scene while the third had a German Renaissance motif. Two showed people in medieval dress while the third showed dwarfs. Two had aphorisms in German beneath each scene.

I have found the numbers 1, 2, 3, 5, 6, 7, and surprisingly, 0 on Westmoreland's steins. Since all that I have seen have been marked, I believe the absence of a number on a stein may indicate another maker.

Indiana/Greentown made at least two steins similar to Westmoreland's, and McKee apparently made one too. In their milk glass book, the Fersons have pictured two steins of uncertain manufacture. I believe their No. 42 will prove to be Greentown's or McKee's, and their No. 216 will prove to be Westmoreland's.

Lidded Mustard Stein

(c. 1905)

Stein has a mould number. Lid is unmarked.

Stein and Lid: 6½" h.

The dealer who sold this to me pointed out it depicted the nine dwarfs who live in the forest to protect the animals. Since I am particularly fond of this stein, I would like to accept her Schweitzerian view. Perhaps the dwarfs were taking a well-deserved day off! There are three scenes and each is framed by a trellised arch. Each shows three of the dwarfs: playing cards, drinking, and bowling, and beneath each scene is a German adage. Westmoreland's imitation of a German pottery stein extends even to the base, which is recessed. The stein was designed to hold 8 ounces of mustard originally. Surprisingly, given the rim shape, this rare surviving lid fits inside the mug and not outside it.

Log Cabin Mustard Bank
Stone House Mustard Bank

(c. 1905)

Both bear original Westmoreland mustard labels.

No mould numbers.

Both the Log Cabin and the Stone House bear their two original labels. The round red mustard labels include this listing of ingredients: "Formula. Mustard seed, brown and yellow, .15; vinegar, .75; salt, .07; herbs, .02; spices, .01; total, 100 percent." There is also square white label which reads, "To use as money bank procure common sealing or paraffine wax from any grocer. Melt and pour around top to secure lid from coming off. Knock out a piece of glass chimney from underside."

In contrast to the simple Log Cabin, the Stone House seems to be a formal, three-bay Georgian ashlar stone house with architecturally correct quoins and lintels. Turn-of-the-century touches are the scalloped slate roof, the five-panel door, and the arched center window. Since roofs on the two will interchange, be careful to notice the difference: Millard (MS 297) has pictured a Stone House with a wooden shake roof from a Log Cabin.

Here, Westmoreland employed the same three colors on both the Log Cabin and the Stone House; however, color variations can be found. For example, the Log Cabin was sometimes painted in a dark, uniform brown and the Stone House was normally painted in two tones of red, which explains (in part) the pseudonym, "Little Red School House" that has been given to it. Considering its construction, though, perhaps we could call it just as reasonably, the "Masonic Lodge"!

"Oriental Boy" Mustard Sugar
Hexagonal Mustard Sugar

Since both of these containers have come down to us with red labels, we can be sure of their Westmoreland mustard origins.

The square sugar pictures an Oriental boy on one side and a junk on the other. While there is a companion sugar that pictures an Oriental girl, there seems to be no corresponding cream for either.

The hexagonal sugar with its Craftsman-like severity, makes an interesting contrast with its rare-surviving domed lid. I have seen several of these sugars — almost always lidless, and always in this same blue color.

(c. 1905)

No mould numbers

Square Sugar: 3⅜"
Hex. Sugar: 3⅝" (without lids)

U. S. Hat

In 1944, Ruth Webb Lee wrote that this hat was "First issued during the campaign of McKinley and Roosevelt" (LVG 422). Since this campaign took place in the fall of 1900, the **U.S. Hat** must have been one of Westmoreland's first pieces of opal glass.

The hat pictured bears the mould number 2 on the inside (plunger side). The number 2 and 3 are most frequently seen in these hats. Since these block-style centered numbers typically appear only in Westmoreland's opal mustard containers, and these hats were originally fitted with tin covers, I believe it is conceivable they were among the first of Westmoreland's long line of opal mustards. I question whether they were sold initially by Westmoreland filled with candy, for Westmoreland's candy packaging evidently did not begin until more than a decade later. However they would surely have been sold as "packers' goods" to others who, in turn, could have resold them with candy in them. Four years earlier in 1896, Westmoreland had made covered McKinley and Bryan jars as packers' goods with pictures of the presidential candidates on the side.

These hats seem to have been made continuously down through the years, and were used and decorated in a variety of ways. For example, "(At Westmoreland's display at the Pittsburgh Exhibit) was an amusing little cigarette holder called 'Uncle Sam's Hat,' made naturally in the form of a tall hat of milk glass with a black glass rim" (L 2/32).

U. S. Hat probably first available in late 1900.

(c. 1902)

1904: Not listed.
1932: Available in crystal, colors, and opal.
1940: Available in opal only. The price was 20% higher than in 1932 (inflation accounted for less than a third of the increase).

Height: 2½"

231 Sleigh (Egg Cover)

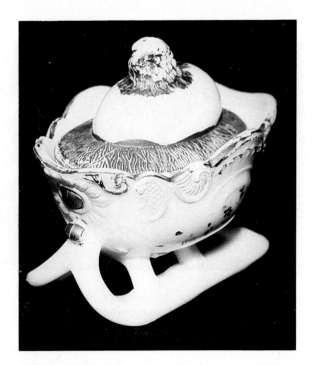

(c. 1905)

1904: **231 Sleigh** listed as an "Opal Novelty."
1932: Not listed.
1940: **1872 Sleigh** listed in opal only.

Length: 5¼"

231 Sleigh (Egg Cover) first available between 1900 and 1904.

The 1904 price list recorded two sleighs under "Opal Novelties": the **227** without a cover (see the Etched Glass section) and the **231** with an egg cover. Because it was not listed, the frequently-seen, and far more logical, sleigh with a robed Santa could be much more recent.

Since the 1932 price list failed to record a sleigh, there was probably a hiatus of several decades in its manufacture. The 1940 price list, however, recorded a 9" sleigh which was given the new number **1872** to go with the **35** or **236** candlesticks of c. 1904 vintage that were also reissued with that number.

In January 1941 the company advertised the 9" sleigh in a trade publication (J 1/41). Then a month later they carried their message direct to the consumer with an ad in *House and Garden*. They wrote, "An exciting revival... after an absence of 50 years... for over 50 years the sleigh bowl mold has been lying in our mould bin and only recently been uncovered...." Except for their "over 50 years," this

could be true. The large sleigh was not available in 1904, and while similar to the 5½" sleigh, there are a number of minor differences. If the 9" sleigh was made from an old Westmoreland mould, however, there should be some early survivors — probably in cold decorated etched crystal.

The egg cover on this sleigh is identical to the egg cover on the flower basket shown earlier in this section. In 1901 Dithridge advertised a "Sleigh Match Box" (L 3/7/01). Like Westmoreland's **231 Sleigh** it has a chick emerging from an egg in a sleigh. But this sleigh differs in two major ways from Westmoreland's: the Dithridge sleigh rim has a pronounced rise towards the back whereas Westmoreland's rim is horizontal. Also, the Dithridge runners have two supports on each side, while Westmoreland's has three.

That same month a Gillinder ad (L 3/14/01) showed a similar egg, with a rabbit emerging from it!

Pottery Effects on Glass

Milk glass has always attempted to imitate pottery. In 1910, Westmoreland decided to extend the imitation by going head-to-head with the expensive pottery steins then being imported from central Europe. Perhaps the idea came from the successful marketing of their little half-pint mustard steins. But Westmoreland needed something that was less symbolic and more functional in this macho age of pre-Prohibition beer quaffing, and their opal tankard set was the answer.

Westmoreland sold these sets — six 10-oz. steins and a 52-oz pitcher — directly, and also through the Butler Brothers wholesale catalog in 1910. Butler Brothers described them as "New in Glass," lending credence to Westmoreland's claim, "… for the first time in glass."

These sets that Westmoreland sold direct were available in the cased colors of brown, green, purple, and perhaps blue, and with a choice of three decorations — "elks," "mottoes," and "drinking scenes." The elk evidently came two ways: while the elk on the purple set pictured were hand-painted, the elk shown on the single brown mug was a monochrome transfer.

The sets sold through Butler Brothers were available only in "Rookwood Brown" and with a choice of a "stag," a "monk," or a "merry maker group." At a cost of just $1.20 a set (1995: $19.30) through Butler Brothers, however, these decorations all had to be monochrome transfers.

The monochrome transfer, or transfer print, is usually associated with china decoration. It was apparently used by Wedgwood as far back as 1761. The transfer is a copy of an original design, and not the original design itself. While the transfer in this respect is no different from a decal, there are two important differences between them: the transfer original exists as an etching on a copper plate, and each copy is lifted from this plate by tissue paper in just a single color. This copy is ordinarily not a complete design, but a design outline intended to be used in conjunction with hand-painting. (This book shows several examples.)

With decalcomania, on the other hand, there is no copper plate, and the decal

colors, the decals are designed to resemble and replace hand painting — not to delineate it. Decals were apparently first used in 1898, but they were not used by Westmoreland in the West period and used only in a limited way in the early Brainard period.

Unfortunately, this early opal was made with phosphates. Because of that it is brittle, and it will rarely, if ever, come down to us without hairline cracks. If these cracks are considered grounds for rejection, a collection will consist of little more than late reissues. Since the tankard sets were never reissued, all of them will show these cracks.

The purple set is also pictured and the color discussed in the Cased Glass section.

copies on special paper are usually purchased. Since each copy comes in various

Vase
Pitcher

(c. 1910)

Vase: 7" h.
Pitcher: 4" h.

Westmoreland also made other imitation pottery pieces in opal glass around 1910. Among these were a variety of vases and jugs without handles, mugs with conventional loop handles, and this little cream pitcher with its rustic handle. While everything about these points to Westmoreland, I have seen many of them attributed to Fostoria. Let's examine the evidence:

1. Both Westmoreland and Butler Brothers claimed this imitation pottery was new in 1910 — and implied it was unique to Westmoreland.

2. Westmoreland was the first to spray glass onto glass, and 1910 seems to be the earliest date this technique was used.

3. While Indians and Arabs, not apparently found on the tankard sets, can be found on Fostoria-attributed pieces, several of Westmoreland's tankard-set transfers can also be found on them as well.

4. Some of the Fostoria-attributed forms can be found with other Westmoreland decorations.

5. Westmoreland's exhibit at Madison Square Garden in August 1910 is pictured in the "What is Westmoreland?" section of this book. Many of the forms attributed to Fostoria can be found in this photograph.

Daisy Bowl
Peach Bowl — Crimped

In 1910, Butler Bros. then pictured this Peach Bowl and referred to it as a "Floral Design." They could have been more specific — the design consists of peach blossoms with peach leaves.

This Peach Bowl, also pictured in the Iridized section, is included here because it was made of white opal glass. This is the way it is nearly always seen. Apparently, Westmoreland chose this glass to help carry out its peach, or peaches and cream, theme.

The Daisy Bowl, made of blue opal glass, was made in the same mould as the Peach Bowl. Only the plungers differed. Refer to the Iridized section for a discussion about the bowl's identifying scallops and mould marks. Any of these bowls found in opal glass will almost certainly be old. Late carnival glass all seems to be black or in transparent colors.

Westmoreland was one of very few companies to iridize opal glass. Two other examples can be seen in the Iridized and Carnegie sections.

Peach Bowl first made 1909 or before.

(c. 1910)

Daisy: 8¼" d. (max.)
Peach: 9" d. (max.)

1933 Vase

(c. 1934)

The **1933** line was an updated interpretation of the highly successful **Lotus** design Westmoreland had introduced ten years before. This accounts for the new number, which was also its year of introduction.

In its outline and decoration this vase suggests the cubist, or martial classicism in vogue at the time (note the chevron silhouette). It seems to have existed in the shadow of the better-known **1933 Footed Bowl,** a companion vase that was described as, "Beauty in formal garb... a ribbed bowl rising from a fold of leaves terminates in curved handles at either side" (L 1/34). This companion vase had an oval, webbed foot, a nearly level rim, and two hooked handles resembling those on a **1211 Octagon Bowl** introduced in January 1928.

An enigmatic third **1933 Vase** was also made. It was a larger and much broader variant of this "Chevron" vase. Since its square foot was somewhat larger, it could not have been made from the same mould.

It was shown in crystal in a 1933 trade publication photograph (L 2/33), and one has come down in the family in opal.

1933 Vases first available in 1933.

1933 was the number assigned to several vases and an open spiral candlestick.

First period **1933 Vases** had ground bottoms.

1932: The **1933 Candlestick** was penned in as well as the **1933 Footed Bowl,** and the **1933 Vase.** All three available in opal. The candlestick also available in crystal.
1940: The candlestick, the "horn of plenty," and the 2-handled vase available in opal. The candlestick also available in crystal. By 1952, this chevron vase was again available.

Height: 10"
Weight: 4¾ lb.

1933 Horn of Plenty

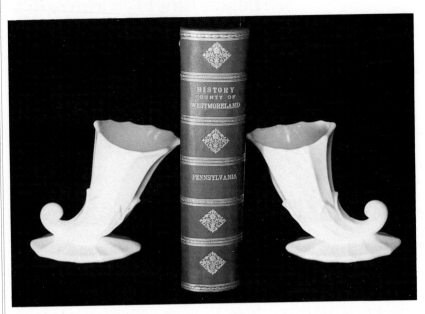

The "horn of plenty" was evidently Westmoreland's fourth and last vase in their **1933** line. It was also the most enduring. Of Westmoreland's five **1933** items, the three large vases had a comparatively short life span. The "horn of plenty" and the **7"** candlestick (where the wax candle was entwined by a spiraling lotus leaf) were made for years, however.

The "horn of plenty" was first pictured in a trade journal photograph in mid-1933 (L 7/33) together with a Westmoreland opal beer mug in the **Rings** design.

In their 1952 catalog, the company described the vase as "reminiscent of the old 'Powder Horn' of Pioneer days."

"2" Stamp Plates — 8"

The importance of these plates is their long-term association with Westmoreland. They were available, perhaps continuously, from the turn of the century until the company's closing in 1984. They were among the first items offered exclusively in opal after Westmoreland began to make this glass.

Throughout the West period, this plate was known by its historic (though less descriptive) name of **"2" Stamp Plate.** The term "stamp plate" was evidently a new one in 1900, for Dithridge & Co. felt the need to define it. In an ad picturing four of them in August of that year, they wrote of their "new line of stamp plates" as "the greatest novelty out. Fancy open rim for inserting ribbon can be put to ornamental uses...." Then the following month a trade journal wrote

that these Dithridge plates were "generally known as stamp plates from the fact that they were first used for decorative purposes by making designs out of clipped postage stamps" (H 9/00). In other words, stamp plates could be characterized by their plain centers where stamps were to be pasted and by their open work ("OW") rims through which ribbons could be strung. While ordinarily made in white, some early stamp plates may also have been made in blue.

Westmoreland may have been only one of three makers of this particular plate design at the turn of the century for there were three distinct versions. Two of the three show sharp breaks at the rim creating shallow wells in the center. While one of the two has a row of beads at this sharp break, the other is smooth.

The beaded version was made in crystal in 1904 with a St. Louis World's Fair design that I believe has been erroneously attributed to Westmoreland. The known Westmoreland plate can be distinguished from the other two by the very shallow drop to the center. This is the way it is shown in the earliest catalog pictures, the way it appears here, and the way it continued to be made during the Brainard years. The version with the beads is shown in Millard (MS 3). The version with the sharp break, but without the beads is shown in Millard (MS 26) and Belknap (BM 21c). The known Westmoreland version is shown in Millard (MS 8) and Belknap (BM 251c). While Canton was probably the maker of one, all three versions have been incorrectly attributed to Canton in these books. It is conceivable that Westmoreland was the maker of all three versions. If so, they were probably also the sole maker and the design innovator as well.

Although Millard would later refer to the design as "Forget-Me-Not, Triple Row," the rosettes are not forget-me-nots, for forget-me-nots have five petals. The same woven-rim design on the plate was used on silver basket and tray rims made in England in the eighteenth century. The rosettes are honesty (*Lunaria*) flowers cultivated both in England and New England for several hundred years. Similar rosettes can be found on leaded fan lights of the late Federal (c. 1810) period where they were used to cover the soldered crossings.

It is interesting to compare these two plates with another I own with a "WG" mark — made 30 years or so later. The diameters are the same, and the upper sides of all three are identical. For stability, however, the foot ring on the bottom was widened by ½" when the mould was remade. Color difference is worth mentioning for the difference may hold true for other pieces as well. All three of these flouride-rich plates are a bright white with no hint of grayness. All of them are dense and opaque. It could be said about all of them that no finer milk glass was ever made. But the two early plates are white, like porcelain, all over, whereas the later plate has just a tinge of blue at the edges. Also, the later plate is "colder" (perhaps a truer white), while the early plates are a creamy white. But without a side-by-side comparison, these differences might not be noticed. Nevertheless, while all three resemble milk, the later plate could be said to resemble skim milk and the earlier plates, Jersey milk.

These two pictured plates were painted by Helen (Mrs. Chas) West after which they were returned to the factory for firing. They were made and painted about 1930.

"2" Stamp Plate first available 1900 or 1901.

(c. 1930)

7" also available in 1901.

"2" was a sequential number. There was also a **"1" Stamp Plate** in 7" and **"4" Stamp Plate** (the "Fleur de Lis" plate).

1904: **"2" Stamp Plate,** 7" & 8" available as opal novelties.
1932: **"2" Stamp Plate,** 7" & 8" available in opal only.
1940: **"2" Lace Edge Plate,** 8" available in opal only. In 1952, 7", 8" & 11" available in white and blue milk glass and in black glass.

Plate: 8⅜" d.
Foot: 4¾" o.d.

1100 Toilet Bottle

(c. 1942)

1100 was an item number for Westmoreland's first toilet bottle.

1100/2 was the same toilet bottle with a cube-shaped stopper. These bottles were pictured in an ad of Oct. 1938, and were then available only in crystal.

1932: About 35 toilet and bathroom bottles available in crystal and colors. Two were available in opal.
1940: About 20 toilet and bathroom bottles available in crystal. Eight were available in opal.

1100 Toilet Bottle first available in 1916 or before.

"(Westmoreland has) *brought out a line of cologne and bathroom bottles. The bottles are etched very lightly in beautiful floral designs. The name of the liquid which the bottle is intended to hold is hand painted at the base, while the stopper and rim are also painted. The line has been brought out in green, blue, and pink glass*" (P 11/9/16).

SEE THE WESTMORELAND LINE

MANY
NEW
WARES

QUALITY
DESIGN
COLORS

No. 1083/545
Modernistic Bottle Set

For 1930, we have prepared a variety of items in shapes, colors and decorations that are bound to be popular.   Additions also have been made to established lines.

WESTMORELAND will offer the most complete array of quality toilet bottles. These bottles come in many shapes as well as in attractive sets.   Decorated to meet your need.

AT THE PITTSBURGH EXHIBIT

JANUARY 13th to JANUARY 25th

WESTMORELAND WARES

Will be shown in the

Assembly Rooms, Hotel Fort Pitt

▼▼

No. 1091
Octagon

WESTMORELAND GLASS CO.

GRAPEVILLE, PA.

No. 1093
Round

No. 1090 Set. Five Pieces

No. 1107 Square

No. 1085 Bull's Eye

No. 1089 Set. Four Pieces

"The Westmoreland Glass Co... are noted for their distinctive creations in toilet bottles" (J 12/28). Perhaps. But earlier that same year a New York importer advertised "Imported Colored Glass Bathroom Sets" decorated with flowers and birds and labeled in English, "Listerine," "Alcohol," "Toilet Water," etc. in what appears to be raised enamel (J 3/28). These imported bottles could be confused with Westmoreland's.

The thin, dull enameling on the pictured opal bottle suggests it was made in the Brainard period, and the gray color of the glass seems to pinpoint the early '40s. Westmoreland used the term "toilet bottles" for those with narrow necks and "bathroom bottles" for those with wide necks.

(L 12/29)

"3" Plates — 8"

"3" Plates first available between 1933 and 1940.

(c. 1942)

In 1940 also available 12",
14" & 16".

"3" was a Westmoreland
line designation.

1932: Not shown.
1940: 8" plates available in
crystal only. However,
most of the **"3" Lace Edge**
line was also available in
opal.

Diameter: 8¼" (max.)

The circle and spear rims on these Westmoreland plates were taken from the foot rims found on Atterbury comport bases. These bases were reproduced by Westmoreland and used with several opal-stem pieces beginning about 1933; two examples are pictured at the end of this section. I believe the plates showing this Atterbury border were first available at the very beginning of the Brainard era — about 1938 or 1939; the well-known candlesticks with this border came later.

The glass used for these plates is thin and gray — even in comparison with the glass used for the early mustard containers. These plates reflect the opal glass being made by Westmoreland during World War II when there was evidently a flouride shortage.

The elaborate decoration on three of the plates also suggests the war years as well. Company records show that extensive decorating was being done at this time to get around price controls that were then in effect. I have found this painting, even though fired, cannot be subjected to strong abrasion.

104 Vase — 15" (Pickle Jar)

(c. 1934)

One of the three pickle jars reissued as vases in 1926. The other two were **102 – 9½"** and **103 – 12½"**.

In 1927, **105 – 9½"** and **106 – 10"** were added.

These item numbers were assigned just to these pickle jar vases.

The vases were all blown.

1932: All five available in crystal and colors. **102, 103,** and **104** also available in opal.
1940: **104** was available in opal only. In 1952, **102, 103, 104,** and **106** were available in milk glass.

"Reproductions of Westmoreland pickle jars (are) made by the Westmoreland Glass Co… in crystal, amber, blue, green, and roselin… (and) in heights of 9, 12, and 15 inches" (L 7/19/26). Between 1926 and 1932 opal was added to this choice of colors. Compare this to an original, pictured in the Colored Glass section. The reissues can be readily identified because of their ground and polished tops; the 1890s originals have jagged, unfinished tops.

This and the three photographs that follow were taken in May 1936 at the West home by Mrs. May Hayes, an artist with the Pennsylvania Project of the WPA. They are part of a collection called the "Index of American Design," and copies are on file at the National Gallery in Washington.

104 – 15" Vase reissued in 1926.

"1" Shell Nappy — 6"

(c. 1934)

"1" Shell Nappy was Westmoreland's original designation.

Plain gold-edged decoration dates from Jan. 1933 (Dec. #915).

1904: Available under both "misc. ware" and "Opal Novelties" (i.e., available in crystal, opal, and possibly in colors).
1932: Available in crystal, colors, and opal. Opal cost 71% more than crystal.
1940: Available in crystal and opal. Opal was lined out in 1941. The 1952 catalog pictured it again in milk glass.

The **"1" Shell Nappy** is pictured in the Etched Glass section with a silver decoration, and is also pictured twice in the Iridized section. While the date span of these four examples is about 25 years, the **"1" Shell Nappy** was probably made continuously from about 1902 down to the time of the company's closing. In this 1936 photograph it is shown in white opal, the glass it could have been made in for more than 80 years.

"1" 6" Shell Nappy first available between 1902 and 1904. #915 decoration first available Jan. 1933.

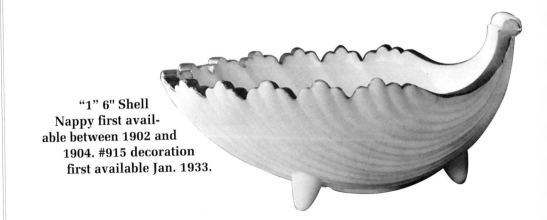

"3" Footed Comport & Cover

**"3" Footed Comport
and Cover probably
first available in 1933.**

(c. 1934)

1932: **"3"** line items not
yet listed.
1940: 37 – **"3" Lace Edge**
items shown, 22 of them
bowls, but not this footed
comport and cover. It reappeared in the 1952 catalog.

Many of Westmoreland's later "Authentic Reproductions" were wholly new forms that shared only design motifs with older pieces. Others, of course, were "Historically Correct" (a 1939 term). This covered comport is a nearly identical copy of an Atterbury original, and it dates from 1936 or shortly before. It shows that Westmoreland's close copying of older glass did not begin in late 1937 — it just accelerated then.

Belknap (BM 119) pictures an Atterbury original that should be compared to this copy. Only minor differences can be seen at the rim, the stem/bowl junction, and the finial. When I returned to Westmore-

land for a visit in the '70s, I noticed a large photograph of this comport on the wall of the gift shop. Stella Brainard, the president's wife, told me that the company had tried to make this comport in later years but had not been successful. Perhaps the problem was with the lead content of the milk glass used. While it softened and extended the working time of the "metal," it had a tendency to cause the glass to sag in the lehr.

A piece like this is a remarkable achievement in glass. The only problem in owning it is having to endure the gnawing thought that out there, some-where, is the real thing!

"3" Footed Bell Bowl

"3" Footed Bell Bowls probably first available in 1933.

(c. 1934)

According to Heacock (HCI 50) Fostoria may have made a number of milk glass pieces of this design (No. 2675) in the early 1960s.

1932: **"3"** line items not listed.
1940: 9" and 12" footed bell bowls available in crystal and opal. Six other **"3" Footed Bowls** also available.

A Westmoreland **"3"** line piece will have a rim with at least one of these two Atterbury motifs: staggered loops, or circles and spears. The first was used for borders around the **"3"** line's many bowls (this was the source of the two Brainard names, **Lace Edge,** and later, **Doric Border**), and the second, usually found along the rims of Westmoreland's comport bases, was adopted as a border on the **"3"** plates and on the widely-sold Brainard period candlesticks. Westmoreland's circle and spears look identical to Atterbury's, but Westmoreland's staggered loops are much coarser. Also, while small, well-defined spheres or nodules protrude from the outer edges of the Atterbury originals (BM 114) (MS 74, 84, 88), they are poorly defined on the Westmoreland's. An 11" plate pictured in

Belknap (BM 251d) appears to be Westmoreland's from the '40s.

A **"3" Bowl** without the stem or foot was pictured in a trade journal as early as 1932 (L 11/32). It was described as a **"9" Belled Bowl."** The Fersons (FF 362) pictured a similar bowl with this same ogee tripodal stem and open round foot which they attributed to Atterbury. Their attribution would be correct, for they pointed out that the Atterbury originals had a vertical support within the stem — and of course, they would have seen this in the one they photographed.

In their 1953 "Reproductions" catalog, the Brainards pictured this footed bowl and described it as "Another graceful piece which Westmoreland has been making… for more than half a century."

"We Originate — Others Follow.... Don't forget we are Originators of Black Glass Flower Bowls, etc" (P 5/25/16). By the time this Westmoreland ad appeared in mid-1916, decorative black glass was apparently being made by Cambridge, Duncan & Miller, Diamond, Northwood, and perhaps Fenton and Lancaster as well. But as late as January 1916 Westmoreland was alone. A trade reporter at the Pittsburgh Exhibit wrote, "What is considered the last word in new glass creations is being shown by the Westmoreland Specialty Co... in Italian Black — the latest development in glass making in this country" (J 1/13/16). To claim that Westmoreland was the pioneer in making black glass would be an exaggeration. Black glass, after all, was made by a number of companies in the nineteenth century, and no doubt before. In their 1904 price list black glass was even one of the colors Westmoreland offered for their developing trays. But Westmoreland does seem to have been the first to use black for ornamental glass such as vases, fern dishes, and candlesticks; and photographs taken of Westmoreland's decorating department in August 1915 show this black glassware was everywhere.

Etched black glass, so closely associated today with U.S. Glass in the '20s was being made by Westmoreland from the start. Also from the start, it was being decorated in a number of different ways. A month before the 1916 Pittsburgh Exhibit a reviewer wrote: "To the line of colored glassware recently brought out by the Westmoreland Specialty Co... the most striking of which is probably the black glassware.... Among the new things in black glass are several styles of footed compote besides bud vases, handled and plain candlesticks, finger bowls and plates, ash receivers and coasters. Several of these are shown in matt black finish.... Among (the) decorations are some handsome floral effects in coin gold.... Then there are some distinctive designs in white enamel and in white and red enamel.... The vogue of colored glassware, particularly among the shops catering to the exclusive trade, was an important feature... during the latter part of the fall season...." (P 12/30/15).

Geo, Lauman West once told me proudly that he came up with a glass color that proved to be such a hit at the Pittsburgh Show that "all the other companies came out with the same thing the following year." In 1915 George Jr. was 20, and

Corner of Westmoreland's decorating department in August 1915. The gentleman standing with the vest is believed to be Gustav Horn, head decorator. (P.J. Rosso)

in his teens he had spent a great deal of time at the plant. Was black this color?

The 1924 Westmoreland decorating department catalog showed 47 individual pieces of black glass. This count includes bowl bases and two bulldogs (see the Miscellaneous section), both made continuously from 1915 on. The following year a trade reporter wrote of Westmoreland's "Satin black, rich and soft finish" (J 1/8/25). This was a period when few companies other than Westmoreland and U.S. Glass were making black glass at all.

Five years later, however, black was back in universal favor. A reporter at the Pittsburgh Exhibit wrote of the glass displays generally: "In glassware... the most widely shown (color) was 'black'.... Not only in occasional and decorative pieces, but also in luncheon sets and dinner sets. The opaque but bright black body of the glassware was relieved by gold, silver, and etched decorations" (L 2/30).

Westmoreland appears to have made black glass continuously from 1915 to the beginning of the Brainard period, and then from sometime before 1952 to the very end.

Black Glass Chemistry

Black glass is evidently not hard to make. It can be made by super-saturating a batch with one of several colorizers — manganese, usually. It is a convenient dumping ground for odd colored cullet (which may explain all those big black Westmoreland bulldogs). Sam'l Brainard West's notebook of glass formulations included the formula for Westmoreland's pre-1937 black:

Sand	500
Soda ash	200
Burned lime	30
Fluorspar	20
Red lead	45
Manganese	15
Cobalt	14 oz.
Sodium bichromate	2½ lb.
Copper oxide	3
Borax	15
Nitre	25

Three colorizers were used. While the formula called for about the same proportion of manganese (purple) as used in the 1926 amethyst, it called for almost four times as much cobalt (blue) and it included copper (green). The minor amount of fluorspar specified shows it was used as a flux and not as an opacifier. This formula shows that Westmoreland's black was clearly not "black milk glass," and strictly speaking not "black amethyst." Despite the three colors used, however, purple seems to predominate.

Dwight Johnson, Westmoreland's chemist and glassmaker from 1965, told me he used just manganese (manganese dioxide) to color his beautiful black. While he originally used 50 pounds in his batch, he found he could cut this to just ten pounds with the addition of a half-pound of potassium bichromate. His late black glass is clearly black amethyst.

Paul Revere Round Nappy — 9"

(c. 1916)

Paul Revere was one of the two colonial lines Westmoreland introduced in 1912.

Line found only in black glass and crystal.

Line not pictured in any catalog after 1917.

"Keystone-W" marked.

Ground and polished bottom.

1932: Line assigned the number **1020**; 20 pieces still listed. Available in crystal only.
1940: Discontinued.

Diameter: 8⅝"

"A striking feature of (Westmoreland's) exhibit is a new line of black glass articles with white embossed decoration…" (L 1/10/16). Pictures taken of Westmoreland's decorating department in August 1915 show an extensive amount of white enameling being applied to black glass at that time.

While the boat shape (inverted here), the jaunty handles (not shown here), and the concave corners were inspired by late Federal period silver, I believe Westmoreland's **Paul Revere** design was original in glass. The boat shape, however, was later used by U.S. Glass in their 15189 line of 1919.

For a detailed discussion of this line see the Cut Crystal section.

Paul Revere Colonial line introduced Jan. 1912. White decoration available Jan. 1916.

98 Vase — 13"

The "**98**" – **13" Vase** was the basis for the blue lamp shown at the end of the Cased Glass section. This black vase was one of two found in the factory decades after it was made.

Like a free-blown vase, this vase shows no mould marks. Nevertheless, it is mould-blown because:

1. There is no pontil mark on the bottom. It was shaped entirely by being blown from the top against the sides of a mould.

2. It bears faint rotational marks on the side showing it was turned in this mould to eliminate the mould marks.

3. There is no irregularity (ovality) around the circumference.

Like the **104 Pickle Jar** shown in the Opaque and Colored Glass sections, it would have had a jagged edge when the top was sheared or "wetted" off. But like the later pickle jars intended for vases, its top was ground and polished, rather than fire-polished, afterwards.

97, 98, 99 Vases first available between 1918 and 1924.

(c. 1929)

Also available 11" (No. **97**) and 15" (No. **99**).

97, 98, 99 were single-item numbers.

Ground and polished rim.

1932: All three sizes available in crystal and colors.
1940: Discontinued.

Height: 13¼"

1012 Candlestick — 8"

Though this candlestick is nearly always found in crystal with cutting, it was shown in the 1910 Butler Bros. catalog with a "solid matt verde green metallic finish." Butler Brothers, a catalog wholesaler, described it as a "Square Colonial" design.

For a discussion about its probable origin, see the Cut Candlestick section.

1012 Candlesticks first available 1910 or before.

(1915 – 1930)

Also available 7".

Ground and polished top and punty.

1932: 7" and 8" available in crystal only.
1940: Discontinued.

Height: 8⅜"

235

1854-2 Chocolate Box & Cover

(c. 1929)

Also available in a smaller size: **1854/1.**

1854 was an item number assigned just to these two boxes.

Ground and polished bottom, pressed star.

1932: **1854/2** available in crystal only. **1854/1** available in crystal and colors. 1940: Both discontinued.

Diameter: 7½"

Unlike the **1854 Chocolate Boxes** found in the Carnegie section, the Gold & Silver section, and the Cased Glass section, the pressed star on this one has not been enriched with etching or cutting.

The forget-me-nots have been painted in raised enamel, confirming this chocolate box was made in the West period.

1854 Chocolate Boxes first available between 1918 and 1924.

1815 Cupped Bowl — 10"
1027 Candlesticks — 8"

(c. 1928)

1815 was the item number for five bowls made from the same mould: 9½" round, 10" cupped, 10½" belled, 11" flared, 11½" rolled edge.

Candlesticks have ground and polished tops.

1932: **1815 Bowls** available in crystal and colors. **1027 Candlesticks** available in crystal only. 1940: Both discontinued.

Bowl: 10½" d.
Foot: 5" o.d.
Candlesticks: 8⅛" h.

The **1027** was one of Westmoreland's Art Nouveau candlestick designs; notice the resemblance of this candlestick to a rose bud on its slender stem. Compare these black-enameled **1027**s to those of engraved crystal in the Cut Candlestick section.

With Currier and Ives chromos as well as Wallace Nutting prints, every copy, while technically hand painted, was nearly identical. Because each artist was given just one color to paint, several people were required to complete each one. At West-

1815 and 1027 both available between 1918 and 1924.

moreland, however, it appears each artist was assigned total responsibility for an entire decoration, and these artists seem to have been given fairly free rein. The differences between these two painted candlesticks is typical of the differences I have found in various pairs of objects — impossible, if they had been simply passed down a long table.

236

1207 Sugar & Cream Set

1207 Sugar & Cream set first available between 1913 and 1917.

(c. 1930)

1207 was an item number used solely for this sugar & cream set.

Optic on the inside (plunger side).

Round pressed star; circumferential groove just above the bottom.

This moderately-priced set never came with a ground and polished bottom.

1932: Available in crystal only.
1940: Discontinued.

Foot: 2¾" d.

I have no reason to believe this silver decoration was applied by Westmoreland. It is the sort of "stamped-out" decoration that could have been applied by

any mass-market decorating house onto any piece of black glass in order to brighten it up. Note the misuse of the term "Sterling" in the design. Sterling is only 92.5 percent pure, whereas plated silver, used here, is 100 percent pure.

A **1207 Sugar & Cream Set** with an etched gold band is pictured in the Gold & Silver section.

1211 Octagon 2-Handled Jelly — 6½"

1211 Octagon line first available between 1918 and 1924. 1211 Jelly first available in 1927.

(c. 1929)

1211 was Westmoreland's **Octagon** line.

A 7" mint bowl, a 7" bon bon, and an 8" cheese plate also made from the same mould — share same handles.

Ground and polished bottom.

1932: Available in crystal and colors.
1940: Discontinued.

Bowl: 5¼" d.
At handles: 6½" d.
Foot: 2¾" o.d.

The rose decoration on this jelly bowl can be tied to the decoration on the red **1700 Candy Jar** in the Flower section; the roses are in raised enamel on both.

Heisey's No. 1229 — 5½" jelly was apparently unmarked and could be mistak-en for this. However, Heisey's handles stick up, not out, and they have two rather than three supports. Finally, Heisey is not known to have made black glass.

237

1211/1 Octagon Bowl — 13" SE (Straight Edge)
1211/1 Octagon Candlesticks — 3"

1211 Bowl and Candlesticks both first available in 1927.

(c. 1929)

Bowl also available 10½" crimped (see colored glass section), 11" belled, and 11" cupped (same mould).

1932: All four **1211/1 Bowls** available in crystal, and colors. The straight-edged bowl also available in opal.
1940: The straight-edged bowl available in opal only.

Bowl: 12⅜" w. (max.)

These Westmoreland **1211 Octagon Candlesticks** are unlikely to be mistaken for any others; they are also pictured in the Reverse Painting section.

Westmoreland's **1211/1 Octagon Bowl** could possible be confused with Fenton's No. 1676. For a comparison of these bowls, refer to the end of the Flower section.

1211 Octagon Sugar & Cream Set

1211 Sugar & Cream Set first available in 1927.

(c. 1929)

1932: Available in crystal and colors.
1940: Discontinued.

Height: 4⅝" (at sugar handles)

The **1211 Sugar & Cream Set** is also pictured in the Cased Glass section. This same raised-enamel decoration can be found on a black glass salver or cake plate pictured in the Miscellaneous section.

The raised-enamel flowers are bleeding hearts.

1211 Octagon Cheese & Cracker — 10"

1211 Cheese and Cracker first available in 1925. This floral decoration available Jan. 1930.

(1930)

Ground and polished plate bottom.

1932: Available in crystal and colors.
1940: Discontinued.

Cheese: 4⅞" w. (max.)
Foot: 3⅛" d.
Plate: 10¾" d. (max.)
Foot: 5¼" o.d.

"As to (Westmoreland's) *colors... (the) newest of all is black. Probably the most noteworthy item in the line is the matt black of a richness almost inconceivable in pressed glass"* (P 11/25/15).

In late 1930 Diamond Glassware advertised a hollyhock decoration similar to this one by Westmoreland which they called, "Jack and the Beanstalk" (P 9/18/30). While it was also shown on black glass, Diamond's decoration was in silver — not raised enamel.

Notice that the sides of the cheese comport rise vertically on the **1211 Cheese and Cracker** pictured. Another cheese and cracker that could be confused with Westmoreland's **1211** has a shallow, cup-shaped cheese dish with no sides. For the origin of the once-popular cheese and cracker set, see the C. West Decoration section.

THE SKILL OF 40 YEARS GLASSMAKING
EXPRESSING THE SPIRIT OF TO-DAY!

TRADE EXTRA W QUALITY MARK

Our 1930 Line

Will reveal new modes of expression in glassware shapes and decorations. Buyers will immediately recognize its sparkling individuality and possibilities for active turnover.

First Showing at Assembly Rooms Fort Pitt Hotel Pittsburgh January 13 to 25

WESTMORELAND GLASS CO., GRAPEVILLE PA.

MANUFACTURERS OF . . .
...AIN-CUT AND DECORATED GLASSWARE FOR TABLE SERVICE-GIFT SHOPS-FLORISTS

(J 12/29)

239

? — 1045 Candlestick — 8"

1045 Candlesticks first available between 1918 and 1924.

(1920s)

Also available 9".

1932: Both sizes available in crystal and colors.
1940: Discontinued.

Height: 7⅞"

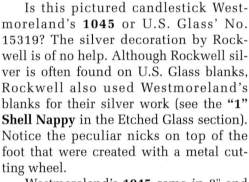

"Colored glassware so popular at the present time is equally as lovely and attractive in the lustrous ebony and especially when the black is decorated with sterling silver deposit... some of which is shown in group No. 246" (JC 1/17/23). "Group 246" shows seven pieces of Westmoreland's black glass decorated with silver.

Is this pictured candlestick Westmoreland's **1045** or U.S. Glass' No. 15319? The silver decoration by Rockwell is of no help. Although Rockwell silver is often found on U.S. Glass blanks, Rockwell also used Westmoreland's blanks for their silver work (see the **"1" Shell Nappy** in the Etched Glass section). Notice the peculiar nicks on top of the foot that were created with a metal cutting wheel.

Westmoreland's **1045** came in 8" and 9" sizes whereas U.S. Glass' 15319 came in 8" and 10" sizes. Both of Westmoreland's **1045** moulds survived at the plant until the late '80s when the 8" size was sold. The 9" mould, which remained there in 1991, is the one that is pictured.

The baluster-shaped stem, which seems to have been derived from a wood turning of the mid-eighteenth century,

was also used by U.S. Glass on one of their comports in the mid-'20s. The "suppressed balls" suggest early Philadelphia furniture.

1211/1 Candlestick — 3"
1038 Candlestick — 9"
1057 Low Candlestick
1009 Candlestick — 7"

1038, 1057, 1009 are candlestick numbers.

1932: **1211/1** and **1057** available in crystal and colors. **1038** and **1009** available in crystal only. Black glass availability not shown in the price list.

1940: All discontinued.

1211/1: 3¼" h.
1038: 9½" h.
1057: 1¾" h.
1009: 7⅜" h.

The **1211/1 Candlestick** is not black glass; the foot is black-cased on the underside of a crystal blank. Notice the candle holder has a simple cut decoration.

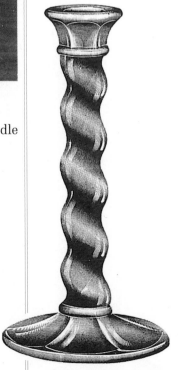

1034 Candlesticks — 9"

1034 Candlesticks first available between 1918 and 1922.

(c. 1930)

Also available 8" & 11".

1932: The three **1034** sizes available in crystal only. 1940: 9" and 11" available in crystal only, then discontinued until 1967.

Height: 9½"

This silver decoration, which may or may not have been applied by Westmoreland, shows a particular sensitivity to the glass form. Note the "hammer blows" beneath the silver on the lip (see the Gold & Silver section).

Westmoreland was the only maker of a candlestick of this design with a solid base. Other examples of Westmoreland's solid **1034 Candlestick** can be seen in the C. West Decoration, the Carnegie, and the Miscellaneous sections.

1034 Candlestick — 9" (Satin Moire)

(1923)

Height: 9½"

"(Out of Westmoreland's 35 new decorating lines) *a majority probably will agree that the new 'Satin Moire' finish glass is the most interesting.... Possibly the best description of the 'Satin Moire' is that it looks like a piece of moire silk had been made of glass instead of silk. The identifying convolutions of moire are truthfully reproduced in the surface of the glass. 'Satin Moire' is especially attractive in black, but it comes also in a number of pleasing colors. The black is shown also with gold and white gold edges and also in combination with ivory. The black moire and ivory make an almost irresistible combination. Shapes include flower bowls, comports, candlesticks, salad plates, salad bowls, cigarette boxes, and aquariums"* (L 1/15/23).

For more on this interesting decoration, including its tie to Wm Jennings Bryan, see the Carnegie section.

The architect Mies van der Rohe used to say he restricted his work to white, black, and gray so that his buildings would never go out of style. Surely he must have been thinking of glassware! Throughout this century and probably for centuries before, there were colored glass periods that alternated with crystal periods. But if the pendulum was kept swinging, it never swung twice in the same plane, for each new color period proved to be unlike the one that went before.

Beginning in the mid-'20s, the glassware industry responded to America's latest craving for color. (In that era, even Henry Ford capitulated: 1927 put an end to his famous, "Any color you want provided it's black!"). The expanded tableware lines the glass manufacturers came out with then were in pastel colors. While some of these colors may have been used in glass before, few, if any, had been used for tableware. By the early '30s, however, when the machine-made glasshouses began to make their glassware in similar colors, the handmade glass market once again demanded crystal and the companies complied. A reviewer at the 1931 Pittsburgh Exhibit wrote, "Crystal... was to be seen more often and in every display. A few years ago little or no crystal was to be seen.... There are many who might say that 'crystal' is a new color" (L 2/31).

Two years later Steuben, the aristocrat of glassmakers, went permanently over to crystal — but a crystal that was suffused with color. 1933 was also the year of Repeal, and Repeal meant a return to crystal. "Crystal glass is easily in the ascendency with colored wares only finding form in the cheaper end.... The liquor interests have sponsored an educational campaign that is already producing results, to educate the public to an appreciation of fine liquors in clear crystal so that the color as well as the taste of the beverage may be appreciated" (P 10/36). During the '30s the few new colors brought out by the hand houses tended to be "heavy colors" such as Westmoreland's ruby in 1933. In 1935 another reviewer wrote, "Colored glassware which has not been very active for some time past is showing a slight tendency to move. In this line of ware, cobalt blue is most popular with amethyst a close second" (B 11/9/35). I once saw a Westmoreland **1038** Candlestick in a deep cobalt blue, clearly from the West period. It was probably made at about this time.

While Westmoreland was probably never in its history a leader in colored glass, the company made a great deal of colored glass from at least the late '90s and may have been one of the last of the hand houses to discontinue color in 1937. We have contemporary press reports, ads, and price lists that tell us what some of these colors were; we also have Sam'l Brainard West's notebook. "Brainard" West, Charles' son, was Westmoreland's secretary from 1921 to 1937, the period when his father was president. After studying engineering at Lehigh, he began a career in Texas with Gulf Oil, but not for long. No sooner did he get to try on his first 10-gallon hat when he received a call from his father asking him to "Come back here and help me run the company."

I understand he took a keen interest in glass formulations, and a surviving notebook of his would seem to bear this out. In it he recorded 84 formulations which included 27 for transparent colors. While some of these are certainly formulas of other companies, the majority can be assumed to be Westmoreland's own. All of Brainard West's entries had to have been made prior to August 1937 when he left the company.

There is an importance to that cut-off date beyond Westmoreland's ownership change. At the end of 1935, less than two years earlier, Dan Jenkins had retired. Since this highly-regarded glassmaker had been Westmoreland's superintendent from 1895, most of these formulas must have been his. At the right is a listing of all 27 colored glass formulas from that notebook.

On the following page is a list of all the transparent colors I am aware of that were made during the West years. It includes some that are not in Brainard West's notebook. My sources were Westmoreland price lists, press reports, ads, and observation.

In August 1937, when Westmoreland's transparent colors came to a belat-

---

S. B. West's Notebook

Greens
  Green (4)
  Reseda Green #1668
  Emerald Green
Roses
  Rose
  Rose – 1928
  Roselind
  Pink
Ambers
  Amber (5)
  Light Amber
  Dark Amber
Yellows
  Yellow (2)
  Canary Yellow #1691
  Topaz
Purples
  Wisteria
  Amethyst
Rubies
  Ruby
  Ruby Dark #1667
Blue
Aventura

ed end, their elimination was a sound business decision then. Opal (milk glass) sales were on the rise, interest in color had waned, and Westmoreland's vast number of product and color options could not be supported by the depressed sales volume of the time.

Year	West Period Colors
1898	Green (an industry-wide color)
1904	Blue (developing tray color)
1904	Black (developing tray color)
1904	Amber (developing tray color)
1904	Bohemian Blue (swung vase color)
1904	Green (swung vase color)
1909	Dark Brown
c. 1910	Turquoise (found on Westmoreland carnival of this period)
c. 1910	Amethyst (found on Westmoreland carnival of this period)
c. 1910	Amber (found on Westmoreland carnival of this period)
c. 1910	Several opalescent colors (found on Westmoreland carnival of this period)
1915	Belgian Blue (first period)
1915	Black (to c. 1937)
1916	"Other colors"
1916	Pink
1916	Canary
1916	Green
1916	Wisteria (pale amethyst) (also made in early 1930s)
1920	Antique Topaz
1922	Antique Canary Yellow
1922	Ruby (probably 1 year)
1922	Dark Green (probably 1 year)
1924	Amber (to mid 1930; then 1932 to c. 1937)
1924	Blue (to mid 1929)
1924	Green (two or more greens) (to c. 1937)
1926	Roselin (a rose color) (to c. 1937)
1928	Aquamarine (a very pale blue) (to c. 1937)
1929	Topaz (a yellow with no brown component) (through 1931)
1931	Moonstone (an opalescent) (to c. 1937) (revived in 1970 with the same name.)
1931	Amethyst
1931	Belgian Blue (darker than in 1916) (to c. 1937)
1933	Ruby (probably one year)
1934	Lemon Yellow

But success in one period can pave the way for failure in another. In October 1962, five years after milk glass sales had begun to fall, one of Westmoreland's manufacturers' reps wrote to J.H. Brainard, "Public demand for Westmoreland is slipping.... Our sales are made almost exclusively to women of middle and old age groups. Milk Glass apparently has little or no appeal to young women... (crystal) is not a type of glassware that would have any special appeal to young women...

(despite) Westmoreland's recent experience with Golden Sunset... colored crystal continues high in public favor and is accounting for strong selling and, presumably, healthy profits for Fostoria, Imperial, and L. G. Wright in pressed lines and Seneca in blown."

Golden Sunset, a red-amber first made in December 1960, was Westmoreland's first colored transparent glass in 23 years. Launched without any market testing, it failed to sell, and this failure seems to have stiffened the Brainard resistance to color. But in 1964, when they finally came out with a green and a blue, Westmoreland's sales and profits turned the corner. The same manufacturer's rep wrote J. H. Brainard in March 1964, "Several women in an antique shop made two purchases... of our new color in stemware... I asked the women how come they preferred the reproductions in the colors in which the original pieces were never made rather than the white milk glass in which they were made, and I was told that the white reproductions had been overdone, to use their words, and the color had not."

Here is a listing of all the colors I am aware of made by Westmoreland from 1960 through 1972. Some of these will prove to be milk glass colors. My sources were company correspondence, board minutes from 1960 – 65, and sales records from 1962 – 73.

First Sold	Early Brainard Period Colors
1961	Golden Sunset (made 12/60 – 3/62)
1963	Ruby (single year: disc. 9/63)
1964	Brandywine Blue (first made 12/63)
1964	Laurel Green (first made 12/63 – disc. 1966)
1964	Amber
1965	Bermuda Blue (disc. 1970)
1965	Olive Green
1966	Flame (two year duration)
1969	Moss Green (single year)
1969	Antique Tan (single year)
1969	Antique Green (two year duration)
1970	Blue and Crystal Moonstone (crystal disc. 1971)
1970	Topaz (single year)
1970	Orange (single year)
1970	New Blue (single year)
1971	Gray (single year)
1971	Brown
1971	Purple and Green Marble (milk)
1972	Plum

Blue Vinegar Bottle

This bottle was found in a corner of the factory with the smell of vinegar remaining in it. Its construction appears to be identical to Westmoreland's mould-blown "G I S" (ground-in stopper) jars made as late as the teen years. However, it is the type of mould-blown bottle commonly made just prior to the use of the Owens automatic glass bottle-making machine of 1904 (MB ch. 6).

The bottle base has a broad, shallow, concave section which may have functioned to help center the bottle in the mould. The circumferential mould seam runs around the outside of the base just above the bottom. Two side seams rise from this and disappear at the base of the neck, which was formed through rotation by tooling. The smooth taper on the inside of the neck suggests it was meant to be corked.

Height: 12½"

1776 Colonial Tall Sweetmeat, Rolled Edge — Amethyst

If the turquoise color in the following photograph resulted from the non-use of manganese, the amethyst color of this sweetmeat resulted largely from its overuse. This deep amethyst seems to have been used for several years just after 1910; in 1916 it was replaced by "Wisteria" — a much paler amethyst color.

But the deeper color may have been brought back 10 years later, for in S.B. West's notebook a formulation called "Amethyst" bore the date of November 1926. It consisted of:

Sand	100 parts
Potash	28½ parts
Soda ash	8 parts
Marble dust	12½ parts
Manganese oxide	4 parts
Cobalt oxide	¾ oz.

Below this was added, "the color of this glass may be modified by changing the proportion of manganese oxide and cobalt oxide in the batch."

Based on this note we might expect to find Westmoreland's amethyst in various hues ranging from predominately blue to predominately red-violet. The formulation for Westmoreland's "Wisteria" was entirely different. It achieved its color through the addition of neodymium (a rare earth). This **1776 Colonial Sweetmeat**, also pictured in the Iridized section, was also available in amethyst without iridescence.

1776 line introduced Jan. 1911. 1776 Sweetmeat first available between 1913 and 1917.

(c. 1914)

1776 was one of Westmoreland's two original colonial lines; four more were to follow.

"Keystone-W" marked.

1932: Available in crystal only.
1940: Discontinued.

Height: 7"

Original Pickle Jar — Natural Glass Color

Unfinished jagged top.

Revived in 1926 as a **104 – 15" Vase.**

The reissues can be found in crystal, opal, and various colors (see the Opaque Glass section).

1932: **104 – 15" Vase** available in crystal, colors, and opal.
1940: Available in opal only.

Height: 15¼"

While Westmoreland apparently made several pickle jars in the 1890s, including this one, there is no clear evidence they made the pickles to go in them. Instead, they were probably sold to the trade as "packers' goods."

The jagged top shows this jar was blown from the top into a blow mould, after which the glass bubble at the top was severed or "wetted off." The circumferential mould mark is on the jar's bottom showing the mould had a raised post (platform) bottom whose function was to keep the vertical hinged "leaves" centered. Three very distinct vertical mould marks rising to the top edge show this mould had three leaves. Because of its design, the jar could not be rotated in the mould to eliminate these marks.

Compare this photograph to the photograph of the same jar in opal in the Opaque Glass section. In 1926 this was one of several pickle jars reissued as vases. These reissues can be recognized not only by their late-'20s colors, but by their finished (ground) tops.

This photograph may appear to show a different jar from the 1926 catalog picture and the opal vase photograph. This is only because they show different sides of the same jar. The German Renaissance design suggests the paneled decoration on one of Westmoreland's mustard steins.

Notice how similar this natural glass color is to the turquoise color Westmoreland used deliberately for some of its carnival glass around 1910. Its color stems from the iron impurities in the sand that were not "filtered" out by the use of manganese in the batch. Because of its clarifying function, manganese has been called "glassmakers' soap."

"77" Hobnail Toilet Bottle — Wisteria

This family **"77"** Hobnail Toilet Bottle proves that Westmoreland brought back Wisteria, a 1916 color, sometime between 1929 and 1937. 1929 was the year the **Hobnail** line was introduced and 1937 was the year the company changed hands.

In 1932 all 59 **Hobnail** items were available in crystal, colors, and "Moonstone" — Westmoreland's new term for opalescent. Color cost 20 percent more than crystal, and Moonstone cost 20 percent more than color.

Westmoreland used the term "Toilet bottles" for those with narrow necks and "Bathroom bottles" for those with wide necks. There was one of each in the **"77"** **Hobnail** line in the early '30s.

77 Hobnail line introduced in 1929.

(c. 1933)

A family piece.

1932: About 34 toilet and bathroom bottles available in crystal and colors. Two available in opal.
1940: About 20 toilet and bathroom bottles available in crystal. Eight available in opal.

Height: 6⅜"

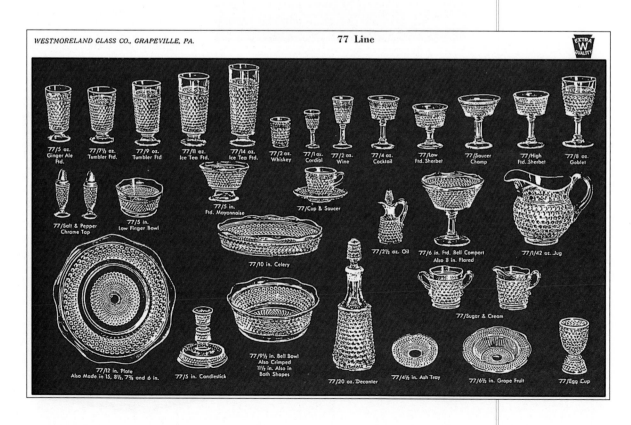

1053 Diamond Foot Candlesticks — 9" — Amber

**1053/9" Candlesticks
first available in 1926.
Amber glass first advertised Sept. 1924.**

(late 1920s)

In 1927, also available 4".

1053 was a candlestick
number.

1932: Available in crystal
and colors.
1940: Discontinued.

Height: 9"

*"(Westmoreland is showing)
new pieces in the shape of bowls,
comports, candlesticks and other
items. This shape has both oval and
round bowls and the feet are diamond shaped"* (L 1/18/16).

These candlesticks were sold to me as "certain unmarked Heisey" because of the shape of their feet. Since the stems came with an inverted baluster shape, perhaps the **1053 Candlestick** was intended for the Australian market!

The amber color, used early in the century, was reintroduced in 1924, phased out in 1930, and reintroduced again in 1932. The "Golden Sunset" of December 1960 was much redder than Westmoreland's late-'20s amber. Golden Sunset resembled Fostoria's amber of the late '20s.

Of the amber formulas in S.B. West's notebook, one of them used 23 pounds of mustard seed to create its yellow-brown color. Another called for 2½ percent brown sugar. Still a third specified oats and sugar.

555 Footed Cream — Topaz

In a 1930 Westmoreland ad: "(To) *our 555 line... we have added recently the jug and footed ice tea. They may be had with crystal, rose, green, amber, or topaz. Quite attractive are the ice tea with foot in black and the jug with handle in black"* (L 6/30).

555 Footed Sugar and Cream first available in 1927. Topaz glass available in 1929 and 1930.

(c. 1929)

555 was Westmoreland's largest tableware line.

1932: **555 Footed Sugar and Cream** available in crystal, colors, and opal.
1940: **555 Footed Sugar and Cream** available in crystal and opal.

Height: 4⅝" (max.)

Sparkling crystal stemware with ebony feet, square and round. Made in Imitation Early American. No. 555 line.

EXCEPTIONAL—

EFFECTIVE—

Every retailer knows the increasing vogue for old designs. This prompted the revival of our hob-nail glassware—a big favorite in years gone by. Today, combined with black feet it is one of the most striking and salable glassware creations on the market.

WESTMORELAND GLASS CO.

GRAPEVILLE, PENNA.

REPRESENTATIVES

New York—H. C. Gray Co., 200 Fifth Avenue.
Chicago—Ira A. Jones Co., 308 W. Randolph Street.
Philadelphia—Fred Stott, 1007 Filbert Street.
Boston—H. P. & H. F. Hunt Co., 72 Summer Street.
Baltimore, Md.—John A. Dobson & Co., 110 Hopkins Place
San Francisco—Himmelstern Bros., 718 Mission Street.
Los Angeles—Himmelstern Bros., 9th & Los Angeles Sts.
Seattle—Himmelstern Bros., Terminal Sales Building.
R. A. Keel, 6400 Wister St., Germantown, Philadelphia.

—Twenty-seven miles east of Pittsburgh on Penna R. R.—

(L 7/30)

Topaz is a yellow with absolutely no trace of amber's red-brown. It was first available in 1929, but it was phased out along with amber the following year. A reporter wrote that Westmoreland's topaz of 1930 was "a shade lighter" than in 1929. A year later, a reporter wrote of the Pittsburgh Exhibit generally: "Nearly every glassware display had either topaz or black or ruby as a new body color.... Topaz seems to be the general term for designating the new gold colored transparent glassware" (L 2/31).

Westmoreland's formula for topaz was:

Quartz (sand)	250 parts
Soda Ash	75 parts
Potash Carbonate	25 parts
Lime	45 parts
Potassium Nitrate	10 parts
Cerium Hydrate	17½ parts
Titanium	7½ parts

This 1930 ad shows **555** stemware pieces available with black (cased) feet. In 1930 and 1931 the **555** line was available in crystal with amber feet as well. The covered urn shown on the top shelf was actually the first piece offered in the new **300 Waterford** line. Note the flutes, which caused problems in the design of some of the **300** pieces such as the cream pitcher and the ice tea glasses.

555 Low Candlesticks — 3½" — Roselin

(c. 1927)

555 Candlesticks also available 9".

1932: Both sizes plus candelabra available in crystal and colors.
1940: Available in crystal and opal.

Height: 3¾"

555 candlesticks first available in 1926. Roselin glass first advertised July 1926.

"Roselin" was a subtle rose or peach color — a pink with traces of both amethyst and amber. Occasionally, however, the color would veer towards a true pink. While they first advertised it in July 1926, Westmoreland formally introduced Roselin at the Pittsburgh Exhibit in January 1927. It was probably made to the end of the West period 10 years later.

These **555 Candlesticks** were among those that Westmoreland introduced in 1925 – 26 in the new, low style (5" and under). The **555 Candlesticks** were Westmoreland's third, following the **Paul Revere Colonial** (1912) and the **Lotus** (1925), to be tied to tableware lines.

1211 Octagon Crimped Bowl — 10½" — Roselin

(late 1920s)

Also available as a 13" straight-edged bowl, an 11" bell bowl, and an 11" cupped bowl (same mould).

1932: All four bowls available in crystal and colors.
1940: All but the straight-edged bowl discontinued.

Diameter: 10" (max.)

1211 line first available between 1918 and 1924. 1211 bowls first available in 1927.

Unfortunately, the formulation for Roselin is not clearly identified in S. B. West's notebook. Roselin may contain lead, for Roselin pieces have a sonic ring, and I have found they weigh slightly more than the same pieces found in other colors.

This bowl was made in the same mould as the 13" straight-edged bowl (shown in this and the Black Glass and Flower sections).

1708 Sugar & Cream Set — Optic — Roselin

1708 Sugar and Cream first available between 1918 and 1923.

(late 1920s)

1708 was an **Optic** line.

1932: Available in crystal, colors, and opal.
1940: Available in crystal and opal.

Height: 2⅞" (at handles)
Foot: 2⅜" d.

The **1708 Sugar and Cream Set** was almost identical to Westmoreland's **294/295** set; the proportions, however, were coarser, and the price (in 1932) was 12 percent lower. (Compare this set to the blue **294/295** set in this section.)

Before 1926 this sugar and cream set was designated **1211** — then it was redesignated **1708.** Beginning in 1926, **1211** was reserved just for items in Westmoreland's growing **Octagon** line. **1708,** a new line number, was called the **Optic** line, but some confusion continued, for many of the **1708** items were available "plain as well as optic" — an option made possible with a simple change of plunger.

Westmoreland Specialty Co.
Grapeville, Pa.

No. 1211 Optic Sugar and Cream Set

Manufacturers of High Grade Glassware
Plain, Cut and Decorated
For Gift Shops, Florists and Table Use

Representatives

NEW YORK	PHILADELPHIA
H. C. Gray Co.	Peacock & Roop
200 Fifth Avenue	1007 Filbert Street
BOSTON	BALTIMORE
H. P. & H. F. Hunt	L. S. Fiteman
41 Pearl Street	404 W. Baltimore Street
SAN FRANCISCO	DALLAS
Himmelstern Bros.	D. D. Otstott, Inc.
718 Mission Street	Southland Hotel Building

(J 3/1/23)

1921 Lotus line introduced June 1924.

(late 1920s)

Lotus patent (65338) granted 7/29/24 to Gustav Horn for 3½ years.

1932: All three items available in crystal, colors, and opal.
1940: Candlestick discontinued. Bowl and plate available in crystal only.

Candlestick: 9" h.
Bowl: 9½" d.
Plate: 13½" w. (max.)

Gustav Horn's 1921 Lotus:
Tall Candlestick — 9"
Cupped Bowl — 9"
Flared Plate — 13"
Roselin

"Candlesticks in the 'Lotus' carry the detail of the flowers on the base as well as in the candleholder proper. The stem is twisted" (L 3/29/26).

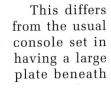

This differs from the usual console set in having a large plate beneath the bowl rather than a small bowl stand (see the Miscellaneous section).

For more on Westmoreland's highly-acclaimed **Lotus** line, see the Etched Glass section.

1707 Sugar & Cream Sets
1820 Handled Tea Tray — 8"
Roselin and Green

1707 was an **Optic** line.

1707 Sugar and Cream Set available optic and spiral.

1820 was Westmoreland's **Flange** line.

Tea Tray and Sugar and Cream set first available in 1927. Green glass first advertised Sept. 1924.

Webbed handles on the sugar and cream; open handle on the tea tray.

1932: Both available in crystal and colors.
1940: Both discontinued.

Tray: 8⅜" l.
Sugar & Cream: 3⅞" (handle to rim)

Westmoreland's **1820 Handled Tea Tray** was available in miniature for salt and pepper. It was also offered full size with four recesses (10") and six recesses (12"). Cambridge made a tea tray similar to Westmoreland's. But Westmoreland's tray has a smooth figure-eight shape, whereas Cam-

bridge's has an angular border and filleted sides that protrude about an eighth of an inch. Both the Cambridge and the Westmoreland **1820** are open-handled in contrast to a third, similar tray that has webbing in the handle.

1901 Fan Vase — 9½" — Green

Westmoreland first advertised their "green" glass in September 1924, but in the '20s and early '30s, they made at least two, and possible three, different greens. Unfortunately, Westmoreland never described their greens in any way in their advertising, and so today we have a problem determining which green came first, or whether several were made at the same time.

There were six green formulas in S.B. West's notebook. While one was identified as "Reseda Green #1668" and another was called "Emerald Green," the rest were unnamed. Chemically they were very different. Reseda green contained reseda green as its colorizer, and emerald green contained uranium and copper sulphate. Others contained copper sulphate alone, copper sulphate with copper scales, and iron oxide with copper oxide.

1901 Fan Vase first available in 1927.

(c. 1929)

The **1901** mini-line was designated **Regular Scallop.**

Fan vase shown and described in the Cut Colored Glass section.

1932: Fan vase available in crystal and colors.
1940: Discontinued.

Height: 9½"

1923 Leaf Salad — 9" — Green

(c. 1929)

1923 was the number of a mini-line.

A family piece.

1932: **1923** line available in crystal and colors (five pieces).
1940: **1923** line available in crystal and opal. A "turned handle bon bon" was added, available in opal only. The 1952 catalog shows the three **1923 Leaf Trays**: 6", 9" & 12" in milk glass.

8¾" x 8¾"

1923/9" Leaf Salad first available in 1927.

"One of the striking things of the Westmoreland display and of the Pittsburgh Exhibit for that matter, was the celery server or pan in the form of a large leaf. The stem of the leaf was turned upward to form the handle, the rough edging and the faithful reproduction of indentations and lines of the leaf made it an article of unusual appeal. This is made in crystal and four colors and is especially striking in green and 'Roselin.' Other colors are amber and blue" (L 3/14/27).

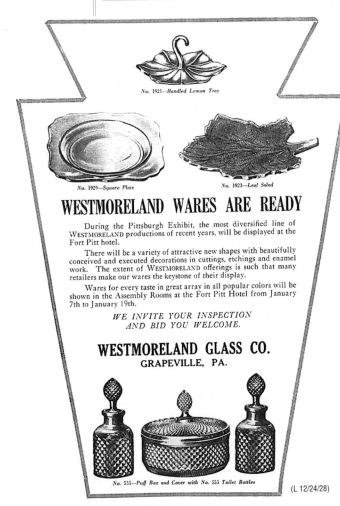

No. 1921—Handled Lemon Tray

No. 1929—Square Plate

No. 1923—Leaf Salad

WESTMORELAND WARES ARE READY

During the Pittsburgh Exhibit, the most diversified line of WESTMORELAND productions of recent years, will be displayed at the Fort Pitt hotel.

There will be a variety of attractive new shapes with beautifully conceived and executed decorations in cuttings, etchings and enamel work. The extent of WESTMORELAND offerings is such that many retailers make our wares the keystone of their display.

Wares for every taste in great array in all popular colors will be shown in the Assembly Rooms at the Fort Pitt Hotel from January 7th to January 19th.

*WE INVITE YOUR INSPECTION
AND BID YOU WELCOME.*

WESTMORELAND GLASS CO.
GRAPEVILLE, PA.

No. 555—Puff Box and Cover with No. 555 Toilet Bottles

(L 12/24/28)

The 9" leaf plate was introduced at the Pittsburgh Exhibit in January 1927. By 1932 Westmoreland had added comparable 6" and 12" plates, 9" and 12" bon bons, and a 4½" x 6" leaf almond.

The veining of these pieces is on the upper side, and what Westmoreland called "mould crackle" is on the bottom. By 1940 Westmoreland offered the line in opaque glass, which highlighted the veining by masking the crackle. The effect of the veins without the crackle can be seen in Belknap (BM 266a).

West Virginia Glass also made a leaf plate, their No. 201. But theirs had no stem and no mould crackle. West Virginia's leaf was a sugar maple, whereas Westmoreland's may have been a cross between an American sycamore and a London plane tree. Both of these trees are related.

555 Candlestick — 9" — Green

This is the taller of the two **555 Candlesticks** which Westmoreland introduced in 1926; the shorter one can be seen in this section in Roselin.

Westmoreland's **555** line was a pressed glass imitation of the American Strawberry Diamond pattern used by a number of cutting houses including Westmoreland (see the Cut Candlestick section). Around 1910 Pairpoint was using this cutting fairly extensively; they called it their "Fire Diamond" cut. At the turn of the century Tuthill was surrounding an eight-pointed cut star with American strawberry diamonds and calling it their "Quilted Diamond and Star" pattern.

Hocking's well-known "Miss America" was not the only Depression-era imitator of Westmoreland's pressed line. I have found that in 1932 Cooperative Flint advertised their "Early American Pattern No. 587" which also shared this American Strawberry Diamond motif.

WESTMORELAND GLASS FOR 1926

No. 555—Footed Bowl and Candlesticks

WE BID YOU COME

You will miss the most interesting display of the Pittsburgh Exhibit unless you visit the *Assembly Rooms* on the *First Floor* and see the many new things WESTMORELAND will show you.

A variety of beautiful new shapes and new designs in Colored, Decorated, Engraved and Cut glassware, as well as attractive new shapes for decorators and cutters will be shown.

We are featuring reproductions of the old Sandwich glass which is enjoying a popular vogue and these will be shown in high grade Crystal and beautiful shades of Amber, Green and Blue.

"EXTRA KEYSTONE QUALITY"

ASSEMBLY ROOMS, FORT PITT HOTEL

January 11th to Jan. 30th, Inclusive

WESTMORELAND GLASS CO.
GRAPEVILLE, PA.

No. 555—Cream and Sugar

(L 12/28/25)

294 Sugar — 295 Cream
Tall Mustard Sugar
Early Belgian Blue

294/295 Sugar and Cream first available between 1905 and 1907. Mustard containers last available mid-1915. Early Belgian blue glass first available in 1915.

(1915)

The blue mustard shows mould numbers in the lid and under the base.

1932: **295 Sugar and Cream Set** available in crystal only. 1940: Discontinued.

Sugar & Cream: 2⅝" h. Mustard: 6½" h.

This important tall mustard was pictured and discussed in the Opaque Glass section. It can be dated precisely, for Westmoreland's mustard operations were ended in mid-1915 and Belgian blue was first made that same year.

This early Belgian blue is lighter in color, overall, than in 1931. But though it is much lighter in thin glass sections, it is just as dark in the thicker sections. This unexpected contrast sets it apart from all other Westmoreland colors.

Compare this **294/295 Sugar and Cream** with its delicate handles to the similar **1708** set in Roselin glass in this section. The **294/295 Sugar and Cream** was available only in crystal by 1932.

1700 Colonial 5" Grapefruit (One Piece)
1776 Colonial Berry Sugar & Cream
Blue

(1924 – 1929)

1700 and **1776** were two of Westmoreland's six colonial lines.

All pieces **"Keystone-W"** marked.

All pieces have ground and polished bottoms. The sugar and cream are ground and polished to the pressed stars.

1932: Berry sugar and cream available in crystal and colors. Grapefruit available in crystal only. 1940: Discontinued. Beginning in the mid-1960s, however, various colonial pieces were reissued in transparent colors.

Grapefruit: 5½" w., 3"h.

1700 Colonial line introduced Jan. 1912. 1776 Colonial line introduced Jan. 1911. Blue glass first advertised Sept. 1924.

"Quite a novelty in (Westmoreland's) *Colonial is a one-piece item consisting of bowl and plate that could be used most effectively for the serving of grapefruit or cantaloupe or could also be employed as a mayonnaise bowl"* (P 2/15/12).

This blue, first advertised in late 1924, was made just five years. It is very similar to a blue used at that time by Fenton. This sugar and cream can also be found in a similar blue ("Brandywine") made from 1964. While the reissues will still show the early **Keystone-W** mark, they will not have finished bottoms. All colonial pieces from the West period will ordinarily have ground and polished bottoms.

700 Modernistic Sugar & Cream
1820 Handled Tea Tray — 8"
Aquamarine Blue

700 Modernistic line introduced Jan. 1927. Aquamarine glass first advertised Dec. 1928.

(c. 1930)

700 Modernistic was a Westmoreland line designation.

Twenty items in the new **700** line were pictured in the 1927 catalog supplement. Five years later 29 were listed.

1932: **700** line available in crystal and colors.
1940: Discontinued. By 1952, however, the sherbets and goblets were being reissued in black glass. Also, Millard (MS 183) shows a piece from that line in milk glass.

Sugar & Cream: 4⅛" h.

Twenty items in this interesting, castellated Modernistic line were first shown in Westmoreland's 1927 catalog supplement. Then, in 1930, Westmoreland advertised: *"Our 700 line… modern? Yes! But so conservative in its interpretation of the new art that it has general appeal…. Made in rose, green, or crystal, and crystal with black or red feet, also in colors with white decoration"* (J 3/30).

Perhaps Westmoreland was anticipating this trade comment written just a year later, *"Many of the new shapes (at the Pittsburgh Exhibit) tended toward the early American or Georgian and were away from the ultra-modern trend of a few years ago"* (L 2/31)

Westmoreland's aquamarine is a blue so light it almost appears colorless. It was introduced at the Pittsburgh Exhibit in January 1929 and it replaced Westmoreland's regular blue that year. It may have been made until 1937.

MODERNISTIC AND ATTRACTIVE

The No. 700 Line rightfully is enjoying a large sale. It has a design and lines of unusual appeal.

Many other items in addition to the Sandwich Tray, Cheese and Cracker and Mayonnaise Bowl and Plate illustrated. Made in all popular colors.

WESTMORELAND GLASS COMPANY

GRAPEVILLE, PA.

◆

REPRESENTATIVES

New York—H. C. Gray Co., 200 Fifth Avenue.
Chicago—Ira A. Jones Co., 308 W. Randolph Street.
Philadelphia—Fred Stott, 1007 Filbert Street.
Boston—H. P. & H. F. Hunt Co., 72 Summer Street.
Baltimore, Md.—John A. Dobson & Co., 110 Hopkins Place
San Francisco—Himmelstern Bros., 718 Mission Street.
Los Angeles—Himmelstern Bros., 643 South Olive Street.
Seattle—Himmelstern Bros., Terminal Sales Building.
R. A. Keel, 30 E. Walnut Lane, Germantown, Philadelphia.

—Twenty-seven miles east of Pittsburgh on Penna. R. R.—

(L 10/29)

1211/1 Octagon Bowl — 13" Straight Edge
1211/1 Octagon Candlesticks — 3"
Aquamarine Blue

1211 Bowls and Candlesticks first available in 1927.

(c. 1929)

Bowl: 12½" d. (max.)

Although this entire floral decoration is in raised enamel, the identical colors visible on the backsides of the glass show that it was a one-step operation.

An identical **1211 Console Set** can be seen in plain black glass in the Black Glass section.

1042 Candlestick — 9" — Late Belgian Blue

1042 Candlesticks first available between 1918 and 1924. Late Belgian blue glass first available Jan. 1931.

(c. 1932)

Also available 6½".

1932: Available in crystal and colors. 1940: Discontinued.

Height: 9¼"

If these **1042 Candlesticks** outnumbered all other items in this book, it is because they can be found with such a variety of decorations. Perhaps, as I wrote in the Cut Colored Glass section, the **1042 Candlestick** was made to be decorated. Yet, I own three undecorated pairs that I value because of their uninterrupted simplicity. Their simple baluster stems mounted on broad, plain, hand-formed feet remind me of so much early pewter where the beauty is in the color and the form.

No one ever made a more patrician glass color than Westmoreland did with their late Belgian blue. While it bears some resemblance to the "Bermuda blue" of the later Brainard years, it has no green component whatsoever. It is generally darker and does not show the sharp contrast between thick and thin glass of the Belgian blue of 15 years before. It is deep. It is transparent. In its thicker sections it seems to be infused with ruby — not violet, ruby. The impression is of light coming through a cathedral window.

Belgian blue was reintroduced at the Pittsburgh Exhibit of January 1931 along with "Moonstone" — an opalescent glass. Both may have been made until the end of the West period.

Tableware lines were made by Westmoreland continuously from early 1891 to mid-1984. While tableware was never so important to Westmoreland's product mix as it was to, say, Fostoria's, it was more important to Westmoreland than it was to Fenton, which never lost sight of its art glass focus.

In the West years tableware had three distinct periods. The first was from 1891 to about 1911. Westmoreland's many lines in those early years were almost all imitation brilliant cut, and I believe further research will confirm that Westmoreland borrowed their ideas more from cut glass houses directly than from competing pressed glass companies whenever their designs were not original. Westmoreland's quality varied from line to line. While some pieces from the early **Waverly** and the very early **15** lines, for example, were beautifully fire-polished, a **228** line goblet I own appears to have been indifferently made by another company. Bottom-finishing, while not usual in this period, can sometimes be found. All of Westmoreland's early lines were built around what was called a "four-piece set" which consisted of a cream pitcher, a vertical spoon holder, a covered butter dish, and a covered sugar bowl.

Westmoreland's second tableware period began with the introduction of their first two **"Keystone-W"** marked colonial lines. ("Colonial" was the industry-wide term for simple paneled or fluted glassware suggesting cut glass of the second quarter of the nineteenth century). In January 1911 Westmoreland launched both their **1776 Colonial** line with many pieces resembling Heisey's and their patented **Floral Colonial** line — an original design. In January 1912, these two were joined by two other colonial lines: the **1770 Colonial,** which suggested Jefferson's Chippendale line with its centered front panels, and the **Paul Revere Colonial** — unlike anything else on the market. Westmoreland displayed their **"Keystone-W"** marked lines in a separate room at the Pittsburgh Exhibit for five years. All of these early colonial pieces have ground and polished bottoms where you would expect to find them, and the crystal glistens with particular spectral fire.

At about this same time, Westmoreland introduced several interesting lines in imitation cut which were not marked and not designated "Keystone Quality" in their catalogs. The press, which had so much to say about the colonial lines, overlooked them. Geared to the conservative buyer, they still had four-piece sets at a time when the spoon and the covered butter and sugar were no longer fashionable. Two of these late imitation-cut lines, the **500** and the **550,** proved to be very durable; some pieces of both, in fact, are still being made today.

Westmoreland's third tableware period began about 1925 when new lines began to supplement the existing lines carried over from the preceding period. For the glassware industry, the Great Depression really got under way five years early. With the belated return in the mid-'20s of fierce competition from central Europe, American glassware companies did whatever they could to survive. They encouraged the American housewife to "Buy American." Some converted to machine operations, while others, as a minimum, turned away from the types of glass that required much hand work. They responded to the color craze of the '20s by coming up with new pastel hues (the Bohemians had typically favored crystal), and what is important to us here, they introduced a spate of new tableware lines — many of them reminiscent of America's glassmaking past. If the many new moulds needed were costly, they at least deflected much of American glassmaking from head-to-head competition with Bohemian blown glass. These new American tableware lines were more comprehensive then they had ever been before. They now included items such as candlesticks, salts and peppers, cups and saucers, and salad plates — pieces that had been sold separately before.

With their heavy emphasis on engraving, enameling, and blown glass, Westmoreland was one of the companies most exposed to this renewed import competition. But rather than abandoning their decorated "Corner Cupboard" glass, Westmoreland used the money they made from their pressed tableware to keep it going. Charles' brother, George, was not so fortunate. The major decorating house he established in 1921, George R. West and Sons, lacking basic glass operations to support it, closed as so many other decorating houses did in the late '20s.

Westmoreland's late tableware lines were the equal of any in the pressed glass industry, and they were probably the most diverse. By the early '30s, Westmoreland had a line — and a color — for just about everybody. But these lines, fine as they were, were really not the glass of Westmoreland's greatness. Westmoreland's premier tableware line was undoubtedly the **1932 Wakefield,** and Westmoreland sold their most expensive Wakefield goblets, with specially cut and polished stems and feet, for $6.00 a

dozen in 1932. But that same year, Hawkes sold their most expensive goblet, their "du Barry," for 100 times as much! At this time, however, the quality of Westmoreland's finest engraving and decorating was unsurpassed.

The following tables list the tableware lines and "near lines" that I have knowledge of that were made by Westmoreland to the eve of the Second World War. Defining a tableware line was easy for the early period, for a full line always included a four-piece set, but from about 1910 on, this no longer held true. I have defined a Westmoreland line as having:

1. Either a four-piece set or a sugar and cream plus a goblet and a salad plate.

2. A distinctive pattern.

3. Ordinarily, a minimum of 20 pieces at some point in time.

Early Tableware Lines

Lines	Dates	Max. Pieces
15	1891 – c. 1905	26 pcs. in 1904
91	c. 1891 – c. 1905	21 pcs. in 1904
Priscilla	c. 1891 – c. 1905	34 pcs. in 1904
Victor	1893 – c. 1910	16 pcs. in 1905
Elite	1895 – c. 1910	52 pcs. in 1904
Sterling	1895 – c. 1910	51 pcs. in 1904
Waverly	1896 – c. 1910	98 pcs. in 1905
98 Westmoreland	1897 – c. 1910	47 pcs. in 1904
160	1899 – c. 1910	21 pcs. in 1904
170	c. 1899 – c. 1910	15 pcs. in 1904
180	c. 1899 – c. 1910	57 pcs. in 1904
185	1900 – c. 1910	25 pcs. in 1904
Star	1901 – c. 1910	34 pcs. in 1904
Daisy	1901 – c. 1910	41 pcs. in 1905
200	1901 – c. 1910	42 pcs. in 1905
210	c. 1902 – c. 1910	40 pcs. in 1905
228	c. 1902 – c. 1910	55 pcs. in 1904
252	c. 1902 – c. 1910	14 pcs. in 1904
400	1903 – c. 1910	101 pcs. in 1904

15

91

Priscilla

Victor

Elite

Sterling

Waverly

98 Westmoreland

160

170

180

185

Star

Daisy

200

210

228

252

400

Other Early Patterns

Patterns	Dates	Max. Pieces
2	1890s – 1902	1 pc. in 1901
4	1890s – 1902	1 pc. in 1901
6	1890s – 1902	1 pc. in 1901
Trilby	1890s – 1905	2 pcs. in 1901
7	1890s – 1905	2 pcs. in 1901
13	1890s – 1905	7 pcs. in 1901
Rambler	1890s – 1905	4 pcs. in 1904
77	c. 1900 – c. 1910	3 pcs. in 1904
98	c. 1900 – c. 1910	2 pcs. in 1904
Rosette	c. 1900 – c. 1910	2 pcs. in 1904
Prosperity	c. 1900 – c. 1910	2 pcs. in 1904
English	c. 1900 – c. 1910	10 pcs. in 1904
Esther	c. 1900 – c. 1910	9 pcs. in 1905
Puritan	c. 1900 – c. 1910	6 pcs. in 1905
165	c. 1900 – c. 1910	18 pcs. in 1904
175	c. 1900 – c. 1910	19 pcs. in 1904
195	1904 – c. 1910	2 pcs. in 1904
205	1904 – c. 1910	9 pcs. in 1905
215	1904 – c. 1910	2 pcs. in 1905
225	1904 – c. 1910	13 pcs. in 1905
226	1904 – c. 1910	6 pcs. in 1905
250	1904 – c. 1910	10 pcs. in 1905
254	1904 – c. 1910	16 pcs. in 1904

2

4

6

Trilby

7

13

Rambler

98

77

Rosette

Prosperity

English

Esther

Puritan

165

175

195

205

215

225

226

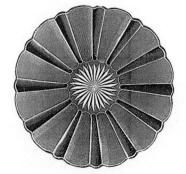

250

254

909

920

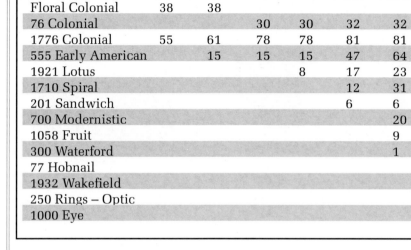

Late Tableware Lines

Lines	Pieces By Year							
	1912	1917	1924	1925	1926	1927	1932	1940
909	10							
920	25							
500	29	29	29	29	31	31	13	12
550	32	32	32	32	32	32		
575	18	18	20	20	20	20		
Floral Colonial	38	38						
76 Colonial				30	30	32	32	
1776 Colonial	55	61	78	78	81	81	103	24
555 Early American		15	15	15	47	64	c. 350	c. 230
1921 Lotus				8	17	23	36	25
1710 Spiral					12	31	34	
201 Sandwich					6	6	?	82
700 Modernistic						20	29	
1058 Fruit						9	19	56
300 Waterford						1	37	41
77 Hobnail							59	71
1932 Wakefield							60	40
250 Rings – Optic							25	
1000 Eye								98

500

550

575

Floral Colonial

76 Colonial

1776 Colonial

555 Early American

1921 Lotus

1710 Spiral

201 Sandwich

700 Modernistic

1058 Fruit

300 Waterford

77 Hobnail

1932 Wakefield

Tableware Lines

1000 Eye

Late Near Lines								
Patterns	Pieces By Year							
	1912	**1917**	**1924**	**1925**	**1926**	**1927**	**1932**	**1940**
Paul Revere Colonial	23	23					20	
1700 Colonial	22	27	32	32	39	39	47	
1777 Colonial		7	8	8	8	8	10	
333		7	7					
444		9	15	15	15	15		
666		10	12	12	12	12		
777		8	7	7	7	7		
122			10	10	10	10		
1211 Octagon			6	12	19	49	69	5
999					10	23		
1909						9	23	
1928						12	12	
1011 Cameo Diamond						8	16	
3 Lace Edge								38

Paul Revere Colonial

1777 Colonial

333

444

1700 Colonial

666

777

122

1211 Octagon

999

1909

1928

1011 Cameo Diamond

555 – 2 Handled Five-Part Relish With Marmalade Center — 12½"

555 Relish first available in late 1932.

(c. 1933)

555 was the original Westmoreland designation for this line — the largest in the company's history.

A family piece.

1932: Relish available in crystal only. Wholesale price was $21/dozen, or $20.50 without the ladle. (1995: $235/$230) 1940: Available in crystal only. Price was $25/dozen, (1995: $275).

Diameter: 13" (at handles)

EXTRA **W** QUALITY

555

LINE *of* Glassware

555 was Westmoreland's designation for the largest, and one of the longest continuously running lines in their history. It was sold as early as 1915 by G. Somers of St. Paul, a wholesale catalog house. Twelve items, evidently made with just six moulds, were offered that year in an assortment called, "Diamond imitation cut glassware assortment... new black diamond cut design." Westmoreland's 1917 and 1924 catalogs show these twelve items plus three more, still made with the same six moulds. Apparently, this line caught the spirit of the "Roaring '20s," for it grew to 64 items in 1927 and peaked at approximately 350 five years later. Even in 1940, 230 items were sill available — many in "opal" or milk glass.

We can be precise about the origin date of this relish, because it was typed into my 1932 price list with a "12/7/32" date. It was the most expensive **555** item both in 1932 and 1940. It consisted of seven separate pieces requiring four moulds to make. The marmalade was available alone; it was advertised with the ladle, a plate, and a chromium-plated brass top by Chase Brass & Copper Co. in 1934 for $2.50 (1995: $28).

200 Cream
200 Footed Oval — 8"

200 line introduced 1901 or before. Opal glass first made late 1900.

(1902 – 1910)

200 was the original Westmoreland designation of this medium-sized line.

1904: 33 pieces listed.

Cream: 5¾" h.
Bowl: 8¼" w.

"No. 200 is a plain line which has proven a great seller…" (L 1/11/02).

Although the trade reporter's comment about this line suggests it predated the Pittsburgh Exhibit of January 1902, the **200** line was not included in Westmoreland's 1901 catalog. The 1905 catalog, however, pictured 42 pieces. The opal cream in this photograph must have been a special mustard cream, for the 1905 catalog pictured the cream without a cover. Lidded pieces were rare in this line. Only three were shown among the 42 items pictured in 1905.

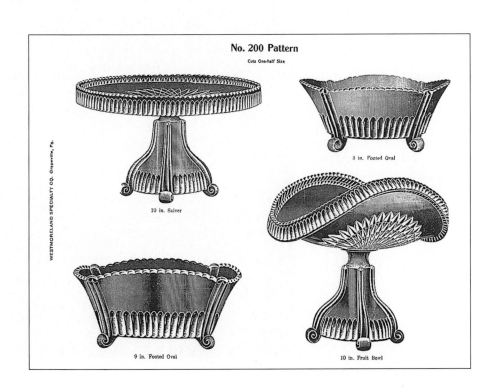

No. 200 Pattern

Cuts One-half Size

WESTMORELAND SPECIALTY CO. Grapeville, Pa.

10 in. Salver

8 in. Footed Oval

9 in. Footed Oval

10 in. Fruit Bowl

Mustard Sugar

(c. 1895)

An unknown early Westmoreland pattern.

More pieces may have been made in this pattern.

Height: 3¼" (to rim)

This mustard sugar has the same foot, the same 20-ray pressed star, the same 2⅝" diameter lid, the same 18-scallop rim, and the same reeded handle as the **Elite** and **Sterling Sugars.** It was probably packed and sold with mustard in the 1890s — the time when Westmoreland's mustard was packaged in crystal containers.

Priscilla Half Gallon Tankard Jug

Priscilla line possibly first available in 1891.

(c. 1898)

Priscilla was the original Westmoreland name for this very early line.

1904: 34 pieces listed.

Height: 9¼"
Weight: 3⅞ lb.

While the **Priscilla** was one of Westmoreland's earliest lines, this jug is beautifully fire-polished, has a "stuck" (hand-formed) handle, and a ground and polished bottom ring. Tumblers in this line, however, are not so well finished.

"15" Celery and Cream

"15" line first made in 1891.

(c. 1895)

"15" was the original Westmoreland designation of this very early line.

1904: 26 pieces listed, but line was no longer shown in the 1905 catalog.

Celery: 7½" h.

"15" was one of Westmoreland's very earliest tableware lines. The Pioneer Glass Co., a short-lived Pittsburgh decorating house specializing in ruby staining, pictured nine pieces of Westmoreland's **"15"** line in their catalog. While Pioneer apparently started in 1891, I understand they were out of business by the middle of the following year. If so, we can date their catalog to those few months of their existence. The Pioneer catalog page showing the nine Westmoreland cleft-log design pieces was headed, "No. 15 Pattern," which clearly establishes Westmoreland as the glassmaker. The celery and the cream pitcher in our photograph are two of the items shown on this page. The celery may have been comparatively short-lived, for it was not included among the 19 line **"15"** items shown in Westmoreland's catalog of 1901.

While Westmoreland seems to have been the first to use this cleft-log motif in a line, they may or may not have been the design originator. In their 1899 catalog, Butler Brothers pictured an assortment of 20 Bryce, Higbee pieces, all of which seem to have had different designs. One of the 20 was a handled bonbon, or nappy, which clearly shows this cleft-log motif on its side. At the turn of the centu-ry, Bryce, Higbee evidently was using this motif on two or more lines of glassware, and one of these lines was named, "Ethol." Heacock has reprinted both the Pioneer and the Butler Brothers' catalog pages in his somewhat inconclusive article, "Who Did Make Cut Log?" (HCI 88–9).

There is a possibility that bamboo shoots rather than cleft logs were the inspiration for this design. There is a surviving Chinese wine ewer of the Ch'ing Dynasty that bears an uncanny resemblance to Westmoreland's water pitcher despite its external spout and lid (CD 133).

Victor Half Gallon Pitcher

Victor line probably first available in 1893.

(c. 1900)

Victor was the original Westmoreland name for this small line.

1904: 14 pieces listed.

Height: 8" (to top of beads)

"(Westmoreland's) new Sterling, a star and diamond pattern, is an exact pressed reproduction of the famous Mt. Washington Glass Co.'s celebrated Bedford cut glass pattern which... has already been esteemed as one of the finest patterns made... the (Sterling) is made plain figured, or in amber or ruby decorations... the firm (also) shows their new Victor, a less showy and expensive line, but one which is meeting with favor" (L 1/15/96).

Claimants from Maine and Canada notwithstanding, Westmoreland was the first with this **Victor** design. Chas West was with Westmoreland from the beginning, and in 1933 when he told Ruth Webb Lee in an interview that the design had originated with his company (LVG 231, 236), he was in a unique position to know. Since the **Victor** line had been out of production for decades, he had no reason then to stretch the truth. This interview must have taken place in late 1933, for in August that year the magazine *Antiques* had a short article on Portland Glass in which the author showed a pitcher similar to the **Victor.** The author referred to it by its later pseudonym of "Shell and Jewel" and she wrote that it was "a very well authenticated Portland product." She was, or course, mistaken, for as she pointed out, Portland went out of business in 1873, and the design clearly suggests a date of origin a generation later.

But Mrs. Lee was also mistaken when she wrote, "Collectors may rest assured that the **Victor** was produced exclusively by Mr. West's company..." (LVG 239). Beginning in 1901, Fostoria also used this design, but not for a line, not for tumblers, only for a three-pint water pitcher. The pitcher was designated their No. 618. The two pitchers can be clearly distin-guished in, perhaps, only one way. While the rows of "eyeballs" along the rim of the **Victor** are perfectly horizontal, those on the Fostoria 618 dip gracefully in response to the angle of the handle and the spout. I have often seen what I have assumed was the Fostoria pitcher sold with tumblers which (if there is no third company) must be Westmoreland's, for Fostoria made only the pitcher. Fostoria seems to have discontinued their pitcher by 1909. The pitcher shown in *Antiques* and attributed to Portland appears to be Fostoria's.

If **Victor's** Westmoreland origin seems clear, its birthdate seems less so. The *China, Glass and Lamps* trade report would seem to establish an introductory date of 1896, which would mean it was first made in 1895 — two years after the 1893 date that has been frequently used. Ruth Webb Lee, again, seems to be responsible for that date, and it had to have come from her 1933 interview. Did Chas West say to her, "We were first — we brought that line out in 1893;" or did he merely say, "We were the first; we originally made that pattern about 40 years ago and here's one of our early catalogs that shows it?" I can truly claim to have been there at the house at the time of Mrs. Lee's interview, but have to confess I was making too much racket to

Victor Pattern

Sugar and Cover

Butter and Cover

SCALE ONE-HALF SIZE

Cream

Spoon

WESTMORELAND SPECIALTY CO., Grapeville, Pa.

Tray for Water Set

Tumbler

8 in. Berry

4½ in. Berry

Half Gallon Pitcher

overhear what was said. You see, I was a year old at the time!

There is another equally plausible explanation for the dating discrepancy. Major lines were seldom launched without trial pieces being made beforehand. Chas West told Mrs. Lee that the **Victor** four-piece set had been used to package Westmoreland's mustard in the 1890s. It would have been very easy for Westmoreland to market-test a line by making trial mustard containers of the new design followed by a formal line introduction if it appeared promising, and I feel sure this is what Westmoreland did. While these **Victor Sugar** and **Cream Mustards** were being made around 1910 in iridized colored glass (see the Iridized section), in the 1890s they all would have been made in crystal or transparent glass.

U.S. Glass later used the name "Victor" — but for a line that bore no resemblance to Westmoreland's **Victor**. U.S. Glass' No. 15046 Victor line, shown in a 1904 catalog, instead, resembled Westmoreland's **Sterling** line of 1896.

"98" Westmoreland Four-Piece Set

"98" Westmoreland line introduced Jan. 1898.

(c. 1898)

"98" Westmoreland was the original Westmoreland designation for this large line.

1904: 47 pieces listed.

Because of its gold-lustre trim, this four-piece set is also pictured in the Gold & Silver section.

The name "Westmoreland" was also used for a line by Gillinder in 1889 — the year this Philadelphia company opened a new plant in Greensburg. The two lines, however, bear no resemblance to each other.

I have mistaken the **"98" Westmoreland** for the frequently-seen "Pennsylvania" line of U.S. Glass.

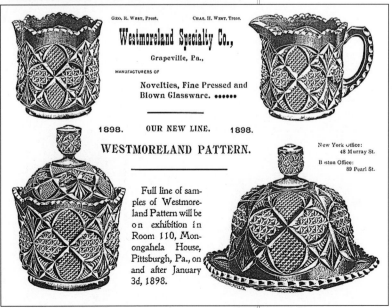

Waverly Berry Bowl — 8"

Waverly line introduced Jan. 1897.

(c. 1898)

Waverly was the original Westmoreland name for this major line.

Ground and polished bottom.

1904: 91 pieces listed.

Width: 8½" d. (max.)

"The Waverly is another new line (in addition to the Elite) *with cut figure near edge, and diamond pointed wheel incuts running in ribs towards the center, which is radiated by an incut star pattern. Decorated in gold the Waverly is a very bright line, and has had a good run thus far wherever shown. The line is especially strong in various shaped styles of berry bowls, nappies, cracker jars, vases, and rose bowls"* (L 1/13/97).

Of Westmoreland's early tableware lines, only the **400,** with more than 100 pieces, outnumbered the **Waverly** with 98 pieces in 1905. The **Waverly's** bat-like design may be unique.

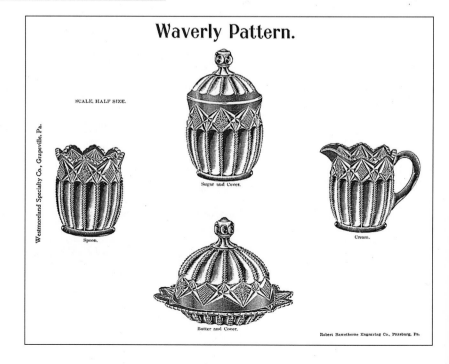

Waverly Pattern.

SCALE, HALF SIZE.

Westmoreland Specialty Co., Grapeville, Pa.

Spoon.

Sugar and Cover.

Cream.

Butter and Cover.

Robert Rawsthorne Engraving Co., Pittsburg, Pa.

160 Triangle Berry

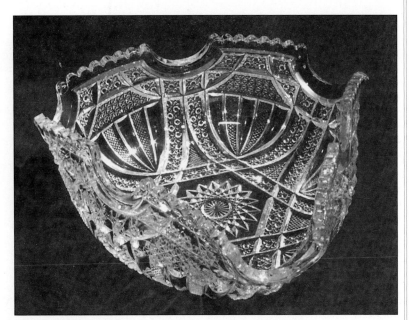

160 was the original Westmoreland designation of this small line.

This bowl was erroneously sold to me as "part cut."

Ground and polished bottom.

1904: 21 pieces listed.

Width: 8½" (max.)

"The Westmoreland Specialty Co. have a new pattern in glassware that they call the '160 line.' It has a shield side with a scalloped edge and a new design on bottom. The trade seems very much pleased with it" (C 12/99).

This line came with few pieces. Perhaps this is because those curious semi-circular cutouts along the rim limited its usefulness. All **160** line pieces I have seen were beautifully fire-polished, and a serving bowl with a set of small nappies I own all have ground and polished bottoms. This was well before Westmoreland's colonial period, when such quality work became commonplace.

A shield motif was also used by Bryce Brothers (a U.S. Glass Co.), but since the Bryce shield resembled the stars and stripes in the American Flag, the two designs are unlikely to be confused.

Heacock wrote that Westmoreland's **160** line was copied from a Libby cut glass design of the period (HCI 89). Since this would have been a pressed glass imitation of a cut glass design, his conclusion is probably true, for Westmoreland did do that sort of borrowing in the West period. However, in his research writings, Heacock regularly assumed, in the absence of dating evidence, that Westmoreland must have been the imitator when he uncovered similar designs of comparable companies. In comparing the glass of Westmoreland to similar pieces of other pressed houses, I have found that more often than not Westmoreland was the originator.

No. 160 Pattern

WESTMORELAND SPECIALTY CO. Grapeville, Pa.

No. 160 ½ Gal. Jug

No. 160 Tumbler

No. 160 4½ in. Nappy

Vase

No. 1 Knife Rest.   Full size

No. 211 Vase, 14 in. to 16 in.   7 in. Foot Vase, also made in 8 in.

Star Berry, Flared — 8"

Star line first made in 1901.

(c. 1902)

Star was the original Westmoreland name for this medium-sized line.

1904: 34 pieces listed.

Diameter: 8¾" (max.)

Westmoreland **Star Bowls** are shown (but not identified) in Millard (MS 87), Belknap (BM 131), and Ferson (FF 289). All show it in early opal (milk glass) — Millard, also, in blue opal. While the quality of this bowl does not compare with the contemporary **Waverly** or **160 Bowls** pictured in this section, both Belknap and Millard mistakenly believed the stars had been cut.

STAR PATTERN

WESTMORELAND SPECIALTY CO., Grapeville, Pa.

8 in. Berry

Tumbler

4 in. Nappy

10 in. Salver

10 in. Fruit Stand

8 oz. Oil

3 Pint Jug

In January 1901 Westmoreland introduced this line at the Pittsburgh Exhibit and sold it with "Bulls' Eyes" (Westmoreland's term) painted in four transparent colors of cherry, green, yellow, and blue. These colors were fired.

In 1904 Westmoreland offered two more decorations: No. 1, which was "gold-on-bull's-eyes"; and No. 2, which was "gold on saw teeth." While both were on crystal glass, Heacock wrote that he had found a **185 Butter Dish** in "deep amber, typically Westmoreland (very dark)" (HCl).

For some reason this bulls'-eye design seems to have engendered a great

185 Sugar
185 Bowl

185 line first made in 1900.

(c. 1901)

185 was the original Westmoreland designation of this small line.

1904: 25 pieces listed.

Sugar: 6" h.
Bowl: 8" d.

Dorflinger cut pattern. The only difference is that the six-sided English hobnails on the Dorflinger are flat across the top while Westmoreland's are capped with hobstars. Notice the Grecian "Bead and Reel" notching — cut on the Dorflinger, and pressed, of course, on the Westmoreland.

deal of proprietary feeling with many companies. Heisey's No. 305 and Cooperative Flint's "Famous" patterns are very similar to each other and to Westmoreland's **185,** yet both the Heisey and the Cooperative Flint patterns were patented. Heisey's 305 can be readily identified because of its oval bulls' eyes. The Cooperative Flint design seems to be a copy of a Becker & Wilson cut design, which was also patented (RA 338). Two other similar cut designs were patented by Benjamin Davies (RA 117) and Andrew Snow, Jr. (RA 57).

Where in this maze does Westmoreland fit in? Westmoreland's **185** design seems to have been taken directly from a

(J 2/21/01)

275

500 Quart Pitcher and Tumblers

(c. 1915)

500 was the original Westmoreland designation for this small but important line.

500 was the longest continuously-running line in the history of American tableware.

1932: 13 pieces listed — 10 available in crystal and opal. Three available in opal only.
1940: 12 pieces listed — available in opal only.

Pitcher: 7½" h. (max.)
Tumbler: 3⅝" h.

500 line apparently first made in 1909.

500 was Westmoreland's designation of what I believe was the longest-running line in the history of American tableware glass. First made in 1909, five or six years before Fostoria's "American" pattern, it was made continuously over the years and some pieces are still being made today.

The **500** was one of Westmoreland's last tableware lines to be introduced

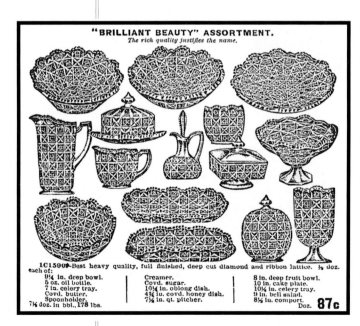

"BRILLIANT BEAUTY" ASSORTMENT.
The rich quality justifies the name.

1C15900—Best heavy quality, full finished, deep cut diamond and ribbon lattice. ⅓ doz. each of:
9¼ in. deep bowl.
5 oz. oil bottle.
7 in. celery tray.
Covd. butter.
Spoonholder,
7¼ doz. in bbl. 178 lbs.

Creamer.
Covd. sugar.
10¼ in. oblong dish.
4½ in. covd. honey dish.
7¼ in. qt. pitcher.

8 in. deep fruit bowl.
10 in. cake plate.
10¼ in. celery tray.
9 in. bell salad.
8½ in. comport.
Doz. **87c**

before their colonial period, which began the following year. Even in 1909 it could have been considered a little old fash-

ioned. It used a complicated imitation-cut design, and it included a dated, covered butter and sugar. Nevertheless, it managed to incorporate those up-to-date Chippendale handles that were then capturing the public's fancy. Never a large line, it peaked with just 31 items in 1926. This was less than a tenth as many items as the **555** line had at its high-point around 1932.

Initially, the **500** line seems to have been available only in crystal, and this early crystal had a clarity and brilliance lacking in later pressings. In the photograph, notice the ground and polished bottom of the tumbler and also the transparency of the ribbons. The Brainards later named the line "Old Quilt" — a superb name for it in milk glass, but singularly inappropriate for its early crystal form. There is nothing "cuddly" about early **500**. The **500** line was made in opal as early as 1932, and continuously from then on.

Care should be taken to examine closely any **500** glass found iridized. Despite the high prices I have seen I believe virtually all iridized **500** is recent: With a single exception, all iridized **500** pieces I have seen so far have been. Assuming period carnival is what the collector is seeking, a knowledge of early glass color and a sensitivity to early iridescent depth will be his protection.

We can be fairly sure about the year the **500** line was first made, for the 1910 Butler Brothers catalog showed it for the first time in five different assortments. In one, a 15-piece crystal assortment was called "Diamond and Ribbon Lattice." In another, a six-piece "Crystal Jewel" set was described as "Brilliant fire-polished crystal, deep miter and relief hobstars, all over ribbon lattice." In a third, an eight-piece "Cold Ribbon Dining Set" was described as, "Fine brilliant crystal, heavy hobstars all over, gold ribbon lattice, burnished gold edges." Clearly, the **500** line was seen at that time in its relation to cut crystal. Fifteen years later, this apparently had not changed. Despite the inroads made by foreign glass, a **500** assortment survived in the 1925 Butler Brothers catalog. This "Brilliant Beauty" assortment

was described as "Finest quality pot glass, diamond and ribbon band design, fine imitation of high grade cut glass."

The origins of the ribboned pattern are nearly as interesting and as tangled as the **185** (Bulls' Eye) pattern. Cambridge introduced such a pattern on their No. 2653 line in 1908, more than a year before Westmoreland. Ironically, Cambridge's pressed imitation-cut design may have spawned a number of similar cut glass patterns. At an unknown but probably later date, Libby came out with a ribbon design. Then in 1909 H.P. Sinclaire patented a ribbon design of their own (RA 184), followed by Hawkes, which patented what they called their "Willow Pattern" in 1911 (RA 186). Finally, Niagara Cut Glass Co. introduced, but probably did not patent, their "Ribbon Pattern" in 1912 (P 9/26/12).

550 Tumbler

The **550** line was brought out at about the same time as the **500** line. Its square-topped Chippendale handles suggest an introductory date of 1907 or after, and yet the line included a then old-fashioned covered butter and sugar. But while the **500** was made continuously over the years, the **550** line was given almost a half-century rest. In the mid-to-late '70s, Westmoreland began to reissue several **550** items in special carnival and opalescent glass for a major customer who apparently sold these pieces under his name. I have found only one **550** item in any of the late Westmoreland catalogs from this period, however. In the 1980 catalog, the 4½" **Footed Bon Bon** was pictured in an assortment of "Crystal Reproductions"; it was designated a **550 Sweetmeat**. I believe all first period **550** was made of crystal and I believe all iridized **550** will prove to be recent.

This line seems to be a simplification of Westmoreland's earlier, rather confused, **228** line. The similar arched feathers on the **550** design are more strongly defined with their crisp outlines and their uniform background of tiny six-sided diamonds that suggest stippling. Of the two, the **550** is perhaps even more assertively Art Nouveau in its feel. Because of this it seems to have been dis-

continued in the late '20s when it would have been viewed as a holdover from another time.

The decoration on the pictured tumbler is probably Westmoreland's, for I have seen a **500 Goblet** which incorporated the same ruby color on its ribbons and had the same gold-lustre rim. Westmoreland used ruby stain until about 1915, and then again from the '50s on. Gold lustre was also discontinued about 1915, but it was brought back again in the late '30s (see the Gold & Silver section).

550 line first made between 1905 and 1912.

(c. 1910)

550 was the original Westmoreland designation for this medium-sized line.

Bottom ground and polished to the Sunburst-design star.

1904: Not listed.
1932: Discontinued.
1940: Discontinued.

Height: 4"

555 — 3 Handled Vase — 8½" — Crimped

555 – 3 Handled Vase first available between 1933 and 1940.

(c. 1937)

Also available plain (uncrimped).

Another has a ground and polished bottom. This one does not.

1932: Vase not listed.
1940: Available in crystal only.

Crimped: 8½" h.
Uncrimped: 9" h.

Resembling a French cathedral with its flying buttresses, this rare and unusual **555 Vase** also suggests the Art Nouveau style from the turn of the century. Notice the smooth inside-champhered curve along the three legs, similar to the handles on Haley's **1016 Candlestick** (see the Cut Candlestick section).

In its manufacture, gradual cooling would have been critical. Another similar vase that I was fortunate to acquire developed a leg crack merely by being left out in an unheated part of my house. The pictured vase was sold from the factory about 50 years after it was made there.

WESTMORELAND GLASS COMPANY, GRAPEVILLE, PA.

555/32 Pce. LUNCHEON SET
CRYSTAL GLASS - BLACK CASED FOOT
EARLY AMERICAN

Consisting of:
4 - Goblets
4 - H. F. Sherbets
4 - Ind. Nuts
1 - Salt and Pepper
4 - Cups and Saucers
1 - Sugar and Cream
4 - Grapefruits or Cereals
4 - 8 inch Plates

201 Plate — 8" (Topaz)

201 line first made in 1925. Topaz glass available in 1929 and 1930.

(1929 – 1930)

201 was the original Westmoreland designation of this Sandwich-inspired line.

Plates also available in 7", 10½", 13" & 18".

Ground and polished bottom.

1932: **201** line pages are missing from my copy. 1940: 82 items listed. All five **201 Plates** available in crystal. 8" & 10½" also available in opal (but the pattern was on the back side where only the dishwasher could appreciate it).

Diameter: 8"
Foot: 5" o.d.

In late 1925 Westmoreland first advertised their new **201 Lace Design** line as "reproductions of the old-time Sandwich Glass which has again come into vogue." It was then offered in crystal, amber, green, and blue (J 12/17/25). This description was an overstatement, for this line was an original Westmoreland design that only suggested one then, apparently, thought to be Sandwich. A generation later, Westmoreland took this claim a step further when they advertised this line as "a faithful copy of a famous old Sandwich design" (House and Garden 10/43).

What was its origin? In 1925 Duncan & Miller introduced a similar line, their No. 41 Early American Sandwich pattern. They advertised it as a "Breath of Early New England" and "Rich in the Traditions of Sandwich." Duncan & Miller must have acquired a plate they then believed had been made by Sandwich, for we now know their No. 41 line is an exact reproduction of a French Baccarat pattern that seems to date from the 1830s (MC 137). Adding to the confusion, in the mid-1870s Bakewell Pears introduced their "Rochelle" line that had a similar design and a similar stippled background on the rim.

In the 1920s, though, Duncan & Miller and Westmoreland were not alone. In December 1925 Indiana Glass advertised their "170 Sandwich" pattern that shared a similar center with Baccarat/Duncan & Miller. Also, D.C. Jenkins made two plates with centers similar to these, and with original rims suggestive of what they must have believed Sandwich could have made (WE 208).

Ten years after their *House and Garden* ad, the Brainards in their 1953 Reproductions catalog referred to the **201** pattern as "A faithful restoration of a lovely old Sandwich creation."

1058 Fruit Design Goblet — 8 Oz.

1058 Fruit line first made in 1926.

(1936)

1058 Fruit Design was the original Westmoreland designation of this line.

1058 was an original 1870s-inspired design.

At the Pittsburgh Exhibit Jan. 1933, shown in opal with gold edges (B 1/14/33).

1932: 19 items listed. Goblet available in crystal and opal. Remainder of line available in crystal and colors.

1940: 56 items listed in crystal. About a quarter of the line also available in opal.

Height: 6¼"

"(Westmoreland's) large bowl is in colored glass and the top is flared out. Pressed in the glass are designs in fruit effect. This is a return to early American ideas of pressing the decorative effect in the glass. (The line) is made in the Westmoreland colors of amber, blue, green, and 'Roselin'" (L 3/14/27).

The specific inspiration for this original Westmoreland design seems to have been the bold double-pear and grape-leaf design used in Adams and Co.'s "Gipsy" line of the 1870s. Because etching over pictorial motifs was common in the 1870s. Gipsy almost certainly was part-etched. During the West period, Westmoreland's **1058 Fruit** line always had etched fruit; any pieces found unetched (except milk glass) will, I believe, date from 1938 or later. In the photograph, notice the care that was used in applying the wax resist to the area surrounding the etching. These goblets have been in the family, and since they were a wedding present, they can be precisely dated to 1936.

From the late '20s to 1937, every item in the line, except for the goblet, was available in color. While "Repeal" in November 1933 was said to usher a return to crystal for drinking, there had to be another explanation, for these goblets were also available in milk glass from 1932 or before. Ruby-stained fruits will date a **1058** piece to the Brainard period — the 1950s or later.

Westmoreland's **1058 Fruit** design could be confused with a similar one made by Duncan & Miller which was also etched. There is a major difference between them, however. While Duncan & Miller's designer was making bananas a prominent part of his arrangement, his Westmoreland counterpart was clearly whistling that 1921 hit tune, "Yes, We Have No Bananas!"

1058 LINE — WESTMORELAND GLASS CO., GRAPEVILLE, PA.

1058/1 Choc. Box

1058/5" Finger Bowl and 1058/6" F. B. Plate

1058 Sugar

1058 Cream

1058 Plate (Made in 9" & 14")

1058/4" Candlestick

1058/8" B. S. Sweetmeat

1058/13" RE Bowl

1058/13" Flange Compart

Chas West's 1011 Cameo Diamond — 2-Handled Bon Bon — 7" (Roselin)

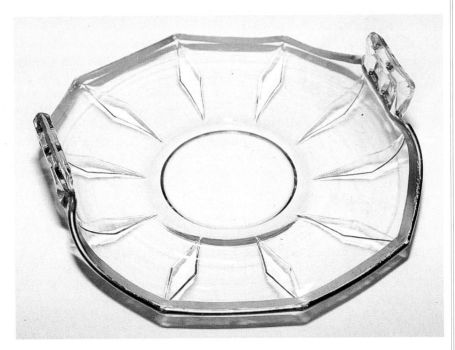

1011 line introduced Jan. 1929. #915 gold decoration available Jan. 1933.

(c. 1933)

1011 Cameo Diamond and **1011 Decagon** were both original Westmoreland designations for this mini-line.

Patent 78370 granted 4/23/29 to Chas West for 3½ years.

Ground and polished bottom.

1932: 6 items listed — all available in crystal and colors. (The cameo diamonds could have been effective in opal, but the line was not offered in this glass.) 1940: Discontinued.

Diameter: 6⅞" – 7⅛"

Although Cambridge had a major decagon line, these few pieces making up the **1011** line are the only 10-sided pieces Westmoreland made. Westmoreland referred to this line as both **1011 Decagon** and **1011 Cameo Diamond** for the raised (cameo) diamonds on the upper surface. Notice the Westmoreland handle that is shaped like a squarish figure-8. This handle was also used on similar **1211 Octagon** pieces (see the Black Glass section). When this line was introduced in 1929, it consisted of eight items that were evidently made from just two moulds. Three years later, however, the number of **1011** pieces had doubled and included both a sugar and cream set and a cup and saucer.

This patented design of Chas West's was the very last of 30 or so patents assigned to Westmoreland or filed by Westmoreland's personnel. In a very real and sad sense, it symbolizes the beginning of the end of Westmoreland's creative years.

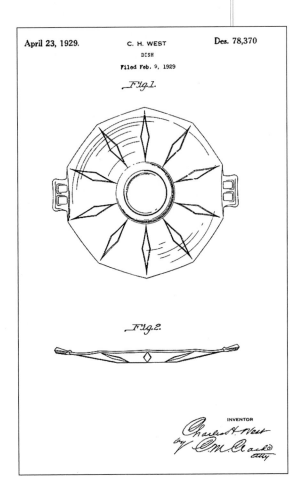

April 23, 1929.   C. H. WEST   Des. 78,370

DISH

Filed Feb. 9, 1929

Fig.1.

Fig.2.

INVENTOR

Charles H. West

1211 Octagon Candy Jar — ½ Lb. (Roselin)

1211 Octagon was the original Westmoreland designation of this line which grew from four bowls and two plates between 1918 and 1924 to 69 items in 1932.

1211 Candy Jar also available in 1 lb.

The unusual resonance of this candy jar suggests lead was used in the glass.

1932: 69 items listed. With three exceptions, entire line available in crystal and colors. 1940: Five items listed. The candy jar discontinued. By 1952, the ½ lb. size was reissued in milk glass.

Height: 8½"

1211 Octagon Candy Jar first available in 1925.

This candy jar is the octagonal sibling of the more common **1707** double-cone design pictured throughout this book. It was introduced in 1925 — four years after the **1707**. Notice that the octagonal cones extend to all parts of this candy jar just as the round cones do on the **1707**. I believe this candy jar was the sole **1211 Octagon** piece that was reissued in the Brainard period, and it was reissued only in milk glass.

In 1926 Westmoreland adapted the conical candy jar shape to their growing **555** line. The **555 Candy Jar** was made continuously well into the Brainard period. The cone shape was used also in 1928 for Westmoreland's **1710 Spiral Candy Jar.** Moulds for this entire **1710** line were drilled out in 1942 to create the hemispheric balls in the **1842 Swirl and Ball** line. Many of these **1842 Candy Jars**, made from the drilled-out **1710** mould can be found in milk glass today.

1932 Wakefield Bell Bowl – 17"
1932 Wakefield Plate, TE – 20"

1932 Wakefield was the original Westmoreland designation for this line.

1932: 60 items listed. Line available only with its own crystal formulation. 1940: 40 items listed. Available in crystal only.

Bowl: 17⅛" d.
Plate: 20" d.
Weight: 15 lbs. (combined)

In October 1930 T.G. Hawkes advertised two goblets calling them "Modern adaptations of old Waterford Glass" (J 10/30). The one they called "Munster Waterford" was the basis of the goblet in Westmoreland's **1932** line the following year. But Hawkes' felicitous marriage of oval eyes or thumbprints and English strawberry diamonds seems to have been used still earlier on a similar cupped tumbler by Thos Webb (MV 79).

The reason for Hawkes' Waterford name is interesting, and it was unrelated to the design of the glass. Samuel G. Hawkes, president of T.G. Hawkes, was a Penrose on this mother's side. Because Penrose was the family that had founded and operated the Waterford Glass Co. when it was in business from 1783 to 1851, Hawkes was incorporating the Waterford name on much of his company's glassware around 1930. For example, there was "Delft Diamond Waterford,"

"Mystic Waterford," "Checquers Waterford," "Belfast Waterford," "Bancroft Waterford," "Walpole Waterford," and many others.

Given the cachet of the Waterford name, it is understandable why Westmoreland might have wanted to use it on their **1932** line, too. The problem was they were already using it on their **300** line — their other prestige line consisting of flutes and American strawberry diamonds. While Westmoreland did, confusingly, call their **1932** line Waterford later, **Wakefield** was its original name. **1932,** the number of the line, was the year of its introduction. It was also the year of the George Washington Bicentenary, and Wakefield was the name of Washington's Virginia birthplace.

From the beginning, **Wakefield** was a special line. It even had its own glass formulation — a Bohemian flint mix. The goblets were available with "cut and polished stems and bases" at twice the price of the regular pressed goblets. Let us put these goblets in perspective. **555** was Westmoreland's "bread-and-butter" line. Eight-ounce goblets in that line whole-saled for $1.75/dozen in crystal in 1932. Pressed ten-ounce **Wakefield** goblets sold that same year for $3/dozen, or $6/dozen with cut feet and stems. Hawkes' "Munster" goblets, however, that were cut all over, were advertised for $50/dozen. (To put these prices in 1995 dollars, multiply them by 11.2). Westmoreland evidently decided to forgo any market testing, for in the year of its introduction the **Wakefield** line consisted of 60 pieces, two of which were this bell bowl and plate.

Despite the ladle shown in the photograph, this bowl was not sold as a punch bowl. A cupped punch bowl was available, however, as were two other plates 19" and 21" in diameter. All five of these immense pieces were made from the same expensive mould, and all five were priced the same: $30.00/dozen (1995: $335). Now the larger a piece of glass, the greater the likelihood that something will go wrong, and the price charged for a particularly large piece should take that into account. Nevertheless, since Westmoreland priced the photographed 20" plate at only double the price of the 14" plate, not even the difference in material and labor was entirely covered let alone the difference in the scrappage rate.

Did Westmoreland unlearn something they understood back in 1904 with their swung vases (see the Iridized section), or is there another explanation? In the '20s and even the Depression years of the '30s, Westmoreland designed and made some spectacular glass; this book pictures a

number of examples. Making money truly was not that important to Chas West, but making the sort of glass he respected was. And I believe he wanted to be able to share his glass with all those he felt would appreciate it. As he once told a local newspaper reporter, he was interested in bringing

"the prices of art and plain goods within reach of the average American's ability to buy and enjoy these wonders of utility, fancy and skill" (JD 1/16/23).

Pieces of this **1932** line are sometimes seen in colored glass, and are often seen in ruby-stained crystal. The colored glass dates from the 1960s and after, and the ruby staining was used from 1962 (though, possibly before) to 1981 and possibly later. This seems to have been the standard way this line was sold in the later Brainard era.

Tableware Lines

1932 Wakefield line introduced Jan. 1932.

(L 1/33)

283

1000 Eye Turtle Box & Cover

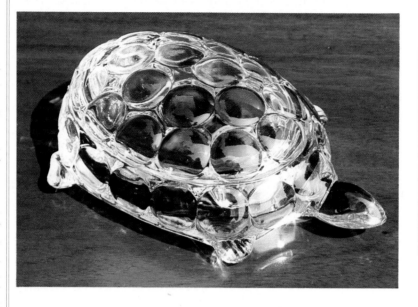

1000 Eye line introduced Jan. 1934.

(Unknown)

1000 Eye was the original Westmoreland name for this major line.

1940: Turtle box and cover, Turtle ashtray (a smaller lidless turtle), and a 6-piece turtle set (box with four ashtrays) available in crystal only. In 1952 they were all available in black glass.

Length: 7½"

"(Westmoreland's) *1000 Eye* — called a 'Modern Antique,' this is today's version of last century's glass design of that name. The 'eyes' are larger than in the old style" (L 2/34).

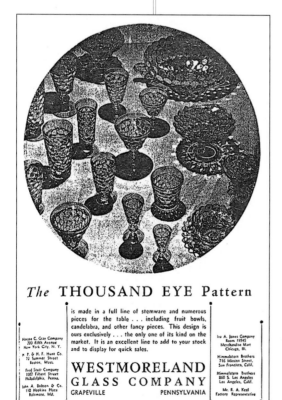

The THOUSAND EYE Pattern

is made in a full line of stemware and numerous pieces for the table . . . including fruit bowls, candelabra, and other fancy pieces. This design is ours exclusively . . . the only one of its kind on the market. It is an excellent line to add to your stock and to display for quick sales.

Horace C. Gray Company
200 Fifth Avenue
New York City, N. Y.

H. P. & H. F. Hunt Co.
72 Summer Street
Boston, Mass.

Ford State Company
1007 Filbert Street
Philadelphia, Penna.

John A. Dobson & Co.
110 Hopkins Place
Baltimore, Md.

Ira A. Jones Company
Room 11545
Merchandise Mart
Chicago, Ill.

Himmelstern Brothers
716 Mission Street,
San Francisco, Calif.

Himmelstern Brothers
860 S. Los Angeles
Los Angeles, Calif.

Mr. R. A. Keel
Factory Representative

WESTMORELAND GLASS COMPANY
GRAPEVILLE   PENNSYLVANIA

(J 9/34)

284

Westmoreland's **77 Hobnail** line, introduced in the late '20s, was little different from hobnail lines of several other companies of the time. On the other hand, the **1000 Eye** line of the '30s was Westmoreland's exclusively. Even the nineteenth-century prototypes bore little resemblance to it. The original **1000 Eye** motifs were made in the 1870s by two companies — Adams & Co. and Richards & Hartley (both later U.S. Glass companies). But Westmoreland made the eyes or roundels much larger, staggered the rows, and placed a little tetrahedron between each cluster of three roundels. These tetrahedrons, or projecting points, can be used today to distinguish Westmoreland's **1000 Eye** from other, later, similar designs.

When I visited Westmoreland in the mid-'70s, the tour guide assured us that

J.H. Brainard, the president at the time, had designed the **1000 Eye** line. Nevertheless, company records show he was first employed at Westmoreland in October 1933 when the line was already in production. It was introduced at the Pittsburgh Exhibit in January 1934, and of course the design and mould work had been done much earlier. The **1000 Eye** line was the last of the major West period tableware lines.

Millard (MS 236) pictured a **1000 Eye Turtle Box** in black and wrote that it was "probably British." It is as British as Westmoreland's well known camel — or maybe its peripatetic Victor pitcher! According to a surviving letter of Walter Brainard's (J.H.'s brother), since **1000 Eye** had just one remaining customer from 1951 on, the line was discontinued by the company in 1956. **1000 Eye Turtles,** however, continued to be made.

1000 Eye was not available in colors in the '30s, and as it was discontinued well before the Brainards introduced their first color in December 1960, it should not be found in colors today. Any turtle boxes that may be found in color are presumably more recent. Crystal **1000 Eye,** however, was available with the King's Jewel decoration of burgundy-, champagne-, and green-lustre staining from the beginning. Later, the pale burgundy was replaced with the more intense ruby.

Syria Shriners Glass

The Shriners, or more formally, the Ancient Arabic Order of the Nobles of the Mystic Shrine, currently has about ¾ million members in North America. Each is either a 32 Degree Mason through the Scottish Rite or a Knights Templar Mason through the York Rite. The photograph of George West was taken in December 1887 when he first "received orders" and became a Knights Templar Mason at the age of 24. He is shown wearing his Commandery, or Knights Templar uniform, and I understand the sword he is carrying in this photograph has been passed down in his family. Because of his partnership in a family dry goods business at the time, his occupation is shown as "merchant" on the Masonic records. While his brother Charles did not become a Shriner until 1919, in all likelihood, George joined shortly after this picture was taken. Today we can be grateful he did, because of the contribution it enabled him to make, both to that organization and to early twentieth century glass art.

Each Shriner member belongs to one of 166 temples. Pittsburgh's Syria Temple is the oldest of seven in Pennsylvania, and the eighth oldest in North America. Even since 1876 the Shriners have held an Annual Meeting or Imperial Session at one of these temples, and Shriners throughout the country who could afford the time have attended. As far back as 1893 souvenir glassware was either sold or presented to the members of the Syria Temple who attended, and evidently to some who did not. (Syria Temple's membership was 19,000 in 1929.) This practice seems to have been continued every year at least through 1918. While never made to be used, all of these pre-Prohibition glass souvenirs seem to have been drinking-related: shot glasses, wine glasses, champagne glasses, whiskey tumblers, etc. In some of the years, a shot glass was combined with another kind of glass making two souvenir pieces.

Westmoreland did not make them all, but it seems Westmoreland made all of the most interesting ones, and perhaps all from 1903 on. George West's keen allegorical sense was never more focused, and the quality of Westmoreland's decorations on these dated, early pieces is remarkable.

Unfortunately, George West and Westmoreland have failed to receive the recognition they deserve, and many of these pieces have been credited to other makers.

Before George West died, he passed his collection of Syria Shriners glass on to one of his sons with the comment, "Here, take my collection of Shriners pieces; we made them all." A distant cousin who once saw this collection can remember there were about 12 to 15 pieces altogether. She clearly remembers the Ruby **1908 St. Paul** with its faggoted wheat, and she remembers the **1910 New Orleans** iridized champagne with the two alligators. We know the **1905 Niagara Falls** glasses (the shot glass and three-handled mug) are Westmoreland's because of surviving moulds. We know the **1906 Los Angeles** and the **1917** iridized **Minneapolis** are Westmoreland's because of surviving moulds. We know the **1906 Los Angeles** and the **1917** iridized **Minneapolis** are Westmoreland's because of surviving paper labels. From all this we can go from piece to piece confirming the others Westmoreland would have made.

There is no reason to believe Westmoreland made any of the glass before 1903. Except for 1900 and 1902, the earlier glass was all generic; that is, the same glass blanks could have been used for any location visited. A 1902 San Francisco cup has survived with its original U.S. Glass label. It is almost generic, but not quite: the cup is supported by a "Golden Gate." Since this can be paired with the 1899 Buffalo as well as the 1900 Washington, U.S. Glass was undoubtedly the maker of all three. From **1903 Saratoga** through **1911 Rochester**, though, all but one of the pressed designs relates to the town or area where the annual Imperial Session was held. 1915 through 1918 are all opal (milk glass) tumblers. The two from 1917 are iridized and one of them has been found with a Westmoreland label. Finally, 1918 is spray-cased in the manner suggesting Westmoreland's "Pottery Effects" of 1910.

George R. West, December 1887 (Avis West).

285

Year 1906 Los Angeles — Pittsburgh

Plate base is ground and polished to a 6-point pressed star.

Plate: 6" d.

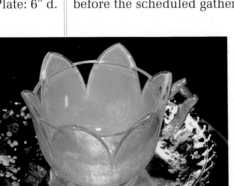

There is an interesting story about this **1906 Los Angeles** cup and saucer: there was no Imperial Session held in Los Angeles in 1906. Less than a month before the scheduled gathering, the earthquake hit San Francisco. Since all normal rail service to the west was curtailed, the Imperial Session had to be postponed and relocated. In the end it took place in Chicago in mid-June.

In this early period Los Angeles was associated with roses and oranges. Westmoreland's rose decoration, later so widely used (see the Flower section), probably had its origin here with the rose spray hand-painted on this plate. Westmoreland's sherbets and punch cups (see the Gold & Silver section) also must have had their origins with these Shriners cups.

The Shriners cup differs from the better known **69 Orange Sherbet** cup in just three ways:

1. The handle is decorated with green enamel, and not lustre gold.

2. The words "SYRIA — PITTSBURGH" are in the pressing on the bottom.

3. While both bottoms were ground and polished, the Shriners cup was ground and polished after the enameling and firing; consequently, it shows a clear foot ring.

This cup still bears its original Westmoreland label. A saucer has also come down to us with its original paper label intact.

Year 1908 St. Paul — Pittsburgh

Souvenir-type lettering.

The only ruby-stained Syria Shriners piece.

Height: 5¼"

This **1908 St. Paul** glass exhibits both lustre gold and ruby staining. Neither of these treatments, however, can be found on Westmoreland-decorated glass from about 1915 to the late 1930s.

Notice the spelling of Pittsburgh with

an "H" three years before it was officially restored. In 1891 an out-of-control bureaucrat with the United States Board of Geographic Names (yes, there was such a thing!) decreed that no town in the United States could end with a Scotch "H." If it was pronounced "burg," it had to be spelled "burg," and even if it was pronounced "boro," it had to be spelled "boro." Well, what happened? The city officially dropped its historic "H," and most Pittsburghers more or less went along. One who wouldn't, however, was a Presbyterian minister who launched a one-man campaign to have the H restored. He gained the whole-hearted support of Pittsburgh's postmaster, followed by the Chamber of Commerce, and finally a U.S. Senator. In 1911 the battle was over and Pittsburgh's "H" was officially restored to its original 1758 spelling. It took 20 years, but in the end the bureaucrat lost, the city won, and the rest, as they say, is history.

The **1908 St. Paul** has been positively identified as being one of the Shriners glasses in George West's collection.

Year 1909 Louisville — Pittsburgh
Year 1910 New Orleans — Pittsburgh
Year 1911 Rochester — Pittsburgh

1909: 4½" h.
1910: 4½" h.
1911: 4⅞" h.

These three champagne glasses have so much in common, the maker of one had to be the maker of all three. The **1910 New Orleans** has been positively identified as being one of the Shriners glasses in George West's collection. It has two supporting alligators — yellow and brown enameled — and also a King of the Mardi Gras with a long white, semi-translucent beard. The inside of the bowl is iridized.

The **1909 Louisville** has four tobacco leaves, amber and blue-gray, stained and iridized — and also a horseshoe. Its lettering size and style, optic bowl, and iridescent color inside the bowl all correspond with the **1910 New Orleans.**

The **1911 Rochester's** colonial foot appears to be identical to that on Westmoreland's footed orange sherbet (see the Gold & Silver section). While its back-sloping lettering does not correspond with the lettering on the other two champagne glasses, it resembles Westmoreland's souvenir lettering. The inside of its bowl is also iridized.

With a panoramic view of Pittsburgh on one side and a corresponding view of Rochester on the other, it is the most elaborately decorated of the three. This champagne glass even manages to find room for a photographer in Rochester taking aim at a camel and rider coming in from Pittsburgh. George West at his absolute best!

Year 1903 Saratoga — Pittsburgh
Year 1904 Atlantic City — Pittsburg

Mould lines are nearly invisible.

Ground and polished bottoms.

In 1903 Pittsburgh was spelled with an H. In 1904 it was spelled without.

Height: 3⅜"
Foot: 1⅞" o.d.

Both the **1903 Saratoga** and the **1904 Atlantic City** had to be made by the same company. Both have bright gold-lustre rims and ground and polished bottoms.

The **1903 Saratoga** shows an Indian head, a peace pipe, two toma-hawks, and two stumps sup-porting the bright scimitar handle.

The **1904 Atlantic City** shows a mermaid holding a scimitar, a sailing vessel, and a silver-lustre fish for a handle. The white on the ship's sails is identical to the curious white on the Mardi Gras King's beard on the **1910 New Orleans** — a known West-moreland piece. The maker had to be Westmoreland.

Year 1905 Niagara Falls — Pittsburgh

Height: 3⅝"

The **1905 Niagara Falls** is the only Shriners glass with hand-painted scenes. A comparison of two of these glasses sug-gests that even the tan delineation in the plaques was painted by hand.

The bottom of this glass is ground and polished to the pressed 8-pointed star. It has no gold on the rim. I have seen others that were gold-rimmed, yet did not have ground and polished bottoms.

Whatever this glass lacks in allegory is more than made up for by a small com-panion shot glass that is in the shape of a barrel! This shot glass is being made today from the original mould. The reproductions, while decorated, lack the gold and silver lustre and finished bot-toms of the originals.

Surviving moulds confirm these **1905 Niagara Falls** glasses were both made by Westmoreland.

Year 1915 Seattle — Pittsburgh
Year 1916 Buffalo — Pittsburgh
Year 1917 Minneapolis — Pittsburgh
Year 1918 Atlantic City — Pittsburgh

Both of the **1917 Minneapolis** glasses are faceted, and both are iridized. The one on the left of the photograph still bears its original Westmoreland label. At the Pittsburgh Exhibit in January 1917, Westmoreland introduced its "Mother-of-Pearl," which was iridized opal (milk glass). (See the Iridized section.)

The **1918 Atlantic City** glass shows the same sprayed casing as the "Pottery Effects in Glass" mugs of 1910.

An interesting thing about this opal assortment is the gold trim. While the earliest of the five glasses, the **1915 Seattle,** is still decorated in bright lustre gold, the others from 1916 on are in the new matt finish "coin gold." If 1916 was the year of Westmoreland's changeover, then it must have been the time when the rest of the industry changed over, too. This could be useful for glass dating.

Miscellaneous

Up to this point all of the Westmoreland glass has fallen rather neatly into one or more categories. Here, though, are about 50 pieces of glass that fall into the cracks: candy containers, lamps, plain crystal candlesticks, diaphanous staining, the George Washington plates, the **300 Condiment Set,** the card and spoon holders, the shelf supports, and, of course, those two quintessential Westmoreland bulldogs.

George West's Suitcase

Westmoreland's opal glass available from late 1900. Suitcase patent filed Feb. 1906.

(c. 1906)

Called a **Glass Receptacle.**

Patent 37851 granted 2/27/06 to George West for 3½ years.

Cold decoration.

Length: 3⅝"

While this suitcase may have been sold originally as a "Packers' Good" or an "Opal Novelty," today it is considered to be a candy container — the first of several patented by George West. The tin-plated bottom is crimped around the glass, covering the 1⅜" x 3¼" x 2¼" interior. In the glass pressing there are leather folds on the two sides and leather grain on the front, back, and top. The suitcase pictured bears the opal mustard mould number 1 on the inside, the words, "PAT APL'd FOR" on the side frame, and the original two-bears decoration in two tones of brown on the front.

Candy Containers

There are at least two excellent books on candy containers that will be familiar to those who collect this glass. Perhaps I can make the following contribution, however:

1. Since the war in Europe, which began August 1914, curtailed the importation of German toys, this field was left wide open to American manufacturers. Because of the surge in demand, Westmoreland decided to expand their West brothers toymaking and candy-packaging operations, and in mid-1915 discontinued their mustard operations in order to do so. Westmoreland's candy-packaging may have begun not long before this.

2. J.H. Brainard later wrote that Westmoreland's candy packaging was "not profitable." This may have been true in the 1930s, but it certainly was far from true in the late teens. Thanks to the cessation of European glass imports generally, and toys and candy containers specifically, these years may have been the most profitable in the company's history.

3. Geo. Lauman West, whose short history began this book, was in charge of the West brothers candy-packaging operations until he left the company with his father in May 1921. He told me the men who made the glass containers were on piecework, and because the rates were set rather low, they found these products as financially rewarding as Westmoreland's owners. He said that during the World War I era you could see glass telephones stacked everywhere as you walked in the plant door.

4. Glass candy containers are, rightfully, most closely associated with George West, for he designed so many of them. Nevertheless, after he left Westmoreland, he never became involved with them again. His brother Charles,

290

however, continued to make them at Westmoreland until the very end of the West period in 1937. As a child in the mid-'30s, I can recall playing with the candy-filled glass lanterns my grandfather brought home to me.

5. By the '30s, the toys' metal parts may have been purchased. Robert Jones, who was first employed at Westmoreland in 1924, told me the company had a tin shop that was moved or dismantled in 1927 (the year of the "Spirit of St. Louis" candy container).

6. In 1980, seven of the "1914 Village" buildings were offered for sale in the *Antique Trader* (11/26/80). A supply had been found unassembled in a barn in Jeannette together with the jigs used to assemble them. They were for sale then for $50 a set ($35 for two or more) with their projected value being "no less than $140" in 1990. Because of this find, these seven should be more frequently seen today than the remaining nine:

Toys and Confectionery Store
1914 Drug Store
1914 Princess Theater
Engine Co. #23
City Garage
2-Story Green House
1914 School House

7. In 1973 Westmoreland reissued 14 "Classics in Glass." They described their assortment as "Typical of wares produced by Colonial Craftsmen." The glass color was not specified. Eight of the fourteen could be classed as candy containers:

Upright Piano
U.S. Mailbox
Happifat on Drum
Standing Clock
Wash Boiler
Doghouse
Penny Trust Co. Safe
Egg Dish

As in the case of the mustard containers, early surviving cold decoration (paint) is the clearest indicator of age.

240 Candlestick

The **240** was one of Westmoreland's earliest, and perhaps their only imitation (brilliant) cut candlestick. It was introduced shortly after 1905 and discontinued between 1918 and 1924. It could be confused with another, made possibly by Imperial. However, Westmoreland's **240** has a round, smooth-sided foot with scalloping at the bottom, a ball centered on the

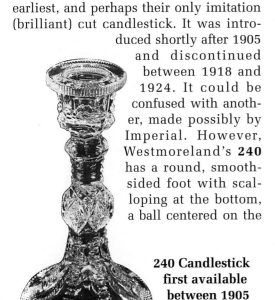

240 Candlestick first available between 1905 and 1912.

shaft, and flat facets on the candleholder; while the variant has 12 "knurled" panels on the side of the foot, a ball high on the shaft and deeply-concaved flutes on the candleholder.

The **240 Candlestick** had a near-mate in the form of a comport that Westmoreland called a **908 – 6" Footed Bon Bon** that was available as late as 1932.

(c. 1910)

240 was an early single-item number.

1904: Not listed.
1932: Discontinued.

Height: 7"

CANDLESTICKS
CUTS ONE-HALF SIZE

No. 220 Swung Vase   No 54 Crucifix   No. 240   No. 1004 Birthday   No. 1005 Birthday, cut full size

1067 Three Ball Candlestick

(c. 1930)

1067 was a candlestick number.

This pictured candlestick was sold from the factory 50 years or so after it was made there.

1932: Available only with the round base (pictured) in crystal and colors.
1940: Available with or without the round base in crystal only.

Height: 3¼"
Base: 4¼" d.

1067 Candlestick first available in 1927.

The **1067** was one of 12 candlesticks Westmoreland introduced in 1927 in the new low style (5" and under). These 12 were Westmoreland's last candlesticks in this era that were not tied to tableware lines.

During the West period, this **1067 Candlestick** came only with the round, flat base that is pictured. In 1940 it was available with the base (**1067**) or without it (**1067/1**) for the same price of $7.20/dozen, but shortly afterwards the base option was eliminated. While the earliest **1067/1**s made without the base will have fully ground and polished bottoms, later ones will not.

This candlestick can be found decorated in the "King's Jewel" pattern (#L130) of burgundy-, champagne-, and green-lustre staining, from about the mid-'30s. Later,

the pale burgundy was replaced with a more intense ruby color. Several other items sharing this **Three Ball** motif were made in the Brainard period and perhaps also, shortly before. They were original and not reproductions.

1034 Candlesticks — 8"

"Three new colors have just been created by the technical department of the Westmoreland factory. These are known as burgundy, champagne, and steel blue. The first is rich red; the second, as might be imagined, a pale straw color with an iridescent lustre, while the third likewise suggests its name. All three colors are brought out in a wide variety of fancy articles, including candlesticks, candy jars, and good night sets" (P 6/20/18).

Although Westmoreland had been staining glassware from the 1890s, their lustre stains were formally introduced in 1918. From three colors in 1918, the number increased to eight by 1924. I believe the two colors pictured are steel blue and burgundy. Lustre stains are characterized by a faint, silvery iridescence.

Westmoreland was the only maker of a candlestick of this design with a solid

base. Other examples of Westmoreland's solid **1034 Candlestick** can be seen in the C. West Decoration, the Black Glass, and the Carnegie sections.

1034 Candlesticks first available between 1918 and 1922.

(Probably 1918)

1034 was a candlestick number.

1034 also available 9" & 11".

Ground and polished punty.

1932: The three **1034s** available in crystal only. 1940: 9" and 11" available in crystal only, then discontinued until 1967.

Height: 8½"

1707 Candy Jar & Cover — 1 lb. — Optic

This **1707 Candy Jar** can be seen in a number of sections of this book; here it is lustre-stained in a burgundy shade. Notice the entire piece is stained except for the handle, which is beautifully offset in crystal.

For a detailed comparison of several similar candy jars see the Cut Crystal section.

1707 Candy Jars first advertised in 1921.

(early 1920s)

1707 was designated an **Optic** line.

Also available plain (not optic).

Also available in ½ lb. size from 1921 & ¼ lb. size from 1926.

1932: All three sizes available in crystal and colors. 1942: ½ lb. size available in crystal only.

½ lb.: 7¾" h.
1 lb.: 9¼" h.

101 Decorated Night Lamp

(c. 1902)

101 was an early item number.

In 1904 the **101 Lamp** was no longer available.

Height: 3¼" (glass only)

"(Westmoreland) are presenting to the trade for the first time two full lines of lamps. They are made in cold decorations, which places them in the front rank of the decorated lamp line for the jobbing trade. Their night lamps, which is also a new feature, are very artistic in design and decoration" (L 1/11/02).

In 1904 Westmoreland offered 26 crystal lamps. All were blown and all had "plaster collars." Eight were from the **Daisy** line, nine were from the **185** line, and nine were varied. By 1904, however, the short-lived opal **101 Night Lamp** had been discontinued.

No. 101 Decorated Night Lamps.

Daisy C Lamp

"(The Daisy) line in gold is one of the most attractive ever placed on the market" (L 1/11/02). This line originally offered plain or decorated in crystal, was also made in opal several years later. The Fersons have pictured an opal tumbler and pitcher (FF 290, 291) as well as four **Daisy Lamps** on an undated Westmoreland catalog page (FF 643).

The lamp pictured seems to be the second tallest of the **Daisy Lamps,** the second of three which shared a No. 2 collar. The tallest, the "D" lamp, was ¾" taller — the font accounting for ¼" and the reeded shaft accounting for the remaining ½" difference in their heights. These lamps were made in blow moulds in two pieces which were then "stuck," or joined, while hot just below the font.

The color of this lamp is a pale lavender, caused by the action of sunlight on the manganese used to counter the green iron impurities in the sand. The evidence for this is the protected underside which is pure white.

There is a curious thing about the **Daisy** design. Westmoreland actually alternated two flowers in their beaded

(c. 1905)

1904: 29 **Daisy** items plus 8 **Daisy Lamps** available in crystal only.
1932: Discontinued.
1940: Discontinued.

Height: 9½" (glass only)

oval plaques: the oxeye daisy of North America and the jonquil narcissus of Southern Europe.

Daisy Pattern
Cuts Half Size.

Westmoreland Specialty Company, Grapeville, Pa.

8 Inch Berry.

10 Inch Flared Berry.

4½ Inch Nappy.

Salt and Pepper.

Tooth Pick.

8 oz. Molasses Can. Nickel Top.

8 oz. Molasses Can. Tin Top.

13 oz. Molasses Can. Tin Top.

13 oz. Molasses Can. Nickel Top.

Robert Rosythorne Engraving Co., Pittsburg, Pa.

1707 Spiral Lamp — 8" (Roselin)
1915 Vanity Lamp — 12" (Aquamarine)
1915 Vanity Lamp — 9" (Green)

1707 and 1915 Lamps first available from 1927. Green glass first advertised Sept. 1924. Roselin glass first advertised July 1926. Aquamarine glass first advertised Sept. 1928.

(c. 1930)

1707 also available 12".

1915 also available 15".

1915 was an item number assigned just to these two lamps.

1932: 43 lamps available (including size variations). Most available in crystal and colors plus some in opal and part opal. All **1707** and **1915** lamps available in crystal and colors.
1940: 42 lamps available (including 9 added after 1932). All **1707** and **1915 Lamps** discontinued.

In their 1927 catalog supplement, Westmoreland pictured 12 "table and boudoir lamps" including five thin-stemmed lamps, five with fonts suggestive of earlier oil or kerosene lamps, and two "water lamps" — lamps intended to be filled with water or other clear or colored liquid. Of the 12, the best known today is the **555 Lamp** still commonly seen in crystal and late '20s colors. By the end of the year, these 12 were joined by four more water lamps bringing their total number to six. A year earlier, Westmoreland had first offered their 9" **Dolphin Candlestick** in an electrified version (**1042/2**) plus what appears to be a modification of their 4" **Dolphin Candlestick** with the substitution of an oil font for the candleholder (**1049/1**).

The late '20s were the beginning of Westmoreland's second lamp period. Like Westmoreland's bath and toilet bottles, Westmoreland's lamps enjoyed continued demand during

the Depression and into the first years of the Brainard era.

Notice the similarity of the **1915 Vanity Lamps** and the **1207 Candlesticks** shown in the Cut Candlestick section. Notice too that the same notched cutting shown on the **1915 Lamp** was used on one of the candlesticks. A great many separate passes against the cutting wheel were required for the notching on this tall six-sided stem.

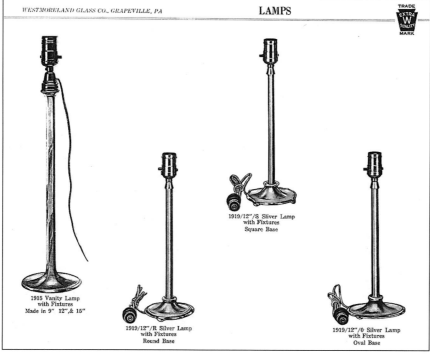

WESTMORELAND GLASS CO., GRAPEVILLE, PA   LAMPS   TRADE W EXTRA QUALITY MARK

1915 Vanity Lamp
with Fixtures
Made in 9", 12", & 15"

1919/12"/R Silver Lamp
with Fixtures
Round Base

1919/12"/S Silver Lamp
with Fixtures
Square Base

1919/12"/0 Silver Lamp
with Fixtures
Oval Base

296

1921 Lotus Lamp — Without Fixtures (Aquamarine)
Unknown Lamp — Without Fixtures (Roselin)
1917 Lamp — 9" — Nickeled Screw Collar (Green)

1921 Lotus line introduced June 1924. 1917 and 1921 Lamps first available 1927.

(c. 1930)

1921 was Westmoreland's patented **Lotus** line.

1917 was an item number used solely for this lamp.

These three West period lamps were sold at the factory auction in 1985.

1932: **1917** and **1921** lamps available in crystal and colors.
1940: **1921** available in crystal only. **1917** discontinued.

Westmoreland's lamps were available to the customer with and without "fixtures." In the late '20s and '30s the customer could specify one of four fixture collars: "Nipple Collars" (which screwed directly into the bottoms of light sockets) and "Screw Collars" (kerosene lamp style). Each of these in turn was available in either lacquered brass or nickel-plated brass. It is hard to understand the illogical combinations often seen of screw collars (which required light socket adapters) on lamps without fonts and nipple collars (which could be used only with lamp sockets) on lamps with fonts. Most Westmoreland collars had double grooves on their sides to help secure them to the white ceramic.

Notice the light bulb-type screw at the end of each cord in the catalog. The base boards of houses at the turn of the century had light sockets with brass covers rather than conventional outlets. In order to use them, you had to have this sort of screw-in plug, or else an adapter. The catalog picture shows that these curious outlets must have been in common use as late as 1927.

Westmoreland expanded its lamp line through the Depression years of the early '30s. The reason is that this was one part of America's glass business that was holding up remarkably well. Between 1929 and 1931, when industry-wide sales of pressed tumblers and goblets plummeted by two-thirds, glass lamp sales were off by just 5 percent (L 10/32). Reflecting the growth of electrical usage at the time, refrigerator sales also held up very well.

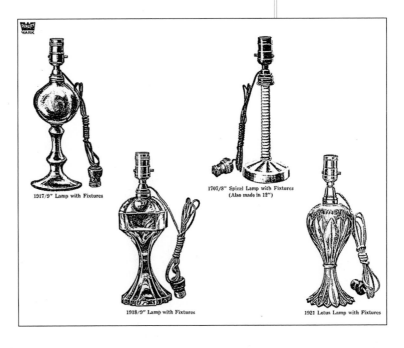

1917/9" Lamp with Fixtures

1707/8" Spiral Lamp with Fixtures (Also made in 12")

1918/9" Lamp with Fixtures

1921 Lotus Lamp with Fixtures

Sandwich Dolphin Candlestick
Westmoreland 1049 Dolphin Candlestick — 9" (Green)
Westmoreland 1049 Lamp — 9" (Roselin)
Czech Copy of Westmoreland's 1049 Dolphin Candlestick

Sandwich c. 1850. 1049 Candlestick first available in 1924. 1049 Lamp first available in 1926. Czech copy late 1920s.

Westmoreland's Dolphin Lamp has a brass screw collar bonded to a glass boss with white ceramic.

1932: **1049 Dolphin Lamp** and **Candlestick** both available in crystal, colors, and opal. The lamp with fixtures was priced about 50% higher than its candlestick counterpart.

1940: **1049 Dolphin Lamp** and **Candlestick** both available in crystal and opal.

Sandwich: 10¼" h.
Westmoreland Candlestick: 9¼" h.
Czech copy: 9½" h.

"Dolphin candlesticks having the hexagonal base are not a Sandwich product but were made in the Pittsburgh area, probably during the 1850s" (LFR 240).

This statement of Ruth Webb Lee's seems to have been a reaction to the later claim that Westmoreland's candlestick was a "Sandwich Reproduction." But ironically, it seems to have been as mistaken as the claim she sought to refute. Westmoreland's **1049 Dolphin Candlestick** dates from late 1924, and at the time the company never claimed it was a copy of anything. They took the dolphin and candleholder directly from an early Sandwich design, and then married this to a Bakewell Pears hexagon base. What was not known in 1924 by Westmoreland, or later by Mrs. Lee, though, was this: Sandwich did make a hexagonal base — one with concave sides, almost identical to Bakewell Pears'. McKearin (MC 196) pictures a dolphin candlestick on a hexagonal base. Clearly shown inside the base in the McKearin photograph are pressed concentric rings that we now attribute to Sandwich based on shards found at the factory site. Because of the

very different proportions of the dolphin, however, this was not the prototype for Westmoreland's **1049 Candlestick**. The dolphin prototype, shown in crystal at the left of our photograph, can be found only on this square base or on a later square-stepped base. In late 1925 Heisey reproduced this square-based Sandwich dolphin candlestick. It was their No. 110 (FO 121). While unmarked, the Heisey can be distinguished aurally because of the lead glass resonance of the original.

Both Sandwich and Mt. Washington came out with similar dolphin candlesticks at roughly the same time, around 1850. Then, I believe Bakewell Pears introduced one of their own about 10 years later. But the design concept of a dolphin supporting a candle may not be American. I understand one of these designs was an adaptation of a French, probably a Baccarat, design from about 1830. Westmoreland, however, seems to have been the glassmaker that revived both the dolphin and the dolphin candlestick in the 1920s.

Beginning about 1925 the American glass industry was confronted for the first time in 10 or 12 years with competition from Europe. In an address to the American Association of Flint & Lime Glass Manufacturers in July 1925, Chas West discussed the problem. He pointed out that following the war and the reconstruction of European industry, the U.S. government felt it was important to encourage imports to help European nations pay their indebtedness resulting from the war. For the American glassware industry, however, this meant going head-to-head with foreign producers whose wages were only a fifth of ours (WC).

As expected, the stiffest competition proved to be with high labor-content glass at the upper end of the market: blown glass, cut glass, decorated glass. But all American glass was affected. Shown on the right of our photograph is a very crude pressed copy of Westmoreland's **1049 Candlestick** with its original paper label still intact. The label reads, "Made in Czecho-slovakia"! (Czechoslovakia seems to have been spelled with a hyphen until the '30s; this may be helpful in dating.)

555 Footed Sugar & Cream

555 Footed Sugar and Cream first available in 1927. Plain gold #915 decoration available Jan. 1993.

(c. 1933)

The **555** line was being sold through G. Sommers, a wholesale catalog house, as early as 1915.

555 was Westmoreland's largest tableware line ever, numbering approximately 350 items in 1932.

1932: **555 Footed Sugar and Cream** available in crystal, colors, and opal.
1940: **555 Footed Sugar and Cream** available in crystal and opal.

Cream: 5⅝" h. (max.)

The original **555 Sugar and Cream Set** dating from 1915 was low and hexagonal in shape; the footed set was available 12 years later. Both types continued to be made over the years.

This highly ornamental, but impractical set must have been made as a display item for the Pittsburgh Exhibit. Since we know the plain, gold-band decoration was used in 1933, this may help us determine its date.

The set was found at the factory and sold in the gift shop "at the time Stella (Mrs. J.H. Brainard) was going around opening up closets." This was just before the Brainards sold the company in 1981.

300 Condiment Set

(c. 1915)

300 was an early item number not to be confused with the **300 Waterford** tableware line of c. 1930.

This set may have been the inspiration of the **555** line of 1915.

1932: Set discontinued. Salt available in crystal only.
1940: Set and salt both discontinued. In 1952, however, the set was offered in milk glass with a chromium-plated shaker top and a ground stopper.

Tray: 3¼" x 4¼"

300 Condiment Set introduced Jan. 1897, then withdrawn c. 1902. Reissued c. 1910, then withdrawn c. 1928. Reissued a second time c. 1950.

"The No. 300 Condiment Set consisting of pepper, salt, tray, and tiny metal spoon, is perhaps the smallest, daintiest set of glassware ever put on the market by anybody anywhere, and has been also one of the largest selling novelties of the past year. The set is put up in separate boxes and has been reduced so as to enable dealers to retail it for ten cents, and John Patterson (Westmoreland's sales manager) *asserts that price will cause over a million of them to be sold this year"* (L 1/13/97).

Despite its initial burst of popularity, the original **300 Condiment Set** was withdrawn at the turn of the century. When it was first reissued around 1910, a cruet was substituted for the salt spoon, and a Britannia metal (thin pewter) shaker top was substituted for the earlier one made of heavy pewter. (The pewter top pictured is from the first period.)

I have seen the shaker in three forms: with a spiral above the strawberry diamonds, with vertical facets (matching the cruet's) above the strawberry diamonds, and with the strawberry diamonds extended to the threads. I cannot account for this difference.

The **300 Salt** had a long and interesting history. After

its initial use with the original condiment set, it was sold alone as a **300 Individual Salt** in 1904 — Westmoreland's first salt cellar. It was reissued in 1917 when it was one of 15 salt cellars offered that year, and it was still available in 1932 as one of the 24 salt cellars then offered. In 1940 only 12 Westmoreland salt cellars remained, and the early **300** was not one of them.

At the West's house sale in 1941, I can recall card tables full of crystal salt cellars of various shapes.

Straw Hat

(c. 1910)

1904: Not listed.
1932: Not listed.
1940: Not listed.

Length: 4¼"

"It is in the novelty section of (West-moreland's) display that one finds the best productions... they range from a straw hat to a spider containing a freshly fried egg... " (L 1/9/09).

While the 1924 ad mentions a black band, the hat pictured, which is perhaps 15 years older, has a red one. On the backside of the band, "Souvenir Hershey Park" has been painted in gold in West-moreland's back-sloping souvenir lettering. On the inside there is a painting of a brown cocoa bean. The bottom of the rim has been painted, like the rest of the hat, in a yellow-straw color. There is no mould number.

(L 5/5/24)

301

Thimble Toy Mug
Soldier Hat
"1" Solid Glass Revolver

1904: Thimble toy mug listed as an opal novelty. Hat and revolver not listed.
1932: "**1**" **Revolver** available in crystal only. Thimble and hat not listed.
1940: **100 Thimble** available in crystal only. Hat and revolver not listed.

Thimble

Originally, this thimble was a shot glass which bore the inscription, "Just a Thimble Full," in raised letters just below the rim. Nevertheless, in both the 1904 price list and the 1905 catalog it was described as a Thimble Toy Mug. When the company reissued it in 1973, it apparently still bore this lettering, and yet in later reissues it appears to have been removed. The thimble pictured is a recent one showing no lettering.

Soldier Hat

This hat was advertised in 1924, and the ad says it was available in "plain crystal or decorated in khaki color with colored cords" (L 5/5/24). A collector wrote me that she owned two such hats and that while one cord was red, the other was gold.

Revolver

"The Westmoreland Specialty Company is making a silver barrel pistol, the handle being done in black. The whole thing is solid glass, and is unlike any specialty of the character now on the market" (P or J 10/17/12). Despite the *"Pat Apl'd For"* on the trigger guard, the patent was evidently not granted.

"A new glass revolver... is considerably larger than the glass gun brought out by the company several seasons back, and would in fact suit a desperado in a Wild West story. The stock is finished black, the balance of the 'weapon' closely simulating steel. It is designed for retailing at 10 cents (1995: $1.50) and should become as popular as the smaller size glass revolver now is" (P 7/20/15).

Still another revolver — hollow, and with no trigger guard — was made by Westmoreland at about this time and used as a candy container. It looks remarkably similar to one made by the newly organized Specialty Glass Co. in March 1889 (J 3/28/89). Specialty called theirs a "Revolver Flask," and like the later Westmoreland candy container, it had a metal screw-cap at the end of the barrel.

The solid glass revolver and the thimble were two of the 14 "Classics in Glass" that the company reissued in 1973. They were described as, "Typical of Wares Produced by Colonial Craftsmen." The glass color was not specified.

"1" Solid Glass Revolver

(c. 1915)

Earliest revolvers were finished in black and silver lustre.

Length: 5"

"… a week ago a burglar was surprised in a residence in Pittsburgh by the lady of the house. Her screams attracted the attention of a youth who had just purchased, in a spirit of fun, one of the glass revolvers put on the market by Westmoreland Specialty Co. Whipping it out, he held up the burglar until the police arrived" (P or J 1/2/13).

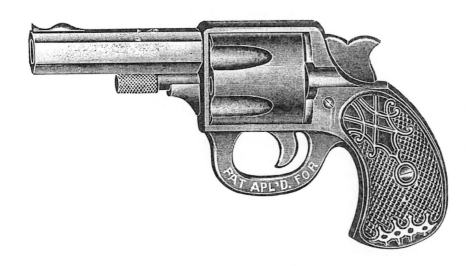

420 Cocktail Glass — 4 Oz.

(c. 1929)

420 was an item number used for this and a 2¾ oz. cocktail glass in 1924 and 1932.

The 1926 catalog pictured identical glasses and described them as **"1801 – 2¾ oz. Cocktail — Plain or Optic"** and **"1803 – 2½ oz. M.C. Cocktail."** I have no explanation for this.

1932: **420 Cocktail Glasses** available in crystal, and in crystal with colored glass feet.
1940: Discontinued.

Height: 3¼"
Foot: 2¼" d.

"(An) item destined for popularity is (Westmoreland's) new cocktail set consisting of an oblong tray and four glasses. This shows a decoration of a colored rooster on the glasses with a red traced line on both glasses and tray. This touch of color is very attractive, making the contrast of the cocktails more tempting. The glasses may be had with or without the tray in any quantity" (J 6/28).

Prohibition notwithstanding, several companies seem to have made cocktail glasses in this general shape with roosters on them in the '20s. The red border, the hand-painted rooster, and the fit in the original mould all point to Westmoreland as the maker of the one shown here.

The glass was blown into the mould pictured. This type of blow mould is sometimes referred to as a "paste mould." The term "paste" refers to the coating the mould is given to keep the molten glass from sticking when it is rotated in order to eliminate the mould scar. The only essential difference between a pressed and a blow mould is the source of the pressure; in a blow mould, air is substituted for a pressed mould's plunger. When a blow mould is opened, the upper portion, the bubble, is cut off and the sharp edge is either ground or else fire-polished in a glory hole. In the case of this cocktail glass, the foot was a separate piece of glass that was afterwards attached like the "stuck" handle of a pitcher. Because of this, Westmoreland's crystal cocktail glasses can be found with glass feet in various Westmoreland glass colors.

In 1991, 439 blow moulds survived at the Westmoreland factory even after two mould scrappings.

1800 Covered Blown Jug — ½ Gallon — Plain
1821 Grape Juice Tumblers — 5 Ounce — Plain
Unknown 11" Tray

Jug and Tumblers first available between 1918 and 1924.

(c. 1932)

1800 — ½ Gallon Jug also available without the lid or lid ledge.

1821 Tumbler also available 3 oz. and 9 oz.

1821 was an item number assigned just to these three tumblers.

Tray **"Keystone-W"** marked. Ground and polished bottom.

1932: Jug and tumblers both available in crystal only. Jug also available in optic (64-oz. size only). The optic on the outside would have required another blow mould.
1940: Both discontinued.

Jug: 7¼" h.
Tumblers: 3⅝" h.
Tray: 10¾" d.

Fortunately, there is a **Keystone-W** mark on the pictured tray which confirms this set was made by Westmoreland. Jugs or pitchers of this same general design were made by a number of glassmakers in the '20s. U.S. Glass made one that was numbered R-115 and one by New Martinsville was numbered 160-6. In 1932 U.S. Glass introduced a second one in optic that was assigned the number 190-5. While most of these others can be distinguished from Westmoreland's **1800** because of different lid finials, there is another pitcher with a teardrop finial identical to Westmoreland's. This near-twin has two vertical mould marks that end at a peripheral mould mark under the foot; also, its finial shows a very prominent vertical mould mark. Because Westmoreland's jug was blown and turned in a paste mould, it has no mould mark. Also, because Westmoreland's handle is stuck, it was made separately and also shows no mould mark. Finally, no mould marks are visible on Westmoreland's lid and finial.

The mustard color found on the finial and the rims is glass enamel and not paint. This edging in a color other than gold suggests an early '30s date. The sprightly wheel-cut design also suggests the same time period.

The dealer who sold the set to me called it a railroad collectible. The keystone proved it was made for the Pennsylvania Railroad.

12 George Washington Plate — 8"
505 George Washington Cut Plate — 3"

"(Westmoreland shows) *an unusually attractive Washington bicentennial plate in quality crystal glass.... The shoulder of the plate shows 13 stars with a panel carrying the signature 'G Washington' and the dates 1732 – 1932. The head of Washington is satin finish on the reverse side making it stand out. The surface of the plate, however, is smooth"* (L 5/32).

George Washington Plates available in 1932.

(c. 1932)

"**12**" and **505** were single-item numbers.

Both plates have etched heads.

Both plates have 1932 terminal dates (1932 was Washington's bicentennial year).

8" plate has a ground and polished bottom.

1932: "**12**" and **505** available in crystal only. "**13**" and "**22**" available in opal only.
1940: **505** available in crystal only. **12** discontinued.

"**12**": 8" d.
505: 3½" d.

The Washington Bicentenary in 1932 seems to have been observed with more fanfare than even the nation's 150th birthday six years before. Washington's year was certainly commemorated at Westmoreland where they introduced one of their premiere tableware lines in 1932 and named it **Wakefield** after Washington's Virginia birthplace. Westmoreland also came out with four Washington plates that year: a **505/3"**, a "**12**"/8" (both shown here) in crystal, and a "**13**"/8", and "**22**"/7" in opal (not pictured). Because the design was on the back of the first two, these plates had to be made of transparent glass. The transparent pair was dated "1732 – 1932" and both had etched intaglio busts of Washington. Presumably the **505/3"** cup plate continued to be made for a while with the 1932 date together with an unetched bust, for Ruth Webb Lee has pictured this combination (LCP 131); later, however, the terminal date was altered to read 1799. Company records show that 1,285 of these Washington cup plates were sold in crystal in 1963 — about a quarter as many as the reproduction "Marriage Day" plates that year. Westmoreland's later "Monticello" and "Martha Washington" cup plates both were original and were based on the Washington cup-plate design.

While the 3" cup plate continued to be made over the years, the 8" plate was retired early. In 1991 I found its mould at the plant with the original 1932 date still in it. If some day any of these 8" plates are found in color, they will be reproductions, for the original was made only in crystal. Also, all of the originals will show ground and polished bottoms.

In their 1953 Reproductions catalog, the Brainards described the cup plate as "'George Washingtons' stippled border. Original belongs to the 1860 period." Both the transparent plates pictured here are Westmoreland originals and both date from 1932. The other two Washington plates, the "**13**" and the "**22**" that share "open-work" 13-star rims, may be original, or may have been made from purchased moulds. If any of these plates are found with "1732 – 1932" dates, this will confirm they are Westmoreland originals and date from 1932.

L.E. Smith also made a Washington plate in 1932 that seems to be a larger version of the Westmoreland cup plate. While it had a scalloped L.E. Smith design border and its decoration was on the top, its stars, stippling, Washington's head, and plaque all look identical to the corresponding parts of Westmoreland's cup plate. But with the design work in cameo on the top, the plunger side of the plate, it was probably a plain L.E. Smith plate reworked for the Birthday year. Years before in 1906, L.E. Smith had been Westmoreland's sales manager just after he left the company that still bears his name.

"75" Small Dogs
1801 Plate — 8½"

"75" Small Dog first made in 1915.

(unknown)

Westmoreland's small bulldog had a collar with the buckle on the dog's left.

1932: Not listed.
1940: **"75" Dog** available in crystal and opal. In 1952 it was available in gloss black, etched black, or milk glass. In 1967 it was available just in milk glass. In 1971 it was also available in black.

Dog: 2⅝" h.
Plate: 8⅝" d.
Foot: 5" o.d.

Westmoreland's **"75" Small Dog** was a smaller version of its bulldog doorstop first made in August 1915 or before. In September 1915, however, Lancaster first advertised their "Toby" — a bulldog similar to Westmoreland's, but with the collar buckle on the dog's right. In their ad, Lancaster claimed that the original model was made by a Swiss artist, and that they had applied for a patent on the design.

The patent was never granted, and the mould seems to have ended up with U.S. Glass, for the small sagacious bulldog they made for some years looks identical to the dog in the "Toby" ad. But there were evidently several other companies involved. I have seen a small bulldog that looks almost identical to Toby, but with no collar. And I understand Fenton at one time made a small dog, but one with a somewhat sunnier mien; it was their No. 307.

While Westmoreland's small dog was still pictured in the 1926 catalog, it was not included in the 1932 price list.

(P 9/2/15)

"78" Dog Door Stop (Amber)
Westmoreland Mustard Grinding Stone

Bulldog

"A five-pound bulldog door-stop is in old ivory and black, with gold collar" (J 1/13/16).
"(Westmoreland's) book blocks are made of glass in two colors — black and ivory. So also are the new bulldog door porters, which like the owls have brilliant eyes. The bottoms are covered with green baize to prevent their slipping or sliding" (P 3/2/16).

The January 1916 press release mentions a gold collar. Then, a Westmoreland catalog of 1924 adds to this by specifically mentioning a brass metal collar and pearl pendant. Finally, the 1926 catalog and a 1930 promotional picture both show a broad gold-colored collar. Today, of course, these collars are almost always missing.

The March 1916 press release mentions the green baize on the bottom, and I can remember this on two I grew up with. The baize resembles the green Victrola turntable covers of the early '20s and before. Any West period dog should have the remains of a green felt pad on the bottom, or at least a few green hairs and the remains of some water-soluble glue. The earlier Brainard period dogs came with black felt pads, but the later ones were apparently not sold with any pads at all.

The March 1916 press release also gives us the bulldog's two original colors, black and white. Today, the majority seen will be black, but some will be white (opal or "carrara") and others will be in various Westmoreland's colors. According to Geo. Lauman West, who worked at Westmoreland from 1917 to 1921, the bulldog was useful for getting rid of excess glass at the end of the day.

The family bulldog pictured is amber, which proves it was made between 1925 and 1937. I saw one in a flea market erroneously attributed to Tiffin that was in a Westmoreland green from the same period. Regardless of color, all West period bulldogs will be etched.

It is hard to write about the Westmoreland bulldog and sidestep the controversy surrounding the claim that another company made it — in '20, in the '20s, in the '20s and '30s, or later. This seems to be a recent claim. Let me make four observations:

1. In Chas West's era (May 1921 – August 1937), there was a closeness among glass manufacturers that is hard to understand today. Judging from the golfing photographs and other contemporary material I have seen, the various companies that made up the Associated Glass & Pottery Manufacturers behaved more like corporate divisions than competing entities. There were certainly favors being done back and forth, and mould lending cannot be cavalierly ruled out. During this period, a mould might have been lent just on the strength of friendship, but before then, George West was in charge. I believe he viewed other glass men more as competitors than his brother did, and I think it is highly unlikely he would have considered such an unbusinesslike arrangement as the loan of a mould.

2. Westmoreland made this bulldog continuously from before August 1915 to sometime after 1930. If there was just one Westmoreland mould, it could not have been lent for more than a brief period at that time, for it was in constant use at Westmoreland. After 1930, Westmoreland's bulldog production is less clear, and so a long-term loan then is conceivable.

3. No one, I understand, has suggested any other company ever made more than a few token bulldogs (one estimate, I believe, is only 100). The Westmoreland bulldog was evidently tricky to make and even trickier to anneal, even for those familiar with it. It is simply inconceivable that a company would borrow a particularly difficult mould (and the tooling to go with it), let their workmen spend time trying to familiarize themselves with it, and then have them use it to turn out a lot of scrap and substandard glass. From the standpoint of economy, if nothing else, a purchase of these dogs from Westmoreland is the only thing that would have made sense.

4. It is not really clear to me why anyone would want to claim to be the originator of Westmoreland's **Victor** line; it is very clear to me, however, why anyone might want to claim to have made Westmoreland's bulldog! If any claimant can come up with a bulldog doorstop in a non-Westmoreland color, I think the claim, then, should be given serious consideration. In the meantime, let it remain Westmoreland's bulldog.

Here is a story about one Westmoreland bulldog that must be told. Early in January 1923 the Wm Jennings Bryans rushed to Johns Hopkins in Baltimore from a visit to Mexico City because of Mrs. Bryan's sudden illness. On January 10th, during the week of her hospitalization, Bryan came to Pittsburgh and spent a day at the Exhibition.

Afterwards Chas West sent him a bulldog door stop and his wife a black console set for which Bryan wrote a letter of thanks. In a personal letter the great "Silver-Voiced Orator" penned this anthropomorphic thought: "The dog is cute and has taken a responsible position as guard at the front door, where he smiles on friends and would, I am sure, frown upon invaders." Twenty-seven years before, Westmoreland had made two mustard jars, one for McKinley and one for Bryan, for their first presidential race in 1896.

Mustard Stone

The amber bulldog pictured is sitting on an original Westmoreland mustard seed grinding stone. At great expense it was first moved from Grapeville to Pittsburgh, then to Fox Chapel, Pa., and finally to Duxbury, Mass., where this picture as taken. Ever since 1915 it has served as a family doorstep.

Mustard seed was poured into a hole in the center of an upper grinding stone just like grain in a grist mill. The upper stone rotated against a stationery lower stone that looked almost identical, but had no center hole. As the seed was ground, the striations that were cut into both of the stones moved the ground seed to the outer edge where it was collected. Until mid-1915, when the mustard operations at Westmoreland came to an end, there was a long row of these grinding stones in the eastern end of the factory kept, I understand, in constant operation.

Miscellaneous

WILLIAM JENNINGS BRYAN
VILLA SERENA
MIAMI, FLORIDA

March 30, 1923.

Mr. Chas. H. West, Pres.,
Westmoreland Specialty Co.,
Grapeville, Pennsylvania.

Dear Mr West:

The glassware sent by you has arrived and I hasten to express for Mrs. Bryan and myself cordial thanks for and appreciation of your generous gift. Mrs. Bryan is very much pleased with the black fruit (or flower)bowl and with the candle sticks, she agrees with me that the work is artistic and the ware beautiful. The dog is cute and has taken a responsible position as guard at the front door, where he smiles upon friends and would, I am sure, frown upon any invaders.

We shall be glad to make known to friends the name of your firm and the merit of your product.

Very truly yours,

Personal

WJB:T

H. J. Bryan

Please let me know the price of the bowl & the dog so I can tell enquirers

100 Wing Sugar & Cream
1211 Octagon Low Foot Salver — 12"

100 Sugar and Cream first available Jan. 1926. 1211 Salver first available in 1927. Black and crystal combinations popular in 1930.

(c. 1930)

100 was an item number assigned just to this sugar and cream.

1932: **100 Sugar and Cream** and **1211 Salver** available in crystal and colors.
1940: **1211 Salver** discontinued. **100 Rooster** available in crystal and opal. The rooster seems to have replaced the winged set.

Salver: 12" w. (max.)

"(Westmoreland's) individual sugars and creams with wing handles and short stem and foot come in a variety of decorative designs" (L 1/18/26).

This winged sugar and cream set was first shown in Westmoreland's 1926 catalog. Except for their wings, they were identical to, and possibly shared the **194/195 Sugar and Cream Set** moulds (see the Iridized section). Because these wings appear to have been "stuck," and not pressed as a unit, the **100 Set** cost 20% more in 1932 than the "Chippendale"-handled **294/295 Set** which was also still listed. And the price was nearly doubled if these winged sugar and creams were sold as **3-piece Bridge Sets** with optional round **1090 7" Trays**. By 1940 the winged set was evidently superseded by the familiar **100 Rooster Sherbet**.

The black glass, Low-Foot Salver, or Cake Plate dates from 1927 or later. It seems to be the only **1211** item with this foot. These same raised-enamel bleeding hearts can be seen on a **1211 Sugar** and **Cream Set** in the Black Glass section.

1024 Shelf Supports — 12" and 15"

"(From Westmoreland) a new item in glass... a standard for supporting glass shelves..." (P 6/26/13).

"A new item in the Westmoreland line... a new glass shelf support. It is customary to use four candlesticks to support a glass shelf, but this new device, being designed expressly for the purpose, saves much valuable room as only two are necessary to a section of shelf" (P 8/21/13).

"The extremely practical shelf support recently put on the market by the Westmoreland Specialty Co. is shown in... three sizes... and there is a new style, designed with a round top" (P 1/29/14).

1024 Shelf Supports first available in 1913.

(c. 1913)

Also available 7" & 9".

1024 was a single-item number.

Both supports marked "Pat Apld For" on bottom.

1932 and 1940: All four sizes available in crystal only.

12": 12¼" h.
15": 15" h.

In 1913 Westmoreland applied for a patent for these unique shelf supports. Today this is helpful to us in dating the earliest supports for they will bear the marking, "PAT APLD FOR" on the bottom surface. Strangely, the patent was never granted, and so Westmoreland seems to have ground out this marking rather than replacing it with the expected, "PATD." Since the unmarked supports may date from as early as 1914, they are more commonly seen today.

The early marked supports were made of particularly fine crystal showing refractory fire. By late 1914 they were also available in Carrara Marble (etched opal glass).

In 1921 this six-sided support was furnished with a circular top to go with Westmoreland's **1026 Display Tray** (L 7/11/21). By 1924 it was also incorporated into Westmoreland's **1047 Rack for Displaying Shoes** (P 1/3/24).

Westmoreland also made a similar **1048 Shelf Support** with eight sides and two crossed support arms in 7" and 12" heights. They also made more conventional spool-shaped supports in five heights from 6" to 15" that were numbered **1037** and **1049**. Some of these were made again in the Brainard years.

NO. 1024 SHELF SUPPORT
Patent Applied for

Made in 7, 9, 12 and 15-inch sizes. Two of these supports will hold safely a glass shelf from 12 to 16 inches wide and from 4 to 6 feet long. Write to us for particulars.

WESTMORELAND SPECIALTY CO.
MAKERS OF HIGH GRADE TABLE WARE
GRAPEVILLE, PA.

(P 12/18/13)

1025 Card Holder
"1" Sanitary Spoon Holder

Card and Spoon Holders first available in 1913.

(1913 or later)

"1" and **1025** are single item numbers.

Card holder shares the design of the **1077** and **1023 Candlesticks.**

Spoon holder has been seen with a finished bottom and a cut decoration.

1932: Spoon holder available in crystal only. Card holder discontinued.
1940: Both discontinued.

1025: 3¾" h.
"1": 4⅛" l. (bottom)

Card Holder

"Another item that is similarly useful (in addition to the 1024 glass shelf support) is a card holder. Two removable wedge-like pieces of glass grip a display or price card so that it cannot become disarranged, and the article in its entirety is very attractive" (P 8/21/13).

Spoon Holder

"A very novel item has been added... by the Westmoreland Specialty Co.... This article consists in a new style of spoon holder quite different from anything heretofore brought out.... The holder is constructed so that the spoons all rest in a uniform pile and in serving they are in such a position as to be readily removed.... It is in plain colonial design..." (P 4/17/13).

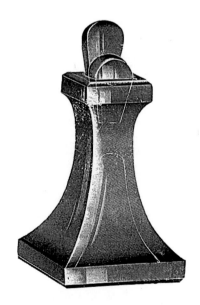

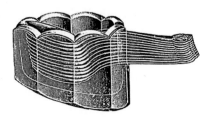

1031 Flower Bowl Stands

1031 Flower Bowl Stand first available between 1913 and 1917. Green and amber glass stands date from 1927 or later.

In 1917 the **1031 Stand** was available in one size in black glass.

In 1921 three sizes were available in black glass.

In 1924 seven sizes, 2¾" to 7½", were available in crystal and black glass.

The black stand pictured is "**Keystone-W**" marked in center of bottom.

1932: Seven sizes available in crystal and colors.
1940: Discontinued.

Westmoreland was one of several companies that made flower bowl stands that resemble the bases of classical columns. U.S. Glass made one that could be confused with Westmoreland's, but U.S. Glass' scotia, or concave portion, is taller. Fostoria also made a similar one with its scotia taller still — so tall in fact, it dominates the Fostoria design. Fenton made one with a profile nearly indistinguishable from Westmoreland's. Both Fenton and Westmoreland also pressed theirs the same way. Nevertheless, Berry Wiggins, a glass researcher, has discovered a way to tell them apart. If you turn them over, you will see three mould marks, one of which is adjacent to one of the feet. Sighting from the bottom, you will find the mould mark on the Westmoreland's just to the right (clockwise) of the foot, and Fenton's just to the left.

These three pictured flower bowl stands were made in black glass, amber glass, and green glass. Since only crystal (though sometimes with cased colors) and black were available through 1926, the two in the foreground must date from 1927 or later.

This photograph may show why amber was such a popular color in the '20s. While amber looks dirty on a white table cloth, no other color can equal its richness against wood, particularly golden oak, which was still in wide-spread use after World War I.

(L 8/15/21)

1032 Flower Bowl Stands

1032 Flower Bowl Stands first available between 1918 and 1924. Through 1926, stand available only in crystal and black glass.

(c. 1929)

In 1924 two sizes, 3½" & 4", were available in crystal and black glass.

1932: Both sizes available in crystal and colors. 1940: Discontinued.

In contrast to the **1031 Bowl Stand** in the preceding photograph, the plain, cove-sided **1032 Stand** may be a unique Westmoreland shape. There is a question, however, about the yellow-stained stand on the right (which appears with a bowl in the Cut Stained section). It is identical in every way to the two known Westmoreland sizes, and if it is Westmoreland's, it would be designated, "**1032/0 – 2¾.**" But the problem is its size. At the factory in 1991, moulds for all ten stands shown on the 1926 catalog page survived; however, there were no moulds for any sizes not pictured. This is one of so many problems that cries out for future research.

114   **STANDS FOR FLOWER BOWLS**   *WESTMORELAND GLASS CO., GRAPEVILLE, PA.*

1031/0—2¾"

Made in Crystal and Black Glass

1032/1—3½"

1031/1—4"

1031/2—5"

1032/2—4"

1031/3—5½"

1031/4—6"

1030 Low Foot Standard

1031/5—6½"

1031/6—7½"

In January 1923 the newly-appointed director of Pittsburgh's Carnegie Museum attended the Pittsburgh Exhibit. Afterwards, a trade reporter wrote that, *"Douglas Stewart, director of the Carnegie Museum, has requested the glass firms who are displaying these lines of ware to select a representative exhibit from the present show to be placed in the museum so future generations may view the beauties of art glass made in 1922"* (B 1/13/23).

Another reporter wrote of it somewhat differently: *"At the request of the Carnegie Museum, manufacturers are to present to the museum annually, one sample piece of their ware, and in the years to come, these will become priceless"* (J 1/18/23). But an article in the *Jeannette Dispatch* was the most comprehensive of the three: *"Charles H. West, president of the Westmoreland Specialty Company of Grapeville, has been invited by officials of the Carnegie Museum to place on exhibition permanently in the museum samples of all the products of Western Pennsylvania in the plain and decorated lines of pottery, china, and glassware. The manufacturer will prepare this exhibit immediately for the instruction of students and the inspection of the public. The museum exhibit will be free and will contain an unusual lot of the finest work of Bohemian designers and decorators... of the Grapeville plant, of which Mr. West is the driving force"* (JD 1/16/23).

Presumably Chas West, who was the newly-elected president of the Associated Glass & Pottery Manufacturers, used his friendship with Douglas Stewart to arrange this display which was to include glass and china from all member companies. He personally contributed "an unusual lot" of Westmoreland glassware, and it certainly ranked, as the Jeannette paper put it, as "the finest work of Bohemian designers and decorators." Carnegie's records show Chas West contributed 49 pieces of art glass to the display — actually 52 if each item is counted separately. These separate pieces make up 34 sets. We can be grateful today this glass was donated and not lent, for it was given the accession number 7058, and this identifying number was painted on the bottom of every piece. It is inter-

esting that the initial Westmoreland donation was made a year before the exhibit was expanded to include other glass and pottery makers. Twenty-nine Westmoreland pieces were donated on February 3, 1922, followed by 20 more over the next several years.

I have been fortunate in obtaining a listing of these 49 pieces:

1. Red glass candlestick.
2. Red glass candlestick.
3. Blue glass candlestick with fish's body for shaft to candleholder.
4. Blue glass candlestick with fish's body for shaft to candleholder.
5. Black glass candlestick.
6. Black glass candlestick.
7. Blue glass candlestick with wide base.
8. Blue glass candlestick with wide base.
9. Glass bowl in form of petals of a flower.
10. Glass candlestick like petals of a flower.
11. Small glass bowl like petals of a flower.
12. Small glass dish like petals of a flower.
13. Blue glass ladle with gold handle, fits with 18?
14. Gold and lavender glass dish with pearl inlay.
15. Clear glass dish and cover.
16. Shallow red glass dish flaring from a base.
17. Shallow blue glass dish flaring from a low base.
18. Stemmed light blue bowl on a swelling base fits with 13?
19. Thin, high-stemmed glass dish.
20. Small blue glass bowl with light blue rim decorations.
21 Blue and gray glass dish on fish body stem.
22. Old rose-colored glass bowl.
23. Red glass bowl.
24. Blue and gold glass dish.
25. Bohemian glass representation vase with lid.
26. Bohemian glass representation vase.
27. Bohemian glass representation vase.
28. Black glass vase with eagles on the side.
29. Black glass base.
30. Black glass base.
31. Black glass base.
32. Red glass base.
33. Blue glass bowl with white festoon panels and roses.

Carnegie Glass

34. Amber glass plate with flying duck in white.
35. Colored glass dish on clear glass stem, flowers, festoons, blue, red, green.
36. Colored glass dish on clear glass stem, flowers, festoons, blue, red, green.
37. Cut glass bowl, clear, with flower baskets around lid.
? Light blue glass.
38. Amber bowl, floral and rose designs in white.
39. Shallow, blue, gold rimmed, and large glass dish.
40. Black glass bowl, mate to 5 and 6.
41. Large amber glass plate with stag center decoration in white.
42. Octagonal plate, gold ornaments and roses.
43. Octagonal plate, gold ornaments and festoons in white.
44. Shallow glass bowl — plate on fish support.
45. Large amber plate, cornucopial and flower bowl decorations.
46. Glass, blueish plate, two dogs, two stags, and a castle in white.
47. Opaque white bowl with gold rim, on stand.
48. Mustard bowl, reddish glass, with plate and spoon.

Many of the painted 7058 numbers will be found with a suffix corresponding to one of the numbers used in this inventory.

Douglas Stewart died in 1926, and presumably all loans and donations ended with his death. Nevertheless, the exhibit remained in the mineral room until it was taken down 11 years later. Dr. James Swauger, who was associated with

Industrial Arts Exhibit, Carnegie Museum, 1924. The Westmoreland case is on the left (L 12/29/24).

Carnegie for many years, told me he began to work there part-time in 1935. His first job was to dust the exhibits. He remembers the glass, "how it sparkled in the light," and recalls packing it away in 1937. Since 1937 was the year Chas West stepped down as president of the Associated Glass & Pottery Manufacturers, there may have been a connection.

In 1950, I understand Carnegie's "decorative arts" (which includes glassware) was assigned to their fine arts (i.e. paintings and sculpture) department which then deaccessioned all of the exhibited glassware. Mark Nye of the National Cambridge Collectors informed me that shortly before they closed, Cambridge received a barrel of their glass from Carnegie. What could be important to other glass clubs is that the other contributing companies still in business in the '50s must have received shipments then, too.

In the late '50s Westmoreland received three barrels from Carnegie. It is my understanding that after these barrels were received at the factory, they remained untouched for several years for "nobody knew what to do with them." Finally, though, they were opened, and the president at the time took some of the pieces he liked home with him, and evidently sold off the rest in his wife's gift shop. Bowls were separated from their stands. Sets were broken up. An important three-piece salon set was broken up when the president took the two vases, but then sold off the center urn.

Today, only a quarter of Westmoreland's Carnegie glass is accounted for. The remaining three-fourths is scattered, and it appears the present owners have no knowledge of the importance of what they own. This is tragic. This glass was Chas West's legacy. It was donated so that future generations could appreciate what his company once produced. The artists understood the importance of their work and where their work was going: the evidence for this is that Racinger seems to have signed all of his Carnegie engraving, and yet signed no other glass from his years at Westmoreland. If there is any downside to this glass, it is that these artists, when asked to do something for posterity, naturally reverted to the early academic styles of their apprentice years. Consequently, much of Westmoreland's

Carnegie glass seems more derivative than original. There are no pointers or cubistic flowers, for example, that I am aware of. But if we find fault with this Westmoreland because it reminds us of its Bohemian roots, then shouldn't we also find fault with Sandwich's notable double-overlay glass for exactly the same reason?

There was an unrelated Industrial Arts exhibit held at Carnegie in 1924; glassware and pottery were figured prominently in this display. One case contained Steuben glass. Another contained Lenox "Belleek" china. One was shared by Heisey, Edmundson Warrin (a New York glass decorator), and C. Reisenstein (a Pittsburgh jeweler). And one was devoted to Westmoreland's glass. The Westmoreland case was described by a trade reporter as having "an appearance of exquisite loveliness" (L 12/29/24). The photograph, which was shown in *China, Glass and Lamps*, shows four of the cases. Westmoreland's is on the left, Lenox's is in the back, and the pottery of various makers is on the right. The large charger in the Westmoreland display appears to be cut in a design that suggests the "Rose Medallion" pattern of nineteenth-century Chinese export porcelain. Since this Westmoreland was simply on loan, none of it would have been marked.

There were two apparently unrelated pieces of glass that Chas West donated to Carnegie in July 1923. They were described by the museum as, "Amber glass bowl carved; blue glass bowl carved," and records show they, too, ended up in the Fine Arts department. Wherever they are today, they will both bear the accession number, 7191.

Carnegie Nos: 7058 – 5, 6, 40
1848 Rolled Edge Bowl — 13"
1034 Candlesticks — 9"
(Satin Moiré)

Most of Westmoreland's decorated glass could hardly be considered subtle; its directness is its charm. But the beauty of this Satin Moiré console set is its calm; it can be properly appreciated only up close. No gold. No silver. No enamel. Frank Chiarenza, a glass scholar and writer, wrote: "I've never seen anything to compare or anything that better defines the true meaning of 'elegant.'"

This pictured black console set had to have been seen by Wm Jennings Bryan when he visited the Pittsburgh Exhibit in 1923, and it is believed to be identical to the one Chas West gave him for his invalid wife. Bryan acknowledged the set in a personal thank-you letter (see the Miscellaneous section) and in a short arti-

cle on Westmoreland in the final issue of *The Commoner* of April 1923 he wrote, "The Westmoreland Specialty Co… have introduced a novelty this year which is attracting a great deal of attention. They are manufacturing glassware covered with beautiful black enamel (it was actually etched black glass)… the black enamel being used to represent watered silk." (See the Black Glass section for another contemporary description of Satin Moiré).

1848 Bowls first available between 1918 and 1923. 1034 Candlesticks first available between 1918 and 1922.

(Donated Jan. 1923)

The date 23-1-18 was painted on the bowl bottom.

The date shows this console set had been on display at the 1923 Pittsburgh Exhibit, and it was then donated to Carnegie immediately afterwards.

The Satin Moiré decoration required multiple hand-blocked etchings.

1932: Five **1848 Bowls** (common mould) available in crystal and colors. **1034** (8", 9", 11") available in crystal only. 1940: **1848** discontinued. **1034** available in crystal only.

Bowl: 12¾" d.
Candlesticks: 9½" h.

Carnegie No: 7058-19
1910 High Foot Comport — 9"

There was a **1910** mini-line of just five pieces, but this comport was not one of them.

This **1910** was a single-item number.

Stem is amber-stained.

1932: Available in crystal and colors.
1940: Discontinued.

Height: 8¾"

1910 HF Comport first available between 1918 and 1924.

This comport is very much in the style of Moser — but a generation late. When Westmoreland's Bohemian-born decorators were asked to do their best work for what was to be a permanent museum display, it is only natural they would return to the design motifs of their early training. Note the similarity between this decoration and that on a console set shown in the Flower and Iridized sections.

Carnegie No: 7058-15
1854/2 Chocolate Box and Cover

1854 Chocolate Boxes first available between 1918 and 1921.

Also available in a smaller size: **1854/1.**

1854 was an item number used just for these two chocolate boxes.

Ground and polished bottom.

Star was pressed, then etched or cut.

1932: **1854/2** available in crystal only. **1854/1** available in crystal and colors.
1940: Both discontinued.

Diameter: 7½"

"The 'show' of the Pittsburgh Glass and Pottery Exposition this season is the display of the lines of the Westmoreland Specialty Co... their 'Bizantine' line of decorated ware is representative of a Cech-Slavonic decoration" (J 1/19/22).

Several years after this review, Westmoreland would be particularly affected by the renewal of glass importation from Czechoslovakia. For 10 or 12 years, first because of the war and then because of reconstruction, the American glassware industry had been protected from competition from Europe. The glass companies that went under during that period were largely limit-ed to the fine cut, English-flint glassmakers such as Dorflinger. The late '20s, however, proved devastating to many American glass decorating houses and financially-leveraged pressed glass companies as well.

Carnegie No. 7058-35
1827 Straight Edge Honey — 6½"

Here, Westmoreland's central European decorators took some of the design elements and colors they used on their traditionally decorated **1910 Comport** and brought them into the jazz age. The result is, I believe, unlike anything that was being done in Bohemia at the time. Notice that the disciplined Moorish border is gone, along with the feeling of preciousness and confinement it conveyed. Notice how the white dots and the husks, or bell flowers, were transformed — and Americanized. Both designs have a surprising amount in common. Notice, both begin with a central six-petal flower and then radiate out from this flower in two alternating groups of six. But while the traditional Bohemian design is bounded by Moorish arches, the "Roaring '20s" American design just seems to keep expanding outward.

1827 items first available between 1918 and 1924.

Also available as a 6" roll edge comport, a 6" straight edge comport, and a 5" bowl.

1827 was an item number used just for these four pieces.

1932: **1827** items available in crystal and colors.
1940: Discontinued.

Carnegie No: 7058-24
1800 Plate — 10"

Two identical plates have come down in the family. One was said to have been shown at a world's fair; the other was exhibited at Carnegie. The "7058" behind this plate shows it was the Carnegie one.

For some reason this plate was returned to Chas West in 1937 when the rest of the exhibit was taken down and packed away. Why the return of a gift and why just this plate? It was one of very few pieces of glass the Wests took with them when they moved to a one-bedroom apartment in 1941.

The backside shows a very complex backing for the gold doily. A white fired-on material was used.

First 1800 Plate available between 1913 and 1917.

1800 was designated a **Plain** line.

1800 plates ranged from 6" to 10".

Ground and polished bottom.

1932: Plate 6" to 8" available in crystal and colors. 10" available in crystal only.
1940: All sizes available in crystal only.

Diameter: 9½"
Foot: 5" o.d.

Carnegie No: 7058-22
1865 Bowl — 9½" (Opal)

1865 Bowls first available between 1918 and 1924.

(Donated Jan. 1923)

Bowl also available 10½" straight sided (same mould).

1865 was an item number used just for these bowls.

Knob foot not ground and polished. No **"Keystone-W"** mark (see Cased Glass section).

Opal iridizing is not "Mother-of-Pearl" (see Iridized section).

The donation date, 23-1-10, has to be in error. Wednesday, January 10th was the day Wm Jennings Bryan visited the Pittsburgh Exhibit. It continued to Saturday the 13th.

1932: **1865 Bowls** available in crystal and colors (but not opal).
1940: Discontinued.

Both the glass blank and the cased and iridized treatments bear a resemblance to a frequently-seen Steuben "Calcite" iridized bowl of this period. Except for Westmoreland's added floral decorations and its foot (Steuben's is larger and more bulbous), these bowls could be confused. In this period Westmoreland's opal (milk glass) was unsurpassed in density and creamy whiteness.

This bowl appears to have been one of only two opal pieces out of the group of 49.

Carnegie Nos: 7058-26, 27
1800 Salon Set (2 Vases Only)

1800 Salon Set first available between 1918 and 1924.

1800 was designated a **Plain** line.

Urn (not pictured) signed "J.W. Racinger 1925."

1932: **1800 Salon Set** discontinued.

Almost all of the glassware in this book was made for the dining room: if not for the table, the sideboard. If not for the sideboard, the corner cupboard. Westmoreland's olympian salon set was made for the mantel. It seems to have been patterned after the five-piece Chinese garniture sets of the Ch'ing dynasty period that we in the west have usually displayed above the fireplace.

Unfortunately, Westmoreland's president in the late '50s kept the two open vases and sold the covered urn. Perhaps he was unaware he was breaking a set. Today, while all three pieces are accounted for, they are in two different collections; and so tragically, this set may never be together again.

Since the covered urn was signed by Racinger and the vases share the same cutting as the urn, we know all three pieces were engraved by him. From these three we can positively connect the cutting of the blue bowl in the Cased Glass

section and the stained plate in the Cut Stained section. In contrast to so many other Racinger designs, the engraving on these was done in the strict academic style of his apprentice period.

This set was among the last of the pieces donated to Carnegie.

1800 Salon Set

321

Carnegie No: 7058-44
1820 Dolphin Comport — 11" (Roselin)

1820 Dolphin Comports introduced Jan. 1925. Roselin glass first commercially available from late 1926.

(1924)

1820 Dolphin Comport also available 7".

Signed, "by J.W. Racinger 1924."

Made two years before Roselin was commercially available.

1932: Both sizes available in crystal, colors, and opal. 1940: Both sizes discontinued in 1940.

Height: 8¼"
Diameter: 11"

I believe Racinger looked at this bowl and saw it as architecture. He saw an inverted cupola and that suggested to him the radiating coffers that are found beneath Roman or Renaissance domes. He would have been familiar with Daniel Burnham's majestic rotunda (1901) in Pittsburgh's Pennsylvania Railroad station just 27 miles from the plant, and that is what I believe was his model. It has the square coffers, and most important, it shares the same broad, shallow proportions of this bowl.

The deep and shaded fruits are in what is often called "Intaglio" cutting. The initial glass removal was done with an iron or an abrasive cutting wheel, and then this was refined with a number of small copper wheels.

This comport is one of the Carnegie pieces that was sold off at the company.

Carnegie No: 7058-38
1820 Low Foot Comport — 11"

1820 Low Foot Comports first available between 1918 and 1921.

(1921)

1820 Low Foot Comport also available 9".

Signed, "J.W. Racinger 1921."

1932: Both sizes available in crystal and colors.
1940: Both sizes discontinued.

Diameter: 11½"

At first glance this bowl seems to be so busy, it is all a blur. But notice how the design forms two interpenetrating triangles like a hexagram or Solomon's Seal. Look again, and you can see how the design comes together near the center. It bears an uncanny visual resemblance to a Baroque trio sonata with its two upper parts constructed over a continuo part in the base. Like a trio sonata, the thematic material here is tossed back and forth in an interweaving of contrapuntal complexity.

Since the bowl is signed and dated 1921, I feel sure it must have been Racinger's presentation piece, made shortly after he was hired by Chas West. In my view, this single piece clearly establishes Joseph Racinger as the Johann Sebastian Bach of glass engraving. Both men could start with tangled threads and end up with tapestry. As artists both were beyond understanding.

Coded References

B *National Glass Budget*

BH Buhler, Katherine C. & Hood, Graham
American Silver, Garvan and other collections in the Yale University Art Gallery
New Haven, 1970

BM Belknap, E. McCamly
Milk Glass
New York, 1949, 1959

C *China, Glass and Pottery Review*

CD "The Arts of The Ch'ing Dynasty"
(An Exhibition organized by the Arts Council of Great Britain and the Oriental Ceramic Society, May – July 1964)
London, 1965

CO Farrar, Estelle Sinclaire & Spillman, Jane Shadel
The Complete Cut and Engraved Glass of Corning
New York, 1979

DD Daniel, Dorothy
Cut and Engraved Glass 1771 – 1905
New York, 1950, 1971

FF Ferson, Regis F. & Mary F.
Yesterday's Milk Glass Today
Greensburg, PA, 1981

FO Felt, Tom & O'Grady, Bob
Heisey Candlesticks, Candelabra and Lamps
Newark, Ohio, 1984

FS Farrar, Estelle Sinclaire
H.P. Sinclaire, Jr., Glassmaker
2 vols., Garden City, NY, 1974, 1975

GG Gardner, Paul Vickers
Glass
Washington, D.C., 1979

H *House Furnisher*

HI Heacock, Wm
Glass Collector I, 1982

HCI Heacock, Wm
Collecting Glass I, 1984

HCII Heacock, Wm
Collecting Glass II, 1985

HCIII Heacock, Wm
Collecting Glass III, 1985

HE Heacock, Wm
"Early Westmoreland Carnival Glass (1908 – 1912)"
Antique Trader Weekly, Dubuque, Iowa, Apr. 7, 1982

HF Heacock, Wm
Fenton Glass, The First 25 Years
Marietta, Ohio, 1978

JMW Heacock, Wm; Measel, James; Wiggins, Berry
Harry Northwood — The Early Years 1881 – 1900
Marrietta, Ohio, c. 1990 (undated)

IL Inness, Lowell
Pittsburgh Glass 1797 – 1891 — A History and Guide for Collectors
Boston, 1976

J *Crockery and Glass Journal*

JC *Jeweler's Circular*

JD *Jeannette Dispatch*
Jeannette Daily Dispatch
Jeannette News
Jeannette News Dispatch

KP Kerfoot, J. B.
American Pewter
Cambridge, 1924

L *China, Glass and Lamps*

LCP Lee, Ruth Webb & Rose, James H.
American Glass Cup Plates
Rutland, VT, 1948, 1985

LFR Lee, Ruth Webb
Antique Fakes and Reproductions
Wellesley Hills, MA, 1938, 1966

LPG Lee, Ruth Webb
Early American Pressed Glass
Wellesley Hills, MA, 1931, 1960

LVG Lee, Ruth Webb
Victorian Glass
Wellesley Hills, MA, 1944

MB Munsey, Cecil
The Illustrated Guide to Collecting Bottles
New York, 1970

MC McKearin, George S. & Helen
American Glass
New York, 1948

MP Montgomery, Charles F.
A History of American Pewter
New York, 1973

MS Millard, Dr. S. T.
Opaque Glass
Topeka, Kansas, 1953

MSM Measell, James & Smith, Don E.
Findlay Glass
Marietta, Ohio, 1986

MV Manley, Cyril
Decorative Victorian Glass
New York & London, 1981

NW Nutting, Wallace
Furniture Treasury Vol. 3
New York, 1933

P *Pottery, Glass & Brass Salesman*

PG *Pittsburgh Post Gazette*

RA Revi, Albert Christian
American Cut and Engraved Glass
New York, 1965

RN Revi, Albert Christian
19th Century Glass
New York, 1959, 1967

WB Wiggins, Berry
Stretch in Color, Book 1
Orange, Virginia, 1971

WC West, Chas H,
"Home Missionary Work"
(an address given by Chas West to the Flint & Lime Glass Manufacturers, Inc., Atlantic City, July 13, 1925)

WE Weatherman, Hazel Marie
Colored Glassware of the Depression Era II
Springfield, MA, 1974

WS Weiss, Gustav
The Book of Glass
Berlin, 1966; New York, 1971

Do all Westmoreland mustard containers show mould numbers?

No. But the presence of a centered block-style number, ¼ to ⅜ inch high, ranging from 0 to 7, is an indication a piece was pressed in a Westmoreland opal container mould from the early twentieth century.

Does the piece have a ground and polished bottom?

If it is by Westmoreland and has a finished bottom, it probably pre-dates 1959. Surviving accounting records from the Brainard years show the separate expense of grinding and polishing ended in 1958. The earlier the Westmoreland piece (back to the early-teens), the more likely it is to have a finished bottom. Heisey made an art form of their bottom finishing. While Westmoreland equaled Heisey's best grinding quality on some of their glassware, a larger proportion of Heisey's glassware than Westmoreland's, from the same era, shows an exceptional standard of bottom finishing.

Is there a round ring about 1" in diameter on the bottom of a jar or vase?

No Westmoreland glass of any era will show such a ring, for it is a cut-off mark made by a machine plunger.

Does the piece have clear mould seams than can catch the fingernail?

This almost rules out Westmoreland from the West period after about 1910. On Westmoreland glassware from this era, the mould seams are as inconspicuous as any that can be found on pressed glass. As moulds wear, however (they are good for about 10,000 pressings), the seams tend to become more obtrusive. Nevertheless, glassware from some other companies always seems to show prominent mould seams, even with apparently new moulds.

Does the piece show striae (parallel heat lines)?

The earlier the Westmoreland glass (back to the early teens), the less likely it is to show these lines. For some reason, Brainard period Westmoreland shows very marked lines in their late transparent glassware, and this is often a way of identifying it. Since it is ever-present, the usual explanation of cold mould temperature cannot be correct, for after only a few pressings the temperature of any mould should rise to the temperature of the molten glass. I have

never seen Duncan & Miller glass that had these disfiguring lines, but I have never seen glass of any other pressed glass company that was all, totally free of it.

Are there faint rotation marks on the bottom center of a plate or bowl?

This suggests the probability of a Westmoreland piece, for Westmoreland's plates and bowls were ordinarily pressed in a "regular" cup shape and then rotated and shaped with a "paddle" or "battledore."

Is there a mould mark across a bowl?

This will rule out Westmoreland. I know of no instance where a joint mould creating such a mark was used for a Westmoreland bowl. Westmoreland always used block or shell moulds for their bowls that left their marks at the outer edge where they could be fire-polished away.

Does the mould line on a stem of a piece veer from a straight line as it descends toward the foot?

This indicates the circular foot was pressed in a "regular" cup shape and then straightened with a battledore as it was turned. This technique suggests Westmoreland and comparatively few other companies.

Does a circular foot on a stemmed piece show a mould mark across it?

This probably rules out Westmoreland. If a foot on a Westmoreland piece could have been rotated and paddled flat, it almost always was; this removed the mould mark across the foot.

Does a circular foot on a stemmed piece suggest plate glass?

If so, the piece is probably Fostoria's. Fostoria seems to have had a unique way of flattening their feet that left no rotation marks. Westmoreland's feet, along with everyone else's, show definite rotation marks on the paddled (bottom) side.

Does a colonial foot have an odd number of sides?

McKee sometimes made a foot with seven sides and Millersburg feet are often seen with nine. Westmoreland's colonial feet, however, are all either six- or eight-sided.

Does the piece show a combination of colored glasses like some Venetian glass or Carder Steuben?

This almost certainly rules out Westmoreland. A great deal of Westmoreland glass was "stuck" or joined with a "wafer," but I know of only one example of two different transparent glasses mated by Westmoreland. Look through the center of an amber, clear-footed Westmoreland piece that may be in question; a clear spot will be evidence of selective staining — common to Westmoreland.

Is the yellow color of a stained piece a light, lemon-yellow rather than a yellow-amber?

Westmoreland's stains in the '20s and '30s varied from amber to medium yellow, but I have never seen a light yellow stain used on a Westmoreland piece. Westmoreland did use a lemon-yellow translucent cased color around 1930, however. But since this glass coating lacks the clarity of the yellow-amber stains, it will probably not be mistaken for them.

Does the Westmoreland amber glass color have a reddish appearance like Fostoria's amber from the '20s?

If so, it is Westmoreland's "Golden Sunset," introduced in December 1960. Westmoreland's original amber, made before 1910 and from 1924 to the late '30s, has an earthy color; mustard seed was one of the colorants used.

Does the green glass seem to fluoresce in direct sunlight?

Both of Westmoreland's late '20s and early '30s greens share this characteristic; nevertheless, Westmoreland's two greens are chemically dissimilar.

Does an etched black piece feel statically charged?

If the piece is very dirty and feels this way, it was probably made by U.S. Glass. However, I have found both Westmoreland's and U.S. Glass' etched black pieces feel this way when washed. Although Westmoreland was the first to make this glass in 1915, U.S. Glass deserves its reputation today as a premier maker of fine etched black glassware in the 1920s.

Does the Westmoreland carnival glass have a turquoise (blue-green) color?

This color, though widely used for Westmoreland's first period (c. 1910) carnival, has not (yet) been used for any late carnival glass. Westmoreland's late carnival, reflecting current tastes, has largely been with glass colors that were never iridized in the first period.

Does the iridizing on a known Westmoreland piece look thin and shiny?

If so, this reflects a single spraying with alcohol rather than acid as the vehicle — the manner in which Westmoreland glass has been iridized over the last 20 years. Period Westmoreland carnival usually has a rich, satiny look, but it sometimes has a deep shine that resembles polished metal.

Is a very subtle iridizing used on an important piece of glassware?

This almost shouts "Westmoreland." Westmoreland continued to iridize some of their finest art glass to about 1930, and this non-carnival iridizing was nearly invisible.

Is the decoration some combination of staining, cutting, etching, casing, iridizing, or enameling?

Any combination of these tends to point to Westmoreland. For example, Westmoreland may have been the only company to combine cutting with sprayed casing, and the only one to combine sprayed casing with iridizing.

If the piece has been sprayed with an opaque or translucent color, does the color come off on a rag if attacked by a strong abrasive?

If the sprayed color is from the West period, it is glass and cannot be dislodged — even with steel wool. Exceptions to this are brushed black bands behind the glass, and gold, silver, and black lines, all of which are perishable.

Does the gold decoration have a brightly polished metallic appearance?

Westmoreland used this "lustre gold" from the 1890s to 1915, and then again from the late '30s on. Between these periods, however, Westmoreland seems to have used only matt "coin gold" in its decorating.

Are the enameled flowers raised, as in Bohemian work?

If so, they are probably Westmoreland's, and will date from the West period. This two-step process, involving double painting with probable double firing and cooling, was discontinued, I believe, in late 1937.

Is the piece decorated with a pantograph (needle) etching?

If so, this will rule out a Westmoreland decoration, and probably a Westmoreland blank.

Revised values compiled by the National Westmoreland
Glass Collector's Club.

Ag	Silver decoration	Gnd.	Ground bottom (milk glass)
Ameth.	Amethyst (dark purple)	HDL	Handle
Aqua.	Aquamarine Blue (from 1929)	HLD	Handled
Au	Gold decoration	HF	High Foot
B'Per	Brainard Period (from 1938)	H.P.	Hand painted
Bl.MG	Blue milk (opal) glass	1'Per.	First period
Bl.		Irid.	Iridized (incl. "carnivalized")
Opalescent	Blue opalescent (white edged, trans. blue glass)	LF	Low Foot
Black	Black (not black cased) glass	MG	Milk (opal) glass
C'Dec.	Cold decoration (paint)	Pr.	Pair (candlesticks)
Col.	Trans. colored glass	RE	Rolled Edge
Cry.	Crystal (clear) glass	Ros.	Roselin (rose or peach from 1926)
Cut.	Cutting or engraving	SE	Straight Edge
Dec.	Decorated/decoration	Trans.	Transparent (not opaque) glass
Des.	Design	Turq.	Turquoise (c. 1910 blue-green)
Enam.	Enamel (fired glass)	W'Per.	West Period (1889 – 1937)
F'Dec.	Fired decoration (glass or ceramic)	Wh.MG	White milk (opal) glass
G&P	Ground & polished (bottom)	Wh. Opalescent	White opalescent (white edged crystal)

Cut Crystal

1776 Colonial Half Gallon Jug (marked). G&P. 1'Per. "Sunburst" & "Grecian" cut. des. . $65.00 – 95.00
1776 Tumbler (marked). G&P. 1'Per. "Grecian" cut. des. . . . . $20.00 – 35.00
1200/1201 Sugar & Cream (marked). 1'Per. "Sunburst" cut. des. . . . . Set $40.00 – 55.00
1700 Colonial Match Holder (marked). G&P. 1'Per. "Grecian" cut. des. . . . . . $35.00 – 45.00
1700 Napkin Ring G&P. 1'Per. "Grecian" cut. des. . . . . $35.00 – 45.00
1700 Vase, 9". 1'Per. "Canada Thistle" & "Grecian" cut. des. . . . . $65.00 – 95.00
1800 HLD Sandwich (early). Gray & gang wheel cutting. . . . . $30.00 – 40.00
1800 HLD Sandwich (late). Gray & gang wheel cutting. . . . . $25.00 – 35.00
1800 Butterball. "Criss-cross" cut. des. w/flowers. . . . . $22.00 – 35.00
752 Basket, 6". Simple medallion cutting . . . . $100.00 – 125.00
1820 5-part Relish. Extensive cutting w/"Hammered Silver" dec. . . . . $85.00 – 125.00
1211 Octagon HLD Sandwich. Radial gang wheel cutting. . . . . $30.00 – 40.00
1211 HLD Sandwich. Floral cutting w/black cased hdl. . . . . $30.00 – 40.00
"Keystone-W" Oval Tray. G&P. Gray cutting . . . . $35.00 – 50.00
1828 Covered Cigarette Box. Racinger "Setter" cut. des. . . . . $300.00+
1822 4-part Relish. Butterfly & floral cutting . . . . $75.00 – 95.00
1700 Vase/Hatpin Holder, 7". 1'Per. "Sunburst" & "Grecian" cut. des. . . . . . $65.00 – 85.00
1700 Vase, 9". 1'Per. "Sunburst" & "Grecian" cut. des. . . . . $65.00 – 95.00
Paul Revere Colonial Berry Sugar (marked). Two gang wheel cuttings . . . . . $70.00 – 95.00
Paul Revere Colonial Berry Sugar (marked). 1'Per. Plain . . . . $35.00 – 50.00
1700 HF HLD Compotier (marked). Gang wheel cutting. . . . . $45.00 – 65.00
1700 HF HLD Compotier (marked). W'Per. Plain . . . . $25.00 – 35.00
1700 "Round Handled" Sugar & Cream. Gang wheel cutting . . . . Set $55.00 – 85.00
1700 "Round Handled" Sugar & Cream. W'Per. Plain. . . . . Set $30.00 – 45.00
1700 Indiv. Celery Holder (marked). Gang wheel cutting. . . . . $45.00 – 65.00
1700 Candy Jars, 2 lb. Two cuttings . . . . $100.00+
1700 Candy Jar, 3 lb. Extensive gray cutting. . . . . $200.00+
1707 Covered Candy Jar, 1 lb. Gray & gang wheel cutting. . . . . $85.00 – 110.00
1209 Sugar & Cream Sets. G&P. Three cuttings . . . . Set $40.00 – 65.00
1801 Straight Comport. Cut. . . . . $65.00 – 85.00
Racinger Wine Set. Post-Westmoreland. Vintage cutting. . . . . Set $350.00+

Cut Crystal Candlesticks

1019 Candlesticks. G&P lips & punties. All cuttings . . . . Pr. $ 100.00+
1016 Candlesticks, 7". G&P lips & punties. Cut. . . . . Pr. $120.00+
1016 Candlesticks, 8". G&P lips & punties. Cut. . . . . Pr. $135.00+
1016 Candlesticks, 7". G&P lips & punties. Plain . . . . Pr. $90.00+
1016 Candlesticks, 8". G&P lips & punties. Plain . . . . Pr. $100.00+
1015 Mission Candlesticks. Cut . . . . Pr. $85.00 – 115.00
1015 Mission Candlesticks. Plain . . . . Pr. $45.00 – 65.00
1012 Candlesticks, 7". Various cuttings . . . . Pr. $50.00 – 95.00
1012 Candlesticks, 8". Various cuttings . . . . Pr. $60.00 – 100.00

1012 Candlesticks, 8". G&P lips. Black. Plain. . . . . Pr. $65.00 – 95.00
1012 Candlesticks, 8". G&P lips. Cry. Cutting on two adj. sides. . . . . Pr. $100.00+
1041 Candlesticks. G&P lips. "Diamonds & Vintage" cut. des. . . . . Pr. $95.00 – 120.00
1023 Candlesticks, 7". Various cuttings . . . . Pr. $40.00 – 55.00
1023 Candlesticks, 7". Cry. Plain . . . . Pr. $20.00 – 30.00
1023 Candlesticks, 7". Black. Plain. . . . . Pr. $40.00 – 55.00
1027 Candlesticks. G&P lips. Cry. Cut stars w/notching . . . . Pr. $75.00 – 115.00
1027 Candlesticks. G&P lips. Black. Plain . . . . Pr. $70.00 – 90.00
1021 Candlesticks. "Grecian" cut. des. . . . . Pr. $65.00 – 95.00
Paul Revere Colonial Candlesticks. All cuttings . . . . Pr. $175.00+
Paul Revere Colonial Candlesticks. Plain . . . . Pr. $75.00 – 100.00

Cut Stained Glass

1708 Covered Sweetmeat. Radial cuts w/flowers . . . . $60.00 – 85.00
1826 Mayo. Radial cuts w/flowers . . . . $60.00 – 85.00
1800 Ladle. Stained. Cut . . . . $15.00 – 20.00
1820 FTD Honey. "Basket & Ribbon" cut. des. . . . . $95.00 – 125.00
1840 Vase, 10". "Basket & Ribbon" cut. des. . . . . $175.00 – 250.00
1840 Vase, 10". "Graceful Scroll" cut. des. $175.00 – 225.00+
Egyptian Jar" Vase. G&P. G&P punty. "Basket & Ribbon" cut. des. w/beads $275.00
1820 Bowl, 11". "Graceful Scroll" cut. des. . . . . $375.00+
1042 Candlesticks. "Graceful Scroll" cut. des. . . . . Pr. $85.00 – 110.00
1042 Candlesticks. "White Rose" cut. des. . . . . Pr. $100.00 – 125.00
1801 Serving Platter, 14". G&P. "Design No. 229" cut. des.;
    1826 Mayo; 1800 Ladle Stained & Cut . . . . Set $185.00 – 240.00
1801 Plate, 9". G&P. "Deer Hunt" cut. des . . . . $85.00 – 100.00
1800 Covered Rose Jar. "Pointer & Pheasant" cut. des. . . . . $750.00+
1800 Vase. "Pointer & Pheasant" cut. des. . . . . $750.00+
1900/2 Bell Bowl, 12". G&P "Directory" cut. des. . . . . $100.00 – 125.00
? - 1900 Bell Bowl. G&P Radial cuts w/foliage. . . . . $75.00 – 95.00
? - 1032/0 Bowl Stand. G&P top. Radial cuts w/foliage . . . . $35.00 – 45.00

Cut Colored Glass

1801 Plate, 9". Green. G&P. "Wreath" cut. des. Cut star . . . . $12.00 – 15.00
1901 Fan Vase. Green. Gang wheel cutting . . . . $40.00 – 60.00
1820 Dolphin Comport, 11". Green. Mitre cutting . . . . $185.00 – 250.00
1820 Dolphin Comport, 11". Ros. "Pirouette" cut. des. . . . . $250.00+
1708 Fan Vase, 8". Amber. Ship cut. des. . . . . $55.00 – 75.00
1042 Candlesticks. Amber. Radial gang wheel cuts . . . . Pr. $65.00 – 85.00
1801 HF Ball Stem Sweetmeat. Amber. Mitre cutting . . . . $55.00 – 75.00
1211 Octagon Ice Tub w/tongs. Ros. Gang wheel cutting . . . . $55.00 – 80.00
'2' Salt & Pepper. Sterling tops. Aqua. "String-of-Pearls" cut. des . . . . . . Set $45.00 – 60.00
1820 LF Comport, 11". Belgian blue. Butterfly cut. des. . . . . $100.00 – 125.00+
1820 LF Comport, 11". Other c. 1930 colors Butterfly cut. des. . . . . $80.00 – 100.00
1042 Candlesticks. Belgian blue. No cutting . . . . Pr. $75.00 – 100.00
1042 Candlesticks. Other c. 1930 colors. No cutting . . . . Pr. $55.00 – 80.00

Etched Glass

'6' Owl Plates. C'Dec. . . . . $30.00 – 45.00
'4' Stamp Plate ('Fleur-de-lis'). C'Dec. . . . . $20.00 – 30.00
227 Sleigh. C'Dec. . . . . $35.00 – 45.00
1820 Flared Bowl. G&P. Egyptian enam. dec . . . . $35.00 – 55.00
1847 Covered Toast. G&P. #470 enam. dec . . . . $150.00+
462 Breakfast (Stacking) Set. #470 enam. dec. . . . . $45.00 – 55.00
462 Breakfast (Stacking) Set. Plain cry. Nickel or pearl tops. W'Per. . . . . $25.00 – 30.00
462 Breakfast (Stacking) Set. Late '20s colors. Nickel or pearl tops. W'Per. . . . $35.00 – 50.00
1921 Lotus Mayo Bowl. Elaborate cased dec. $25.00 – 35.00
1921 Lotus Mayo Plate. Elaborate cased dec. $25.00 – 30.00
1921 Lotus Cupped Bowl, 9". Late '20s colors . . . . $25.00 – 35.00
'1' Shell Nappy, 6". Rockwell Ag dec. . . . . $75.00 – 95.00
Floral Colonial Round Nappy (marked). G&P. Etched flowers . . . . $50.00 – 80.00
Floral Colonial Round Nappy (marked). G&P. Plain . . . . $40.00 – 65.00
1042 Candlesticks. Stained. "Graceful Scroll" cut & etched des. . . . . Pr. $85.00 – 110.00
1708 3-FTD Plate. Aqua. #C542 cut. des. . . . . $35.00 – 55.00
1801 Comport. Ros. Hand-blocked etching . . . . $55.00 – 75.00
1905 Bell HF Bowl. Stained. Hand-blocked etching . . . . $85.00 – 110.00
1700 Colonial Candy Jar, 2 lb. "Engine turned" etching . . . . $75.00 – 90.00
1800 RE Frappe. "Engine turned" etching w/enam. flowers & Au. . . . . $60.00 – 80.00
1816 Covered Urn. "Engine turned" etching w/Au. . . . . $80.00 – 100.00
1820 LF Comport, 9". Blue. "Engine turned" etching . . . . $50.00 – 75.00
1049 Dolphin Shell. Ros. Hand-blocked etching . . . . $250.00 – 300.00
1049 Dolphin Shell. Ros. Without etching. $150.00 – 200.00

Tankard Sets:

Tankards. Purple cased. H.P. F'Dec...................................$325.00 – 400.00
Tankards. Brown cased. Transfer dec..................................$150.00 – 160.00
Mugs. Purple cased. H.P. F'Dec. ....$ 60.00 – 75.00
Mugs. Brown cased. Transfer dec......................................$ 40.00 – 50.00
1019 Candlesticks. "Mahogany Glass" dec. .... Pr. $125.00 – 150.00
1832 HLD Nut Bowl, 9". Etched & cased ....$25.00 – 40.00
1921 Lotus Low Candlesticks, 2½". W'Per. Cased ....Pr.$ 35.00 – 50.00
1921 Lotus Tall Candlesticks, 9". W'Per. Cased ....Pr. $50.00 – 75.00
750 Basket, 6". Cased..$65.00 – 80.00
1840 Vase, 10". Cased #1 dec..$50.00 – 70.00
1211 Octagon Sugar & Cream Set. Cased Enam. dec. .... Set $35.00 – 45.00
1854/2 Covered Chocolate Box. G&P. Cased w/Au dec. Etched star .... $40.00 – 60.00
1707 Covered Candy Jar. Cased w/Au dec. ....$30.00 – 45.00
1777 Colonial Grapefruit. G&P. Cased w/Au dec. Cut star ....$30.00 – 40.00
1800 Mayo. Cased w/Au dec. ....$25.00 – 35.00
1800 Ladle. Cased w/Au dec. ....$7.00 – 12.00
1820 Bowl, 13½". Cased w/enam. fruits...............................$60.00 – 85.00
"Egyptian Jar" Vase. G&P punty. "Transparent Green" casing.
    "Graceful Scroll" cutting ....$250.00 – 350.00
HF Sweetmeat. "Transparent Green" casing. "Graceful Scroll" cutting..... $95.00 – 125.00
1707 Covered Candy Jar, Half lb. "Transparent Rose" casing. Cutting....... $45.00 – 60.00
1865 Bowl, 9½". "Transparent Rose" casing. Elaborately cut.............$90.00 – 125.00
1042 Candlesticks. "Transparent Rose" casing. Elaborately cut .... Pr. $100.00 – 125.00
1031/0 Bowl Stand. Cased ....$12.00 – 20.00
1820 LF Comport, 9". "Transparent Blue" casing. "Deer Hunt" cutting....$175.00 – 225.00
1848 RE Bowl, 13". G&P. "Transparent" casing. Cut.....................$95.00 – 125.00
HF Sweetmeat. Stained, etched, cut. Opaque green casing...............$65.00 – 90.00
HF Sweetmeat. Stained, etched, cut. Opaque black casing...............$65.00 – 90.00
1800 FTD Vase. Stained, etched, cut. Opaque green casing ....$100.00 – 135.00
"Egyptian Jar" Vase. G&P. G&P punty. Stained, etched, cut. Blue cased ... $150.00 – 185.00
1820 LF Comport, 11". Stained, etched, cut. Blue cased.................$75.00 – 100.00
1840 Vase, 10". Stained, cut, black cased............................$175.00 – 225.00
1211 Octagon Ice Tub w/tongs. Cut & black cased ....$120.00 – 145.00
1902 LF Comport. Carnation cutting. Black cased.......................$80.00 – 100.00

1910 Tall Comport. Two cased colors ....$35.00 – 55.00
1034 Candlesticks, 9". G&P punty. Cased..............................Pr. $50.00 – 65.00
1038 Candlesticks, 9"...Pr. $60.00 – 75.00
1909/1 Bowl. G&P. Cased ....$35.00 – 55.00
1042 Candlesticks. Cased ....Pr. $50.00 – 65.00
1031/2 Bowl Stand. Black..$12.00 – 20.00
1848 Belled Bowl. G&P. Cased ....$50.00 – 65.00
1002 Candlesticks. Cased ....Pr. $55.00 – 70.00
1820 Cheese & Cracker. G&P. Cased. Bronze trim ....$50.00 – 70.00
1865 Flower Bowl (marked). G&P.......................................$40.00 – 60.00
1865 Flower Bowl (marked). G&P w/wrought iron stand ....$100.00+
1800 Cracker & Cheese Plate. G&P. Etched & cased.....................$65.00 – 85.00

1007 Candlesticks. Cry. C'Dec. ....Pr. $40.00 – 60.00
1208 Sugar & Cream. Cased. Enam. dec. w/Au trim .... Set $30.00 – 40.00
1708 Fan Vase, 9". Cased. Enam. dec. w/Au trim ....$35.00 – 45.00
1707 Covered Candy Jar, Half lb. Cased. Enam dec. w/Au ....$50.00 – 65.00
1800 Mayo. Cased. Enam. dec. w/Au...................................$25.00 – 40.00
1800 Ladle. Cased ....$7.00 – 12.00
1849 Butterball. Cased. Enam. dec. w/Au ....$25.00 – 35.00
1707 Covered Candy Jar, 1 lb. Enam. dec. on black band w/Au...........$60.00 – 75.00
1708 Covered Sweetmeat. Enam. dec. on black band w/Au ....$60.00 – 75.00
1820 HLD Sandwich. Cased. Enam. dec. w/Au...........................$30.00 – 45.00
1700 Colonial Candy Jar, 3 lb. Single rose w/Au dec..................$150.00 – 200.00
1700 Colonial Candy Jar, 2 lb. Single rose w/Au dec..................$125.00 – 150.00
1820 LF Comport, 11". Ros. Cased. Single rose w/Au dec..............$50.00 – 70.00
1060 Candlesticks. Ros. Cased. Single rose w/Au dec. ....Pr. $65.00 – 85.00
1900/2 Re Bowl. G&P. Cased. Single rose w/Au dec. ....$45.00 – 65.00
1042 Candlesticks. Cased. Single rose w/Au dec. ....Pr. $55.00 – 80.00
1849 Butterball. Cased. Single rose w/Au dec. ....$30.00 – 40.00
857 Covered Honey. Cased. Single rose w/Au dec......................$45.00 – 55.00
1503 Covered Bonbon. Cased. Single rose dec. w/Au trim..............$45.00 – 55.00
1700 Candy Jar, 2 lb. Cased. Single rose w/Au dec. ....$125.00 – 150.00

Cased Glass

Chas West's Decoration

Enameled Flowers

1835 Comport. Etched & cased. Single rose dec. on Au band............$40.00 – 60.00
1033 Candlestick. Single rose dec. on blue band w/Au trim............$100.00 – 125.00
1841 HF Comport, 6½". Single rose dec. on Au band.................$35.00 – 55.00
1700 Candy Jar, 2 lb. Double rose dec. on black band w/Au trim.........$125.00 – 150.00
1800 Mayo. Double rose dec. on black band w/Au trim.................$25.00 – 40.00
1800 Ladle. Raised enam. dec. w/black & Au trim.....................$10.00 – 20.00
1800 Cracker & Cheese, 10". G&P. Cut star. Double rose dec. on black band w/Au trim. $60.00 – 75.00
1800 Syrup w/Lid & Plate. Double rose dec. w/Au.....................$50.00 – 70.00
1800 Cracker & Cheese, 10". Aqua. Double rose dec. w/cutting & etching....$75.00 – 95.00
1700 Candy Jar, 2 lb. Silver cover. Triple rose dec....................$135.00 – 160.00
'23' Bowl. Cased. Raised enam. flowers.............................$35.00 – 50.00
1849 Butterball. Ros. Enam. w/wide Au band..........................$35.00 – 45.00
1827 SE Honey. Raised enam. dec. w/Au trim.........................$35.00 – 50.00
1211 Octagon FTD Sweetmeat. Enam. dec. w/Au trim..................$50.00 – 65.00
1211/1 SE Bowl, 13". G&P. Cubist enam. dec. w/red trim................$100.00+
1042 Candlesticks. Rococo enam. dec w/Au trim..............Pr. $60.00 – 90.00
1700/2 Urn. Multiple dec's.......................................$150.00+
1038 Spiral Candlesticks. Multiple dec's......................Pr. $150.00+

Reverse Painting

1900 Flange Bowl, 14". G&P. "Spanish Dec." w/Au trim.................$50.00 – 80.00
1054 Candlesticks. "Spanish Dec." w/Au trim...................Pr. $40.00 – 55.00
1707 Covered Candy Jar, Half lb. "Spanish Dec." w/Au trim............$40.00 – 55.00
1211/1 Octagon Candlesticks. Cry. w/Leaf & Au dec..............Pr. $40.00 – 55.00
1054 Candlesticks. Cry. Cased w/Leaf dec....................Pr. $35.00 – 45.00
1909/1 Belled Bowl. G&P. Etched & Cased. Fruit dec. w/Au trim........$50.00 – 75.00
1211 HLD Sandwich. Cased. Pheasant & Peony dec. w/Au trim...........$40.00 – 55.00
1849 HLD Sandwich. Cased. Pa. Dutch dec..........................$40.00 – 55.00
1820 LF Comport, 9". Cry. Oxidized band w/Cubist flowers............$55.00 – 75.00
Zodiac Plate, 9". Lustre stained w/ruby. B'Per......................$110.00 – 135.00
Zodiac Plate, 15". Lustre stained w/ruby..........................$85.00 – 110.00

Iridized & Crackled Glass

Filigree Sugar & Cream. Crystal..........................Set $75.00 – 95.00
Filigree Sugar & Cream. Wh. Opalescent...................Set $150.00 – 175.00
294/295 Sugar & Cream. Amethyst.........................Set $20.00 – 40.00
294/295 Sugar & Cream. Cry. "Verde Green Metallic"..........Set $20.00 – 40.00
294/295 Sugar & Cream. Crystal..........................Set$ 20.00 – 40.00
Paneled Pattern Rose Bowl. Turquoise......................$75.00 – 95.00
Paneled Pattern Rose Bowl. Amethyst......................$65.00 – 85.00
Paneled Pattern Salad or Fruit Dish. Turq...................$40.00 – 65.00
Polka Dot Bowl. Amber.................................$30.00 – 50.00
Polka Dot Bowl. Amethyst..............................$40.00 – 60.00
Peacock Optic Bowl. White Opalescent.....................$75.00 – 100.00
Peacock Optic Bowl. Blue Opalescent......................$150.00 – 200.00
Peacock Optic Bowl. Blue MG...........................$275.00 – 325.00
Peacock Optic Finger Bowl. Amethyst......................$30.00 – 40.00
Peacock Optic Finger Bowl Plate. Ameth....................$55.00 – 85.00
Peach Bowl. Wh. Opalescent. 1'Per........................$175.00 – 225.00
Peach Bowl. Cry. (Irid.) W'Per...........................$50.00 – 75.00
Daisy Bowl. Blue MG. 1'Per.............................$500.00+
Daisy Bowl. Wh. Opalescent. 1'Per........................$350.00+
Daisy Bowl. Blue Opalescent. 1'Per........................$400.00+
252 LF Comport, 6". Turquoise...........................$60.00 – 90.00
Ribbed Swung Vase. Amethyst...........................$30.00 – 45.00
Ribbed Swung Vase. Turquoise...........................$40.00 – 55.00
"Jester's Cap" Swung Vase. Turq..........................$75.00 – 100.00
"Jester's Cap" Swung Vase. Ameth.........................$60.00 – 90.00
Ribbed Flat Spoon. Amber..............................$50.00 – 75.00
Reeded Bowl. Turquoise................................$40.00 – 65.00
Footed Jelly (Paneled Stem). Ameth........................$45.00 – 70.00
Footed Jelly (Polka Dot). Wh. Opalescent....................$90.00 – 125.00
High Comport (Acanthus leaves). Amber.....................$50.00 – 75.00
High Comport (Acanthus leaves). Turquoise..................$60.00 – 90.00
'1', 6" Shell Nappy. Turquoise............................$50.00 – 65.00
'1', 6" Shell Nappy. Amber stained.........................$40.00 – 45.00
'1', 6" Shell Nappy. Amethyst............................$35.00 – 50.00
4" Shell. Turquoise...................................$60.00 – 70.00
1001 (Spool") Candlesticks. Amber stained..............Pr. $15.00 – 25.00
"Basket Weave" Cream or Sugar w/lid. Stained...............$ 40.00 – 60.00

"Peacock" Cream or Sugar w/lid. Ameth. W'Per. . . . . $ 45.00 – 60.00
Victor Cream or Sugar w/lid. Turquoise. W'Per. . . . . $ 50.00 – 65.00
Elite Bowl. Wisteria. W'Per. . . . . $50.00 – 65.00
Elite Bowl. Turquoise. W'Per. . . . . $60.00 – 75.00
1776 Colonial Sweetmeat (marked). Ameth. W'Per. . . . . $100.00+
1700 Colonial HLD Compotier (marked). Ameth. W'Per. . . . . $100.00+
1865 Bowl, 9½". Gray cased w/Au band . . . . $55.00 – 80.00
1867 Covered Urn. Green cased w/Au . . . . $60.00 – 85.00
1700 Candy Jar, 1 lb. MG "Mother-of-Pearl" w/Au B'Per . . . . B'Per $30.00 – 40.00
1023 Candlesticks. Amber stained . . . . Pr. $50.00 – 65.00
? - 1043 Candlesticks. Blue . . . . Pr. $60.00 – 75.00
1700/2 Urn. Multiple decs. . . . . $150.00+
1038 Spiral Candlesticks. Multiple decs. . . . . Pr. $150.00+
1841 HF Comport, 6½". Cry. Cased & engraved . . . . $150.00 – 200.00
300 Square Foot Vase. Cry. Lustre stained . . . . $60.00 – 85.00
1900/1 Bell Bowl, 9½". Cry. w/Au trim . . . . $45.00 – 60.00
'23' Bowl, 8½". Cry. w/cut star & cased lines . . . . $45.00 – 60.00
1031/2 Bowl Stand, 5". Black . . . . $15.00 – 20.00
750 Basket, 5". Cry. Crackled. Lustre stained . . . . $85.00 – 110.00
1865 Bowl, 9½". (marked). Dark Green. Crackled . . . . $60.00 – 85.00

Gold & Silver

'98' Westmoreland 4-piece Set. Cry. w/Au Lustre . . . . Set $175.00+
Puriton 4-oz Mug. Cry. w/Au Lustre . . . . $15.00 – 25.00
Filigree Puff Box. Cry. w/Au Lustre . . . . $15.00 – 25.00
'69' Orange Sherbet. G&P. 1'Per. F'Dec w/Au Lustre hdl. . . . . $8.00 – 15.00
'69' Orange Sherbet. G&P. 1'Per F'Dec w/green hdl. "Syria - Pittsburgh" . . . . $40.00 – 55.00
FTD Orange Sherbet. F'Dec. . . . . $8.00 – 15.00
1820 Dolphin Comport, 11". MG. F'Dec. w/Au Lustre . . . . $250.00+
1835 Comport. Cry. w/Au rim . . . . $25.00 – 35.00
1810 Flower Bowl. Cry. w/Au rim . . . . $55.00 – 85.00
1823 Covered Comport. Cry. w/Au rim . . . . $35.00 – 55.00
1800 Mayo. Cry. w/Au rim . . . . $25.00 – 35.00
1800 Ladle. Cry. w/Au rim . . . . $5.00 – 10.00
1700 Colonial 4-part Relish & Comport. Cry. w/Au trim. . . . . $50.00 – 75.00
1705 HLD Candy Jar. Cry. w/Au trim. . . . . $55.00 – 75.00
1800 Mayo. Cased cry. w/Au rim . . . . $25.00 – 40.00
1820 Sugar & Cream. Cry. w/Au rims. . . . . Set $30.00 – 50.00
1820 5-Part Diamond Relish. Ros. w/Au trim . . . . $40.00 – 65.00
1820 5-Part Diamond Relish. Ros. w/Ag dec. . . . . $40.00 – 65.00
1207 Sugar & Cream. Cry. w/Au band . . . . Set $30.00 – 45.00
1207 Sugar & Cream. Black w/Ag dec. . . . . Set $40.00 – 55.00
1854/2 Covered Chocolate Box. G&P. Cry. cased w/Au dec. . . . . $60.00 – 75.00
1854/2 Covered Chocolate Box. G&P. Black w/raised enam. dec. . . . . $60.00 – 75.00
1042 Candlesticks. Blue cased w/Au Leaf dec. . . . . Pr. $60.00 – 85.00
1042 Candlesticks. Pastel cased w/Ag & Au band . . . . Pr. $45.00 – 65.00
1042 Candlesticks. Cry. w/E. Warrin Ag dec. . . . . Pr. $65.00 – 90.00
1042 Candlesticks. Black w/E Warrin Ag dec. . . . . Pr. $100.00 – 125.00
1042 Candlesticks. Cry. Plain . . . . Pr. $40.00 – 50.00
199 Colonial Mustard. Cry. w/Ag dec. . . . . $35.00 – 45.00
1840 Vase, 10". Blue cased w/Ag dec. . . . . $70.00 – 95.00
1800 HF Sweetmeat. Yellow & blue cased w/Ag dec. . . . . $45.00 – 70.00
1042 Candlesticks. Purple cased w/Ag dec. . . . . Pr. $65.00 – 90.00
1849 HLD Sandwich. Ros. w/Lotus Co. Ag dec. . . . . $45.00 – 55.00
1849 HLD Sandwich. Black w/Lotus Co. Ag dec. $90.00 – 110.00
1820 Oval Relish. G&P. Cry. Cut star & Ag dec. . . . . $40.00 – 65.00
1902 LF Comport. Cry. w/etching & Ag dec. . . . . $60.00 – 75.00
1820 5-Part Relish. Cry. Elaborate cutting. "Hammered Silver" dec. . . . . . . $85.00 – 125.00
1208 Sugar & Cream. Cry. Cut. "Hammered Gold" dec. . . . . Set $35.00 – 55.00
1841, 9" Comport. Cry. Cut. "Hammered Gold" dec. . . . . $50.00 – 75.00
750 Basket, 5" (marked). Cry. Elaborate Ag Dec. $125.00 – 150.00+
1700 Colonial Lily Vase, 6". Cry. Ag dec. . . . . $50.00 – 65.00
1800 Butterball Cry. Cut. Watson Co. Sterling band . . . . $125.00 – 175.00

(Cold decoration in exceptional condition can add 50 – 100% to the value of an early piece.
Original label can add 50 – 100% to the value of a mustard container.)

Opaque Glass

'7' Rabbit Plate. C'Dec. "Pat.Appl'd For." 1'Per. . . . . $50.00 – 60.00
'7' Rabbit Plate. Plain B'Per. . . . . $25.00 – 30.00
Rabbit Plaque. C'Dec. 1'Per. . . . . $75.00 – 90.00

'5' Cat Plate. C'Dec. 1'Per. . . . . $40.00 – 50.00
'5' Cat Plate. Plain. B'Per. . . . . $25.00 – 30.00
'6' Owl Plate. MG. C'Dec. "Pat'd July 2, 1901" . . . . $45.00 – 60.00
'6' Owl Plate. Cry. Etched. C'Dec. 1'Per. . . . . $30.00 – 45.00
'6' Owl Plate. MG. Plain. B'Per. . . . . $25.00 – 30.00
'15' National Plate. C'Dec. "Pat.Sept 8, 03 36538". . . . . $40.00 – 55.00
'15' National Plate. C'Dec. Wyoming plunger . . . . $125.00 – 150.00
'15' National Plate. C'Dec. R. Williams plunger. . . . . $125.00 – 175.00
'8' Cupid Plate. C'Dec. 1'Per. . . . . $30.00 – 40.00
'14' Easter Chick Plate. C'Dec. 1'Per. . . . . $45.00 – 55.00
9' Niagara Falls Plate. C'Dec. 1'Per. . . . . $35.00 – 45.00
'12' Garfield Mem. Plate. C'Dec. 1'Per. . . . . $35.00 – 45.00
'17' Donkey Plate. C'Dec. 1'Per. . . . . $35.00 – 45.00
Rope Edge Mustard Cream. Blue MG . . . . $25.00 – 40.00
'1' Basket w/'257' Peep Cover. C'Dec. 1'Per. Plaque w/dec. . . . . $125.00 – 175.00
'1' Basket w/'257' Peep Cover. C'Dec. 1'Per. No plaque. . . . . $100.00 – 125.00
'2' Basket w/Chick Cover. C'Dec. 1'Per. No plaque . . . . $75.00 – 125.00
'2' Basket w/Chick Cover. C'Dec. 1'Per. Plaque w/dec. . . . . $100.00 – 150.00
Hen. 1'Per. Wh MG. C'Dec. . . . . $30.00 – 50.00
Hen. 1'Per. Bl MG. . . . . $50.00 – 60.00
Hen. 1'Per. Bl MG & Wh MG . . . . $70.00 – 80.00
Hen. W'Per. Amber & Wh MG . . . . $175.00 – 195.00
Hen. W'Per. Black & Wh MG . . . . $200.00 – 225.00
Hen. W'Per. Wh MG w/Black head . . . . $225.00+
Hen. W'Per. Cobalt blue & Wh MG. . . . . $300.00+
Rooster. 1'Per. Wh MG. C'Dec. . . . . $40.00 – 60.00
Rooster. 1'Per. Bl MG . . . . $80.00 – 90.00
Rooster. 1'Per. Bl MG & Wh MG . . . . $100.00 – 110.00
Dog. 1'Per. Wh MG. C'Dec. . . . . $60.00 – 70.00
Dog. 1'Per. Bl MG . . . . $85.00 – 95.00
Dog. 1'Per. Bl MG & Wh MG . . . . $80.00 – 95.00
Lion. 1'Per. Wh MG. C'Dec. . . . . $60.00 – 70.00
Lion. 1'Per. Bl MG & Wh MG. . . . . $85.00 – 95.00
Duck. 1'Per. Wh MG. C'Dec. . . . . $50.00 – 65.00
Duck. 1'Per. Bl MG. . . . . $70.00 – 80.00
Duck. 1'Per. Bl MG & Wh MG. . . . . $125.00+
Cat. 1'Per. Wh MG. C'Dec. . . . . $45.00 – 55.00
Cat. 1'Per. Bl MG & Wh MG. . . . . $70.00 – 80.00
Lamb. 1'Per. Wh MG. C'Dec. . . . . $70.00 – 80.00
Lamb. 1'Per. Bl MG . . . . $110.00 – 140.00
Lamb. 1'Per. Bl MG & Wh MG . . . . $100.00 – 120.00
?-Dolphin Mustard. C'Dec. . . . . $80.00+
Square Shaped Sugar & Cream. 1'Per. C'Dec. . . . . Set $45.00 – 55.00
Cornucopia Sugar. Wh MG or Bl MG. C'Dec.. . . . . $ 60.00 – 75.00
Cornucopia Cream. Wh MG or Bl MG. C'Dec. . . . . $ 75.00 – 90.00
Shell Sugar. C'Dec. . . . . $35.00 – 50.00
Tall Mustard Sugar or Cream. Trans. Blue. . . . . $ 20.00 – 30.00
Tall Mustard Sugar or Cream. Bl MG . . . . $ 30.00 – 50.00
Swan Sugar or Cream. Lidless. 1'Per. C'Dec. Bl MG. . . . . $ 35.00 – 40.00
Swan Sugar or Cream. Lidless. 1'Per. C'Dec. Wh MG. . . . . $ 30.00 – 35.00
(Swan lids add 50%)
Stein. Lidless. 1'Per. C'Dec. Wh MG. . . . . $35.00 – 40.00
Stein. Lidless. 1'Per. C'Dec. Blue or Green MG . . . . $40.00 – 50.00
(Stein lids double the value)
Log Cabin. Correct roof. Both labels . . . . $75.00 – 135.00
Stone House. Correct roof. Both labels . . . . $100.00 – 165.00
Oriental Boy/Girl Sugar. 1'Per. C'Dec.. . . . . $ 75.00 – 100.00
Oriental Boy/Girl Sugar. 1'Per. Paint stripped. . . . . $35.00 – 70.00
Hex Sugar. Lidded. Bl MG . . . . $30.00 – 40.00
Hex Sugar. Lidless. Bl MG . . . . $20.00 – 30.00
US Hat. 1'Per. C'Dec. Lidless . . . . $50.00 – 75.00
US Hat. 1'Per .C'Dec. w/tinned lid . . . . $85.00 – 125.00
231 Sleigh (Egg Cover). Wh MG. 1'Per. C'Dec.. . . . . $70.00 – 85.00
Tankards. Purple cased. H.P. F'Dec. . . . . $325.00 – 400.00
Tankards. Blue/Green cased . . . . $200.00 – 275.00
Tankards. Brown cased. Transfer dec. . . . . $150.00 – 160.00
Mugs. Purple cased. H.P. F'Dec. . . . . $60.00 – 75.00
Mugs. Blue/Green cased. . . . . $50.00 – 60.00

Mugs. Brown cased. Transfer dec. . . . . $40.00 – 50.00
"Pottery Effects" Vase. Brown cased. Transfer dec. . . . . $30.00 – 50.00
"Pottery Effects" Cream. Brown cased. Transfer dec. . . . . $45.00 – 55.00
Daisy Bowl. 1'Per. Bl MG. Irid. . . . . $500.00+
Daisy Bowl. 1'Per. Wh Opalescent. Irid. . . . . $350.00+
Daisy Bowl. 1'Per. Bl Opalescent. Irid. . . . . $400.00+
Peach Bowl. 1'Per. Wh Opalescent. Irid. . . . . $175.00 – 225.00
Peach Bowl. 1'Per. Crystal. Irid. . . . . $50.00 – 75.00
All Large 1933 Vases. Wh MG. W'Per & B'Per. . . . . $90.00+
1933 Horn Vase. Wh MG. Gnd. W'Per & B'Per. . . . . $ 35.00 – 45.00
1933 Horn Vase. Wh MG. Not Gnd. B'Per. . . . . $ 30.00 – 35.00
1933 Spiral Candlesticks. Wh MG. W'Per & B'Per. . . . . Pr. $25.00 – 35.00
'2' Stamp Plate, 8". Wh MG. Plain. W'Per & B'Per. . . . . $20.00 – 30.00
'2' Stamp Plate, 8". Black. Plain. W'Per & B'Per. . . . . $25.00 – 40.00
1100 Toilet Bottle. Wh MG. H.P. B'Per. . . . . $45.00 – 65.00
'3' Plates. Wh MG. H.P. B'Per. . . . . $20.00 – 35.00
'3' Plates. Wh MG. Plain. B'Per. . . . . $7.00 – 15.00
'104' Pickle Jar Vase. Wh MG. W'Per & B'Per. Gnd top . . . . $125.00+
'104' Pickle Jar Vase. Trans. colors. W'Per. Gnd top . . . . $135.00+
Original Pickle Jar. Natural glass color. Rough top. . . . . $150.00+
'1' Shell Nappy. Wh MG. W'Per & B'Per. . . . . $20.00 – 30.00
'3' FTD Comport. Wh MG. W'Per & B'Per. . . . . $50.00 – 60.00
'3' FTD Bell Bowl. Wh MG. W'Per & B'Per. . . . . $25.00 – 40.00

Black Glass

Paul Revere Colonial Round Nappy, 9". G&P. Raised enam. dec. . . . . $100.00 – 150.00
'98' Vase. G&P. top. Plain. . . . . $80.00 – 95.00
1012 Candlesticks, 8". G&P. lip & punty. Plain. . . . . Pr. $65.00 – 95.00
1854 Covered Chocolate Box. G&P. Raised enam. dec. w/Au trim . . . . $50.00 – 75.00
1815 Cupped Bowl, 10". F'Dec. w/Au trim . . . . $50.00 – 75.00
1027 Candlesticks, 8". G&P. lip. F'Dec w/Au trim . . . . Pr. $90.00 – 120.00
1207 Sugar & Cream Set. Ag dec. . . . . Set $40.00 – 55.00
1211 Octagon 2-HLD Jelly. G&P. Raised enam. dec. w/Au trim . . . . . . $45.00 – 65.00
1211 SE Bowl, 13". Plain. . . . . $30.00 – 40.00
1211/1 Candlesticks. Plain. . . . . Pr. $35.00 – 45.00
1211 Sugar & Cream Set. Raised enam. dec. w/Au trim . . . . Set $40.00 – 65.00
1211 Cheese & Cracker. G&P. Etched. Raised enam. dec. w/Ag trim . . . . . . $50.00 – 70.00
? - 1045 Candlesticks. Etched. Rockwell Ag dec. . . . . Pr. $125.00 – 150.00
1211/1 Candlesticks. Cry. black cased w/cutting . . . . Pr. $35.00 – 50.00
1038 Candlesticks, 9". Plain . . . . Pr. $40.00 – 60.00
1057 Low Candlesticks. Plain . . . . Pr. $15.00 – 25.00
1009 Candlesticks, 7". Plain . . . . Pr. $40.00 – 55.00
1034 Candlesticks. "Hammered" lip. Silver dec. . . . . Pr. $100.00 – 125.00
1034 Candlesticks. "Satin Moire" etched dec. . . . . Pr. $125.00 – 175.00

Colored Glass

Original Pickle Jar. Natural glass color. Ragged top . . . . $150.00+
104 Pickle Jar (same). MG. W'Per & B'Per. Gnd top . . . . $90.00+
104 Pickle Jar (same). Late '20s colors. Gnd top . . . . $100.00+
1776 Colonial Sweetmeat - RE (marked). Ameth. Irid. W'Per . . . . $100.00+
77 Hobnail Toilet Bottle. Wisteria. W'Per . . . . $50.00 – 75.00
77 Hobnail Toilet Bottle. Other c. 1930 colors. . . . . $40.00 – 60.00
77 Hobnail Tumbler. G&P. c. 1930 colors . . . . $15.00 – 18.00
1053 Diamond Foot Candlesticks, 9". Amber . . . . Pr. $65.00 – 85.00
1053 Diamond Foot Candlesticks, 9". Other late '20s colors . . . . Pr. $65.00 – 85.00
555 Sugar & Cream. Topaz . . . . Set $40.00 – 55.00
555 Sugar & Cream. Other c. 1930 colors. . . . . Set $30.00 – 45.00
555 Sugar & Cream. MG. W'Per & B'Per. . . . . Set $15.00 – 25.00
555 Low Candlesticks, 3½". Ros. . . . . Pr. $30.00 – 45.00
555 Low Candlesticks, 3½". Other late '20s colors. . . . . Pr. $30.00 – 45.00
1708 Sugar & Cream. Ros. Simple cutting . . . . Set $25.00 – 45.00
1211 Octagon Crimped Bowl. Ros. . . . . $30.00 – 40.00
1921 Lotus Flared Plate, 13". Ros. Plain. . . . . $55.00 – 80.00
1921 Lotus Cupped Bowl, 9". Ros. Plain . . . . $25.00 – 35.00
1921 Lotus Tall Candlesticks, 9". Ros. Plain . . . . Pr. $25.00 – 35.00
1707 Sugar & Cream. Late '20s colors. Plain . . . . Set $25.00 – 45.00
1820 HLD Tea Tray. Late '20s colors. Plain . . . . $20.00 – 30.00
1901 Fan Vase. Green. Cutting . . . . $35.00 – 50.00
1901 Fan Vase. Green. Plain . . . . $25.00 – 35.00
1923 Leaf Plate, 9". Green. W'Per . . . . $18.00 – 28.00

1923 Leaf Plate, 6". Green. W'Per . . . . $12.00 – 20.00
1923 Leaf Plate, 12". Green. W'Per . . . . $25.00 – 35.00
1923 Leaf Plate, 9". MG. B'Per . . . . $15.00 – 20.00
555 Candlesticks, 9". Late '20s colors . . . . Pr. $65.00 – 80.00
555 Candelabra. Cry. W'Per & B'Per.. . . . . Pr. $60.00 – 80.00
555 Candelabra. MG. B'Per. . . . . Pr. $68.00 – 85.00
294/295 Sugar & Cream. Early Belgian blue. Plain . . . . Set $20.00 – 40.00
Tall Mustard Sugar or Cream. Early Belgian blue. C'Dec. . . . . $ 20.00 – 30.00
1776 Colonial Sugar or Cream (marked). G&P. Late '20s colors. Plain . . . . . . $ 20.00 – 40.00
1700 Colonial 1-Piece Grapefruit (marked). G&P. Late '20s colors. Plain. . . . . $35.00 – 50.00
700 Modernistic Sugar & Cream. c. 1930 colors. Plain . . . . Set $25.00 – 45.00
1820 HLD Tea Tray. Aqua. Plain . . . . $20.00 – 30.00
1211/1 Octagon SE Bowl, 13". Aqua. Raised enam. dec. w/Au trim . . . . $45.00 – 65.00
1211/1 Candlesticks. Aqua. Raised enam. dec. w/Au trim . . . . Pr. $40.00 – 55.00
1042 Candlesticks. Late Belgian blue. Plain. . . . . Pr. $75.00 – 100.00
1042 Candlesticks. Other early '30s colors. Plain . . . . Pr. $55.00 – 80.00
1042 Candlesticks. Cry. Plain . . . . Pr. $40.00 – 50.00

Tableware Lines

555 2-HLD 5-Part Relish. Cry. . . . . $150.00+
555 Water Goblet. Cry. W'Per & B'Per . . . . $7.00 – 14.00
555 Ice Tea Glass. Cry. W'Per & B'Per . . . . $12.00 – 16.00
555 Torte Plate, 20½". G&P. Cry. B'Per. . . . . $75.00 – 100.00
200 Cream w/lid. MG. C'Dec. . . . . $35.00 – 50.00
200 Cream w/lid. MG. Plain . . . . $20.00 – 40.00
200 FTD Oval. Cry. Plain . . . . $20.00 – 35.00
Unk Mustard Sugar. Cry. . . . . $15.00 – 25.00
'15' Celery. Cry. . . . . $35.00 – 50.00
'15' Cream. Cry. . . . . $25.00 – 40.00
Priscilla Tankard Jug. G&P. Cry. . . . . $45.00 – 65.00
Priscilla Tumbler. Cry. . . . . $10.00 – 15.00
Victor Pitcher. Cry. . . . . $40.00 – 60.00
Victor Tumbler. Cry. . . . . $10.00 – 15.00
'98' Westmoreland 4-Piece Set. Cry. w/Au Lustre . . . . $175.00+
'98' Westmoreland 4-Piece Set Plain . . . . $85.00 – 135.00
Waverly Berry Bowl. G&P. Cry. . . . . $25.00 – 45.00
160 Triangle Berry. G&P. Cry. . . . . $40.00 – 60.00
Star Berry, Flared, 8". Cry. . . . . $25.00 – 45.00
Star Berry, Flared, 8". MG. 1'Per. Plain . . . . $60.00 – 80.00
Star Berry, Flared, 8". Black. 1'Per. Plain. . . . . $75.00 – 90.00
185 Covered Sugar. Cry. Stained "Bulls' Eyes.". $60.00 – 85.00
185 Bowl. Cry. Stained "Bull's Eyes." . . . . $55.00 – 75.00
500 Pitcher. Cry. 1'Per. . . . . $30.00 – 50.00
500 Pitcher. Ameth. Irid. 1'Per. . . . . $2700.00+
500 Pitcher. G&P. Cry. 1"Per. . . . . $10.00 – 15.00
550 Tumbler. G&P. Cry. w/ruby stain & Au lustre. . . . . $40.00 – 55.00
550 Tumbler. G&P. Cry. Plain. . . . . $12.00 – 18.00
555 3-HLD Vase. Cry. (Undamaged) . . . . $100.00+
201 Plate, 8". G&P. Topaz. W'Per. . . . . $20.00 – 30.00
201 Plate, 8". G&P. Other c. 1930 colors. . . . . $18.00 – 28.00
201 Water Goblet. Cry. W'Per & B'Per. . . . . $12.00 – 18.00
1058 (Fruit) Water Goblet. Cry. Etched. W'Per. $30.00 – 40.00
1058 (Fruit) Water Goblet. Cry. Plain. B'Per. . . . . $10.00 – 15.00
1058 (Fruit) Water Goblet. Cry. w/ruby stain. B'Per. . . . . $20.00 – 30.00
1011 Cameo Diamond, 2-HLD Bonbon. Ros. w/Au rim. . . . . $20.00 – 30.00
1211 Octagon Candy Jar. Ros. Plain . . . . $40.00 – 55.00
1211 Octagon Candy Jar. MG. Plain. B'Per. . . . . $25.00 – 35.00
1932 Wakefield Bell Bowl, 17". G&P. Cry. W'Per. . . . . $85.00 – 125.00
1932 Wakefield Plate, 20". G&P. Cry. W'Per. $85.00 – 125.00
1932 Wakefield Water Goblet. Cry. W'Per & B'Per. . . . . $10.00 – 15.00
1932 Wakefield Water Goblet. Cry. w/cut foot & stem. W'Per. . . . . $15.00 – 30.00
1000 Eye Covered Turtle Box. Cry. W'Per & B'Per. . . . . $35.00 – 55.00
1000 Eye Covered Turtle Box. Black. B'Per.. . . . . $55.00 – 70.00

Syria Shriners Glass

Certain Westmoreland:
1903 Saratoga. . . . . $90.00 – 115.00
1904 Atlantic City . . . . $90.00 – 115.00
1905 Niagara Falls. 1'Per. Dec. . . . . $90.00 – 115.00
1905 Niagara Falls Barrel Shot Glass. 1'Per. G&P. Au Lustre . . . . $275.00 – 350.00

1906 Los Angeles, Cup. Green Hdl. . . . . $40.00 – 55.00
1906 Los Angeles, Saucer. Dec. . . . . $40.00 – 55.00
1907 Los Angeles Blown Goblet . . . . $95.00 – 100.00
1908 St. Paul . . . . $75.00 – 85.00
1908 St. Paul Wheat Shot Glass . . . . $275.00 – 300.00
1909 Louisville. Irid. . . . . $95.00 – 100.00
1910 New Orleans. Irid. . . . . $95.00 – 100.00
1911 Rochester. Irid. . . . . $95.00 – 100.00
1915 Seattle. MG . . . . $100.00 – 125.00
1916 Buffalo. MG. . . . . $100.00 – 125.00
1917 Minneapolis. MG. Irid. . . . . $100.00 – 125.00
1918 Atlantic City. MG. Spray Cased . . . . $100.00 – 125.00

Miscellaneous

Suitcase. MG w/wire hdl, tinned bottom & surviving bears dec. . . . . $125.00+
240 Candlesticks. Cry. . . . . Pr. $35.00 – 45.00
3-Ball Candlestick w/Base. Cry. . . . . Pr. $25.00 – 35.00
3-Ball Candlestick w/Base. Cry. w/"King's Jewels" lustre staining. . . . . . . Pr. $35.00 – 45.00
3-Ball Candlestick w/Base. Colors. W'Per. . . . . Pr. $45.00 – 55.00
1034 Candlesticks. Lustre stained. W'Per. . . . . Pr. $70.00 – 85.00
1034 Candlesticks. Cry. Plain. W'Per. . . . . Pr. $40.00 – 55.00
1707 Covered Candy Jar, 1 lb. Lustre stained. W'Per. . . . . $40.00 – 55.00
101 Night Lamp. MG. C'Dec. . . . . $95.00 – 115.00
Daisy Lamp, No. 2 Collar. MG . . . . $250.00 – 350.00
Daisy Lamp, No. 2 Collar. Cry. C'Dec. $100.00 – 200.00
Daisy Pitcher, ½ Gal. MG . . . . $100.00 – 150.00
1707 Spiral Lamp, 8". Ros. w/cutting. . . . . $35.00 – 55.00
1915 Vanity Lamp, 12". Aqua. w/cutting. . . . . $60.00 – 80.00
1921 Lotus Lamp. Late '20s colors. . . . . $90.00 – 120.00
1921 Lotus Lamp. Crystal. . . . . $70.00 – 90.00
1049 Dolphin Candlesticks, 9". Late '20s - early '30s colors . . . . Pr. $70.00 – 140.00
1049 Dolphin Candlesticks, 9". MG. W'Per or B'Per. . . . . Pr. $70.00 – 85.00
1049 Dolphin Candlesticks, 9". Black. B'Per. . . . . Pr. $90.00 – 130.00
1049 Dolphin Candlestick Lamp. Late '20s - early '30s colors. . . . . $ 80.00 – 175.00+
1049 Dolphin Candlestick Lamp. MG. W'Per or B'Per. . . . . $ 80.00 – 110.00
1049 Dolphin Font Lamp. Late '20s - Early '30s colors . . . . $ 80.00 – 175.00+
555 Tall Sugar & Cream. Cry. Spec. Au Dec. W'Per. . . . . Set $45.00 – 65.00
555 Tall Sugar & Cream. MG. Plain. B'Per. . . . . Set $15.00 – 25.00
300 Condiment Set, 4-Piece. Cry. W'Per. . . . . Set $50.00 – 60.00
300 Condiment Set, 4-Piece. MG. Chrome top. B'Per. . . . . Set $40.00 – 50.00
Straw Hat. MG. Red Band. C'Dec. 1'Per. . . . . $60.00 – 75.00
Straw Hat. MG. Black Band. W'Per. . . . . $50.00 – 65.00
Soldier Hat. Cry. F'Dec. W'Per. . . . . $90.00+
Revolver (Solid). Black w/Ag Lustre. 1'Per. . . . . $125.00 – 175.00
Revolver (Solid). All Black. W'Per & B'Per. . . . . $70.00 – 80.00
420 Cocktail Glass. Cry. F'Dec. . . . . $15.00 – 20.00
420 Cocktail Glass. Cry. w/Col. foot. F'Dec. . . . . $20.00 – 30.00
Grape Juice Set. Cry. w/cutting & cased trim. . . . . Set $95.00 – 150.00
505 G. Washington Cup Plate, 3". Cry. Etched. 1932-dated . . . . $35.00 – 45.00
'12' G. Washington Plate, 8". G&P. Cry. Etched. 1932-dated . . . . $45.00 – 70.00
'75' Small Dog. Wh. MG or Black. Etched. Glass eyes. C'Dec Au Collar W'Per & B'Per. . $35.00 – 50.00
'78' Dog Door Stop. Black, white, or col. glass. Etched. Glass eyes.
    Worn green or black felt. Unchipped. . . . . $450.00 – 550.00
'78' Dog Door Stop. Black, white, or col. glass. Etched. Glass eyes.
    Worn green or black felt. Unchipped. w/early collar. . . . . $500.00 – 600.00
100 Wing Sugar & Cream. Cry. w/black cased feet. W'Per. . . . . Set $40.00 – 60.00
1200 Octagon LF Salver. Black. Raised enam. dec. W'Per. . . . . $35.00 – 65.00
1024 Shelf Supports ("Pat Apld For" mark). Cry. 1'Per. 7" . . . . Pr. $40.00 – 50.00
1024 Shelf Supports ("Pat Apld For" mark). Cry. 1'Per. 9" . . . . Pr. $50.00 – 60.00
1024 Shelf Supports ("Pat Apld For" mark). Cry. 1'Per. 12" . . . . Pr. $60.00 – 75.00
1024 Shelf Supports ("Pat Apld For" mark). Cry. 1'Per. 15" . . . . Pr. $100.00+
1024 Shelf Supports ("Pat Apld For" mark). "White Carrara Marble"
    (etched MG). 1'Per. . . . . 2½ x above prices
1048 Shelf Support (Crossed arms), 7". . . . . $35.00 – 45.00
1025 Card Holder. Cry. W'Per. . . . . $15.00 – 25.00
'1' Sanitary Spoon Holder. Cry. W'Per. . . . . $25.00 – 40.00
'1' Sanitary Spoon Holder. G&P. Cry w/cutting. . . . . $50.00 – 75.00
All Flower Bowl Stands. Cry., Black, Colors. 2¾ – 5½" . . . . $12.00 – 20.00
All Flower Bowl Stands. Cry., Black, Colors. 6 – 7½" . . . . $20.00 – 30.00

NATIONAL WESTMORELAND GLASS COLLECTORS CLUB

Invites you to become a part of our exclusive organization dedicated to the preservation of Westmoreland Glass and its rich history

Dear Collector:

In 1889 a group of men founded a company not knowing whether it would survive or be just another investment gone sour. Today we know that company which produced its wonderful glass for nearly 100 years as Westmoreland Glass Company of Grapeville, Pennsylvania. Just imagine how proud those men would feel if they were with us now. Those men didn't just start a company, they touched all of our lives by giving us the beautiful handmade glassware we all collect and cherish.

On October 7, 1989, a group of Westmoreland Glass collectors gathered and founded what is now the National Westmoreland Glass Collectors Club. The main goal of the N.W.G.C.C. is to enrich and preserve the history and glass of that company through a bi-monthly newsletter and meetings where members can share information. By expanding our knowledge and educating all those who are interested we will be able to keep Westmoreland Glass alive through our collections and in our hearts. We invite you to join us in continuing where the founders of that company left off.

The club membership fee of $12.00 a year entitles you to the bi-monthly newsletter *The Towne Crier,* and full club privileges. For an additional $6.00 each, any other individuals in your household can also belong and attend the monthly meetings.

Meetings are held at Colonial Grille, 333 Main Street in Irwin, Pennsylvania, at 7 pm. on the second Tuesday of each month. The club also maintains a room for members only at the Remember When Antique Mall, Main Street, Mt. Pleasant, PA 15666 in which members can sell items for a small fee.

TO APPLY FOR MEMBERSHIP

Send your name, address, city/state, zip code, phone number, and the date along with your check, made payable to N.W.G.C.C., and remit to: National Westmoreland Glass Collectors Club, P.O. Box 100, Grapeville, PA 15634